GENDER IN DEBATE
FROM THE EARLY MIDDLE AGES
TO THE RENAISSANCE

THE NEW MIDDLE AGES

BONNIE WHEELER, *Series Editor*

The New Middle Ages presents transdisciplinary studies of medieval cultures. It includes both scholarly monographs and essay collections.

PUBLISHED BY PALGRAVE:

GENDER IN DEBATE FROM THE EARLY MIDDLE AGES TO THE RENAISSANCE

Edited by

Thelma S. Fenster and Clare A. Lees

palgrave

First published 2002 by
PALGRAVE™
175 Fifth Avenue, New York, N.Y. 10010 and
Houndmills, Basingstoke, Hampshire, England RG21 6XS.
Companies and representatives throughout the world.

PALGRAVE is the new global publishing imprint of St. Martin's Press
LLC Scholarly and Reference Division and Palgrave Publishers Ltd.
(formerly Macmillan Press Ltd.).

ISBN 0–312–23244–6

Library of Congress Cataloging-in-Publication Data
Gender in debate from the early Middle Ages to the Renaissance / edited
by Thelma S. Fenster and Clare A. Lees.
    p. cm – (The new Middle Ages series)
    Includes bibliographical references and index.
    ISBN 0–312–23244–6
    1. Sex role in literature. 2. Women in literature. 3. Literature,
Medieval—History and criticism. 4. European literature—Renaissance,
1450–1600. I. Fenster, Thelma S. II. Lees, Clare A. III. New
Middle Ages series (Palgrave (Firm))

PN56.S52 G46   2002
809'.93353—dc21

2001048211

A catalogue record for this book is available from the British Library.

Design by Letra Libre, Inc.

First edition: March 2002
10 9 8 7 6 5 4 3 2 1

Printed in the United States of America.

TABLE OF CONTENTS

SERIES EDITOR'S FOREWORD

The *New Middle Ages* contributes to lively transdisciplinary conversations in medieval cultural studies through its scholarly monographs and essay collections. This series provides focused research in a contemporary idiom about specific but diverse practices, expressions, and ideologies in the Middle Ages; it aims especially to recuperate the histories of medieval women. *Gender in Debate from the Early Middle Ages to the Renaissance,* a model collection of essays edited by Thelma S. Fenster and Clare A. Lees, is the twenty–fourth volume in this series. These essays range widely over medieval Western experiences but keep focused squarely on one central issue: how were women, as individuals and as a group, objects of interpretation in the Middle Ages? How was the status of women—a favorite topic—debated? What purposes were achieved by "thinking through gender," and invoking the full apparatus of the conventional "woman question"? These vivid essays by noted scholars provide sophisticated yet accessible responses to these questions.

Bonnie Wheeler
Southern Methodist University

In memory of
Jack Lees (1932–2001)

ACKNOWLEDGEMENTS

We wish to thank Fordham University, and former Dean of the Graduate School of Arts and Science Robert F. Himmelberg in particular, for generous funding of the March 1999 conference at Fordham University, at which most contributors to this volume were able to exchange ideas and perspectives. We thank too Roland Greene, and the Program in Comparative Literature at the University of Oregon, for their support.

We would also like to express our gratitude to the contributors to this volume, both for their willingness to think through the difficult issues raised by focusing on medieval "debate" and gender and for their expertise at wrestling the subject to the ground, for now. We hope that their efforts will inspire further investigation, as the best writing often does. Jim Craddock has continued to lend his strong support. Cora Maude and Jacob Lees Weiss provided welcome distraction (sometimes even at the right moments).

LIST OF ILLUSTRATIONS

INTRODUCTION

Thelma S. Fenster and Clare A. Lees

As [Simone de] Beauvoir shows, the question of what a woman is instantly raises the question of the relationship between the particular and the general.

—Toril Moi, *What Is a Woman?*
And Other Essays[1]

Toril Moi's *What Is a Woman?*, which makes a strong case for liberating the word "woman" from its "binary straitjacket" of essentialism on the one hand and social constructivism on the other, marks an important stage in modern theoretical debates about women. Those who argued for the constructivist view had often interpreted Simone de Beauvoir's thinking in *The Second Sex* as providing crucial support, but Moi brings a welcome qualification to that idea, stating that for Beauvoir the "body both is a situation *and* is placed within other situations."[2] Moi points out that "most feminist theories today rely on a universalized and reified concept of 'femininity,'" whereas Beauvoir herself had written: "Surely woman is, like man, a human being, but such a declaration is abstract. The fact is that every concrete human being is always in a specific situation."[3]

The essays collected in *Gender in Debate* explore the particular, that is, the local (both temporal and geographic) inflections of a larger human preoccupation with self-definition in terms of gender and, even more pertinently, with the uses to which that can be put. Medieval and early modern debates about women were conducted overwhelmingly by men (always excepting Christine de Pizan, of course, to whom we will return shortly, and a number of humanist-trained women in Italy who wrote in Latin during the Trecento and Quattrocento[4]), with all that may imply reflexively, if silently, about their authors' notions of self. Modern theoretical debates, conducted largely by feminist women scholars, necessarily stand in a different relation to medieval ones. It goes without saying, however, that medieval debate literature is a historic part of the ways in which "woman" is put into question in the West; that narrative, however much it may be bound up with the history of misogyny, has significance for modern debates. It is a history rich with continuity—for example, debates over woman's "sameness" or "difference" with respect to men, which is discussed even today[5]—as well as discontinuity, by apparent progress as well as by regression. After all, *What Is a Woman?* was published during an extensive (and ongoing) period of sociopolitical backlash against feminism.

Our collaborators on *Gender in Debate* locate other resemblances between medieval and modern debates about women. In varying ways, both stated and implied, the articles engage with modern feminist thought, converting the recovery of a past debate—important in its own right—into a present dialogue about women. As Moi emphasizes, Beauvoir recognized how the question of woman always raises a further question, that of "the relation between the particular and the general." This collection, therefore, which emphasizes the historical and theoretical particularities of literature about women, also points toward Beauvoir's statement, toward understanding it in ways that make sense in both medieval and modern contexts.

Not Just Christine

If Simone de Beauvoir's *The Second Sex* can be said to initiate modern feminist intellectual philosophy (as Moi argues), then the moral genre of the *querelle des femmes,* or debate about women, is often said to have begun in France in the early fifteenth century with Christine de Pizan's participation in the *querelle de la Rose* [debate of the *Rose,* 1401–04] or perhaps with her slightly earlier *Epistre au dieu d'Amours* [Letter of the God of Love, 1399], a courtly, narrative poem in which Cupid "excommunicates" men who vilify or trick women. Perhaps because the *Rose* debate was conducted by real people who exchanged letters written in prose and not in courtly verse, and perhaps because Christine was a woman, the debate about gender that it transmits is frequently interpreted as a foundational event without precedent in French or in other medieval cultures.[6] Conjointly, Christine has been praised for the content and shape of the defense arguments she deploys, particularly in the *Epistre,* then later in such works as the *Cité des dames* [City of Ladies]. In these ways, Christine's particular work is made to stand in for the more general and diffuse cultural debate. In the past few years, however, new research, and in particular Alcuin Blamires's *The Case for Women in Medieval Culture,* has contributed to undermining that view by showing that a body of material in Latin and in French preceded Christine. Unquestionably, Christine took the debate into new territory; at the very least, her intervention as a historically situated, actual woman with a palpable commitment to articulating a defense in ways relevant to her and to her public anchors the discussion in the "real" world in a way that had not been done before. Nonetheless, it is easy to lose sight of the fact that Christine de Pizan did not begin the debate, nor is she in herself representative of the breadth and depth of it. Julian Weiss's bibliography of debate literature in medieval Spain in this volume, even if it had to stand alone as demonstration, would indicate how misleading the emphasis on Christine—and on France (or concomitantly, England)—can be from the perspective of medieval studies. For all these reasons, we include no single article on Christine alone, although, as is appropriate in a collection that explores the relationship between the general and the particular, her work is present in word or in spirit throughout.

Shaping a Debate[7]

Alcuin Blamires's *The Case for Women in Medieval Culture,* to which a number of essays here refer, reconstructs in outline the juridically fashioned and theological-sounding defense or 'case' for women in Christian tradition, whose formal features appear in one combination or another in much debate literature. Blamires defines these formal features as follows:

> The formal case has a quasi-judicial flavour and expressly sets out to promote women's cause and to exonerate them from slander. Its typical features are these: it questions the motives and morality of misogynists, who seem to forget that women brought them to life and that life without women would be difficult; it denounces antagonistic generalization; it asserts that God showed signs of special favour to women at creation and subsequently; it revises the culpability of Eve; it witnesses women's powerful interventions throughout history (from the Virgin Mary and scriptural heroines to Amazons and modern notables); and it argues that women's moral capacities expose the relative tawdriness of men's.[8]

To this we add the observation that such debate, centered on Adam and Eve in the Genesis story, reflects rather a medieval Christian view. That is, Jewish commentary on Genesis "focuses on different moments, explores different options, and asks different questions."[9] In Christian tradition the issue of Eve's purported pride and desire to equal God was much debated, from Augustine to Aquinas and beyond. By contrast, according to one modern understanding of Genesis commentary in the Midrash, it is the snake, not Eve, who appears to be prideful, for in his arrogance he hopes to remove Adam and seduce Eve.[10]

A good example of a formal debate from the French corpus—that is, paired pieces pro and con—can be found in the short narrative poems called the *Bien des fames* [Virtues of Women] and the *Blasme des fames* [Vices of Women], which have been arranged to resemble a debate by their placement together in three extant manuscripts (London, British Library, Harley 4333; Paris, Bibliothèque Nationale, fonds français 837; Rouen, Bibliothèque Municipale 671 [ancien A. 454]). The *Bien,* just under one hundred lines, leans toward a courtly platform (lauding women for inspiring men to great martial deeds, as well as to dancing and to writing songs celebrating women), but also toward a biblically derived idea of sweetness and kindness in women, as well as toward women's motherhood of men; it claims that Christ raised the Virgin Mary above the angels (see further below, the "privileges" of women). The *Blasme,* a little more than one hundred lines and arguably more vigorous than the *Bien,* takes the opposite tack: The snake re-formed woman in its image; women cause strife and make men take up swords; woman is sweet on the outside, evil on the inside; she tricks and takes advantage of men; she's weak-minded, irrational, and given to anger. Read in conjunction, these texts exemplify the binary modes into which literature about women in this period is often distributed: Arguments for and against turn on different sides of the same binary coin.

It is striking, however, that a defense of woman alone can put the more general conversations about women circulating in the Middle Ages into the particular shape of a debate, and not only because of the chronological precedence of accusatory literature. As Pamela Benson in her essay here suggests, a defense, even when it did not explicitly rehearse the arguments against women before refuting them, necessarily implied its opposite, for making full sense of a defense required knowledge of the accusatory corpus—and, as woman's imperfections constituted a medieval cultural given, such knowledge could be safely assumed. Authors for the defense, therefore, could not have avoided tacitly reminding audiences of the arguments against women.

Seen from the perspective of an emerging cultural space for exploring the question of woman, such arguments, whether defamatory or defensive, were remarkably fluid and adaptable, lending themselves to a range of courtly, learned or semi-learned, didactic, and moralizing discourses (not always themselves neatly cordoned off from one another, of course). The dynamic variation of their manuscript contexts confirms the adaptability of this material, as the contents of the three extant manuscripts containing the *Bien des fames* and the *Blasme des fames* make plain. In the London manuscript, said to have been compiled in the late thirteenth century, the *dit* is in the company of a number of short works on mixed subjects: fabliaux, short stories, a religious play (*Miracle de Théophile*), poetry by Rutebeuf, and of course the anti-woman *Blasme des fames.* In the

Paris manuscript, however, dated from the late thirteenth or early fourteenth century, the *Bien des fames* appears in learned company, that is, with
a large number of theological works in Latin as well as with some works
in Old French, including two sermons, and again, the *Blasme des fames;* in
the opinion of one of its modern editors, the *Bien* and the *Blasme* are "no
doubt included to provide additional material for sermons."[11] The Rouen
manuscript, executed in the second half of the thirteenth century, records
vernacular works with a didactic thrust, such as Marie de France's
Fables—as well, of course, as the *Evangile des fames,* an anti-woman text.
Equally interesting is the manuscript configuration of Robert de Blois's
L'Honneur des dames, a one-hundred and fifty line poem that, in one manuscript, occurs near the beginning of a "Miroir" poem written to advise
the nobleman on right acting; in another, it acts as prologue to the same
work, but in two other manuscripts it accompanies a poem concerned
with women's behavior, called the *Chastoiement des dames.*[12] Scrutiny of
manuscript contents, and especially of the way they place or arrange those
contents, can be richly revealing in other crucial ways, as Ann Marie Rasmussen here demonstrates for German material.

New Words

As we have already indicated, we want to avoid having Christine de Pizan's
writing speak for other work about women in modern critical thinking on
the debate. Nonetheless, without appearing to backslide, the French corpus can sometimes be used, with judicious selection and a critical eye, as a
tool with which to explore other debate literature. Many essays in this volume, for example, take a large and somewhat uniform corpus like the
French one[13] as their starting point, frequently to show how discourses of
gender differed elsewhere. Yet even a cursory look at the history of this
material usefully illustrates how its principal themes find their parallels,
necessarily modified, in other medieval cultures. We can argue for a pan-
European genre of debate literature, therefore, so long as we pay attention
to its particular instances, and to the critical tensions that are generated by
moving from particular to general, and vice versa.

We begin with the French defense texts that started to appear in pro-
fusion in the thirteenth century and were preceded in the twelfth by Latin
passages flattering to women, such as those found in writing by Peter
Abelard and Marbod of Rennes (who, working in the tradition of the binary mode, also wrote a text *against* women). Because they were composed
in Latin, however, these works belonged to an "international" clerical culture more than they did to any proto-national culture.[14] But at the same
time, the increasing status of the French vernacular beginning in the

twelfth century and the taking up of gender issues in courtly compositions created a wider audience for formal debates. In the thirteenth century, French became established as a language of learning, elbowing out Latin for some things. Jean de Meun's scholastically informed *Roman de la Rose,* widely regarded in the French Middle Ages as *soubtil,* or "learned," is probably the best-known example, especially apt in the context of this volume. Even speakers of other European languages chose to write learned works in French, such as the Italian author Brunetto Latini, who wrote his *Livre dou Tresor*[15] in French; presumably, its encyclopedic thrust would otherwise have dictated composition in Latin. Differences between secular and learned, Latin and vernacular modes of debating, defending, or asserting knowledge about women are crucial to understanding the nature of debate literature in other cultures too, as the essays by Blamires (for Middle English), Rasmussen (for German), and Weiss (for Spanish) illustrate.

Latin material also points to the ways in which different institutional modes shape and transmit material that comprises the conventional content of much debate literature. Abelard, for example, used (but did not invent) a set of defense arguments that, in modern criticism, have come to be known as the privileges.[16] In formal defenses they became pervasive. For the purposes of this brief discussion, we shall let them represent the larger "defense of women." These advantages, honors, or favors, as they may also be seen, focused on the Creation story in the Book of Genesis, just as women's detractors did, and they tapped features of the Creation narrative that could be fashioned into points flattering to women. The two most popular arguments for women's superiority were that God had made Eve out of bone, whereas Adam was composed of mud, and that Eve had been created in Paradise, whereas Adam had not. Two others argue that Christ was born of woman and chose to reveal himself first to a woman after the Resurrection. Yet another, not in Abelard's corpus, holds woman to be God's triumph, for she was created last.[17] (It was left to the twentieth century to rephrase that idea to fit on bumper stickers and T-shirts: e.g., "When God made man, he was only practicing.") This set of refutations, give or take one or two, resembles somewhat the concept of 'redoctrination' that Blamires in this volume imputes to work by Chaucer and Marie de France: that is, the deriving of "profeminine hypotheses (of a sort) from various misogynistic notions of feminine deficiency." Whereas redoctrination stands negative beliefs on their heads, however, the privileges rely upon finding aspects of the Creation narrative that had not been tapped previously to enhance woman's image. The privileges made the rounds, cropping up again in Latin but also in Italian vernacular literature, in Middle English, in Catalan, and no doubt elsewhere.

The privileges were not a medieval discovery. They were instead a form of traditional knowledge about women formulated by the church fathers and institutionalized by clerical culture. The argument-from-place, to take one example, can be found in the *De paradiso* by Ambrose, bishop of Milan and Augustine's contemporary, but Ambrose did not construe it to suggest woman's goodness.[18] In fact, he seems to have thought of it as a conundrum: Why did God create Eve in Paradise and Adam outside it, given that Adam was the superior being? Ambrose concluded that the dignity of place meant little compared with inherent virtue: Adam, created in an inferior place, was better than Eve, who had let herself be seduced by the snake.[19]

Ambrose's thinking was, along with Augustine's, often cited in the Middle Ages. Just the same, about nine hundred years later the Dominican preacher Humbert of Romans presented the argument-from-place in a different light. As a Dominican committed to the importance of preaching, Humbert compiled a collection of *ad status* model sermons in Latin to be drawn upon by other preachers, who would then deliver them in the vernacular. One of these, designated "For Women in General," begins by stating that "the Lord has given woman many advantages . . . even over men."[20] He then lists the privileges[21] and concludes: "All of this ought to encourage women to love the God who gave them all this, and to pursue for love of him all that is good in a woman; it should also deter them from all that is evil."[22] Women who would follow Humbert's advice were required to be devoted to God as well as modest in dress, restrained in speech, kind toward the poor, and industrious; and they should not go gadding about or tell fortunes. Humbert's recording of the privileges in his sermon has prompted his modern biographer to comment upon the "more constructive approach" of the sermons, for Humbert's other writings and his activities as fifth master general of the Friars-Preachers, which involved him in the *cura mulierem* dispute, show that he shared with his contemporary male religious a view of women as "a species which members of religious orders would do well to avoid completely."[23] In other words, the privileges never seemed to suggest to Humbert that the Church should revise its thinking about relative gender status or about gender roles, nor is there reason to suppose that Humbert's own religious view of women departed in any important way from Ambrose's. Humbert's particular stand conforms to a point made here more generally by E. Ann Matter, who states that in the medieval church itself there was no "properly theological" debate about women and their status as created beings. Matter's essay amply exposes the ideological contradictions upon which much clerical thinking about women rested, whereby aspects of female behavior (their spirituality, for example) were overvalued in a system that formally undervalued women. It is striking that secular imaginative literature, not religious treatises, surfaced to point a way beyond that impasse, a point amply demonstrated in the essays by Helen Solterer and Alcuin Blamires, which we shall come to below.

Humbert's sermon gives us a glimpse at how the church in France contributed indirectly to the growth of debate literature in this culture by encouraging the use of French, not Latin, for the dissemination of biblical knowledge (of course, that also made the Church responsible for a two-tiered system of exclusive theology in Latin on the one hand, and its vulgarization on the other). Jacques Le Goff and Jean-Claude Schmitt have referred to the "parole nouvelle" of the thirteenth century, meaning in part the use of the oral vernacular in preaching, and with it the elaboration of advice to preachers on effective language for reaching their audiences.[24] Consequently, as orders like the Dominicans took the title of "preaching brothers," the word of God as interpreted into the vernacular was heard beyond church walls, in open spaces such as the *grande place* of the city.[25] Even earlier, however, the monastic reforms effected in Anglo-Saxon England in the late tenth century had aimed at a similar dispersal beyond the monastery of clerical knowledge in the vernacular.

Humbert's sermon does accord to women a small measure of official approval in the rhetoric of later preaching absent from the earlier evidence, however. Rarely indeed does the early medieval church address women as a collective group, as Humbert urges preachers to do. In fact, Lees and Overing here query, on the basis of Anglo-Saxon material, whether early medieval clerics had even formulated "woman" as a general category.[26] Yet, as we know, Humbert's concessions (like similar concessions evident in defense literature) had little or no impact on social structure, either secular or religious. Matter reminds us that the question of women's status stood as Augustine's reading of Genesis had left it: Even though men and women were theoretically equal in their humanity, the order of creation also allowed for men's superiority and women's subordination. Men's superiority and women's subordination thus remained naturalized. What we might call a "real" or material exchange on the issues, that is, one with social, political, or economic consequences, was never contemplated. In granting women a measure of goodness, therefore, Humbert promised women something that could be activated only within the framework of Christian teaching, and only for as long as women remained obedient to it. Humbert's sermon reminds us that what woman "is"—how she is viewed and what gender work she performs—depends heavily on the nature of the institution that frames her. In the cases both of the early medieval clerical literature and of Humbert of Romans we see how the church worked to maintain, and thus contain, a very particular (that is to say, partial) form of knowledge about women as a general tradition.

Woman, Knowledge, Power

If the defenses (whether or not formally staged as debates) were to have no direct, material effect on women's status, for what reason were they written? Principally—and arguably even in the case of Christine de Pizan—debates encouraged good conduct on women's part and exhorted men to treat women better, but they never advocated a political upheaval in the established social order. Perhaps, when we consider aspects of debate literature in the way that Lees and Overing do—its deliberate deferral of closure, for no winner is announced; its control of the moral sphere and moralized knowledge; concomitantly, its foregrounded display of learning (in the sense of book learning) as a means of maintaining both class and superiority—it becomes clear that men, those theologians, preachers, and secular poets and writers who talked or wrote about women, could in this way reaffirm their claim to knowledge of women, and therefore their intellectual supremacy, while conceding the moral need to respect women. The contradictory nature of knowledge about women (when deployed in the intellectual or moral spheres, for example) made it all the more important to control. Supremacy therefore lay in circumscribing knowledge, sharing it with an elite caste of other men and apportioning it out to women (and to men in general). No doubt there is some general truth in this, but at the same time some essays here also suggest that thinking about the category of 'woman' is also a means of thinking about other categories with which that of woman is imbricated, such as sexuality, ethnicity, belief, and governance. Barbara Weissberger, by recovering the historical particularities of Isabel the Catholic's reign that the generalities of debate literature serve, highlights some of the ideological functions both of queenship and of woman in late medieval Spain. Rasmussen, by contrast, demonstrates how thinking about gender as a category can help elucidate the particularities of medieval manuscript compilation and variation. Then again, Helen Solterer's article on freedom suggests the power of imagining a different status for women.

Weissberger's essay on the literature of the reign of Isabel the Catholic strikingly lays bare the ideological uses to which knowledge about women can be put by both women and men. Isabel, according to Weissberger, fosters a contradictory sense of herself and of her queenship that performs useful and, it must be said, conservative political work for her. Analysis of Spanish debate literature, when contrasted with Christine de Pizan's defense of women in France, for example, also underlines its broad national, proto-national, and geopolitical uses. In another register, comparison of Christine with Humbert of Romans helps us to understand more clearly the general context of Christine's interventions. In fact, Christine would probably have found nothing to disagree with in Humbert's sermon on women. The very same arguments advanced by Humbert, or their spirit, can also be found in her writing, and more than once. In this instance, then, what is the difference between his sermon and Christine's own ethic? If at least one of the points about this literature was to display knowledge and hence affirm it, then Christine, having demonstrably mastered "men's" knowledge, could now herself display what she knew, and she was in a position to dispense moral knowledge generally as it affected *both* men and women,[27] which she did, in work after work. In spite of great distance over time, comparisons between Christine and Simone de Beauvoir seem inevitable, as we have already implied. Moi, probably Beauvoir's most sustained modern supporter, borrows a concept from Stanley Cavell to talk about the philosopher's arrogation of voice: that is, as Moi defines it, "to claim for oneself the right to appeal to the judgment of others." Cavell's formulation deliberately conflates *arrogation,* or the presumption of undue claim, with *arrogance.* Moi therefore writes about Beauvoir that: "[t]he arrogance in her claim lies in the fact that she dares to speak at all, that she arrogates to herself the right to speak."[28] Christine de Pizan was not a philosopher but a moralist, and like medieval moralists she was not so much appealing to others' judgment as she was to their sense of rightness, which all Christians could be presumed to share. Nonetheless, like Beauvoir, Christine markedly "arrogated" to herself the right to speak. The question of voice, of the claim to speak for women, is central to critical analysis of the debate literature. Beyond this, however, and taking the long view, the issue is not simply that a woman arrogates the right to speak (as does Christine), but how many centuries have to pass, how many ideological formations have to change, before the category of woman can be explored without its traditional accompanying structure of defense.

Nevertheless, some changes in debate literature are discernible within the medieval period itself. In Anglo-Saxon England as in later medieval Germany, for example, conversations about women and gender did not take the shape of defense or debate. But even in France, as Roberta Krueger argues here, looking only at formal debate literature limits the available cultural evidence: Courtly genres, for example, make ample use of the woman question. Indeed, with the elaboration of courtly literature in Old French, theological discourse was borrowed into the secular realm, perhaps not too surprisingly, given its ready adaptability to the sort of rumination about gender that courtly literature was already engaged in. The development of certain romances, with their persistent foregrounding of issues on gender—what Krueger describes as an invitation to readers "to ponder the nature of sexual identity and to reflect on gender as cultural production"—acted sometimes as antecedent, logical corollary, and companion to the explosion of French debate texts. The didacticism alone of some courtly works, particularly of rich and sophisticated narratives such as those of Chrétien de Troyes, could make the romance (for one) closer in spirit to debate texts than they might otherwise seem; but Chrétien's deep concentration upon the requirements for aristocratic manliness makes absolutely clear his concern for male and female gendering.

Weiss takes our earlier point about the enmeshing of the category of woman with other ideologies a couple of stages further when he argues, using Castilian evidence, that this convergence not only made it impossible to isolate 'woman' as a category, but was also a remarkably effective hegemonic effect of misogyny:

> Indeed, when we peruse the relevant texts from fifteenth-century Castile, we soon see that although the debate over gender is most explicitly a debate over "woman," it is never exclusively so. Occurring in a variety of discursive situations (within the court; within the medical and academic professions; in sermons, and so forth), the praise and blame of woman is often a way of rationalizing or naturalizing hierarchies within a particular "field." . . . The debate over woman certainly does enact patriarchal ideologies of gender, and no feminist will underestimate its debilitating effects upon the lives of real women. But the debate is also inextricably intertwined with a range of other ideologies that structure social castes and classes, notions of race, morality or medicine, or such practices as courtliness and the literary . . . It is this complex interweaving of ideologies that makes misogyny so powerful and pervasive, such a towering, yet also such an elusive target: like the Woman it despises, "la misoginia è movile."

Weiss's observations are borne out by other essays in this collection. Defining women is often a means of defining men, of a certain standing. Pamela Benson's study of the 'cases' for women in the literature of Trecento Florence and Margaret Franklin's art historical discussion of two portrait panels, studies that complement each other, offer parallels with the Castilian evidence. Benson explicitly links changing definitions of woman with the passage from a feudal to a republican ethic. She shows that vernacular texts in the earlier part of the century, whose courtliness was associated with a feudal aristocracy in which women could and did inherit, better tolerated a view of woman as not necessarily man's inferior. The mercantile values that dominated Florence later in the Trecento, however, offered women no opportunities for public action and therefore squelched whatever potential for reform *may* have existed in the earlier defenses. (That potential was in fact taken up by Petrarch and Boccaccio, according to Benson; we might add that Christine de Pizan's *Book of the City of Ladies,* which now tends to eclipse Boccaccio's catalogue of women in modern feminist thinking, might arguably have not been written without Boccaccio's *Concerning Famous Women;* in spite of Boccaccio's ambivalence about women, disinterested historical investigation would concentrate upon outlining what was rather a *European* phenomenon exhibiting both continuities and disruptions and, above all, multiform expression.) Franklin takes the discussion into the Quattrocento to demonstrate that republican and aristocratic values clashed in visual portrayals as well, in this instance portrait panels of mythographic women. When Franklin contrasts these portraits with those of mythographic men, we see how important gender is in the articulation of political values.

Men on Women

The preceding considerations can be supplemented by reflection upon events related more specifically to male gendering. Feminist historian Jo Ann McNamara has argued that a restructuring of gender relations occurred in the century between 1050 and 1150. That is, new professions created by the Church, as well as by the growth of towns and of secular government, required "new identities that had to be gendered as well as classed."[29] These changes undermined any easy definition of masculinity, such as exploitation of the "most obvious attributes of manhood" (e.g., being a warrior) granted. What could these new men do to continue defining themselves above all as "not women"? As McNamara asks, "If a person does not act like a man, is he a man?" And in the case of the clergy, how could men who repudiated relations with women still be men? Further, for men to be men, women themselves had to remain gendered as women, or else "the whole male effort would collapse."[30] McNamara's argument offers interesting food for thought. On the one hand, it is clear that the category of 'man' is qualified by class or status, as is that of 'woman'; on the other hand, that there is no genre of literature about men as highly developed as that for women makes clear the imbalance between these two categories. By naturalizing these powerful ideological asymmetries, by making it seem perfectly ordinary to discuss only the woman question, debate literature often serves misogynist interests.

An understanding of the asymmetries between the categories of man and woman also qualifies the ways in which we think about voice. What happens, for instance, when a male voice arrogates the right to speak about women? Could a secular, perhaps courtly, male author have written an enlightened and benign defense of women without seeming to eradicate the boundaries between himself and woman, thus not only compromising his own masculinity but also the hegemony it and his status gave him? A preacher like Humbert could peg his defense to a higher authority like the

Bible, arrogating the voice of the church, and therefore presumably leave his own personal masculinity unquestioned. But what of the individual courtly poet taking up the defense of women: Would he risk being thought too much like a woman himself, thus effeminate, or not fully heterosexual, or would such risks be effectively naturalized by the "arrogance" of his class and learning? What is clear is that the debate acted as an effective means of accumulating cultural capital, as Weiss observes.

Karen Pratt's essay here illustrates what can happen when a male authors a courtly work in defense of women. In some instances, medieval authors have given an authoritative voice in defense of women to a female character, and sometimes the device seems genuine—but not in the hands of Jean LeFèvre in his long work in defense of women called the *Livre de Leesce,* which Pratt concludes is best understood as a form of "play." From the beginning, the *Leesce* shows its courtly, masculine point of view by praising women's physical beauty and implicit sexual desirability (it seems banal to say so, but by comparison, no such portrait of women can be found in Christine de Pizan's work). According to Pratt, LeFèvre deploys a number of strategies to undermine his defense; chief among these is what he does to reduce Leesce's effectiveness as an advocate for women.

On the other hand, we may also want to ask what, if any, cultural work is achieved by using a playful stance? Does it, at the very least, "indicate the impossibility of discussing in serious terms the proposition of women's equality," as Ian Maclean proposed some time ago[31] (a point also dealt with, though differently, by Benson in her book)?[32] Indirectly, Pratt's essay raises another issue, discussed here by Helen Solterer: the resonance of courtly texts in the "real" world. In her analysis of Franchise in Alain Chartier's *Belle Dame sans merci,* Solterer argues for the "promise of fiction," that is, its power to change "the ways of evaluating people symbolically." Chartier's poem provides an imaginary space where women could contest the principle of freedom, for before freedom could happen, it had to be truly envisaged. Solterer's original take on the nature of fiction here breaks through a dead end, an impasse, in the study of debate literature, for it intersects with a vision of what debate literature—specifically Chartier's—could effect extratextually. We might push her particular argument in a more general direction: Despite all the caveats we feminist medievalists may issue about masculinity, class, and misogyny, and in spite of what we believe authors may have intended, the literature on gender breaks off from its creators and breathes on its own. It exists as a cultural space wherein the woman question can be imagined, handled, articulated, and tested; this in turn recalls Émile Durkheim's observation about the "imaginary" he envisaged, a place where the mind was offered no "resistance."[33] It is this creation of a cultural space, however it is used, that perhaps makes medieval gender debates the antecedents of their modern counterparts.

Since the articles in this volume show how multivalent are the uses to which the woman question was put in the medieval and early modern periods, we cannot draw from this collection any single or overarching conclusion: In this way, modern critical analysis seems to mimic the open-ended nature of the debates themselves. The essays collected here explore the idea of gender debate in roughly three ways, however: First, some articles (such as those by Benson, Franklin, Weiss, and Weissberger) tell us how elements of the debate in its formal contour spread beyond the French and Middle English cultures, the ones generally assumed to be the central if not the exclusive witnesses; second, some articles abandon the category of form as it has been given in order to discern a "debate" being conducted in other ways (such as those by Krueger, Lees and Overing, Rasmussen, and Franklin); third, some articles also address or challenge the ways in which modern criticism has approached the categories of debate (for example, Blamires and Matter). In this third category, the analysis of debate literature can be a critical tool for exploring, and hence beginning to change, the traditional dominance of certain fields and certain genres within medieval studies, as Rasmussen points out. It would thus appear that some essays travel a long way from the study of the woman question. To the contrary, however, Rasmussen's essay, like the collection as a whole, confirms the structure of the category of woman as comprising in itself both the particular and the general. This structure can be seen as both problem and potential: Woman in debate literature can be the object of the most virulent misogyny, but she can also be the way, however tentative, of imagining a new order of things, a new relation between the particular and the general.

Notes

1. Toril Moi, *What Is a Woman? And Other Essays* (Oxford: Oxford University Press, 1999), p. 9.
2. Moi, p. 65.
3. Moi, p. 8; Moi's translation corrects J. M. Parshley's in *The Second Sex* (New York: Vintage, 1989; reprt. of Knopf edition, 1952), p. xx; Parshley translated, erroneously: "The fact is that every human being is always a singular, separate individual." In this Beauvoir appears to have anticipated modern gene research. Sarah Blaffer Hrdy quotes sociobiologist Mary Jane West-Eberhard: "Nothing is genetically determined in the sense of determined by genes alone. No gene is expressed except under particular circumstances. . . . It's a kind of biological illiteracy to talk about a gene *for* anything other than a particular protein molecule" (West-Eberhard, lecture, University of California, Davis, May 4, 1998; comprehensive treatment in preparation; Hrdy, *Mother Nature: Maternal Instincts and How They Shape the Human Species* [New York: Ballantine, 1999], p. 56). Hrdy sees as

unjustified the charge of "genetic determinism" leveled against early sociobiologists, who well understood that "genetics does not equal biology" (p. 66).

4. See Margaret L. King and Albert Rabil, Jr., *Her Immaculate Hand: Selected Works by and about the Women Humanists of Quattrocento Italy,* Medieval and Renaissance Texts and Studies (Binghamton, N.Y.: Center for Medieval and Early Renaissance Studies, 1992).

5. For the period from the French Revolution forward, see Joan Wallach Scott's penetrating critique in *Only Paradoxes to Offer: French Feminists and the Rights of Man* (Cambridge, Mass.: Harvard University Press, 1996.

6. See for example Joan Kelly, "Early Feminist Theory and the *Querelle des Femmes,*" in *Women, History and Theory: The Essays of Joan Kelly,* introduced by Blanche W. Cook, Alice Kessler-Harris, Clare Coss, Rosalind P. Petchesky, Amy Swerdlow (Chicago: University of Chicago Press, 1984; Women in Culture and Society series), pp. 65–109. In this connection, Alcuin Blamires has stated in his book: "The existence of substantial antecedents [to late medieval authors such as Boccaccio, Chaucer, Christine de Pizan, and Jean LeFèvre], especially for Christine's arguments, has not been adequately recognized. There is a tendency to think of her as *sui generis,* as constituting in herself the roots of feminism" (*The Case for Women in Medieval Culture* [Oxford: Clarendon, 1997], p. 3).

7. On this subject, see Helen Solterer's book *The Master and Minerva: Disputing Women in French Medieval Culture* (Berkeley and Los Angeles: University of California Press, 1995). A more general recent discussion of "contraries" in medieval literature is Catherine Brown, *Contrary Things: Exegesis, Dialectic, and the Poetics of Didacticism* (Stanford, Calif.: Stanford University Press, 1998).

8. Blamires, *The Case for Women,* p. 9.

9. Gerald J. Blidstein, *In the Rabbis' Garden: Adam and Eve in the Midrash* (Northvale, N. J., and Jerusalem: Jason Aronson, 1997), p. xii. Here Blidstein also says: "Certainly the Jewish tradition—if we may mount so brazen a generalization—approaches the genesis narrative differently than does Christianity . . . Adam and Eve are, quite frankly, less central to Judaism as a whole, which finds its foundational figures and locates its significant narrative elsewhere." See also John A. Phillips, *Eve: The History of an Idea* (San Francisco: Harper & Row, 1984), which reads Eve from the Christian perspective and remarks that "the stories of Adam and Eve do not occupy for Judaism the crucial position they occupy for Christianity" (p. 30).

10. Blidstein, esp. pp. 1–51.

11. *Three Medieval Views of Women: La Contenance des Fames, Le Bien des Fames, Le Blasme des Fames,* ed. Gloria K. Fiero, Wendy Pfeffer, Mathé Allain (New Haven, Conn.: Yale University Press, 1989), p. 9; this portion by Wendy Pfeffer.

12. See Blamires, *The Case for Women,* pp. 26–27, and Roberta L. Krueger, "Constructing Sexual Identities in the High Middle Ages: The Didactic Poetry of Robert de Blois," *Paragraph* 13 (1990): 105–31; at pp. 114–15.

13. The fullest discussion of works that make up this corpus appears in Blamires, *The Case for Women,* esp. pp. 26–49.

14. Recent studies of medieval Latin literature, even clerical culture, point to its specific local and national uses, however. See for example David Townsend's "Omissions, Emissions, Missionaries, and Master Signifiers in Norman Canterbury," *Exemplaria* 7.2 (1995): 291–315, and more generally *The Tongue of the Fathers: Gender and Ideology in Twelfth-Century Latin,* eds. D. Townsend and Andrew Taylor (Philadelphia: University of Pennsylvania Press, 1998).

15. As Nadia Margolis points out in "The Rhetoric of Detachment in Christine de Pizan's *Mutacion de Fortune,*" *Nottingham French Studies* 38, no. 2, autumn 1999 [autumn 2000]: 170–81; at p. 175.

16. The term "privileges" appears to be a translation from the Latin term as used, for example, by Jacques de Vitry in his sermon *ad coniugatos.* He says: "Noluit igitur deus feminam homine conculcari, quam tribus privilegiis specialiter exornavit: unum, quia mulier facta est in paradiso, vir autem factus est extra. Aliud, quia homo factus est de limo, femina de pulchra costa. Tertium, quo deus voluit habere feminam matrem, et non hominem patrem" [Therefore God did not want woman to be despised by man, for he especially adorned (*exornavit*) her with three privileges: One, because woman was made in Paradise; man on the other hand was made outside it. Another, because man was made of slime (*limo*) while woman was made of a fine (*pulchra*) rib. The third, because God wanted to have a woman as his mother, not a man as his father]" (David d'Avray and M. Tausche, "Marriage Sermons in *Ad Status* Collections of the Central Middle Ages," *Archives d'histoire doctrinale et littéraire du Moyen Age,* 47 (1980 [1981]): 71–119). A manuscript identified by Paul Meyer contains a list in Latin of what Meyer calls theological arguments in favor of women ("des arguments théologiques en faveur des femmes"). These are: that Adam was made of the mud of the earth, Eve from bone; that Adam was made outside Paradise, Eve in Paradise; that woman conceived God, which man was not able to do; that Christ appeared first to a woman, namely, Mary Magdalen, after the Resurrection; that woman, in the form of Mary, is exalted above the chorus of angels (Paul Meyer, "Les manuscrits français de Cambridge, ii: Bibliothèque de l'Université," *Romania* 15 (1886): 236–357.

17. This privilege seems to rely upon the kind of reasoning from temporality that Augustine applied in interpreting the biblical Creation story. Augustine read Genesis 2.7, 22, in which God is said to have made Eve from the bone of Adam, as *conformatio:* As woman was made *from* man and thus depended on him to provide the matter of her body, relations between man and woman would necessarily take the same form, and woman would be subordinate to man. If Eve was therefore really the best thing God ever made, then the conclusion most logically in keeping with Augustine's type of reasoning in the *conformatio* would be that man should be subordinate to woman in some real sense; that, as we know, was never seriously suggested.

18. For a useful recent discussion of Ambrose's views on women, see John Moorhead, *Ambrose: Church and Society in the Late Roman World* (New York: Longman, 1999), pp. 40–70. Moorhead makes clear Ambrose's advocacy of virginity but comments that whereas Ambrose is "generous in the dignity he offers virgins, he holds back from genuine empowerment" (p. 69).

19. Saint Ambrose, *On Paradise*, in *Hexameron, Paradise, and Cain and Abel*, tr. John J. Savage (New York: Fathers of the Church, 1961), pp. 285–356; at p. 301. Cited by Marie-Thérèse d'Alverny, "Comment les théologiens et les philosophes voient la femme," *Cahiers de civilisation médiévale* 20 (1977): 105–29; at p. 108; and by Moorhead, op. cit., p. 45.

20. Humbert of Romans, "XCIV, For Women in General," *Early Dominicans: Selected Writings,* ed. Simon Tugwell, O.P., Classics of Western Spirituality (New York: Paulist Press, 1982), p. 330.

21. The privileges were not an entirely fixed collection. Humbert's group of privileges is as follows: Eve was made in Paradise, whereas Adam was not; she was made of bone, whereas Adam was made of mud; and she was made from the middle of Adam's body, not from his feet, and was therefore man's companion, not his servant.

22. Loc. cit.

23. Moorhead, *Ambrose,* p. 68.

24. Jacques Le Goff and Jean-Claude Schmitt, "Au XIIIe siècle une parole nouvelle," in *Histoire vécue du peuple chrétien,* ed. Jean Delumeau. 2 vols. (Toulouse: Privat, 1979; here, vol. 1, pp. 259–78).

25. Le Goff and Schmitt, p. 268.

26. The contrast with Humbert becomes clearer when we consider how infrequent are direct addresses to women even in the vernacular preaching literature of the early Middle Ages. For a discussion of women in the clerical literature of Anglo-Saxon England, see Clare A. Lees, *Tradition and Belief: Religious Writing in Late Anglo-Saxon England* (Minneapolis: University of Minnesota Press, 1999), chap. 5.

27. Christine's control and distribution of moral knowledge is the subject of Rosalind Brown-Grant's *Christine de Pizan and the Moral Defence of Women: Reading beyond Gender* (Cambridge: Cambridge University Press, 1999).

28. Moi goes on to say: "But there is another form of arrogance here too, an ambitious wish to make us all agree with her, regardless of our own specific positions in the world" (*What Is a Woman?* pp. 234–35).

29. "The *Herrenfrage:* The Restructuring of the Gender System, 1050–1150." In *Medieval Masculinities: Regarding Men in the Middle Ages,* ed. Clare A. Lees, Medieval Cultures 7. (Minneapolis: University of Minnesota Press, 1994), p. 4.

30. Ibid., p. 5.

31. *The Renaissance Notion of Woman: A Study in the Fortunes of Scholasticism and Medical Science in European Intellectual Life,* Cambridge Monographs on the History of Medicine (Cambridge: Cambridge University Press, 1980), p. 91.

32. In *The Invention of the Renaissance Woman: The Challenge of Female Indepen-dence in the Literature and Thought of Italy and England* (University Park: Pennsylvania State University Press, 1992), Pamela Benson has identified the Renaissance defense in Italy (along with panegyric, eulogy, and the like) as in fact a "genre of self-defense," because "it [self-defense] appears as a subtext of restraint that results in the taming of the independent woman who is created in the explicit defense. It is the compromise by means of which authors seek to establish for themselves and their society a livable relationship with the threatening notion that women are equal to men" (p. 47).

33. Émile Durkheim, *The Rules of Sociological Method* (New York: Free Press, 1964), p. 17; French: *Les règles de la méthode sociologique,* 18th ed. (Paris: PUF, 1973), p. 18; as quoted in Pierre Bourdieu, *Outline of a Theory of Practice,* trans. Richard Nice, Cambridge Studies in Social Anthropology 16 (Cam-bridge: Cambridge University Press, 1977), p. 74; French: *Esquisse d'une théorie de la pratique* (Geneva: Droz, 1972).

CHAPTER 1

THE CLERICS AND THE CRITICS: MISOGYNY AND THE SOCIAL SYMBOLIC IN ANGLO-SAXON ENGLAND

Clare A. Lees and Gillian R. Overing

"The Clerics and The Critics" explores the evidence for debates about gender in Anglo-Saxon textual culture, arguing that different forms of gendered knowledge are at work in this period as contrasted with later medieval periods.

What's to Debate?

What can Anglo-Saxon culture contribute to our understanding of the debates about women that were conducted by and large in the later medieval period? How useful is it to talk of such material in terms of only one debate (*the* "querelle des femmes," or *the* "formal" debate, for example)? Since modern critical investigation of medieval debates about gender tends itself to take the rhetorical form of a debate, how and to what extent do modern debates shape and dictate the parameters of our inquiries into the medieval material?

As a general rule, Anglo-Saxon culture barely enters modern critical consciousness about medieval debates on gender. Accordingly, this period is not seen as making an identifiable 'case' for, or against, women. However much modern critical discourse about medieval gender debates is also cast in juridical language, the evidence from the Anglo-Saxon period—often similar in content to that used in later medieval debates—does not take such a form. Nor is Anglo-Saxon culture routinely incorporated by medieval studies into

its engagements with issues such as sexuality or gender, which offer the main
critical contexts for understanding medieval debate literature about gender.
Anglo-Saxon culture would thus seem poorly situated to answer the questions we posed in our introductory paragraph. Indeed, Anglo-Saxon England
is not commonly viewed as "a promising place to think about sex," as one
of us has noted elsewhere.[1]

Despite such unpromising beginnings, we argue here that the Anglo-
Saxon period has a great deal to contribute to both of these debates—that
is to say, the historical debates about women in the medieval period, and
the modern critical debates about them. These often conflicted conversations between the clerics and the critics raise the crucial question of the
complex interrelationship between the history of forms and the forms of
history. When we ask what there is to debate about gender in the Anglo-
Saxon period, what forms might it take if not the juridical, and why, we
are asking questions about the rhetoric of misogyny and its relation to social and cultural modes in any given period. By attending to this relation,
we begin to understand the ways in which modes of knowledge in general and forms of gendered knowledge in particular are expressed, codified,
and organized. And when we adjust our critical lens to focus on issues of
rhetoric and form in the Anglo-Saxon period, we see that there's plenty of
sex about, not to mention gender, sexuality, and misogyny.[2]

In much the same way that R. I. Moore argues that persecution and
heresy did not just appear in the later medieval period but rather were the
products of a series of specific sociopolitical circumstances, we argue first
that misogyny too has its history, which can be traced through the language and rhetoric of a period as well as through its gender politics.[3] In
sum, misogyny acts in the domain of the social symbolic. Careful attention
to the operations of rhetoric, its liaison with the symbolic forms of the social, and its relationship with history in the Anglo-Saxon period offer the
opportunity to watch structural misogyny develop—socially, intellectually,
rhetorically, and indeed, cognitively. This in turn clarifies the extent to
which later medieval debates about gender, equally firmly rooted in other
historical and cultural forms of the symbolic, are in fact aspects of the
complex ways in which misogyny maintains its hegemony within medieval discourses of knowing. Our second and interrelated point is that attention to those Anglo-Saxon modes of knowing that structurally organize
misogyny also provides an opportunity to examine the rhetorical categories of our own critical language. Hence our title: The critics are as significant to this project of understanding gender debates as are the clerics.
In order to detect the means by which misogyny, sexuality, and gender distinctions are culturally produced, we need to ask questions different from
the ones critics currently ask.

After all, the Anglo-Saxon period does not offer clear prescriptive catego-
rizations for or about women cast in binary forms of praise and blame, enco-
mia or vilification, familiar from the later medieval evidence. Similar to the
situation outlined in this collection by Ann Marie Rasmussen for medieval
Germany, Anglo-Saxon England provides no equivalent of that splendid
'querelle' between Christine de Pizan and her clerics, let alone a vernacular
version of the topos of *molestiae nupturarum;* neither do we have incontro-
vertible evidence for the "privileges of women," or even anything like Boccaccio's *De mulieribus claris.*[4] Later material of that kind and its incorporation
into literary juridical forms such as the debate employs different sets of binaries to those we find in the Anglo-Saxon period. There is plenty of evidence
for debate as a genre in Anglo-Saxon literary culture, of course, although this
genre is not routinely used as a vehicle for the exploration or reinforcement
of categories of male and female.[5] The mere fact that the genre of debate exists, however, points to the use of different structures of knowledge for exploring gender in the period.[6] Accordingly, we argue here that there are no
cultural sites in the Anglo-Saxon period to tell us what "woman is," as is exemplified by that strong component of the later medieval debate literature:
The *mulier est* tradition. Instead, we get glimpses of "woman should" (that
powerful Old English verb form, *sceal*), "woman does," "woman can't," as well
as "woman equals . . . ," in the sense of her worth, her value. And let's be quite
clear about it: When we speak of medieval debates about gender, we're really
talking about the ways in which proscriptive knowledge about the marked
category of "woman" is produced and maintained, granted that "woman" is
produced relative to the unmarked category of "man."

Proscription and Definition

We start with examples from the genres of wisdom and epic poetry; that
is, from those genres most closely associated with the court and the aristocracy, albeit inflected by the clerical caste responsible for the preserva-
tion and promotion, if not composition, of such literature. In both genres,
the proscriptive, circumscribed social category of wife or queen is what
counts. In the Old English *Maxims,* as in *Beowulf,* we learn how to tell the
difference between a good and a bad queen, and what she should and
shouldn't do.[7] In *Maxims I,* from the Exeter Book, the king must procure
a queen with cash, with "bunum ond beagum" [goblets and rings, line
82], while the queen must be perky at all times, "leohtmod wesan, / rune
healdan" [be light of mood, keep confidences, 85–6], and know how to
spend, spend, spend: "rumheort beon / mearum ond maþum" [be openly
generous with horses and with treasures, 86–7]. The queen is also the perfect hostess:

> meodorædenne
> for gesiðmægen   symle æghwær
> eodor æþelinga   ærest gegretan
> forman fulle   to frean hond
> ricene gercæcan,   ond him ræd witan
> boldagendum   bæm ætsomne (87–92)

[in counsel about the mead and in the presence of the band of warriors, she must always and everywhere greet first the leader of the princes and instantly offer the cup to her lord's hand, and she must know what is wise for both of them as rulers]

In *Beowulf,* the queen should be similarly well versed in social etiquette and alert to her role as a very particular social actor. She knows what to wear—gold is always appropriate—and who or what to serve—her sons and the cup, respectively. These are the conventions of queenship enacted by the gold-adorned ("goldhroden") wife of Hrothgar, Wealhtheow.[8] By contrast, Modthryth, according to Klaeber, is not "ladylike" (his translation of *cwenlic,* "queenlike," l. 1940) because she insists on murdering her suitors when they presume to look at her. Other women in the poem, like Hygd, know their job better. Although relatively young and inexperienced, Hygd passes the cup without recrimination (in contrast to Wealhtheow, who passes the cup but seizes the opportunity of the ceremony to make her own points, ll. 1168–91).[9] Like queens, noblewomen had better be careful if they want to retain their currency in *Maxims II*

> Ides sceal dyrne cræfte
> fæmne hire freond gesecean, gif heo nelle on folce geþeon
> þæt hi man beagum gebicge (43–5)

[the noblewoman must visit her lover with secret craft, if she will not thrive among her people so that someone will purchase her with rings]

Secrecy is the price a noblewoman pays for love when she will not pay the social price required of her (that is, of looking good, or thriving), so that she can be bought (that is, married, perhaps unwillingly). But in *Maxims I,* it is wives not queens who do the washing and wait at home for their husbands. When the so-called Frisian husband, the welcome beloved ("leof wilcuma," 94), returns, the wife leads him in, washes his dirty clothes, and gives him clean ones (97–8).[10] More proscriptions follow. A woman should stick with her embroidery ("fæmne æt hyre bordan geriseð," 62), but a "roving woman" ("widgongel wif," 63), unlike the Frisian wife who waits at home, risks gossip and—what's more—poor skin:

word gespringeð, oft hy mon wommum bilihð
hæleð hy hospe mænað, oft hyre hleor abreoþeð (64–5)

[she gives rise to talk, is often accused of sordid things; men speak of her in-
sultingly; and often her complexion deteriorates]

This latter example of the "roving woman" (a commonplace of misogynist
literature) and her bad skin offers us a tantalizing hint of the rhetorical syncretism of body with moral action in Anglo-Saxon literary culture: We will
explore it in detail in a later section of this article. For our purposes now,
it is important to note that these instances of what women should and
shouldn't do are enacted, proscriptively, on and through the female body.
The female body is what matters most in misogynist discourses. And, indeed, another obvious part of woman should do is reproduce, as *Maxims I*
states, stressing "woman" by putting her first in the utterance: "sceal wif
ond wer in woruld cennan / bearn mid gebyrdum," [woman and man will
bring forth children in birth into the world, ll. 24–5].

As these examples of "woman should" and "shouldn't" demonstrate,
wisdom literature (a tradition exemplified by the *Maxims* and incorporated
into *Beowulf*) is a particular form of knowledge. It is, to paraphrase the
opening lines of *Maxims I,* a matter of exchanging secrets in order to
deepen understanding: "gleawe men sceolon / gieddum wrixlan," [wise
men must exchange sayings] as *Maxims I* puts it (4). The category of wise
men, however, rarely includes that of wise women, as we shall see. Equally
importantly, proscriptions about women—or rather, wives, lovers, and
queens—are a subsection of the general category of wise knowledge. Such
knowledge is expansive indeed, not to mention seemingly redundant: It
includes knowing that every mouth needs food (124), frost must needs
freeze (71), and an arrow needs a bow (153), as well as that a woman must
keep her promises to a man at all costs (100). The gap between the expectations of modern critics and those of the Anglo-Saxon clerics about gendered knowledge can be measured by the latters' startlingly heterodox (at
least to modern eyes) categories of knowing.[11] Our sense of what seems
redundant—that frost freezes, or that a sick man needs a doctor—shifts
suddenly when we discover a woman must keep her promises to a man at
all costs. Redundancy, moreover, is one means whereby traditions of
knowledge—including misogynist traditions—are maintained by a society
characterized more by orality than by literacy.[12]

If we move to modes of knowing other than wisdom literature, we see
that similar proscriptions about women, their duties, responsibilities, and
roles prevail. While the form that gendered knowledge takes may change,
the way that it is structured as a proscription stays the same—and often the

content of the proscription remains broadly similar. This is a dynamic common to later medieval forms of gendered knowledge as well. It is from the Anglo-Saxon laws, for example, that we discover what women of various classes can and cannot do, and what it costs (not to mention the telling contrasts with what men can and cannot do). Take this example of the classification of sexual (mis)behavior (or of "woman can" and "woman can't") according to social rank (or "woman equals . . .") from the ninth-century laws of King Alfred: "If a betrothed maiden commits fornication, if she is of *ceorl* birth, sixty shillings compensation is to be paid to the surety . . . if she's a woman of six hundred wergild, 100 shillings are to be given to the surety . . . if she's a woman of twelve hundred wergild, a 120 shillings are to be paid to the surety. . . ."[13] It is from the Anglo-Saxon penitentials, however, that we learn how women, class, guilt, and penance are inextricably connected: "If a mother slays her child, if she commits homicide, she shall do penance for fifteen years and never change except on Sunday . . . if a poor woman slays her child, she shall do penance for seven years. . . ."[14] And from Old English homiletic discourse, we (re)discover the routine classifications of women according to sexual status—wives, widows, maidens—and the ethical rewards of the thirty-fold, sixty-fold, and a hundred-fold fruits attached to each station in the next life.[15] In each case, the structure of the prohibition defines "woman" according to class or sexual status: "Woman" is noble wife or lower-class maiden; she is worth x amount, whether measured materially or spiritually; but she rarely is defined as "woman."

Regardless of the form it takes, knowledge about women is thus structured proscriptively, oriented toward role and class, and morally inflected. And yet, in spite of the uniformity of structure of gendered knowing across these examples from Anglo-Saxon poetry, the laws, the canons, and religious discourse, the collection is itself is utterly random. By compiling material from a variety of sources, we have in fact created a new form appropriate to the subject of this essay collection: That of the category of "woman." There is no such equivalent *category* in Old English writing, although there's plenty to be learned about women from the forms of knowing that do comprise Anglo-Saxon vernacular writing, including the poetry, the laws, the homilies, and so forth. Furthermore, the genres of praise, blame, and debate so familiar from the later medieval period do not offer any formative principle of collation for gendered knowledge in the Anglo-Saxon period. Taken together, these Anglo-Saxon routines of misogyny in the social symbolic say more about social action and its classification ("woman should," "woman does," "woman can't," and "woman equals" in a quantifiable sense—legally, morally, and materially) than they tell us about "woman is." It is absolutely central to our project that the question of "what is woman," which would result in the answer: "Woman is . . . ," is *not* posed by the Anglo-Saxon vernacular literature (and, to the best of our knowledge, nor is it in the Latin). A woman in this culture is a wife, a queen, a relative of a man or his family, a lover, but she rarely is "woman" in either the misogynist or existentialist senses of the term.[16]

What's the Difference?

Indeed, in the particular instance of knowledge about gender, before we look at why the question of "what is woman" does not have cultural currency in the Anglo-Saxon period, we need to look at the critical debate that seeks to give or take away that currency. As already noted, most scholars working with the debate about women in the Middle Ages simply do not recognize the difference of the Anglo-Saxon material and the absence of the question about "what woman is" from this material. Ergo, Anglo-Saxon England is not a promising place to think about sex. Ergo, Anglo-Saxon England is routinely omitted from critical debate. Those medievalists who elide the Anglo-Saxon period from the medieval debate about women have something in common, however, with the many Anglo-Saxonists who similarly recognize only their own questions. By a fine irony, Anglo-Saxon criticism in the name of feminism often borrows from the other critical traditions a dynamic of debate (pro–and anti-woman) and imposes it on the period. Critical debate about the status of women in Anglo-Saxon England, for example, seems mired in assessing women's relative freedom or powerlessness in spite of the fact that the very framing of the question in these terms seems alien to the Anglo-Saxon evidence itself. Indeed, the question of "what is woman" is arguably far more pressing in later centuries than it is in the tenth. "What is woman" is not a universal question, equally relevant in all periods and cultures; it is one with its own particular inflections—it can be posed misogynistically and existentially, for example—and its own history.[17] Yet, the extent to which feminist criticism of the Anglo-Saxon period replays the same binary assumptions prevalent in later debate literature is remarkable. That is, in the critical literature, "woman" may escape to some extent the period's proscriptions (as only noble wife or lower class maiden, for example) but she is reclassified as either/or: She may be active or passive, powerless or powerful, good or bad, etc.[18] The problem here of course is not simply that these binary categories appear to be imposed on the Anglo-Saxon evidence, nor that such a critical paradigm fails to recognize historical difference; it is that the very elision of historical difference precludes the recognition of other rhetorical modes aside from these binaries of good or ill at the same time as it forecloses critical engagement with paradox and ambiguity.

Let us look first and somewhat briefly at this issue of the difference of the historical period.[19] The Anglo-Saxon period itself is constructed by means of an ongoing, largely unexamined, and often unconscious critical process of differentiation. The period is differentiated from other periods by means of its status as an originary culture (and its connections to European and North American nationalism) for example; it is also differentiated by periodization itself (that is, it is not post-Conquest England); so too by social formation (tribal to civil state); by language (not Latin, not Middle English); by religion (pagans and/or Christians); by gender (the so-called "golden age" of Anglo-Saxon women); and by sexuality (no sex please, we're Anglo-Saxon).[20] Add to these examples of what we might call negative differentiation a master narrative of history that often elides the early medieval period altogether, and historians must (and do) wait until the twelfth and thirteenth centuries to recognize the emergence of the individual (and the heretic), as well as of familiar clerical and secular institutions (Gregorian reforms, Lateran councils, clerical celibacy, marriage, the universities, towns, a money economy).[21] In such a narrative, the medieval world starts to resemble, however precariously, the modern only *after* the Anglo-Saxon period. Similarly it is *after* the Anglo-Saxon period that the structure of misogyny starts to take on a form that medievalists identify— whether we choose to recognize or to deny it—a form that is also informed by our critical questions and identifications. The "case" for (and against) women is thus rhetorically structured within the parameters of traditional historical periodization.

Furthermore, we cannot reconstruct or assess the category of "woman," which is so central to knowledge of gender in the Middle Ages (as well as to our argument here), without consideration of a second major index of difference presented by Anglo-Saxon period: That of the idea of the self. Our work on Anglo-Saxon culture has persuaded us that this idea of the self must include the highly conventionalized and often ignored *cultural* notion of Anglo-Saxon Christian identity.[22] This cultural notion informs our understanding of the Anglo-Saxon cleric as a subject (one who may be responsible, for example, for the compilation of *Maxims I*) as much as it appears to inform contemporary clerical understanding of their subjects, their congregation and their fellow clergy, as Anglo-Saxon and Christian. Accordingly, we stress here too the importance of historicizing Christianity and the subjects of that history—male or female—in specific terms. Anglo-Saxon didactic literature, with its profound emphasis on sanctity as well as on traditions of Christian exegesis and moral exhortation, may appear unpromising material for any investigation into the historical nature of such a subject. To ignore this evidence, however, is to assume that questions of subjectivity can be framed only by modern debates about the formation of identity, gender, and sexuality.[23] When we recognize the performative power of Christian rhetoric to create a moral agent and a psyche that cannot be dismissed by such modern assumptions about psychological interiority, we admit this Christian agent into conversations about the history of the subject and/or self in later periods. It is here that the *Maxims* meets *Beowulf,* and both meet the didactic religious writing of the period. However much the content of *Beowulf* appears alien to a Christian sensibility (and there's been plenty of critical argument about *that* over the years), and however much the explicitly Christian sentiments of parts of the *Maxims* seems at odds with other more folkloric, or heroic, elements, both share an interest in the conventions and commonplaces of subjects— in what people should or should not do. This characteristically syncretic terrain of the Christian and the heroic or folkloric parallels that of Christian didactic literature as well, which has its own explicitly conventional, performative notions of the self, its duties and its responsibilities.[24] (Syncretism—the melding of Christian with non-Christian, Germanic, heroic and/or folkloric traditions—is a well known feature of Anglo-Saxon culture in general and of its belief systems in particular.) In sum, belief and its sociohistorical formations are of prime relevance to historical questions of identity, gender, and subjectivity.

Concepts of Anglo-Saxon subjectivity are related historically and dialectically to concepts of gender—to concepts of "woman," for example— because components of self, psyche, and body are most obviously at work in Christian didactic literature. This literature thus offers us a glimpse into the social imaginary of the Anglo-Saxons, as evidenced in its clerical writings. We do not underestimate the power of the church over this social imaginary. Didacticism is predicated on a notion of a desiring and volitional self, we argue, a self that is educable through such disciplinary processes as exegesis (spiritual interpretation of Scripture, sermons, and saints' lives) and ritualized behavior (monastic rules, attendance at mass, public penance, almsgiving, tithing, etc). The subjectivity of the Anglo-Saxon monastic cleric is inevitably constructed by such processes, and the cleric seeks in turn to reproduce a similar subjectivity in those under his pastoral care. This relationship between pastor and souls is structured institutionally and discursively by means of a hierarchical reciprocity that binds the teacher and the taught, the priest and his congregation. Didactic literature endlessly replays and re-enacts this hierarchy.[25] In consequence, in acknowledging that didactic discourses enact a Christian subject, it is crucial that the rhetoric of didacticism and the power of its metaphors, both of which are heavily influenced by patristic conventions, be closely scrutinized. Such discourses have tremendous power: They create the rhetorical parameters by which knowledge is created, processed, and transmitted, and they thereby structure the terms by which categories of subjects (whether of man, woman, king, or cleric, etc.) can be understood, at the most profound level of cognition. In order to engage with the issue of why the question "what is woman" does not exist in the Anglo-Saxon period, therefore, we have to admit this didactic material into the debate.

Our approach therefore takes language very seriously, acknowledging its ability to create the social symbolic in close tandem with the religious. Yet although rhetoric is important, its operations are far from straightforward and, of course, there is no necessarily direct correlation between representation and the real without the mediation of ideology. While "roving" may or may not improve the complexion of the errant woman in *Maxims I,* to pick one example already mentioned, this textual female body is clearly a site of, and for, moral inscription in the social symbolic in much the same way that "woman" is enjoined to bear children in the same text. Time and again in the Anglo-Saxon cultural record (which is by and large a clerical record), the female body is used as a site of representation, and in many ways. All these ways, however, are dependent for their meaning on the utter absence of the "real" woman and her material body; in this sense, the one subject so central to much later debate literature is profoundly absent from Anglo-Saxon culture. The examples of Christine de Pizan (as female author) or Isabel the Catholic (discussed by Barbara Weissberger in this volume) remind us how women can affect the shape of later medieval and early modern debates about gender. The female body's continual, repeated entry into the Anglo-Saxon social symbolic as a site of representation, however, does not necessarily signify its increased absence or presence, or its "actual" freedom or restraint in the culture (as is so often argued by those critics who detect more—or less—freedom for Anglo-Saxon women in this record). Examining how the female body is produced rhetorically in various social formations and how that body relates to the subjects of real women—its representation and referential modes— may indicate instead a change in the relation between these modes. In short, we need to scrutinize the liaison between specific ideological discourses and the historicized instance in order to identify those areas of tension between representation and reference, bodies and metaphors, subjects and objects. In these sites of tension and often paradox, we can gain an enhanced understanding of the historical body's multivalence as a site of knowledge and meaning. Put another way, in order to situate "woman" in her own time, we need to look at the categories of knowing and representing within the period, while at the same time examining our own rhetorical categories of definition. These are precisely the places where we will recognize the limitations of imposed binary categories and the inappropriateness of the "woman is" question for the Anglo-Saxon period.

In fact, Anglo-Saxon textual culture is crammed full of rhetorical sites where we can detect the various ways in which "woman" as body enters the social symbolic. Such sites challenge the structure of binary definition (a structure often shared by medieval debates about women and modern critical debate) with a remarkably rich ambivalence. The popular clerical genre of Latin and Old English riddles, for example, offers instances of the representation of women and the feminine that are so closely related to the theme of knowledge that they enable us to pose the question of the relation between women and knowledge.[26] After all, riddles are ways to explore the world and its structures of knowing. In a number of examples from the riddles, we see that the female body is somewhere present at the site of representation, but present as a condition for signification, as a metaphoric ground; the body's meaning and functions are contained, and are produced as textual effects predicated on the very absence of the material body. A good example of this conundrum is the metaphorically pregnant book-cupboard of Aldhelm's seventh-century Latin Riddle 89. Pregnancy is perhaps the most obvious and common female condition signifying creativity co-opted for clerical metaphoric manipulation within knowledge systems. Nonetheless, as the riddle unfolds, the pregnant book-cupboard ("gestant praecordia") becomes sterile; it is transformed into an image of ignorant instrumentality, the cupboard finally a mere vessel of meaning:

Nunc mea divinis complentur viscera verbis
Totaque sacratos gestant praecordia biblos;
At tamen ex isdem nequeo cognoscere quicquam:
Infelix fato fraudabor munere tali,
Dum tollunt dirae librorum lumina Parcae.[27]

[Now my inwards are filled with holy words, and all my entrails support sacred books. And yet I am unable to learn anything from them. Unfortunately, I am deprived by fate of such a gift, since the deadly Parcae take away the illumination (that) books (provide)][28]

The disappearance-in-process of the creative female body as metaphor evident in Aldhelm's Latin riddle appears to be completed in the later vernacular Exeter Book collection of the tenth century. Exeter Book Riddle 49, for example, an analogue for Aldhelm's book-cupboard, shows no rhetorical trace of the feminine.[29] The vessel-subject in this case is simply "deafne, dumban" [deaf and dumb, line 2], vomiting knowledge as an "eorp unwita" (11), or "sombre nitwit," as one translator puts it,[30] but not recognizably female. How seriously shall we take language in such riddles, and what power to perform a subject shall we acknowledge? In Aldhelm's

Latin riddle, the feminine symbolizes a vehicle of knowledge (the book-cupboard), but there is no knowing female subject here. In the Old English, even this problematic conflation of knowledge and the feminine disappears. In riddles such as these we may begin to identify the structures of misogyny that co-opt the feminine and the female for use in other symbolic structures (as metaphoric commonplaces, for example), but this only begins the project of demystifying the naturalizing forces of patristic rhetoric and its power to structure cognition. This is the language of gender in debate in the Anglo-Saxon period.[31]

The Woman Question: Who Wants to Know?

If the riddles pose the question of the relationship between women and knowledge as an enigma, a mystery—as a riddle, in short—other sites within the culture confirm that knowledge itself can be metaphorically feminine. One particularly intriguing example that we report on here is the opening item from Pseudo-Bede's Latin *Collectanea*.[32] This collection of seemingly ad hoc clerical jottings is probably of Insular origin (that is, produced by an English or Irish cleric, either in the British Isles or in Continental circles known to have British connections), and is dated variously between the late eighth and tenth centuries (the resistance of the *Collectanea* to dating and provenance is a useful indication of the traditionality of the knowledge it encodes):

> Dic mihi, quaeso, quae est illa mulier, quae innumeris filiis ubera porrigit, quae quantum sucta fuerit, tantum innundat? Mulier ista est sapienta. (item 1)
>
> [Tell me, please, who is the woman who offers her breasts to innumerable sons, and who pours forth as much as she is sucked? This woman is wisdom]

The site of signification for wisdom here is an image of the female body as nourishing, sexed, maternal, even intellectual; at the same time, however, this spectacularly complex image of plenitude makes it plain that (in the obverse of the later *mulier est*) this wisdom is no woman. The *Collectanea* would appear to agree: Later items assert that "[m]ulierum frequens uisus mollificat mentem, et hebetat sensum, et sapientum esse non patitur" [constant sight of women softens the mind and dulls the judgment and does not allow a man to be wise (item 203)]; pose this formally unanswered question: "Mulierem sapientem quis inueniet?" [Who can find a wise woman? (item 204)]; and swiftly admonish that "[s]apiens uir eunctam mulierem respuit, stultus uero concupiscit eam, miserabiliterque decipitur ab ea" [The wise man shuns every woman, the fool desires her and is wretchedly deceived by her (item 206)]. While this latter item indicates that there is a category of wise men ("sapiens uir"), women are threats to wisdom and its acquisition; they fail to acquire it, even as they offer an image of it. Note too that it is "innumerable sons" who suck the milk from wisdom's breast—we are only too aware how few women in this period had access to the kinds of learning that the *Collectanea* symbolizes.

If women cannot be wise (for who can find a wise woman), then what of wisdom's femininity? Wisdom in the *Collectanea* is also imaged as a well-spring and nurse (item 144), in an echo of that overdetermined and indiscriminate mother with her many sons of the first item; as a key (item 26); as better than gold (item 63); and as a golden fountain (64)—another example of idealized fluidity. Where 'woman' appears to be the referent, as opposed to personified metaphor, we find her as a subcategory of, for example, the holy or the prophetic (the *Collectanea* poses questions about the first holy woman and the first prophetess).[33] She also appears as the womb, one of the three things that are never satisfied (together with hell and earth in item 38)—not all forms of plenitude are as desirable as wisdom, clearly—and as the source of domestic chaos as well as temptation. "Quid peius est domo, ubi foemina imperium habet in uirum?" [What is worse than a house where woman has control over man?] muses one item (193), while another advises, "Noli attendere in faciem muleris, ne te scandalizet uultus eius" [Pay no heed to a woman's appearance, lest her face tempt you to evil (214)]. The juxtaposition of two other items (or "factoids" as we might now call them), which appear sequentially in the text, is particularly satisfying when we consider the disjunction between woman-as-referent and woman-as-metaphor evident in the other examples: "Memento semper quod paradisi colonum mulier depossessione sua iecit" [Remember always that it was a woman who expelled the first inhabitant of Paradise from his inheritance] and "Tres sunt filiae mentis: fides, spes, charitas" [There are three daughters of the mind: faith, hope, and charity (both item 248)].

Most of these items are quite clearly commonplaces, whether from Scripture, the church fathers, or Insular learning, and all have parallels with the kinds of knowledge proffered about women in later medieval praise-or-blame traditions. The *Collectanea* hardly forms part of these later discourses, whether praise, defense, or blame, however, nor is it usefully described as one instance of the "incidental" case for the defense of women, as Alcuin Blamires has reconstructed it. What the evidence of the *Collectanea* points to instead are the ways in which gendered knowledge is embedded in modes of knowing that are historically and culturally specific. Early medieval modes, and the evidence of gendered knowledge they offer, are inevitably different from other medieval formations, but their difference does not compel us to dismiss them from discussion of the later debate material. Rather, we need to reconfigure that later material so as to see it as a variety of expressions—rooted in time and place—of a long-lasting inquiry into the relation between women and knowledge. That inquiry in our period is conducted by the clerical and aristocratic class and is, in the final instance, a means of maintaining misogyny as an acceptable branch of knowledge.

As an instance of one form of clerical learning, the structure of the *Collectanea* is homologous with that of the *Maxims,* discussed earlier, while individual items within the collection frequently take the form of the riddle. In much the same way as the *Maxims,* the items about women and wisdom that we have explored here are neither central nor incidental to the *Collectanea.* The collection comprises some 304 items, with a subsequent "appendix" of a further 84 items, sometimes arranged in groups, often not. As a result, the *Collectanea,* like the *Maxims,* does not have a center, and therefore none of its items, whether pro- or antifeminine, are incidental to it. It might be best described as a clerical anthology of wisdom literature, heavily influenced by the form of the patristic florilegium (so popular between the eighth and tenth centuries) and combined with a healthy dash of the "joca" tradition (clerical question and answer texts, which were equally popular in the early medieval period); hence its editorial title, the *Collectanea.* Wisdom literature, clerical patristic florilegia, and question and answer texts were all central to traditions of knowing that ordered knowledge-as-commonplace in the early medieval period, whether in Latin or in English. The *Maxims,* the riddles (both in Latin and in English), and the *Collectanea* are homologies of this tradition. In part because of the commonplaces it promoted, this tradition was a powerful social process in the early Middle Ages; yet, like many other traditional forms, its specificities (its structures, its use of commonplaces, and its rhetorical modes) are at present not well understood.[34]

What the *Collectanea,* the *Maxims, Beowulf,* and the riddles exemplify are some of the modes of knowing that incorporate knowledge about women in the Anglo-Saxon period. As we have already insisted, such modes are specific to period, culture, and social formation—that is, they are thoroughly historical and so too must be our methods of analysis. The *Maxims,* the riddles, *Beowulf,* and the *Collectanea* remind us that modes of knowing do not necessarily take the relation between gender and knowledge as their ordering principle. What the *Collectanea* also recalls for us is that women can be both subjects of, and for, knowing, but, at the same time, women are obstacles to knowledge (recall that "the wise man shuns every woman") *and* vehicles for knowledge (woman-as-wisdom, woman-as-womb). Furthermore women never generate knowledge, unlike men. Recall the man impeded by the sight of a woman in his pursuit of wisdom that we have already mentioned (item 203), or consider item 142, "Vir sapiens non putat se mori, sed migrare; nec amicos relinquere, sed mutare" [The wise man does not think he will die, but pass over; not leave his friends, but change them]. Insofar as they are gendered as "vir" or "homo," men in the *Collectanea* are embedded into discourses of morality, learning, and ignorance: "Multi apud homines sunt reprobi, apud Deum autem electi" [Many are despised among men, but chosen with God] asserts item 83, while another suggests: "Melior est patiens uiro forti, et qui dominatur animo suio expugnatore uerbium" [It is better to be rebuked by a wise man than to be deceived by the flattery of fools (item 32)]. Given such gender asymmetries in the relation of subjects to knowledge, the items on women in the *Collectanea* invite meditation more generally on the complex relations between woman as subject and as object, as metaphor and referent, in discursive formations. These are relations of rhetoric, knowledge, and power that cut across the more familiar binary structure of the praise-or-blame tradition of later texts.

Items about women in the *Collectanea* do not always fall readily into binary categories. Although some quite clearly idealize or denigrate woman and/or the feminine, others—such as the items that correlate wisdom and woman—blur the category, and few fall into a binary *structure* (of, for example, the genre of the good woman/bad woman). Since this is also the case in *Maxims I,* we might ask from whence come the binary structures that often ground knowledge about women in the debate literature of the High Middle Ages? In some cases (such as Marbod's *De matrona* and *De meretrice*), the binary structure of a quasi-juridical 'case' holds.[35] Knowledge about women (often virtually the same knowledge) in such examples can occupy either pole of the binary with only slight modification; such material is not simply for or against, it is, in fact, for *and* against (as Blamires's work elucidates). This twofold structure, however, derives from and reveals more about scholastic practices of argument and rhetoric than it does about any necessary relation between the feminine and the binary. In much later debate literature (and here too Marbod's texts are good examples), the elements of rhetorical display and mastery over a given subject need to be correlated with that choice of subject and sociopolitical domain. Woman, in some examples, may simply yield a good text over which the clerical class can argue; that good text may, in other words, say more about structural misogyny in the symbolic order than about the virtues of any pro- or antifeminine debate. Modern reconstructions of this literature as praise or blame, defense or attack, risk imposing a binary structure and an overarching narrative where the medieval example has none, or where a juridical structure is subordinated to another (which is as much the case with Anglo-Saxon clerical literature as it is with later courtly examples).

The liaison between specific discourses that encode gendered knowledge and their referents is complex food for thought. What is at stake here are the questions with which we began this article. The Anglo-Saxon material offers a useful way to reopen the question of definition: Is it in fact useful to talk in general terms of *one* debate about women in the medieval period? We can use the literature of the clerics to challenge the potentially singular vision of the critics. The careful synchronic analysis of the specific historical example is therefore the only way forward. The Anglo-Saxon evidence challenges too our understanding of concepts of historical change and periodization. It is simply not enough to overlook this evidence because it is prior or incidental to the later material, when we realize that the later material is itself hardly unitary. At the same time, however, we cannot afford to lose sight of diachronic change, even if the model we adopt is ultimately one of continuity and change. For there is change, as evidenced for example by the gradual shift in the literature from attributing wisdom to women (attribution of a state) to commenting on the teaching or preaching of that wisdom by women (attribution of an activity).[36] Such well-known shifts as these, however, are contested by asymmetrical and oppositional modes, whereby (to continue with our example) the attribution of wisdom to women (whether as state or process) is contested not only by the attribution of wisdom to men, or by the highly contentious issue of whether women could teach, but also by the broader and more commonplace use of the feminine to personify wisdom for a largely clerical (that is, male) audience in texts such as the *Collectanea* or, to draw on a better known example, Boethius's *Consolation of Philosophy.* Here too we might note that King Alfred's Anglo-Saxon version of Boethius's allegorically feminine Philosophy is, in part, the abstract *masculine* virtue of "wisdom."[37] No linear narrative will accommodate these shifts in what might best be described as the history of the disappearing and reappearing woman.

There is, moreover, an intriguing relation between this unstable, nonlinear history and the decentralized apparatus of feudal relations.[38] How feudal relations produce and maintain certain forms of knowledge as hegemonic, thereby producing and disciplining desire for that knowledge as a correlative of social, gendered identity, is an important area for continuing research. To state the utterly obvious, sociocultural modes of knowing are not limited to that literature, which is cast in the genre of debate. The Anglo-Saxon material demonstrates how a literature that produces, controls, and disseminates knowledge about women is part of a web of discursive formations that produce, control, and disseminate knowledge more generally. Structural features such as the lack of resolution or closure in the later debates and the use of rhetoric as a social practice of display of learning and hence caste, together with the fundamentally moral nature of knowledge—none of these are unique to debate literature but all are reminders of the hegemonic forms of knowing with which that literature intersects and engages. Medieval modes of knowing women may idealize, abject, and naturalize issues of sexuality, race, ethnicity, and dominant structures of belief and class, but they do so only when we ignore the workings of power these modes encode and their intersection with other structures of knowing. This is perhaps most profoundly illustrated by the ways in which clerical literature in the Anglo-Saxon period works to render the woman question ("what is woman?") moot. Such literature, because of the power of its rhetorical engagement with dominant forms of knowledge, helps maintain dominant social relations: As we have already shown, "woman," as opposed to "wife" or "queen" for example, hardly comprises a subject in Anglo-Saxon England. How knowledge about women is embedded in, related to, transformed by, or excluded from other forms of knowing is crucial to our understanding of misogyny. Crucial too, therefore, is how and why these forms, with their powerful rhetoric, do so little to transform the real lives of women and men.

There are many different ways in which misogyny becomes rhetorically routine. Our point here is quite simply that to impose a single unified concept, such as that of the woman question, onto the Anglo-Saxon material and chart its absence is to ignore the massively complex relation between representation and reality in this, and any other, period. Such a methodology stops us from recognizing the hegemony of structural misogyny. To us, the denial, silencing, and elision of women's agency in the Anglo-Saxon cultural record at this structural level is so pervasive as to seem utterly naturalized. This is not to say that women in Anglo-Saxon England were not out there living their lives productively in both social and cultural spheres; but it does say that the more apparent the forms of naturalization (of suppression, of denial, of silencing of "women"), the clearer the rationale for further research into the multiple processes of misogyny.

We close by reemphasizing that the Anglo-Saxon period has a great deal to contribute to the debate about women in the Middle Ages and beyond, precisely because it differs so radically in its representations of the "case" for or against women. In his conclusion, Alcuin Blamires notes that the "case" as he has outlined it does not make any effective contemporaneous dent in "structural misogyny"[39]—even Christine de Pizan was subject to and a subject of the very rhetoric she sought to challenge. So too there was a lot of misogyny about in Anglo-Saxon England as in the Middle Ages more generally, and to better understand that misogyny, we need better answers to the question of "woman." Who wants to know, indeed.

Notes

1. Clare A. Lees, "Engendering Religious Desire: Sex, Knowledge, and Christian Identity in Anglo-Saxon England," *Journal of Medieval and Early Modern Studies* 27.1 (1997): 1–29 (at p. 1).

2. To an important extent, this essay builds upon the thinking and writing we have done together over the years about these critical questions. Wherever we have drawn upon previous publications, they are so noted.

3. R. I. Moore, *The Formation of a Persecuting Society* (Oxford: Blackwell, 1987). For an important critique of Moore, see David Nirenberg, *Communities of Violence: Persecution of Minorities in the Middle Ages* (Princeton, N.J.: Princeton University Press, 1996). R. Howard Bloch's *Medieval Misogyny and the Invention of Western Romantic Love* (Chicago: University of Chicago Press, 1991) offers a useful introduction to the topic of misogyny in the medieval period, although it omits the Anglo-Saxon period from analysis.

4. For all these issues, see Alcuin Blamires, Karen Pratt, and C. W. Marx, eds., *Woman Defamed and Woman Defended: An Anthology of Medieval Texts* (Oxford: Clarendon Press, 1992), and Blamires, *The Case for Women in Medieval Culture* (Oxford: Clarendon Press, 1997).

5. For examples, see *The Prose Solomon and Saturn and Adrian and Ritheus*, ed. James E. Cross and Thomas D. Hill (Toronto: University of Toronto Press, 1982), and the poetic *Solomon and Saturn I* and *Solomon and Saturn II*, ed. Robert J. Menner, *The Poetical Dialogues of Solomon and Saturn* (New York: The Modern Language Association of America, 1941). Also related are the monastic debates in both Latin and Old English used as classroom exercises; see, for example, G. N. Garmonsway, ed., *Ælfric's Colloquy* (Exeter: University of Exeter Press, 1978), and Scott Gwara, ed., *Latin Colloquies from Pre-Conquest Britain* (Toronto: Pontifical Institute, 1996). For an introduction to the literature that clusters around the tradition of debates between the body and the soul, see Stanley B. Greenfield and D. G. Calder, *A New Critical History of Old English Literature* (New York: New York University Press, 1987), pp. 235–7.

6. This is an area much in need of further research, but see Martin Irvine, *The Making of Textual Culture: "Grammatica" and Literary Theory, 350–1100* (Cambridge: Cambridge University Press, 1994) for a mapping of monastic textual culture in this period.

7. For *Maxims I*, see *The Exeter Book*, eds. George Philip Krapp and Elliott van Kirk Dobbie, Anglo-Saxon Poetic Records 3 (New York: Columbia University Press, 1936), pp. 156–63; for *Maxims II*, see *The Anglo-Saxon Minor Poems*, ed. van Kirk Dobbie, *Anglo-Saxon Poetic Records* 6 (New York: Columbia University Press, 1942), pp. 55–7; and for *Beowulf*, see Father Klaeber, ed., *Beowulf and the Fight at Finnsburg*, 3rd ed. (Lexington, Mass.: D. C. Heath and Co., 1950). All translations are our own unless otherwise stated.

8. Cf. *Maxims I*, lines 125–6, where gold is described as fitting jewelry for a queen. For analysis of the relation between Wealhtheow and the world of

objects—cups and treasures—in *Beowulf*, see Gillian R. Overing, *Language, Sign, and Gender in "Beowulf"* (Carbondale and Edwardsville: Southern Illinois University Press, 1990), pp. 42–67.

9. For discussion of Wealhtheow's behavior at this point in the poem, see Overing, *Language, Sign, and Gender*, pp. 91–101. For an important analysis of the many roles of a queen, see Pauline Stafford, *Queen Emma and Queen Edith* (Oxford: Blackwell, 1997), esp. pp. 55–64.

10. The wife's activities are described as "charming" by Christine Fell, *Women in Anglo-Saxon England* (Oxford: Blackwell, 1984), p. 70.

11. For the genre of poetic wisdom literature, see T. A. Shippey, *Poems of Wisdom and Learning in Old English* (Cambridge, Eng.: D. S. Brewer, 1976), and for discussion, see Carolyne Larrington, *A Store of Common Sense: Gnomic Theme and Style in Old Icelandic and Old English Wisdom Poetry* (Oxford: Clarendon Press, 1993).

12. This point about the need for redundancy as a means of maintaining knowledge in traditional societies was best made by Walter Ong, *Orality and Literacy: The Technologizing of the Word* (London: Methuen, 1982), pp. 31–75.

13. The laws of Alfred (871–99), 18.1–18.3, quoted from Dorothy Whitelock, ed., *English Historical Documents c. 500–1042* (London: Eyre & Spottiswoode, 1955), p. 376.

14. From the penitential of Theodore of Tarsus, conveniently translated in *Medieval Handbooks of Penance*, trans. John T. McNeil and Helena M. Gamer (New York: Columbia University Press, 1938, repr. 1990), p. 197, sections 25, 26. When we broaden the context to include sections 24 and 27, we see how Theodore is staking out the differences between homicide and abortion with these proscriptions.

15. For discussion, see Clare A. Lees, *Tradition and Belief: Religious Writing in Late Anglo-Saxon England* (Minneapolis: University of Minnesota Press, 1999), pp. 133–53.

16. This failure to recognize this instance of Anglo-Saxon culture as different from other, later medieval instances and hence to elide or sidestep the Anglo-Saxon instance altogether is an aspect of a more general problem for the critics, which we explore in *Double Agents: Women and Clerical Culture in Anglo-Saxon England* (Philadelphia: University of Pennsylvania Press, 2001).

17. For a feminist reclamation of this question, which moves away from the Scylla of essentialism and the Charybdis of determinism that has dogged attempts to discuss "woman," see Toril Moi, *What Is a Woman? And Other Essays* (Oxford: Oxford University Press, 1999), esp. pp. 3–120.

18. For discussion, see Overing, *Language, Sign, and Gender in "Beowulf,"* pp. 68–107, and "On Reading Eve: Genesis B and the Readers' Desire," in *Speaking Two Languages: Traditional Disciplines and Contemporary Theory in Medieval Studies*, ed. Allen J. Frantzen (Albany: SUNY Press, 1991), pp. 40–51, and Lees, "At a Crossroads: Old English and Feminist Criticism,"

in *Reading Old English Texts*, ed. Katherine O'Brien O'Keeffe (Cambridge: Cambridge University Press, 1997), pp. 146–51.

19. Our comments here and for the next three pages are heavily influenced by
    our article "Before History, Before Difference: Bodies, Metaphor and the
    church in Anglo-Saxon England," *Yale Journal of Criticism* 11 (1998):
    315–34.

20. For discussion and references, see "Before History, Before Difference," pp.
    316–17.

21. "Before History, Before Difference," p. 317.

22. "Before History, Before Difference," pp. 317–18, and for a longer study of
    the Christian subject, see Lees, *Tradition and Belief*, pp. 106–32.

23. "Before History, Before Difference," p. 317.

24. See Lees, *Tradition and Belief*, pp. 127–32.

25. *Tradition and Belief*, pp. 120–27.

26. Our argument about the riddles is abbreviated from that in chap. 2 of *Double Agents: Women and Clerical Culture in Anglo-Saxon England*.

27. R. Ehwald, ed., *Aldhelmi Opera*, Monumenta Germaniae Historica 15
    (1919), p. 138.

28. Translated by Michael Lapidge and James L. Rosier, *Aldhelm: The Poetic
    Works* (Cambridge: D. S. Brewer, 1985), p. 89.

29. *The Exeter Book*, ed. Krapp and Dobbie, p. 206.

30. See *The Exeter Book Riddles*, trans. Kevin Crossley-Holland (Harmondsworth, Middlesex: Penguin, 1979), p. 71.

31. We've taken up this issue of the relation between women and knowledge
    in greater detail in *Double Agents: Women and Clerical Culture in Anglo-Saxon
    England*. We consider, for example, the plain but problematic narratives of
    charters and wills; the tortured description of female saintly bodies; the salvation history of Bede; the idiosyncratic narratives of Asser as examples of
    clerical metaphorization of mothering; and Alfred's re-masculinization of
    the conventionally feminine persona of Wisdom in his translation of
    Boethius's Consolation of Philosophy.

32. See *Double Agents: Women and Clerical Culture in Anglo-Saxon England*, chap.
    5, for a fuller discussion. For the *Collectanea*, see *Collectanea Pseudo-Bedae*,
    eds. Martha Bayless and Michael Lapidge, Scriptores Latini Hiberniac XIV
    (School of Celtic Studies: Dublin Institute for Advanced Studies, 1998); all
    references are to this edition and translation, by item. For the vexed issue
    of the dating and provenance of the *Collectanea*, see the introductory (and
    sometimes contradictory) essays.

33. Respectively, Mary, sister of Abraham, item 7, and Dina, daughter of Jacob,
    item 8.

34. For preliminary comments on the role of tradition in early medieval culture, see Lees, *Tradition and Belief*, intro. and chap. 1.

35. For translations of these works, see *Woman Defamed and Woman Defended*,
    eds. Blamires et al., pp. 100–3 and 228–32.

36. For the debates about women preachers, see Blamires, *The Case for Women in Medieval Culture,* pp. 184–97.

37 See further *Double Agents: Women and Clerical Culture in Anglo-Saxon England,* chap. 5.

38. We are fully aware of Susan Reynold's contestation of the term "feudalism" in *Fiefs and Vassals: The Medieval Evidence Reinterpreted* (Oxford: Oxford University Press, 1994). We chose to continue to use the term in its broad Marxist sense (for which see Reynolds, pp. 1–16).

39. *The Case for Women in Medieval Culture,* pp. 231–44.

CHAPTER 2

THE UNDEBATED DEBATE: GENDER AND
THE IMAGE OF GOD IN MEDIEVAL THEOLOGY

E. Ann Matter

This essay examines the strange lack of debate about women's role in the classical theological treatises of the Middle Ages. The reason for this may well be the predominant influence of Augustine of Hippo, who set up a condition in which women are equal to men (and therefore in the image of God) according to our humanity but NOT according to our female embodiment. The consequences of this paradoxical formulation can be seen in women's spiritual writings from medieval Europe.

No theological tenet of medieval Latin Christianity had greater impact on the thinking about gender relations than the question of whether both man and woman had been equally created in the image of God. This question is deeply troubling from a modern perspective, but it did not arouse much debate in the Middle Ages. The solution proposed by Augustine (roughly put, that women *qua* humans were created in God's image, but women as specifically female were not) traveled uncontested throughout the medieval period. Such theological debates as occurred were not undertaken within the framework of the medieval ecclesiastical structures: monastic and cathedral schools, homilies by bishops and popes, and, eventually, the universities. Perhaps it will be surprising to readers of this collection that there was no properly theological debate of any real consequence about whether women were in the image of God, it being understood that women both were and were not, as Augustine had argued.

On the other hand, the activities of many spiritually gifted medieval Christian women suggest that they found something of a solution to their exclusion from full participation in the image of God in the way they positioned themselves as living in (and in some ways performing) the image of God. Their lives unfolded in the context of various types of religious communities where there was a certain spiritual equality between men and women; so, even though their actions may have presented a challenge to accepted dogma, the potential conflict never erupted into an articulated debate. Nonetheless, the fact of being able to represent the image of God created a sure alternative position for women to the one the church had foreordained, and it opened a seam that the church carefully and jealously watched for signs of increase.

The theological importance of the creation of human beings in the image of God has a clear basis in the two human creation stories in the book of Genesis: In Genesis 1.26–7, God makes human beings "ad imaginem et similitudinem nostram" [in his image] and gives them power over all the beasts of the earth, air, and seas. In the next chapter, Genesis 2.21–3, God fashions a companion for the original (male) human, Adam, by taking a rib from his side and turning it into a woman. When he sees his new companion, Adam calls her "bone of my bone and flesh of my flesh", and says (according to the Vulgate version of the Bible), "Haec vocabitur Virago, quoniam de viro sumpta est" [I will call her Virago because she has been taken from a "vir"].

The double story of the creation of human gender has been read in different ways to support specific ideas about gender relationships. Twentieth-century feminist biblical criticism, for example, has prioritized Genesis 1, especially the explicit reference in verse 27 to the co-creation of men and women as equally in the image of God.[1] The description can actually be read in various ways since the language is somewhat ambiguous: "Ad imaginem Dei creavit illum, masculum et feminam creavit eos" [In the image of God created He him, male and female created He them]. Especially when read with an eye to the story that follows in Genesis 2, this seems to imply that Adam was created first, in the image of God, and then Eve was created from Adam. So is Eve (and are women) also in the image of God?

The question becomes even more vexed when, in the very next chapter of Genesis, Adam and the woman eat from the forbidden tree of the knowledge of good and evil and thereby bring suffering and death into the world. The curses of Genesis 3.16–17 are explicit about the connection of our earthly woes to the original sin of our first parents: Women will have pain in childbirth and will be subordinate to their husbands, and men and women both will ultimately die and return to the dust. Adam is specifically chided for letting the woman lure him into eating from the fruit of the tree. His curse (to wrest his living by the sweat of his brow from the earth and then return to it) begins, "Quia audisti vocem uxorem tuam" [Since you listened to the voice of your wife]. The equivalence of women with carnality and spiritual and intellectual weakness is a commonplace of Latin Christianity, from Tertullian in the late second century to the late-fifteenth-century *Malleus Maleficarum* [The Hammer of Witches].[2] The Dominican authors of this treatise revert to the first three chapters of Genesis to explain why women are inferior to men (because the first woman was made from a bent rib, and so she is bent in a contrary direction to that of man) and offer us the etymology "femina" = "fe minus", because women are, by their very nature, weaker in faith than men.[3]

When scholars consider the development of these ontological questions about gender, blame for this reading of Genesis and the consequent relegation of women to second-class status in relation to the image of God often comes to rest squarely on Augustine of Hippo. In fact, the arguments pro and contra Augustine on women have been quite heated.[4] Is the basic subordination of women to men in Western Christian culture all the fault of Augustine? Or was he, especially for a man of his age, actually rather favorably disposed to women? Here I will try neither to damn Augustine nor to save him, but will investigate his role in the debate about the divinely revealed gender distinctions that led to the subordination of medieval women. Whatever Augustine may have actually thought, and however his writings may be interpreted from the context of late antique Latin theology, his statements in this regard, as in so much of Latin theology, were enormously influential.

First of all, it was Augustine who showed why the issue was so important. As Gerald Bonner has pointed out, a central feature of all of Augustine's theology was the fashioning of man in the image of God, since it is precisely the verisimilitude of man and God that is the basis for the elements of salvation theology, namely, the Incarnation and the mediation of Christ in the church.[5] For our purposes, then, it is worth paying some attention to Augustine's understanding of the nature of woman according to the order of Creation. I will use the suspect term "woman" in the abstract as opposed to "women," that is, actual female humans. As I will show below, woman is in fact a more accurate term given that Augustine was concerned about definitions of human nature and had no sense of women as in any way the equal of men.

In a much-quoted passage from *De Genesi in litteram*, Augustine defines the role of women in creation as totally bound up with fertility and childbirth. This was the reason God created the woman from the rib of Adam in Genesis 2: "If one rejects giving birth to children as the reason why woman was created, I do not see for what other help the woman was made

for the man."[6] Women's subordination to men is, therefore, a natural consequence of the order of Creation, even before it is confirmed by the sad
event of original sin. Augustine makes it clear that women are intellectually inferior to men, even though some women, notably his mother Monica, are able to reach a level of philosophical sophistication.[7]

At the ontological level, though, the situation is more complicated. When
the nature of female human beings is considered in relation to the saving fact
of the Incarnation of God as the man, Jesus Christ, the problem becomes: If
women cannot be in the image of God, then can women be saved? In an
important passage in De trinitate, Augustine answers "yes and no":

> Woman together with man is the image of God, so that the whole substance
> is one image. But when she has the role of helpmate, which pertains to her
> alone, she is not the image of God. But with regard to man alone, he is the
> image of God, just as fully and completely as he is joined with the woman
> into one.[8]

A number of scholars have read this statement in a positive light, pointing
out that it includes the category "woman," if not the lives of specific women,
in the definition of human being (homo).[9] Augustine is understood to have
been working in a philosophical framework deriving from Platonism, in
which the distinction between body and spirit is also mirrored in the division between levels of the human mind. A woman as an embodied being
(femina, mulier) does not participate in the image of God, but as part of the
category "human being" (homo), she does. The category "woman," furthermore, is understood by Augustine to be a manifestation of the active mind
(scientia), in contrast to the masculine part of the mind, the meditative wisdom of God (sapientia). Since the active mind always leads back to Creation,
only the masculine principle (sapientia) can truly image God.

Women, therefore, are spiritually equal to men only in their creation as
human beings. In terms of the Genesis myth of Creation, this would be
understood as existing in the time before the separation of the woman
from Adam's rib. Women lose the image of God specifically in those physical attributes that make them women. The physical origin of the spiritual
inferiority of women is counterbalanced, as it were, by the reassurance that
women are equal to men in basic humanity, as opposed to female physicality, and will stand equally before God at the resurrection of the body.[10]

The Augustinian model of gender relations, therefore, provides a basis
for male superiority and misogyny even as it allows room for Christian
women to strive for ultimate union with God. This formula was widely accepted throughout the Latin Middle Ages and formed the basis for most
theological discussions about the nature of creation of men and women,

the spiritual relationship between the genders; it also informed the consequent laws and customs governing women's roles in Christian society. Thomas Aquinas, for example, worked out his careful discussion of the nature of human bodily creation and how human bodies can reflect the image of God by starting with Augustine's formulae.[11] Such ready acceptance of Augustine's position could certainly be understood as evidence of its usefulness to the patriarchal establishment of medieval Christianity; that is, Augustine's position kept on being useful to the church as a way of continually reiterating its position on (male) sacramental authority and hence on the institutional procedures that arose from this fundamental point. This is where theology and institutional politics (the need for an institution to maintain and reproduce itself across time) collaborate.

This solution to the problem, that women are spiritually equal to men and therefore in the image of God with regard to humanity but not with regard to femininity, was never formally debated in medieval theological circles. That is, there are no theological treatises from the Middle Ages arguing that women are fully in the image of God according to the physical creation of a woman's body. The reason is obvious: This understanding of Genesis provided both the theological underpinnings and the justification for the roles of women in the medieval church. Women were categorically excluded from sacramental leadership in the church, that is, from positions like the priesthood, which centered on symbolic activities in the place of Christ [in loco Christi], because of cultural expectations about gender roles, which rarely gave women position of authority over men.[12]

Yet, in spite of the lack of open debate about this issue, there was a way in which medieval Christians managed to emphasize women's spiritual abilities. For one thing, women were baptized, of course, and therefore capable of attaining salvation; thus they participated in some way in Christ's Incarnation. Furthermore, women often manifested great spiritual abilities, to the extent that there developed a system of female visionary experience mediated (and controlled) by male amanuenses.[13] Women's embodiment also became symbolically associated with spiritual metaphors of healing, feeding, and giving life—all things associated with the body of Christ both in the Incarnation and as present on earth in the church, and all things inherent in women's carnality.[14] To modern sensibilities, the resulting spiritual roles played by women may seem almost subversive, but in a medieval theological context, and especially from an Augustinian point of view, the contradictions made perfect sense.

For example, the twelfth-century abbess and polymath Hildegard of Bingen presented herself as a mouthpiece for the voice of God (as a prophet, in other words) even while accepting her status as a "poor little female."[15] It was a monastic convention to speak of oneself in as lowly terms as possible, and to take on the role of prophet as a directly inspired, but not sacramentally ordained, type of leadership, since many important monastic authors were not ordained to the priesthood.[16] Hildegard was a deeply intelligent and creative person who clearly took advantage of this way of claiming spiritual authority. But even she was watched over by male ecclesiastics, as is evident from the contrasting ways in which she and her two male biographers speak about her spiritual gifts and powers. Hildegard's *Vita* is a most interesting document in this regard. It was begun (rather unusually) while she was still alive by Gottfried of Disibodenberg, who had served Hildegard and her community as a secretary and provost. When Gottfried died in 1176, three years before Hildegard's death, he left one short book of nine chapters. The project was completed after Hildegard's death by Theodoric of Echternach (Trier), who wrote two more books, added prefaces, and appended to the text four letters about Hildegard.[17]

A telling aspect of this hagiographical treatise lies in the inclusion by both authors of long passages from Hildegard's writings, thus making the *Vita* a composite of three voices: Gottfried's, Theodoric's, and Hildegard's. Most of the passages from Hildegard come from the *Scivias,* her first mystical book, written between 1141 and 1151.[18] Hildegard's self-descriptions in the *Vita* thus come from a book dedicated to describing her interactions with the divine Word, and they have an immediate and unselfconscious air to them.

It is easy to see, as several scholars have pointed out, how different Hildegard's biblical models are from those of her biographers.[19] Notably, Hildegard compares herself with only biblical *men,* and with quite a parade of them: Noah, Joshua, Jacob, Joseph, Moses, Samson, David, Solomon, Jeremiah, Zacchaeus, and even Paul.[20] The only biblical woman with whom Hildegard compares herself in these passages selected by her biographers is Susanna, who stood up against false witnesses. Hildegard may thus have characterized herself as a "poor little woman" but she also portrayed herself among the Fathers.

In contrast, it is clear that Hildegard's biographers, especially Theodoric, want to portray her in the tradition of bridal mysticism. In a striking departure from Hildegard's own self-referential language, Theodoric portrays Hildegard at least six times as the Beloved of the Song of Songs, and refers at least twice to Christ as the Heavenly Bridegroom.[21] This disparity suggests, as Barbara Newman has noted, that Hildegard sees herself in the tradition of biblical prophecy, while Theodoric wants to portray her in the tradition of bridal mysticism.[22] In other words, Hildegard assumes for herself a prophetic leadership modeled most often by men, while her biographers cast her as the submissive female Bride of Christ. It is true that medieval men, especially in the monastic tradition, also used this bridal language to describe themselves in love relationships with Christ,[23] but they did so in a theological context in which they assumed that they were also in the image of God, and, insofar as some were priests, able to stand *in loco Christi*. That Hildegard could not assume any of this about herself might have had much to do with how she chose to describe herself.

The life of Catherine of Siena shows the same disparity between the way a medieval holy woman saw herself and the way she was portrayed for posterity by the male ecclesiastical elite. Catherine was the daughter of a well-to-do cloth dyer of Siena. Her father's house, now a museum dedicated to its most famous daughter, was just down the hill from San Domenico, the central Dominican church in Siena. Catherine's private devotions were shaped by this literally looming Dominican presence. Until the age of twenty-seven, she directed her piety to her own neighborhood, the Contrada dell'Oca, the section of the town that sponsored the green-clad horse and jockey with the goose mascot in the annual Pallio. She joined the *mantellate*, the Dominican-guided lay Sisters of Penance, caring for the poor and sick and acting as a local peacemaker.[24] She had her earliest religious experiences at home, in front of religious objects reminiscent of the Passion of Christ, such as the crucifix. As Karen Scott has shown, Catherine saw herself as an apostle."[25] This is an especially apt description for the last six years of her life, between the age of twenty-seven and her death at thirty-three (that is, 1374–1380), when Catherine traveled through central and northern Italy and southern France preaching peace and repentance to a world filled with political turmoil and conflict. These were the years in which the papacy had established itself at Avignon in the south of France, and Catherine is probably most famous for her special pleading with Pope Gregory XI to return the papacy to Rome. She was ultimately successful in that endeavor, although it must also be noted that this in turn led to the papal schism known as the Babylonian Captivity of the church, with rival papal courts in Rome, Avignon, and for a time also in Pisa.

Catherine may have been able to read, but she probably did not know how to write. Her letters and her one "book," the *Dialogue*, were probably dictated to a series of scribes.[26] The *Dialogue* is a serious work set as a conversation between a questing soul and God. The central part is an extended metaphor of the body of Christ as a bridge between heaven and earth. God says to the soul:

> This bridge, my only-begotten Son, has three stairs. Two of them he built on the wood of the most holy cross, and the third even as he tasted the great bitterness of the gall and vinegar they gave him to drink. You will recognize in these three stairs three spiritual stages. The first stair is the feet, which

symbolize the affections. For just as the feet carry the body, the affections carry the soul. My Son's nailed feet are a stair by which you can climb to his side, where you will see revealed his inmost heart. For when the soul has climbed up on the feet of affection and looked with her mind's eye into my Son's opened heart, she begins to feel the love of her own heart in his consummate and unspeakable love. [. . .] Then the soul, seeing how tremendously she is loved, is herself filled to overflowing with love. So, having climbed the second stair, she reaches the third. This is his mouth, where she finds peace from the terrible war she has had to wage because of her sins.[27]

This is the traditional Christian language of meditation on the sufferings of Christ as a means of spiritual development.[28] The passage is reminiscent of the claim of Catherine's biographer, Raymond of Capua, that she participated graphically in the imitation of Christ when, at the age of twenty-eight, she received the stigmata, visible by her own request only to herself.[29] It is also a clear example of the sort of *imitatio Christi* that follows from an Augustinian understanding of the relationship between the creation of human beings in the image of God and the incarnation of God in human form. The mimetic element of entering into Christ's sufferings was a very important part of Catherine's self-conscious spirituality, but this is not the tradition Raymond chose to emphasize in his portrait, perhaps because he saw it as too threatening (given that his famous confessee was a female), or perhaps because he wanted to stress another view of Catherine: the traditional role of the Bride of Christ.

The relationship between Raymond and Catherine was very complicated.[30] One thing that does seem clear is that after Catherine's death, Raymond's hagiographical intent was to portray her as a holy woman in the model of bridal mysticism rather than as the fierce *Apostola* she considered herself to be. An excellent example of this is the stark image Catherine gives in several of her letters of Christ marrying her with the foreskin of his circumcision (that is, with his bodily sacrifice), a graphic bit of symbolism that becomes for Raymond a ceremony presided over by the Virgin Mary and witnessed by a host of saints, in which Catherine gets a gold ring with pearls and diamonds, as shown in a painting from around 1900 by Alessandro Franchi.[31]

Raymond's concern to portray Catherine in the model of girl saint is evident from other stories in his *Vita,* such as the young Catherine cutting off her hair out of humility, or being visited by the Holy Spirit in the form of a dove (a miracle witnessed by her father Jacopo), or her ability to say the Ave Maria and fly miraculously up the stairs, as her mother Monna Lapa testified.[32] Catherine was a pragmatic church reformer who took on many male privileges (preaching, advising the pope, traveling back and forth between Rome and Avignon attempting to resolve the Great Schism). As a member of the Dominican Penitent movement, however, Catherine was supervised by male Dominicans, notably by her confessor Raymond.[33] Raymond's hagiographical vision of Catherine is our major source for her life and has been combed for details by generations of scholars and faithful, although it may well be a more useful index of the public religious environment of fourteenth-century Siena than of Catherine's personality or spiritual life. Just as Theodoric turned Hildegard the Prophet into Hildegard the Bride of Christ, so Raymond stresses Catherine's mystical marriage to Christ, although the practical, plainspoken, and blunt Catherine never described herself that way. Even at the beginning of the second part of the *Life,* when Raymond describes the difficulties and persecutions Catherine encountered in her lay apostolate in the world, he lavishly evokes the Song of Songs 5.1, where the Bride languishes awaiting the Bridegroom so that she can open to him.[34]

The examples of Hildegard and Catherine are meant to suggest some ways in which medieval Christian women of special spiritual gifts managed to find a way to act out the full implications of Christian teachings about the importance of humanity fashioned in the image of God. The fact that there never was an open theological debate on this issue may seem odd in the face of medieval debates about women, men, and gender in medieval vernacular literature. On the other hand, it is also obvious that the theological realm is one place where women had no official role and not even the possibility of a full education. Only the religious life (in the various forms it took during the long centuries of the Middle Ages), and particularly the mystical and visionary traditions, offered women a chance to be in the imitation of Christ. Yet, even in these realms, the male privilege of being explicitly in God's image and therefore worthy of serving in priestly roles was jealously guarded.

A letter of Pope Innocent III dating from a few decades after Hildegard's death shows just how rigorous this exclusion could be. Innocent writes to two Spanish bishops regarding the behavior of abbesses in their regions:

Recently certain news has been intimated to us, about which we marvel greatly, that abbesses, namely those situated in the dioceses of Burgos and Palencia, give blessings to their own nuns, and they also hear confessions of sins, and, reading the Gospel, they presume to preach in public. This thing is inharmonious as well as absurd, and not to be tolerated by us. For that reason, by means of our discretion from apostolic writing, we order that it be done no longer, and by apostolic authority to check it more firmly, for, although the Blessed Virgin Mary surpassed in dignity and in excellence all the Apostles, nevertheless it was not to her but to them that the Lord entrusted the keys to the kingdom of heaven.[35]

This letter was intended for a situation in which women were already exercising a significant degree of authority in their communities and beyond. One monastery for which this warning was evidently intended was Las Huelgas, a Cistercian house of women that was founded with royal and papal sanction. The abbesses of Las Huelgas had a good deal of power, exercising civil jurisdiction over sixty-four villages, and quasi-episcopal authority in a wide variety of circumstances.[36]

It is ironic to note that reading the Gospel in public and preaching, two of the functions Innocent III wanted to deny the abbesses, were in the early church duties assigned to deacons. It was by no means novel for medieval women to be performing some of these diaconal duties. In fact, there was a well-documented order of deaconesses in the first centuries of Christianity that gradually merged into the early medieval monastic orders; even in the twelfth century, there was an acknowledged connection between the roles of abbess and the deaconess of the early church.[37]

Another irony is the future of this letter in documents of canon law. It is quoted in its entirety in the *Decretals* of Pope Gregory IX, under the heading "An abbess cannot bless monastics, hear confessions, and preach in public."[38] The standard gloss (*glossa ordinaria*) for this section refers the reader to another part of the *Decretals,* where a letter of Pope Honorius II to the abbesses of the diocese of Halberstadt, dated 1222, forbids them to excommunicate their subject nuns and clerics.[39] Bernard of Parma's gloss on this passage is extremely rich, offering a broad commentary on the role of women according to church law. Crucial to the argument is the statement that women do not have the legal right of jurisdiction. Therefore, even though abbesses preside over their own communities, they do not have full legal powers as men do.[40] Further, the gloss links the letters of Innocent III and Honorius II in order to give the overarching rationale for these prohibitions: "A woman should not have such power, since she is not made in the image of God, but man is the image and glory of God, and the woman should be subject to the man and should be his handmaid."[41] Scholars have pointed out that the canon law tradition has been essential to the tradition of denying women's sacramental roles in the church.[42] But the ingredients of this denial were in place long before Innocent III.

There are several conclusions I would like to suggest from the material I have gathered here:

First, there was no theological *debate* per se about the nature of gender in the Middle Ages because medieval theology was based on an Augustinian reading of Scripture, especially of the first chapters of Genesis, which do not grant that women were created, as men were, in the image of God.

Second, although women did not have either the theological training or the intellectual context for undertaking such a debate, they did have the teaching of that very same Augustine that all human beings by virtue of their humanity are in the image of God, and that this humanity is taken on by Christ in the Incarnation.

Third, medieval women obviously saw that this opportunity for spiritual self-assertion could be argued from the great importance of the imitation of Christ among a certain type of spiritual elite. The ecclesiastical power elite knew this full well, and managed to control and even exploit spiritually gifted women, although they often chose to portray their charges in submissive terms.

Finally, however, the other side of the formula was always available, waiting in the wings: Any time women were thought to transgress their status, they could be forcibly reminded of their secondary status in the order of creation. Medieval Christianity was more than a "religious tradition" in our modern sense; it was a cultural construct that informed all aspects of life. Theological issues were discussed on a theoretical level by the magisterium of the church, but just as importantly, they were acted out in daily life not just out of a sense of "obedience" to a theological structure, but because that was how the natural world was understood. This meant that the question of the relationship between female existence and the image of God was a tool that could be used by medieval ecclesiastical leaders to effectively squelch debate on the subject of gender in Christian theology.

Notes

1. See especially Phyllis Trible, *God and the Rhetoric of Sexuality* (Philadelphia, Pa.: Fortress Press, 1978).
2. For Tertullian, see *On the Veiling of Virgins,* Alexander Roberts and James Donaldson, eds., in *Ante-Nicene Fathers* 4 (Grand Rapids, Mich.: Eerdmans, 1982; repr. of 1885 Edinburgh edition). See also Francine Cardman, Women, Ministry, and Church Order in Early Christianity, in *Women and Christian Origins,* ed. Ross Shepard Kraemer and Mary Rose D'Angelo (New York: Oxford, 1999), pp. 300–29. Sprenger and Kramer's *Malleus Maleficarum* has been translated into English by Montague Summers (London: The Pushkin Press, 1948) and widely anthologized. My citations are from *Witchcraft in Europe: 1100–1700: A Documentary History,* ed. Alan C. Kors and Edward Peters (Philadelphia: University of Pennsylvania Press, 1972), pp. 105–89.
3. *Malleus Maleficarum,* part 1, question 6, in Kors and Peters, eds., p. 121.

4. For a discussion of these divergent readings of Augustine, see E. Ann Matter, "Women," in *Augustine through the Ages: An Encyclopedia*, ed. Allan D. Fitzgerald (Grand Rapids, Mich.: William B. Eerdmans Publishing Company, 1999), pp. 887–92; E. Ann Matter, "Christ, God and Woman in the Thought of St. Augustine," *Augustine and His Critics: Essays in Honor of Gerald Bonner*, ed. Robert Dodaro and George Lawless (London and New York: Routledge, 2000), pp. 164–175; and Kim Power, *Veiled Desire: Augustine on Women* (New York: Continuum, 1996).

5. Gerald Bonner, "Christ, God and Man in the Thought of St. Augustine," *Angelicum* 61 (1984): 268–94, at p. 293; reprinted in *God's Decree and Man's Destiny: Studies on the Thought of Augustine of Hippo* (London: Variorum Reprints, 1987, II), pp. 268–94.

6. *De Genesi ad litteram* 9.5.9.

7. *De Genesi ad litteram* 11.42, *De vita beata* 2.10.

8. *De trinitate* 12.7.10

9. K. E. Børresen, *Subordination and Equivalence: The Nature and Role of Woman in Augustine and Thomas Aquinas*, tr. C. H. Talbot (Washington, D.C.: The University Press of America, 1981); idem, "In Defence of Augustine: How Feminine is Homo?" in *Collectanea Augustiniana: Mélange T. J. van Bavel*, ed. B. Bruning, M. Lamberigts, and J. van Houtem (Leuven: Institut Historique Augustinien, 1990) [= *Augustiniana* 40 (1990): 411–28]; S. Sonnecken, *Misogynie oder Philologie? Philologisch-theologische Untersuchungen zum Wortfeld Frau bei Augustinus* (Frankfurt-am-Main/New York: Peter Lang, 1993); J. A. Truax, "Augustine of Hippo: Defender of Women's Equality?" *Journal of Medieval History* 16 (1990): 279–99; F. E. Weaver and J. Laporte, "Augustine and Women: Relationships and Teachings," *Augustinian Studies* 12 (1981): 115–31; T. J. van Bavel, "Augustine's Views on Women," *Augustiniana* 39 (1989): 5–53; idem, "Woman as the Image of God in Augustine's *De trinitate* XII," in *Signum Petris: Festgabe für Cornelius Petrus Mayer OSA zum 60. Geburtstag*, ed. A. Zumkeller (Würzburg: Augustinus-Verlag, 1989), pp. 267–88; R. J. McGowan, "Augustine's Spiritual Equality: The Allegory of Man and Woman with Regard to *Imago Dei*," *Revue des études augustiniennes* 33 (1987): 255–64.

10. See, for example, Augustine's *Epistula* 147 for further elaboration of this ultimate equality.

11. Børresen, *Subordination and Equivalence*, pp. 155–78.

12. For the fullest discussion of the monastic world, in which women did sometimes assert authority over men, see Penelope D. Johnson, *Equal in Monastic Profession: Religious Women in Medieval France* (Chicago: University of Chicago Press, 1991). This authority stopped at the sacramental level, however, where the question of acting in the place of Christ became an issue.

13. See, for example, John Coakley, "Friars as Confidants of Holy Women in Medieval Dominican Hagiography," in *Images of Sainthood in Medieval Europe*, ed. Renate Blumenfeld-Kosinski and Timea Szell (Ithaca and London: Cornell University Press, 1991), pp. 222–46.

14. Caroline Walker Bynum, *Holy Feast and Holy Fast: The Religious Significance of Food to Medieval Women* (Berkeley and Los Angeles: University of California Press, 1987).

15. Barbara Newman, "Hildegard of Bingen: Visions and Validations," *Church History* 54 (1985): 163–75, and Newman's *Sister of Wisdom: St. Hildegard's Theology of the Feminine* (Berkeley and Los Angeles: University of California Press, 1987).

16. A dated but still useful overview of the monastic spirituality of the Middle Ages is Jean Leclercq, *The Love of Learning and the Desire for God: A Study of Monastic Culture,* trans. Catharine Misrahi (New York: Fordham University Press, rev. 1974).

17. Sabina Flanagan, *Hildegard of Bingen, 1098–1179: A Visionary Life* (London and New York: Routledge, 1989), pp. 1–2; *Vita Sanctae Hildegardis,* ed. M. Klaes, Corpus Christianorum, Continuatio Mediaevalis 126 (Turnhout: Brepols, 1993); *The Life of the Holy Hildegard,* trans. J. McGrath (Collegeville, Minn.: The Liturgical Press, 1980).

18. Hildegard of Bingen, *Scivias,* ed. A. Führkötter, Corpus Christianorum, Continuatio Mediaevalis 43, 43A (Turnhout: Brepols, 1978).

19. Catherine Mooney, "Disentangling Voices: Medieval Women Writers and Their Male Interpreters," lecture at Harvard University, April 1992; Barbara Newman, "Hildegard and Her Hagiographers: The Remaking of Female Sainthood," in *Gendered Voices: Medieval Saints and Their Interpreters,* ed. Catherine M. Mooney (Philadelphia: University of Pennsylvania Press, 1999), pp. 16–34.

20. Most of these references are from *Vita* II, 14, which is concerned with the battle between the spirit and the flesh.

21. For references to the bridal mysticism of the Song of Songs, see *Vita* I, 9; II, 1, 3, 17.

22. Newman, "Hildegard and Her Hagiographers," pp. 26–27.

23. E. Ann Matter, *The Voice of My Beloved: The Song of Songs in Western Medieval Christianity* (Philadelphia: University of Pennsylvania Press, 1990). For an excellent medieval example, see Walter Daniel, *Vita Ailredi Abbatis Rievall (The Life of Aelred of Rievaulx),* ed. Maurice Powicke (Oxford: Clarendon Press, 1978).

24. See Karen Scott, "Urban Spaces, Women's Networks, and the Lay Apostolate in the Siena of Catherine Benincasa," in *Creative Women in Medieval and Early Modern Italy: A Religious and Artistic Renaissance,* ed. E. Ann Matter and John Coakley (Philadelphia: University of Pennsylvania Press, 1994), pp. 105–19.

25. Karen Scott, "Catherine of Siena'" *Apostola, Church History* 61 (1992): 34–46.

26. Catherine of Siena, *The Dialogue,* trans. Suzanne Noffke (New York: Paulist Press, 1980). See Noffke's introduction for a discussion of how Catherine may have composed her works.

27. Catherine of Siena, *The Dialogue,* trans. Noffke, p. 64.

28. The literature on this theme is vast, but see most recently Ellen Ross, *The Grief of God* (New York: Oxford University Press, 1997).

29. Raymond of Capua, *De S. Catharina Senensi virgine de poenitentia S. Dominici* pars 2, caput 7, *Acta Sanctorum* 12 (April 30), p. 910.

30. John Coakley, "Friars as Confidants of Holy Women in Medieval Dominican Hagiography," pp. 222–46.

31. Caroline Walker Bynum, *Holy Feast and Holy Fast,* pp. 174–75, quoting from Catherine's Letter 50 and Letter 221; see note 135, pp. 376–77. Franchi's painting is in the museum dedicated to Catherine in her parental house in Siena.

32. Raymond of Capua, *Vita* pars 1, caput 2 (p. 874 D), pars 1, caput 2 (p. 875 D), pars 1, caput 1 (p. 870 E). The Catherine museum in Siena includes nineteenth-century paintings of all of these scenes.

33. Maiju Lehmijoki-Gardner, *Worldly Saints: Social Interaction of Dominican Penitent Women in Italy, 1200–1500* (Helsinki: Suomen Historiallinen Seura, 1999), for Dominican Penitent women in general. Lehmijoki-Gardner is preparing a volume of translations of writings by Dominican Penitents for the Paulist Press series *Classics of Western Spirituality.*

34. *Acta Sanctorum,* April 30: 891 (II.i.118).

35. Innocent III, *Epistula* 187 (11 December, 1210) PL 216: 356.

36. Las Huelgas was founded in 1187 by Alfonso VIII of Castile and his wife Leonora. The jurisdiction of the abbess was confirmed by Pope Urban VIII and not suspended (in spite of Innocent III's letter) until 1873, when Pius IX voided all exempt monastic jurisdictions in Spain. See J. M. Escriviá, *La abadesa de Las Huelgas* (Madrid: Editorial Luz, 1944).

37. The great care with which Peter Abelard discussed the proximity of the role of the abbess to the ancient order of deaconesses is discussed by Mary Martin McLaughlin, "Abelard and the Dignity of Women: Twelfth-Century 'Feminism' in Theory and Practice," in *Pierre Abélard, Pierre le Vénérable* (Cluny: Abbaye de Cluny, 1972), pp. 288–334. On women deacons, see Ida Raming, *The Exclusion of Women from the Priesthood: Divine Law or Sex Discrimination?* trans. N. R. Adams (Metuchen, N. J.: Scarecrow Press, 1976), and, more recently, Mary Rose D'Angelo, "Diakonia," in *Dictionary of Feminist Theologies,* ed. Letty M. Russell and Shannon Clarkson (Louisville, Ky.: Westminster/John Knox, 1996), pp. 66–67; J. G. Davies, "Deacons, Deaconesses and the Minor Orders in the Patristic Period," *Journal of Ecclesiastical History* 14 (1963): 1–2; and Cardman, "Women, Ministry, and Church Order in Early Christianity."

38. Gregory IX, *Decretals Corpus iuris Canonici,* lib. 5, tit. 38, *De Poenitentia* ch. 10, "Nova," ed. J. Friedberg (Leipzig: Bernhard Tauchnitz, 1928) 2: 886–87.

39. Gregory IX, *Decretals,* lib. 1, tit. 33, *De Maioritate et Obedientia* cap. 12, "Dilecta," ed. Friedberg, 2:201.

40. "Dicas quod abbatissa habet iurisdictionem talem qualem, non ita plenam, sicut vir habet, Bernard of Parma," *Glossa in Decretal,* lib. 1, tit. 33, cap. 12, "Dilecta", no. C, "Iurisdictione," ed. A. Nardi (Lyons: Huegeton et Barbier, 1671) 2:431.

41. Ibid., 432.

42. Joan A. Range, "Legal Exclusion of Women from Church Office," *The Jurist* 34 (1974): 119. It is startling to note that part of Innocent III's letter was quoted in the 1977 Vatican document *Declaration on the Question of the Admission of Women to the Ministerial Priesthood;* see *Women Priests: A Catholic Commentary on the Vatican Declaration,* ed. Leonard Swidler and Arlene Swidler (New York: Paulist Press, 1977), p. 40, and the commentary on the passage by E. Ann Matter, "Innocent III and the Keys to the Kingdom of Heaven," pp. 145–51.

CHAPTER 3

REFIGURING THE "SCANDALOUS EXCESS" OF MEDIEVAL WOMAN: THE WIFE OF BATH AND LIBERALITY

Alcuin Blamires

In medieval debate about gender, moral claims and counter-claims were a lively medium of contention through which subtle reversals could be wrought. This essay shows how Chaucer uses the Wife of Bath's discourse to gender the ethical concept of "liberality" feminine, especially in the realms of counsel and of sexuality. The Wife of Bath's Prologue and Tale thus convert the misogynous notion of feminine "excess" into a positive, a strategy here termed "redoctrination."

Medieval defenses of women can seem strangely heterogeneous: Bizarre conglomerations of biblical observation, judicial logic, physiology, anecdote, exemplum, moral polemic, topped off with a colorful froth of psychoanalytical speculation about the motives of detractors. Yet there is an underlying continuity, which is to be found in the moral or ethical dimension of the debate. This is explicitly so, of course, where a writer tries to claim particular virtues for one sex and to demonize the other sex by ascribing contrary vices, as in the case of wrangling over whether men or women are more sexually depraved. The moral preoccupation is sustained with regard to the contentious crux of the relative guilt of Adam or Eve. Gender issues remain moral issues when exempla of all sorts are invoked in defense of women or against them. The present essay will show that although moral implications may not always be very apparent to us, medieval gender discourse invokes particular "vices and virtues" categories in nuanced ways. We shall enhance our understanding even of such heavily discussed works as *The Wife of Bath's Prologue* and *Tale* if we retrieve the strategies of moral dialectic that they incorporate.[1]

The element of moral dialectic within the gender debate that may yet prove most interesting—for there are discoveries to be made—is the strategy whereby medieval defenders of women translated alleged moral deficits of women into moral credits. Since from our perspective medieval constructions of women appear generated and sustained through persistent indoctrination, it might be apt to use the term *redoctrination* to designate the strategy that reverses normative paradigms of deficits and credits. Of course, these reversals could readily be referred to as "paradoxes." The disadvantage of thinking in terms of paradox is that commentary on early gender polemic often reads paradox as a self-mocking trope, one that draws skeptical attention to the sheer brazenness with which it switches traditional weaknesses into strengths.[2] Interpreted thus, paradox used in defense of women dwindles into an intellectual juggling act, or what Helen Solterer calls a "two-timing discourse" for the entertainment of the cognoscenti.[3] That it was occasionally so should not forestall inquiry into the serious (though not necessarily solemn) revisionary moves that the rhetoric of reversal could accomplish. Adoption of the fresh term "redoctrination" may encourage us to appreciate afresh the radical intervention in gender prejudice that proponents of reversal sometimes sought to achieve.

Specimen medieval examples of this redoctrination, deriving profeminine hypotheses (of a sort) from various misogynistic notions of feminine deficiency, would be: That the ascribed "weakness" or "fragility" of women fosters a peace loving disposition, as against the violence that masculine "hardness" induces;[4] and that the imputed "inferiority" of woman's judgment logically implies that Adam must be held more guilty in the Fall than Eve.[5]

I should like to investigate here another, quite drastic instance of redoctrination, one that discloses a fascinating collision of moral impulses lurking within misogyny, near the heart (even) of gender debate in the Middle Ages. The justification for claiming so much would be that the instance I have in mind focuses on excess. The expression "scandalous excess" in the title of this paper is borrowed from Howard Bloch's 1987 article on medieval misogyny.[6] By "scandalous excess" Bloch means extravagance in dress and ornament such as misogyny anciently pilloried in women—an excess characterized as "surplus," and which he identifies as a corollary of the secondariness of woman in Creation.[7] For in woman's status as "supplement" to Adam, Bloch detects the core of a misogynous paradigm that holds women supplementary, literally an "excess," in all respects. (Actually Bloch is too mesmerized by this paradigm of supplementarity;

he elides the difference between "supplementary" and "second." After all, to the argument that the male had prime position in Creation, there was from early times the ready retort that woman was created second to an improved formula;[8] or, in the bibliographic analogy delightfully proposed by Constantia Munda in 1617, woman was the "second edition" of God's best creation—presumably with the import that second editions remove the defects found in the first.)[9]

Yet "scandalous excess" is a resonant expression for quite other reasons than Bloch indicates. Excess, in the ethical tradition that the Middle Ages received from antiquity, was the malfunction of a given virtue in one direction; deficiency was the malfunction in the other direction. The principle was Aristotelian, but the Middle Ages did not have to wait for the complete translation of Aristotle's *Ethics* in the thirteenth century to know of it, for it percolated through other channels, such as the *sententia* voiced in Chaucer's *Canon's Yeoman's Tale:* "That that is overdoon, it wol nat preeve / Aright . . . it is a vice" (VIII.645–6).[10]

Now innumerable readers have come across the sort of dyspeptic rhetoric produced by medieval writers about alleged vices of excess and deficiency in women. There are notorious and shrill examples in the last part of Andreas Capellanus's *De amore.* Women are there held to be driven by *rapacitas,* addicted to gain, to the extent that they consider it a virtue to hoard whatever they get [*omnia reservare*] and to give it to none [*nemini largiri*].[11] As against the deficiency of generosity shown in this material avarice, they are also held to display a contrary excess of sexual generosity, for they are driven by lust and "unable to deny" their bodies [*neque sui corporis solatia denegare*], so no man could satisfy their libido.[12] A further classic allegation of excess in Andreas concerns speech. It is the complaint that women can't keep quiet. Secrets burn them up inside; women cannot restrain their tongues from talking.[13]

Familiarity with this material breeds neglect, but what happens if we delve into the categories of excess and deficiency here glimpsed in Andreas, and into their relations to gender stereotypes? We shall focus on the virtue of liberality, or largesse—*liberalitas* and *largitas* being, it must be emphasized, interchangeable names in the Middle Ages for the virtue of generosity: "Another word for liberality [*liberalitas*] is bountifulness [*largitas*]."[14]

In certain crucial ways, of course, the chief medieval womanly virtue was guarding or keeping, not giving. It was a social hypothesis of ancient origin, still urged by Christine de Pizan in *Le Livre des trois vertus,* that while a man's role is to acquire goods for the household, a woman's is to "conserve" such goods through prudent domestic management (Latin *conservare,* Middle English *kepen*).[15] She should steer prudently between parsimony and wastefulness, for, as *The Merchant's Tale* hypothesizes, she

"kepeth his good, and wasteth never a deel" (IV.1343). This arrangement
tended to reserve to males the prerogative of conspicuous material liberality[16] and therefore the charisma of what was often reckoned a particularly
fine virtue of humanity.[17] That *largesse* "makes" the noble man was a medieval maxim, as one could read on the authority of Boethius.[18] Conversely, in Lydgate's *Fall of Princes* it is axiomatic that in the case of a lord
who abandons "largesse," "negardship exilith ientilesse."[19] The classic medieval story of competitive *liberalità* (taken up by Chaucer in *The Franklin's
Tale*) explores the magnanimity of three males. The woman in the story, the
Dorigen figure, apparently has no claim in the competition.[20]

Since some readers of courtly literature will primarily be aware of
largesse as a defining feature of social class, it is important to observe at this
point that largesse/liberality was not a concept discussed only with reference to class (i.e., the nobility, who clearly could afford to be generous).
Rather, as this study seeks to show, it had a wider scope, which derived in
part from biblical advice; it also had an asymmetrical gender application.
Even the world of literary courtship, where generosity served to distinguish noble from *vilein* behavior, tended to reinforce an insinuation that
largesse was masculine. The *Romance of the Rose* commands male lovers to
give "largement."[21] The lover in Gower's *Confessio amantis* fanatically com-
plies—he would shower his lady with gifts if she would let him—"Als fre-
liche as god hath it yive, / It schal ben hires"[22] (V.4769–70). Giving as
lavishly as God has given: It is a significant formulation, as we shall see.

How much did the patterns of thought we are following *exclude*
women from the prerogative of practicing liberality? Christine de Pizan,
repudiating misogynous suppositions of female greed, pointedly asserts in
her *City of Ladies* that she could dwell on the endless *largesces* and *liberalités*
of women, who are only too happy to see money used with wise generosity rather than hoarded away in some chest by a miser.[23] In this respect,
Christine makes the classic reactive move in the debate about women: She
recovers for women a virtue that the other side alleges they lack. But
equally, as the passage implicitly discloses, Christine is aware that many
women are not in a position to practice the virtue of liberality because
they are kept on a tight rein financially by miserly husbands.[24] They "guard
the little that they can have" for the sake of the household, she suggests,
but their reward is perverse—they acquire a reputation for graspingness.[25]
Unwittingly echoing Christine, Andrée Blumstein deduces that historically there is a social causation for stereotypes of womanly "greed" in the
structured financial dependence of women on men, which fixed women
in the position of petitioning males for money.[26] Christine herself would
have found the stereotype rehearsed in one of her sources, the *De
mulieribus claris* of Boccaccio, who confirms an assumption that women are

innately parsimonious even as he expresses enthusiasm over exceptions.[27] Christine protests that this imputed vice should be revised into a virtue: Using the other classic debating move, which I have dubbed redoctrination, she proves the alleged "avarice" to be "prudence" instead. Such behavior "is not at all avarice or greed, but is a sign of great prudence."[28]

Small wonder that wives are heard in *The Canterbury Tales* insisting that one of the top seven qualities women want in husbands is generosity: They should be *free,* and *no nygard*.[29] But however generous a husband might be, a wife was supposed to "conserve" her husband's goods on his behalf just as she conserved her body on his behalf, since her body constituted another category of his "goods." A kind of wordplay reinforced the principle of double conservation. In Boccaccio's Latin, it is a matter of being both *servatrix pudicitiae* [guardian of her sexual modesty] and *servatrix thesaurum* [guardian of the family treasures].[30] In English, it is a matter of the wife "*keeping* goods": In Chaucer's *Shipman's Tale,* a merchant urges his wife to "kepe oure good" scrupulously, just when she has in fact decided to offer a sexual part of it elsewhere (VII.241–3). Generosity in a woman might carry a certain danger. There should be some keeping in a lady's giving.[31]

However, if some cultural impulses favored a feminine generosity that was scrupulously calibrated, other cultural impulses constructed the feminine to be a beneficent, abundant source of bounty and radiance. One such cultural impulse that is pertinent here linked the feminine with the dissemination of goodness. It came through medieval lyric tradition and was of a Neo-Platonist kind, derived from sources such as Pseudo-Dionysius. Pseudo-Dionysius offers the following definition of divine goodness: "The Essential Good, by the very fact of its existence, extends goodness into all things." Like the sun, which "gives light to whatever is able to partake of its light," the originary principle of Good "sends the rays of its undivided goodness to everything with the capacity . . . to receive it."[32]

The significance of this in the present context is that it contributes powerfully to a concept of liberality that Chaucer reaches for when he wants to memorialize a woman, Duchess Blanche, in his elegiac poem *The Book of the Duchess.* In this text, the Black Knight eventually describes his dead wife as a paradigm of abundance. True, he has to accommodate the proprieties of more inhibiting feminine virtues before winning through to that thought. We are assured that her charismatic and magnetic look was consistent with "mesure" ; it was never "foly sprad" (line 874), and it bespoke a "brotherly" love for decent folk. In *this* sort of love "she was wonder large" [marvellously generous, ll.891–3].

Yet Chaucer finally allows the discourses of Neo-Platonism and liberality to triumph over the discourse of decorum. When Blanche relaxed, he says,

> . . . she was lyk to torche bryght
> That every man may take of lyght
> Ynogh, and hyt hath never the lesse.
> Of maner and of comlynesse
> Ryght so ferde my lady dere;
> For every wight of hire manere
> Myght cacche ynogh, yif that he wolde,
> Yif he had eyen hir to biholde. (ll.961–70)

Here is the familiar Neo-Platonic concept of rays of goodness (in Blanche's case, her "manere"), which can be "caught" by every person with the capacity to do so ["Yf he had eyen . . ."]. But here also is a simile powerfully associated with liberality: The simile of a distribution of fire or light from a source (in this case, a torch) that remains unimpoverished by such distribution.

The locus classicus for this analogy is Cicero's ethical treatise, the *De officiis* I.16. Cicero finds the elementary principle of *liberalitas*—what he calls *vulgaris liberalitas*—enshrined in the offering of common property for the common benefit. He exemplifies this through a quotation from Ennius: "To give directions to another who's lost, is to light another's lamp by one's own: No less shines one's own lamp after lighting another's." The principle is reiterated in the maxim "let anyone who will, take fire from fire." Other maxims reinforcing the point are that water should be freely given from a flowing source, and (something to note in relation to *The Wife of Bath's Tale*) that one should give good advice to anyone in doubt. Cicero argues that ideal liberality with private property actually conforms to the same principle, that is, it does not seriously deplete one's means—otherwise liberality consumes the basis for further liberality.[33]

In ethical literature, accordingly, liberality is always delicately poised between parsimony (deficient liberality) on one hand, and prodigality (excess liberality) on the other:

> Tak Avarice and tak also
> The vice of Prodegalite;
> Between hem Liberalite,
> Which is the vertu of Largesse,
> Stant and governeth his noblesse.[34]

True, Christian moral treatises tirelessly repeated that if you had much, you should give lavishly, mindful of the *largesse* of God to humanity[35]—a divine abundance that is itself memorably imagined by the writer of the Middle English *Pearl* in terms of water poured out of a bottomless gulf.[36] God's largesse was a model of *un*calculating charity—and definitions of largesse overlapped considerably, albeit a little uncomfortably, with those of charity. The ethic of giving uncalculatingly might be said to have been always in tension with the received reverence for moderation. "In Charity," as Sir Francis Bacon was to assert, "there is no Excesse."[37]

Sometimes in medieval discussion there lurks a beguiling hypothesis that if you emulate unrestrained divine abundance, God will enhance your resources to sustain such generosity. When the personification of Largesse is described in *The Romance of the Rose*, Guillaume de Lorris writes that "God caused her wealth to multiply, so that however much she gave away, she always had more."[38] But if human generosity here fortunately accelerates, as it were, the divine supply, it was more normal to urge, unlike Sir Francis Bacon, that liberality be moderated according to the Ciceronian (and Aristotelian) golden mean. The right use of riches meant avoiding excess or *foollargesse* on one side and parsimony on the other.[39] The crux was the first of these: A self-impoverishing generosity was not largesse—it was prodigality.

The wonder of Chaucer's Blanche is that her personality is a torchlike phenomenon that is at once private yet *undepletable*. She herself, or her radiant personality, is (in modern idiom) an infinitely "sustainable resource." What the remainder of this paper will argue is that the Wife of Bath models herself, or is modeled, in much the same way.

Chaucer's Wife of Bath carries out a policy of bodily *largesse*. She formulates this in the terms appropriate to the moral discourse of liberality. Liberality, after all, is about the right *use* of riches. Everyone, she recalls from Scripture, has some special gift from God (III.103–4). She proposes to utilize whatever bountiful sexual resources she has received. It is precisely the sort of argument found in moral exhortations to generosity and charity. "So bids St Peter [as *The Book of Vices and Virtues* puts it] that the graces that God hath lent us, that we should deal forth to our neighbours" in the interests of "common profit."[40] The underlying ethical principle was that whatever superabundance some people have, they have in order to gain the merit of "dispensing it well" [*bona dispensatio*].[41]

It is in this spirit that the Wife of Bath sees herself as using her "instrument" as "frely" as God has given it (ll.149–50)—indeed, she says she uses it free of pedantic calculations about her partner's size, color, degree of poverty, or humble social status (ll.622–6). In the same spirit, she represents herself bestowing her body as refreshment, so as to emulate the Lord's own miracle of supplying five undepletable barley loaves that could feed five thousand.

All of which is brought to a sensational focus in Alisoun's own adoption of the old Ciceronian liberality topos. Declaring women's desire to be free and expansive, ["at oure large," l.322], she argues that husbands should be contented with a sufficiency from wives, and generous-minded about any surplus:

> Ye shul have queynte right ynogh at eve.
> He is to greet a nygard that wolde werne
> A man to lighte a candle at his lanterne;
> He shal have never the lasse light, pardee.
> Have thou ynogh, thee thar nat pleyne thee. (ll.332–6)

Chaucer may have picked up this knowingly sexual application of the
"torch" image from one of his favorite authors, Ovid, in *Ars Amatoria,* or
from Jean de Meun, who, in the *Romance of the Rose,* suggests that such an
application is notorious.[42] One's first thought may be that it is a spurious
travesty of the social imperative of generosity, or of what was admired in
Blanche.[43] Blanche, of course, radiates her charisma unselfconsciously, in a
stringently *involuntary* way,[44] which corresponds rather precisely with the
Pseudo-Dionysian notion of goodness as a source exerting raylike benefi-
cence by virtue of its sheer existence, not as a matter of active choice. By
contrast, the Wife flaunts her bounty self-consciously, laced with a mischievous nuance of threat ["ye *shul* have ynogh"]. Small wonder that this
is the side of *The Wife of Bath's Prologue* that prompts even well-disposed
critics to splutter censoriously about the Wife's "theatrical exaggeration of
female sexuality," her "licentious charity," and her "false analogies" that
"pervert" orthodox positions.[45]

Must that be our response? Might not Chaucer have become genuinely
interested in asking why personal physical "superabundance" should not
come under the rubric of liberality? When Boccaccio does almost the
same thing in a story in the *Decameron,* the fictional audience, albeit at first
amused, concludes unanimously that the point is accurately made. Again
the context presents a spirited woman protesting her moral obligation to
give away whatever sexual surplus her husband is unable to respond to.
This is the tale of Madonna Filippa, who is arrested for adultery but re-
solves to defend herself with "the truth." Her defense is that the law on
adultery bears inequitably on women, who in any case can satisfy more
male partners than vice versa. Thus, having satisfied her husband sexually,
"What is she to do with what is left over?" Is it not better for her to "present it to a gentleman who loves her" rather than "throw it to the dogs" or
let it "turn bad or go to waste"?[46] Implicitly invoked here as the opposite
of good practice in liberality is a stereotype of niggardliness—the skinflint
who hoards food only for it to go off.[47] Such hoarding amounts in medieval moral discourse to a defrauding of those who might otherwise have
benefited from it.[48]

Technically it might be easy to puncture the moral delight of both
Madonna Filippa and Alisoun in their sustainable bodily largesse. For one
thing, although liberality did not consist only in material goods, but in other

forms of assistance too, sexual favors are not a medium of generosity that the discourse of liberality normally contemplates. For another, according to strict doctrine, Alisoun's body is not hers to give: The lantern owner in her analogy is her husband.[49] Ethical discourse insists, moreover, that liberality is to be applied in the "right way" to the "right recipients,"[50] whereas Alisoun confesses to observing "no discrecioun" in her choice of recipients (ll.622–6). Above all, there is the catch that moralists knew that the characteristic trick of prodigality was to pass itself off as liberality. Each vice can be masked as a virtue, and so, according to Alan of Lille, "a harlotlike relationship with Prodigality lyingly advertises itself as a tribute to Generosity."[51] Alisoun's generosity certainly sounds more like prodigality when she later associates herself with Venus's love of "ryot and dispence" (III.700).

Even if it were conceded, however, that the Wife of Bath is disguising prodigality as generosity, she would retain more sympathy in terms of ethical discourse than the miser. Aristotle had already noted that prodigality resembles liberality, that actually the prodigal has the natural inclination toward liberality, and even that a prodigal is distinctly preferable to a miser because "he benefits a number of people," whereas the niggard "benefits nobody" (a concession echoed by Aquinas).[52] This is rather crucial because the Wife of Bath is representing tightfisted lantern owners (her husbands) as "niggards," as part of her overall campaign to project men as a miserly species intent on locking all women and cash away in the safe. At least her natural bent toward liberality benefits somebody.

It is not just that the Wife's prodigality *resembles* largesse. Her attitude conforms in another important respect with that virtue, in that she thinks in terms of "not withholding." Witness her famous suggestion that she "koude noght withdrawe" her "chambre of Venus from a good felawe" (III.617–18). A characteristic of largesse, though one that always took it riskily near prodigality, was that true generosity makes it hard to hold back one's goods. Vernacular writers were aware of this, but the point is formally and etymologically made by Aquinas, who explains that *largitas* and *liberalitas* are synonyms because both signify a "letting go" rather than a "retention."[53]

Such evidence may not of itself remove skepticism. It might be felt that this exploration of the liberality discourse merely confirms that the Wife's *Prologue* is a lurid parody of (or at least a joke about) these ethical issues— and that at the end of the day Chaucer does no more than highlight with a snigger a disproportion between female and male sexual capacities. Yet a reason for tempering skepticism arises if we recall that the Ciceronian passage that is a matrix for the torch/lantern figure links it with other gestures of liberality: In particular, with giving directions to someone lost, or giving good advice to someone in doubt. It was not necessary to go back to Cicero to know that liberality encompassed kind advice. "Largesse does

not consist only in material gifts, as a wise man has said, but also in com-
forting words," as Christine de Pizan generalizes.[54] Moreover, an association of the torch figure with freely given counsel was especially
conspicuous in the Middle Ages at a high point of the ubiquitous Alexander narrative: Alexander, having heard that the abstemious King Dindimus
frowns on his own lifestyle, somewhat rashly invites Dindimus to counsel
him about it. Alexander adds that by giving such counsel Dindimus will
not diminish his own wisdom any more than a "blazing brand" or "bright
candle" is diminished by igniting other lights.[55]

The availability of such a connection in the late Middle Ages opens the
possibility, at a stroke, of a new way of understanding the relation between
the sexual liberality banteringly mooted in the Wife's *Prologue,* and the liberality of counsel that is offered at two points by the old woman of *The Wife
of Bath's Tale:* First when she whispers a secret answer to the despairing
knight (who is indeed "lost") in order to save his life; and second when she
counsels him about his prejudices after he has been obliged to marry her.
Readers often wonder whether in disclosing the secret she epitomizes medieval stereotypes of women as "incontinent of speech," as "overflowing
mouths."[56] Alisoun tempts us with that stereotype by introducing a story of
Midas's wife, who could not contain the secret that Midas had grown ass's
ears.[57] Yet the point of this much-discussed allusion, I suggest, is that Midas
was a byword for *avarice.*[58] Mrs. Midas epitomizes the antithesis of that
avarice: To her it seemed that her knowledge "swal so soore aboute hir herte
/ That nedely som word hire moste asterte," and Alisoun comments: "out it
moot" (III.967–8, 980). This un-withholdability should not be written off
as sheer indiscipline. It further articulates liberality's "letting go" as opposed
to "retention." So too the old woman's liberality with her counsel in the tale
deploys the nondiminishing resource of words to save a life, and such liberality is to be associated with Alisoun's bodily generosity.[59]

Counsel was certainly associated with generosity in medieval moral literature, however unexpected that link may be to us.[60] In *The Book of Vices
and Virtues* it is the spiritual Gift of Counsel, vested particularly in the elderly, that is held to dispel the sin of avarice and to promote the virtue of
mercy or *pitee,* which people can primarily enact by being *large and curteis*
to each other, as opposed to keeping shut purses like covetous men.[61] As
it happens, this is quite a good description of the efficacy of the elderly
woman's counseling of the knight in the *Wife of Bath's Tale.*

Miserliness, not largesse, is gendered masculine by Alisoun. Through her
is expressed an idea that women stand against masculine miserliness in three
of life's most important departments: money, sex, and speech. The ethic of
largesse is here decisively regendered feminine. The sensual largesse in Alisoun is unrestrained, but a woman's unrestraint is what saves the knight's

life in the tale. Admittedly there is a contradictory current in Alisoun's self-presentation—her *Prologue* speaks of "winning" and "selling" and even "ransom."[62] This is a reminder that her *Prologue* discourse produces emphases of such inconsistency as to build what Arthur Lindley calls a "haystack of contradictions," and the disconcerting oscillation between generous and mercantile impulses is one of its facets.[63] But whereas the intermittently mercantile impulse has been widely noted, neither the full extent of Alisoun's impulse of liberality nor its subtle continuity between *Prologue* and *Tale* has been well understood. Besides, her tough trade talk constitutes at least in part a survival tactic adopted in reaction to masculine oppression. The trigger that can switch off feminine reactiveness and *enable men to understand women's liberality* is a change in men's own perception of women, a removal of the scales from the eyes: "Cast up the curtyn, looke how that it is," to quote the old woman at the end (III.1249).[64] To reach this stage, it seems that feminine largesse has to save men from themselves.

If the exploration of these ideas in *The Wife of Bath's Prologue* and *Tale* gives grounds, hitherto unnoticed, for a positive ethical interpretation worth pondering in itself, such exploration also raises some wider questions touching on gender and essentialism. In particular, we might ask whether the refiguring, or redoctrination, of female "excess" as "liberality" escapes the frying pan of one misogynistic stereotype only to fall into the fire of another kind of essentialism; and more broadly, there is the problem of whether the whole notion of appropriating moral attributes seriously advanced any profeminine position in medieval debate about women.

It is as well to begin by heading off one sinister possibility. What we have seen are two male writers, Chaucer and Boccaccio, redefining an untamable sexual impetus, something that misogyny fears in women, as a form of admirable generosity. The whole thing could be interpreted as the misogynous trick of the male author: What men cannot own of women's sexuality through conventional doctrines of chastity, they seek to gain "on the side" by invoking an alternative doctrine of liberality that authorizes women to distribute their surplus urges freely (blissfully oblivious, meanwhile, to outcomes such as pregnancy).

The catch here is that male writers are joined by female in this project. Marie de France writes a whole *lai* (*Lanval*) in which a woman's material and sexual bounty pointedly shows up deficiencies in Arthurian society. In this story a mysterious woman offers Lanval her love when he has been neglected by the court. She becomes a source that emulates the undiminishable quality of God's abundance; for when Lanval commits himself to her, she gives a double boon that "however generously [*largement*] he gave or spent, she would still find enough for him"; and wherever love might be made, there he would find her, ready.[65] When he fails the sole condition she places on this bounty, and discloses this secret love, her generosity still extends to saving him from the wrath of Arthur and Guinevere. She transports him out of society altogether. Although this tale raises questions about male sexual fantasy, and although it hints that the woman's liberality is a phenomenon somehow incompatible with the cynical state of normative society (it is an ideal unattained even by so elevated a woman as Arthur's queen), the impression that nevertheless Marie deliberately locates the principle of largesse of all sorts in a woman remains hard to resist. As Regula Evitt puts it, "The woman's 'giving gift' establishes a paradigm of concatenating, reproductive generosity: one that Marie associates with the feminine autonomy that Celtic myth regularly ascribes to the otherworld. The woman gives so that Lanval can give; she, in turn, will give more if Lanval will give more as well."[66]

Of course, any suggestion that generosity might be a special virtue of women would nowadays strike many readers as an essentializing move, and one liable, moreover, to essentialize that virtue in ways convenient to men. Doubtless the same risk attaches to the much more recent, and extremely pertinent, discussion of "giving" by Hélène Cixous in her well-known piece entitled "Sorties." Cixous suggests that what men want out of their giving is to prove something, to gain "plus-value of virility, authority, power," and that men can't help this because that is "how society is made." But where a woman is concerned, "How does *she* give?"

> She too gives *for.* She too, with open hands, gives herself—pleasure, happiness, increased value, and enhanced self-image. But she doesn't try to "recover her expenses." She is able not to return to herself, never settling down, pouring out, going everywhere to the other. She does not flee extremes; she is not the being-of-the-end (the goal), but she is how-far-being—reaches.

A paragraph later, Cixous is developing a similar view of libido, arguing that a woman does not "create a monarchy of her body or her desire"; hers is not a "party dictatorship." "Her libido is cosmic, just as her unconscious is worldwide."[67] A few lines further on, Cixous adds a familiar *verbal* dimension to this vision of liberality: "Her tongue doesn't hold back but holds forth, doesn't keep in but keeps on enabling." Obviously what is provocative here in relation to what we have discussed is both the convergence of certain liberational drives that are held to constitute something centrally "feminine," and the consciously insurrectionist, patriarchy-subverting tonality with which they are asserted.

The presence of these emphases in Cixous's writing demonstrates that the redoctrination that refutes the misogynous charge of feminine excess by self-consciously celebrating that excess as liberality articulates a defense of the feminine that is having a long history. And just as Cixous worries some feminists by seeming to "run the risk of constructing a universal model of femininity,"[68] so the medieval profeminine alternative to the alleged female vice of "excess" leans distinctly toward an essentializing version of woman as icon of sexual and material sustenance.

Notwithstanding that, there is a case for saying that in the context of a culture in which Andreas and others could wield their bullying rhetoric with impunity, any challenge to misogyny is nevertheless worth hearing about. The redoctrination strategy had, I suppose, a kind of disconcerting or destabilizing efficacy. The same can be said of Christine de Pizan's assertion that what men stereotyped as women's tightfistedness was really prudence—a necessity for women who didn't want households to be ruined by their husbands' self-indulgences. Not only does the "vice" become a "virtue," it becomes a virtue that bracingly exposes a latent masculine complacency.

Redoctrination is not, therefore, a negligible instrument of moral dialectic in medieval gender debate. Modern readers who are sensitized to feminism feel uncomfortable with most of the moral wrangling in the medieval debate about women. It smells of a patriarchal and priestly methodology for consigning women to passive or emasculating virtues that keep them under control: In other words, it threatens women with virtues they do not want. And yet, moral discourse was not only an unavoidable "master" discourse, the general terrain across which medieval debate of all sorts, including gender debate, was inevitably conducted. It was sometimes a democratic weapon too, always capable of sudden levelings, sudden challenges to the patriarchal cast of mind. As Christine de Pizan realized, women might ultimately benefit more from a complete cessation in the use of gendered moral labeling. Nevertheless she, and other profeminine voices before her (and if I am right, Chaucer too), also realized that in a climate saturated by moral analysis, valuable structures of argument lay close at hand in the "vices and virtues" field, which was culture's most massively disseminated instrument of analytical discourse.

The moral argument went on anyway. The virtue of liberality was still being enigmatically appropriated for women by a writer calling herself (or himself) Jane Anger in the treatise *Protection of Women* in 1589, and with this I close. "That we are liberal, men will not deny since many of them have received more kindness in one day at our hands, than they can repay in a whole yeare." So far, that is not enigmatic: but then Anger adds, with a mischievous Wife-of-Bathly gleam in the eye, "Some have so glutted themselves with our liberality as they cry, No more."[69]

Notes

1. The present essay originated as a paper developed through conferences of the New Chaucer Society (Sorbonne, 1998) and Fordham University (New York, 1999), and was presented also as a Lansdowne lecture (University of Victoria, 2000). I should like to thank Norm Klassen, Thelma Fenster, and Elizabeth Archibald for providing these opportunities.

2. See, for example, Ian Maclean, *The Renaissance Notion of Woman* (Cambridge: Cambridge University Press, 1980), p. 91, and Linda Woodridge, *Women and the English Renaissance: Literature and the Nature of Womankind, 1540–1620* (Urbana: University of Illinois Press, 1984), p. 59. For further reflections on the balance of facetiousness and seriousness in the debate, see Alcuin Blamires, *The Case for Women in Medieval Culture* (Oxford: Clarendon Press, 1997), pp. 5–7, 36–7, and 124.

3. Helen Solterer, *The Master and Minerva: Disputing Women in French Medieval Culture* (Berkeley and Los Angeles: University of California Press, 1995), p. 148.

4. Blamires, *The Case for Women,* pp. 83–9.

5. Blamires, *The Case for Women,* pp. 32, 114–19.

6. R. Howard Bloch, "Medieval Misogyny," *Representations* 20 (1987): 1–14.

7. Ibid., 13.

8. Blamires, *The Case for Women,* pp. 96–8, 105. For other critical discussions of Bloch's essay, see Elizabeth A. Clark and others, "Commentary on Bloch, 'Medieval Misogyny'," *Medieval Feminist Newsletter* 7 (1989): 2–16.

9. Constantia describes woman as the "second edition of the Epitome of the whole world," and the "second Tome of that goodly volume compiled by God"; *The Worming of a Mad Dogge,* in *The Early Modern Englishwoman,* pt. 1, vol. 4, *Defences of Women,* introduced by Susan G. O'Malley (Aldershot: Scolar; Vermont: Ashgate, 1996), p. 2.

10. All Chaucer quotations are from *The Riverside Chaucer,* ed. Larry D. Benson (Boston: Houghton Mifflin, 1987); *The Canterbury Tales* are cited by Roman numeral and line number in the body of my text. The *Riverside* note to VIII.645–6 cites a manuscript gloss supplying the common proverb "Omne quod est nimium vertitur in vitium"; though a specific *Ethics* reference is not impossible—cf. "Vertu is the mene, / As Etik seith," *Prologue to the Legend of Good Women,* "F" 165–6. See Aristotle, *Ethics,* II. vi, trans. J. A. K. Thomson (Harmondsworth: Penguin, 1953), pp. 100–2. Jill Mann cites the partial medieval Latin translation circulating in the thirteenth century, ed. R.-A. Gauthier, *Ethica Nichomachea, Aristoteles Latinus* (Leiden and Brussels: E. J. Brill and Desclée de Brouwer, 1972): "Medietas autem, duarum maliciarum, huius quidem secundum superfluitatem, huius vero indigenciam. Et adhuc, quoniam hee quidem deficiunt, hee autem superhabundant, eius quod oportet, et in passionibus et in operacionibus, virtus autem medium et invenit et vult," in "Satisfaction and Payment in Middle English Literature," *Studies in the Age of Chaucer* 5 (1983): 17–48 (pp. 18–19).

11. *Andreas Capellanus on Love,* ed. and trans. P. G. Walsh (London: Duckworth, 1982), pp. 310–11.

12. Walsh, pp. 318–21. Andreas thus articulates a view that women "exhaust male substance" both in the financial and physiological domains. Physiologically women's sexual demands "weaken" men's bodies by intercourse (Walsh pp. 304–5), and cf. Chaucer's *Parson's Tale,* X.147, and D. Jacquart and C. Thomasset, *Sexuality and Medicine in the Middle Ages,* trans. M. Adamson (Cambridge: Polity Press, 1988), p. 56.

13. Walsh, pp. 316–19.

14. "Unde et alio nomine liberalitas largitas nominatur," St. Thomas Aquinas, *Summa theologiae,* IIa IIae q. 117 on Liberality, in *Summa theologiae,* gen. ed. Thomas Gilby, O.P., 60 vols., vol. 41, *Virtues of Justice in the Human Community,* ed. and trans. T. C. O'Brien (London: Blackfriars, in conjunction with Eyre and Spottiswoode; and New York: McGraw-Hill, 1972), pp. 224–5. See also Chaucer, *Parson's Tale,* X.464, where among signs of *gentillesse* listed by the Parson is "to be liberal, that is to seyn, large."

15. "Vous devez mettre grant peine [. . .] de mettre a proufit les biens et la chevance que vos mariz, par leur labour [. . .] ameinent ou pourchacent. Et est l'office de l'omme d'acquerre et faire venir ens les provisions; et la femme les doit ordonner et dispenser par bonne discrecion [. . .] sans trop grant escharceté, et aussi bien se garder de fole largece [. . .]. Et doit bien aviser en toutes choses que gast n'en puist estre fait, ne s'en attendre du tout a la meisgnee; ains elle meismes doit etre dessus et s'en prendre souvent garde, et de ses choses vouloir avoir le compte" [You ought to devote very great care (. . .) to using to the best advantage all the goods and provisions that your husbands by their labor (. . .) obtain for the home. It is the duty of the man to acquire all the necessary provisions (. . .). Likewise the woman ought to manage and allocate them with good discretion (. . .) without too much parsimoniousness, and equally she ought to guard against foolish generosity (. . .). She should understand that nothing must be wasted, and she should expect all her household to be frugal. She herself must be in overall charge and always watchful]; *Le Livre des trois vertus,* ed. Charity Cannon Willard and Eric Hicks (Paris: Champion, 1989), III.1, p. 173, and *The Treasure of the City of Ladies,* trans. Sarah Lawson (Harmondsworth: Penguin, 1985), p. 146. For further discussion of this topos, see Blamires, *Case for Women,* pp. 91–3.

16. In *The Shipman's Tale,* the merchant "heeld a worthy hous, / For which he hadde alday so greet repair / For his largesse" (VII.20–22); and "Free was daun John, and manly [so *Riverside,* though "namely" in the earlier Robinson edition] of dispence" (VII.43).

17. "Dear son (. . .) generosity [*largesce*] is the mistress and queen that gives lustre to every virtue," *Cligés* 188–90, ed. Alexandre Micha (Paris: Champion, 1978); and *Chretien de Troyes, Arthurian Romances,* trans. D. D. R. Owen (London: Dent, 1987), p. 95; Alan of Lille's Natura sees *largitas* as the means whereby the human mind becomes "a palace of virtues" and

whereby people "bind themselves together" in love; *The Plaint of Nature* XVIII, trans. James J. Sheridan (Toronto: Pontifical Institute of Mediaeval Studies, 1980), p. 213. Andreas writes that "omnis sine largitate virtus nulla putatur" [every virtue without generosity is regarded as nothing] (Walsh, pp. 304–5).

18. "Largitas maxime claros facit," Boethius *De consolatione philosophiae*, II. pr. 5 ("largesse maketh folk cleer of renoun" in Chaucer's *Boece*, II. pr. 5, 10). See also *Cligés* (197), "Par soi fet prodome largesce" [Liberality on its own makes a worthy man]. Sir Gawain describes *larges* as one of the attributes "þat longez to kny3tes," *Sir Gawain and the Green Knight*, line 2381, ed. J. R. R. Tolkien and E. V. Gordon, 2nd ed. by Norman Davis (Oxford: Clarendon Press, 1967). ·

19. Part of a protest by "Glad Pouert" against Fortune in John Lydgate, *The Fall of Princes,* III.372–5, ed. Henry Bergen (pt. ii), Early English Text Society. Extra Series 122 (London: Oxford University Press, 1924).

20. Boccaccio's discussion of *liberalità* in his two versions of this narrative (the *Filocolo* IV.4 and *Decameron* X.5) is expertly reviewed in N. S. Thompson, *Chaucer, Boccaccio, and the Debate of Love* (Oxford: Clarendon Press, 1996), pp. 251–7.

21. "Li amant / Doignent du lor plus largement / Que cil vilain" ; Guillaume de Lorris and Jean de Meun, *Le Roman de la Rose,* ed. Daniel Poirion (Paris: Garnier-Flammarion, 1974), l. 2214; all further quotations are from this edition. Cf. "Resoun wole that a lover be / In his yiftes more large and fre / Than cherles that can not of lovyng" ; in the Chaucerian *Romaunt of the Rose,* ll. 2331–3.

22. *Confessio,* V.4769–70, in *The English Works of John Gower,* ed. G. C. Macaulay, Early English Text Society, Extra Series 81–2 (London: Oxford University Press, 1900–1).

23. Christine says to Droitture that she has seen "de femmes moult hommourables en discrete largesce de ce que elles povoyent" and knows women joyful over money "bien employé, que nul aver ne pourroit avoir de tirer a soy et mettre en coffre," in *Le Livre de la cité des dames,* ed. Maureen Curnow, Ph.D dissertation, Vanderbilt University (1975), Xerox University Microfilms (Ann Arbor), II.66.2, pp. 963–4; see also *The Book of the City of Ladies,* trans. Earl Jeffrey Richards (London: Pan Books, 1983), p. 210; and Droitture responds, "de inffinies largesces, courtoysies et liberalités de femmes te pourroye dire," II.67.2 (Curnow p. 965, trans. Richards p. 211).

24. So in the *Livre des trois vertus* Christine suggests that some wives "si ne pourroient ycelles par effect, quelque bon vouloir que elles eussent, user de celle vertu de largesce" [cannot practice this virtue of generosity, even though they may have good will], ed. Willard and Hicks I.21, p. 81, trans. Lawson I.20, p. 80.

25. "On les reppute avaires [. . .] je te promet qu'il est assez de femmes [. . .] que, se elles aveyent de quoy, ne seoyent pas escharces ne averes en hon-

neurs faire et donner largement . . . On les tient communement si a de-stroit d'argent que ce pou que elles en pueent avoir le gardent [. . .]." They have to complain about the wastefulness of husbands who are "larges gas-teurs de biens," *Cité,* II.66.1 (ed. Curnow pp. 962–3, trans. Richards p. 209).

26. Andrée K. Blumstein, *Misogyny and Idealization in the Courtly Romance* (Bonn: Bouvier, 1977), p. 7.

27. See remarks in *De mulieribus claris,* ed. Vittoria Zaccaria, in *Tutte le opere,* vol. X (Verona: Mondadori, 1970), pp. 274–8 and 314–19; *Concerning Fa-mous Women,* trans. Guido A. Guarino (New Brunswick, N.J.: Rutgers University Press, 1963), pp. 150–1 and 173–5.

28. "Sy n'est mie tel chose avarice ne escharceté, ains est signe de tres grant prudence," *Cité,* II.66.1 (ed. Curnow pp. 962–3, trans. Richards p. 209).

29. "We alle desiren . . . To han housbondes hardy, wise, and free, / And secree, and no nygard, ne no fool, / Ne hym that is agast of every tool, / Ne noon avauntour," says Pertelote in the *Nun's Priest's Tale* (VII.2913–17); and "yet me greveth moost his nygardye, / And wel ye woot that wommen naturelly / . . . wolde that hir housbondes sholde be / Hardy, wise, and riche, and therto free, / And buxom unto his wyf, and fresshe abedde," says the wife in *The Shipman's Tale* (VII.172–7).

30. Boccaccio discusses the relationship between Zenobia's munificence and her caution as servatrix in *De mulieribus claris,* ed. Zaccaria, pp. 410–12; trans. Guarino, p. 228. In *The Monk's Tale* Chaucer abbreviates into one de-scriptive phrase, "large with mesure" (VII.2299).

31. Gower's Amans labors to articulate the complicated generosity that the ideal lady discreetly shows toward others: "Sche takth and yifth in such degre, / That as be weie of friendlihiede / Sche can so kepe hir wom-manhiede / That every man spekth of hir wel," *Confessio Amantis,* V.4753–7.

32. Pseudo-Dionysius, *The Divine Names,* in *The Complete Works,* trans. Colm Luibheid (London: 1987), pp. 71–2.

33. Cicero, *De Officiis,* I.16, ed. and trans. Walter Miller (London: Heinemann; and New York: Macmillan, 1913), pp. 52–6.

34. Gower, *Confessio,* V.7644–48.

35. In a discussion of Mercy, *The Book of Vices and Virtues* notes the "grete largenesse" of God who gives generously to all "after þat þei ben, as seynt Iame seiþ, & makeþ his sonne schyne vpon þe goode and vpon þe schrewen, as he seiþ in the gospel." Since God is so "large" to us, giving us "alle þe goodes þat we haue, we schulde be large and curteis eche of vs to oþer," as urged in the Gospel: "Beþ merciable, as ȝoure fadre is merciable"; ed. W. Nelson Francis, Early English Text Society, Ordinary Series 217 (London: Oxford University Press, 1942), p. 193. Under "De cupiditate" in *Jacob's Well* there is a discussion of *nygardschippe* that cites Tobit 4.7 ("Ex substantia tua fac eleemosynam, et noli avertere faciem tuam ab ullo pau-pere"), and urges "ȝif þou haue myche, ȝyue þou plentyvously; ȝyf þou

haue lytel, gladly 3eue þou part therof to þe poore": see also ch. 50, "De paupertate spiritus, & de largitate," which cites Christ as exemplar of generosity, his arms symbolically open on the cross; ed. Arthur Brandeis, Early English Text Society, Ordinary Series 115 (London: Kegan Paul, Trench, Trübner, 1900), pp. 121–2, and pp. 307–11.

36. "For þe gentyl Cheuentayn is no chyche, [. . . He] laue3 his gyfte3 as water of dyche, / Oþer gote3 of golf þat neuer charde. / Hys fraunchyse is large" ; *Pearl* (ll. 605–9), ed. E. V. Gordon (Oxford: Clarendon Press, 1953).

37. See Essay XIII, "Of Goodnesse, and Goodnesse of Nature," in Sir Francis Bacon, *The Essayes or Counsels,* ed. Michael Kiernan (Oxford: Clarendon, 1985), p. 39: "*Goodnesse* answers to the *Theologicall Vertue Charitie,* and admits no Excesse, but Errour. The desire of Power in Excesse, caused the Angels to fall; The desire of Knowledge in Excesse, caused Man to fall; But in *Charity,* there is no Excesse; Neither can Angell, or Man, come in danger by it."

38. Trans. Frances Horgan, *The Romance of the Rose* (Oxford: Oxford University Press, 1994), p. 18 [Et Diex li fesoit foisonner / Ses biens, si qu'ele ne savoit / Tant donner cum el plus avoit; ed. Poirion, ll. 1136–8].

39. The point is elaborated in Chaucer's *Tale of Melibee,* which urges that riches are to be used "in swich a manere that men holde yow nat to scars, ne to sparynge, ne to fool-large—that is to seyen, over-large a spendere. / For right as men blamen an avaricious man by cause of his scarsetee and chyncherie, / in the same wise is he to blame that spendeth over-largely" (VII.1596–1600). This exposition of the use of riches derives from a brief hint in chapters 43 and 45 of Albertano's treatise, and takes up his invitation to draw on a chapter, "De acquirendis et conservandis opibus," in his *De amore et dilectione dei et proximi et aliarum rerum et de forma vitae.* See *Albertani Brixiensis Liber consolationis et consilii,* ed. Thor Sundby, Chaucer Society, 2nd ser. Viii (London: Trubner, 1873); and *Sources and Analogues of Chaucer's* Canterbury Tales, ed. W. F. Bryan and Germaine Dempster (Chicago: University of Chicago Press, 1941), p. 563.

40. *Vices and Virtues,* p. 146; see also the treatise's further discussion of "largenesse" on pp. 193 and 212–16.

41. Aquinas invokes Ambrose on the point that *superabundantia* is bestowed upon some so that they can gain the merit of *bona dispensatio* [good stewardship] whereby the *liberalis* spends on others more than self; *Summa theologiae* 2a 2ae q. 117, art. 1, on "whether liberality is a virtue." For similar statements, see Chaucer, *Boece,* II. pr. 5; *Dives and Pauper,* VII.12, ed. Priscilla Barnum, I, pt. 2, Early English Text Society, Ordinary Series 280 (Oxford: Oxford University Press, 1980), p. 160. For a survey of the doctrine of wealth as stewardship, see Miri Rubin, *Charity and Community in Medieval Cambridge* (Cambridge: Cambridge University Press, 1987), ch. 3, "The Idea of Charity Between the Twelfth and Fifteenth Centuries," pp. 54–98.

42. Poirion, ll. 7405–14. Jealousy is berated for greediness: "It is foolish to hoard such a thing, for it is the candle in the lantern, and if you gave its

light to a thousand people, you would not find its flame smaller" (trans. Horgan, pp. 113–14). A moderately wide dissemination of the figure is attested in Bartlett J. and Helen W. Whiting, *Proverbs, Sentences, and Proverbial Phrases from English Writings Mainly Before 1500* (Cambridge, Mass.: Harvard University Press, 1968), C24, "One Candle can light many." The antecedent in Ovid is: "Sufficit et damni pars caret illa metu. / Quis vetet adposito lumen de lumine sumi? / Quisve cavo vastas in mare servet aquas?" [That part endures, and has no fear of loss. What forbids to take light from a light that is set before you? or who would guard vast waters upon the cavernous deep?]; *Ars amatoria,* III.88ff, in *Ovid II: The Art of Love, and Other Poems,* ed. and trans. J. H. Mozley, 2nd ed. revised by G. P. Goold (Cambridge, Mass.: Harvard University Press; and London: Heinemann, 1979), pp. 124–5. For an extended discussion of the Ovidian link, see Michael Calabrese, *Chaucer's Ovidian Arts of Love* (Gainesville: University Press of Florida, 1994), pp. 81–111.

43. For manipulation of ethical commonplaces elsewhere in Chaucer, see e.g., *The Miller's Tale,* I.3530.

44. This aspect of Blanche's representation is well elicited by Priscilla Martin, *Chaucer's Women: Nuns, Wives and Amazons* (Basingstoke: Macmillan, 1990), p. 25.

45. Lee Patterson, "'For the Wyves love of Bathe': Feminine Rhetoric and Poetic Resolution in the *Roman de la Rose* and the *Canterbury Tales,*" *Speculum* 58 (1983): 656–94 (p. 680); Martin, *Chaucer's Women,* pp. 70, 96. However, an alternative view links the Wife's sexual generosity with the philosophy of "plenitude" promoted by the school of Chartres; Paul G. Ruggiers, *The Art of the Canterbury Tales* (Madison: University of Wisconsin Press, 1965), pp. 198–200.

46. *The Decameron,* trans. G. H. McWilliam (Harmondsworth: Penguin, 1972), pp. 499–500 [Le done . . . le quali molto meglio che gli uomini potrebbero a molti sodisfare; . . . domando io voi, io che doveva fare o debbo di quel che gli avanza? Debbolo io gittare ai cani? Non è egli molto meglio servirne un gentile uomo che piú che sé m'ama, che lasciarlo perdere o guastare?], *Decameron* VI.7, ed. Cesare Segre (Milan: Mursia, 1984), pp. 398–9.

47. Keeping food like this is cited under *nygardschippe,* a subcategory of *Cupiditas,* in *Jacob's Well,* p. 121. Christine de Pizan urges that prudential vigilance in the household entails care that no food goes bad (so nothing is wasted that could have helped the poor), *Livre des trois vertus,* ed. Willard and Hicks, III.1, p. 176, trans. Lawson, p. 148.

48. "For al that þe ryche man hat pasynge hys nedful lyuynge aftir þe stat of his dispensacion it is þe pore mannys;" *Dives and Pauper* VII.12, ed. Barnum, p. 160.

49. The woman who gives her body to someone other than her husband therefore commits "theft" ; see *Parson's Tale,* X.876–77. Cicero points out

that giving as a result of robbing another is not liberality (*De Officiis*, I.14, pp. 47–9).

50. Aristotle, *Ethics*, IV.i, trans. Thomson, p. 110.

51. *Plaint of Nature*, XVIII; trans. J. J. Sheridan, p. 214. The fourteenth-century English treatise *Speculum Christiani* explains that "wast ouerspens is called largys and fredam of hert;" see Thomas Bestul, *Satire and Allegory in* Wynnere and Wastoure (Lincoln: University of Nebraska Press, 1974), p. 21, citing *Speculum Christiani,* ed. Gustaf Holmstedt, Early English Text Society, Ordinary Series 182 (London: Oxford University Press, 1933), p. 232. Bestul also cites Isidore, *Sententiae* 2.35 1–3, PL 83.636–7.

52. *Ethics*, IV.1, trans. Thomson p. 146; Aquinas, *Summa theologiae* IIa IIae 119.3, Responsio, trans. O'Brien, pp. 273–5.

53. "[. . .]the bountiful do not hold back but let go" [quod largum est, non est retentivum sed est emissivum], and "when someone lets something go [emittit] he liberates it [liberat] from his care and control"; *Summa theologiae* IIa IIae 117.2, Responsio, trans. O'Brien, p. 225. See also a passage from Wace, *Brut* (ll. 3685–9), cited by David Burnley in *Courtliness and Literature* (Harlow, Essex: Addison Wesley Longman, 1998), p. 71: "Bledudo was more generous than his father" [plus larges fu de duner] and "did not know how to refuse or retain anything of his own" [Nule rien ne saveit veer / Ne a suen ués rien retenir].

54. [. . . largece ne s'estant mie tant seulement en dons, come dit un sage, mais aussi en reconfort de parole], *Livre des trois vertus,* ed. Willard and Hicks, I.20, p. 78, trans. Lawson, I.19, p. 78. Christine elsewhere reports her father's view that learning was a treasure that one could keep giving away, without losing any; *Le Livre de la Mutacion de Fortune,* I.3, trans. Kevin Brownlee in *The Selected Writings of Christine de Pizan,* ed. Renate Blumenfeld-Kosinski and Kevin Brownlee (New York: W. W. Norton, 1997), p. 91. I am grateful to Renate Blumenfeld-Kosinski for bringing this detail to my attention.

55. Alexander writes to Dindimus, King of the Brahmans, that he understands that Dindimus frowns on his own laws and lifestyle, and that the Brahmans' *manars* differ profoundly from those of other people: "Bott deyned it ȝour doctryne bedene vs to write, / ȝoure customes & ȝourc conscience & of ȝour clene thewis, / We miȝt sum connynge, per ca, chach of ȝoure wordis, / And ȝour lare of a leke suld neuire þe les worth. / Slike similitude of science is sett, as of kynde, / As of a blesand brand or of a briȝt candill. / For many liȝtis of a liȝt is liȝtid othirequile, / And ȝit the liȝt at þam liȝtis is liȝtid as before," *The Wars of Alexander,* ll. 4354–61, ed. Hoyt N. Duggan and Thorlac Turville-Petre, Early English Text Society, Special Series 10 (Oxford: Oxford University Press, 1989). This and most other Middle English translations closely follow at this juncture the Latin of the *Historia de preliis,* a late-twelfth-century interpolated version of a narrative going back to Greek romance.

56. So Sheila Delany, "Strategies of Silence in the Wife of Bath's Recital," *Exemplaria* 2 (1990): 49–69 (p. 51); and Calabrese, *Chaucer's Ovidian Arts of Love,* p. 108.

57. "[. . .] hir thoughte that she dyde, / That she so longe sholde a conseil hyde" (III.965–6).

58. Midas appears in Gower's section *de avaricia,* in the *Confessio Amantis* beginning at V.141. Keats (Sonnet 17) bids poets be "Misers of sound and syllable, no less / Than Midas of his coinage." It has been customary to derive negative readings of the Wife of Bath from the interpolated episode of Midas's wife, as does R. L. Hoffman, *Ovid and the Canterbury Tales* (Philadelphia: University of Pennsylvania Press, 1966), pp. 145–9, though more ambiguous possibilities are glimpsed in Patterson, "'For the Wyves love of Bathe',", pp. 657–8.

59. Women's divulgence of secrets in the tale has not I think been seen in this light before, though it has been held by Susan Signe Morrison to herald "a community of power"; "Don't Ask, Don't Tell: The Wife of Bath and Vernacular Translations," *Exemplaria* 8 (1996): 97–123 (p. 117); and see Karma Lochrie's important analysis of "gossip" in the Wife of Bath's performance, in *Covert Operations: The Medieval Uses of Secrecy* (Philadelphia: University of Pennsylvania Press, 1999), pp. 56–61.

60. The connection was consolidated through commentary on the Beatitudes, which from Augustine onward had forged links between the "spirits" listed in Isaiah 11.2–3 and the Beatitudes in the Sermon on the Mount (Matt. 5.3–10). *Beati misericordes* (Matt. 5.7) was conventionally linked with *spiritus consilii* (Isa. 11.2).

61. *Vices & Virtues,* pp. 188–93; and see p. 145 for *conseil* as an aspect of *charite.* In *Jacob's Well,* ch. 50, "De paupertate spiritus, & de largitate, & elemosina, & misericordia, & dono consilii," *largenesse* is said to embrace the gift of "counseyl," which itself prompts and inspires one how best to be generous, p. 311.

62. Paralleling the generous motives already discussed is Alisoun's impulsive gift of all her property to her young fifth husband (III.630–1); but a contradictory mercantile thread is exemplified in her prior eagerness to obtain her elderly husbands' land and treasure, claiming to have endured their desire because "al is for to selle" as a "raunson" (ll. 411, 414)—even the bran that succeeds her flour with age (l. 478). Such brash engagement in marketability needs to be read, of course, in the context of a society acutely attuned to dowry negotiation.

63. "'Vanysshed Was This Daunce, He Nyste Where': Alisoun's Absence in the *Wife of Bath's Prologue and Tale,*" *English Literary History* 59 (1992): 1–21 (p. 9) repr. in *Chaucer: The Canterbury Tales,* Longman Critical Reader, ed. Steve Ellis (Harlow: Addison Wesley Longman, 1998), pp. 100–120 (p. 108).

64. Perception is an important concept in the *Tale:* fire remains fire unseen in a dark room (III.1139–43); poverty is a "spectacle" enabling one to see

friends (ll. 1203–4); and, after the casting up of the curtain, the "knyght saugh verraily," ll. 1249–50.

65. "Ja cele rien ne vudra mes / Quë il nen ait a sun talent; / Doinst e despende largement, / Ele li troverat asez" (ll. 136–9), and "Ja ne savrez cel liu penser. . . . Que jeo ne vus seie en present / A fere tut vostre talent" (l. 163), *Lais,* ed. A Ewert (Oxford: Blackwell, 1978); *The Lais of Marie de France,* trans. Glyn Burgess (Harmondsworth: Penguin, 1986), pp. 74–5.

66. "When Echo Speaks: Marie de France and the Poetics of Remembrance," in *Minding the Body: Women and Literature in the Middle Ages, 800–1500,* ed. Monica Brzezinski Potkay and Regula Meyer Evitt (New York: Twayne, 1997), pp. 77–101 (pp. 95–6). Although it would be a simplification to attribute a systematic female gendering of liberality to the *lais,* the evidence of *Lanval* is supplemented by conspicuous acts of generosity by women in *Le Fresne* and *Eliduc.*

67. "Sorties: Out and Out: Attacks/Ways Out/Forays," in *The Feminist Reader,* 2nd ed., ed. Catherine Belsey and Jane Moore (Basingstoke: Macmillan, 1997), pp. 91–116 (pp. 95–7).

68. Belsey and Moore, p. 11.

69. Jane Anger, *Her Protection for Women* (London: 1589), in *The Early Modern Englishwoman,* pt .1. vol. 4, *Defences of Women,* introduced O'Malley, fol. Cv.

CHAPTER 4

BEYOND DEBATE: GENDER IN PLAY
IN OLD FRENCH COURTLY FICTION

Roberta L. Krueger

Many courtly fictions, thought of as a site for articulating and promulgating normative gender roles, also debated, and sometimes (temporarily) destabilized, gender identities. Just at a time when formal debates about women circulated in Latin and Old French, a number of courtly texts questioned the nexus of gender, language, and power. Marie de France's Guigemar, *the chantefable* Aucassin et Nicolette, *and Heldris de Cornualle's* Roman de Silence *serve as illustration.*

If the inner truth of gender is a fabrication and if a true gender is a fantasy instituted and inscribed on the surface of bodies, then it seems that genders can be neither true nor false, but are only produced as the truth effects of a discourse of primary and stable identity

—Judith Butler

The vernacular narratives of twelfth- and thirteenth-century francophone courts can be read as a vast textual laboratory in which the gender roles of elite culture were articulated, examined, and put to the test. To paraphrase Simone de Beauvoir, knights and ladies are not simply born in courtly fiction, they are most particularly formed within the course of adventures that shape comely damsels into submissive wives, like Enide, or bold youth into accomplished knights, like Perceval and Lancelot. In keeping with their

strongly didactic function, romances and other narratives tended to reproduce and promulgate a traditional binary division between masculine and
feminine traits and "essential" male and female natures.[1] Romance's conventional sex roles bolstered aristocratic projects of marriage and lineage and
conformed to clerical notions of sex differences, at least in theory.

But in practice and within the unfolding events of many narratives the
binary division of male and female was often temporarily destabilized.
Given the remarkable irony, ambiguity, rhetorical sophistication, and narratorial self-consciousness for which Old French courtly fictions have been
celebrated,[2] it should not surprise us that their representation of men and
women is complex.

Critics have not failed to demonstrate how romances and other fictions
promulgated the hierarchical asymmetry of the sexes and normalized the
abjection of women.[3] But others have also pointed out the inherent ambiguity of gender representations and have demonstrated that medieval
texts do not always reproduce gender as a stable, immutable category.[4] In
thinking about gender ambiguity in medieval fictions, Judith Butler's notion of gender identity as performative—articulated over a decade ago in
the context of disputes within contemporary feminist politics—has proved
to be especially useful.[5] Butler cautions that the distinction between "sex"
(the "natural" body) and "gender" (the social construction) is specious, because the body is always apprehended within a discursive system. If body
and its constituted role are inseparable, then gender is best viewed not as a
construct imposed on a neutral body, but as "performative," constitutive of
the body that enacts it in gestures and words.[6] Gender identities are embedded within the discursive system and political matrix in which beings
speak and act, but they are also inherently plastic and dynamic.

Butler's idea of gender as performance seems particularly apt as a lens
to view the representation of gender in courtly texts, for the stories themselves were performed aloud before a mixed audience of clerics, knights,
and ladies. And like romance characters, the men and women in historical
courts played roles whose costumes, speech, and gestures were marked for
sex and class. Any hint that gender roles were in fact malleable within the
literary performance might draw attention to gender's status as a cultural
production, rather than a divinely ordained distinction, in the sphere of the
court. By calling attention to gender as a linguistic, cultural or discursive
production, courtly fictions could invite critique of social practice in the
world of the romance and beyond.

Such metacritical performances took a number of forms, as demonstrated in recent analyses of the interrogation of gender in Old French literature: in transvestite narratives;[7] in correspondence;[8] in romances from
Chrétien de Troyes onward;[9] in conduct books;[10] in the literature of

"courtly love;"[11] and in clerical representations of the "woman's response."[12] Viewed from the perspective of this scholarship, Old French courtly literature appears to be a dynamic forum in which questions of gender were frequently brought into play.

Moreover, such "gender play" in Old French courtly literature proliferated during the time that the formal debates about women circulated in French and Latin.[13] Indeed, courtly fictions sometimes incorporate elements of formal debate into their exploration of male and female natures. But, as we shall see, these texts often stage the debate about gender in such a way that its foundational categories are called into question and the relationship between gender, language, and power comes under scrutiny.

Close analysis of the literary techniques and rhetorical strategies that "produced" gender in courtly texts shows how the neat opposition of male versus female could be obfuscated, questioned, and even subverted in the course of the experiment. Narrators might expressly raise the differences between men and women as a subject for discussion. But they often did so in ways that moved beyond what Alcuin Blamires has called the "quasi-judicial" terms of debate.[14] Some fictions portrayed sexual identity as enigmatic; others called attention to the rhetorical strategies by which gender distinctions were created, or analyzed the political structures delimiting discursive practice. Such deft moves invited readers to move beyond debate to ponder the nature of sexual identity and to reflect on gender as cultural production, as we shall observe in three exemplary texts that span roughly a century: Marie de France's *Lais*, the anonymous *Aucassin et Nicolette*, a chantefable, and Heldris de Cornuälle's *Le Roman de Silence* (both mid-thirteenth century).

The Enigma of Gender: Marie de France

In her *Lais*, written in the 1160s, probably at the court of Henri II Plantagenet, Marie de France assembles twelve stories with crisscrossing motifs and themes whose characters subtly defy traditional social categories, often blurring or transgressing easy distinctions between male and female, human and beast.[15] Although she presents a gallery of remarkable female figures, whose resourcefulness, generosity, patience, and charity are often exemplary (the daughter in *Fresne*, the maiden in *Deux Amants*, the wife in *Eliduc*, to name only a few examples), she complicates the categorical definition of woman's nature as either virtuous or evil, or of man's nature as either naturally protective of or oppressive toward women. The wicked wives of *Equitan* and *Bisclavret*, the spiteful and cowardly mother in Fresne, the self-absorbed lady of *Chaitivel* offer powerful counterexamples to female virtue, in which women scheme for their own interests and manipulate or deceive men, abusing their sexual powers or abrogating their maternal responsibilities. Throughout the collection, Marie confounds the straightforward identification of gender with moral action, and invites her readers to ponder conflicted sexual identities, desires, and motivations, as an early scene from *Guigemar* exemplifies.

Near the beginning of *Guigemar*, which is the first *lai* in London BL. Harley MS 978 (the only manuscript containing all the *lais*), the narrator relates how the eponymous hero, having disdained love for hunting, receives a wound in the thigh when his arrow rebounds after striking an androgynous doe with stag's horns. As the *biche* dies, she declares that Guigemar can be healed only by a woman who will suffer more pain out of love for him than has ever been suffered, just as he will for her. The injured nobleman is carried off by a magical ship to a distant land where he will meet the unhappily married lady whose love will cure him. In recounting the unfortunate situation of the *mal mariée*, Marie offers an extended description of the chambre in which the lady has been enclosed by her jealous husband:

> Li sire out fait dedenz le mur,
> pur metre i sa femme a seür
> chambre; suz ciel n'aveit plus bele.
> A l'entrée fu la chapele.
> La chambre ert peinte tut en tur.
> Venus, la deuesse d'amur,
> fu tresbien mise en la peinture;
> les traiz mustrot e la nature
> cument hom deit amur tenir
> e leilment e bien servir.
> Le livre Ovide, u il enseigne
> coment chascuns s'amur estreigne,
> en un fu ardant le getout,
> e tuz icels escumenjout,
> ki ja mais cel livre lirreient
> ne sun enseignement fereint.
> La fu la dame enclose e mise.[16]

[In order to guard his wife securely / the lord had constructed a room inside a wall; / no more beautiful room could be imagined. / The chapel was at the entrance. / The room was completely painted all around (by murals). / Venus, goddess of love, / was very clearly portrayed in the mural; / she showed the traits (or arrows) and the nature of love / and how man should serve love loyally. / She was casting into a burning fire the book of Ovid, where he teaches / how each one should constrain love, / and she excommunicated / all those who would read this book / or follow its teaching. / This is where the lady was placed and kept]

The oppositional nature of this passage and its rejection of traditional authority are striking. Marie, female author who has named herself in the *Guigemar* prologue (p. 3), creates a scene in which a female goddess of love throws a book by the best-known authority on that subject into the flames and banishes all those who would follow his teachings. A female potentate has replaced a male *magister* in an incendiary scene that has not failed to provoke commentary from readers who gloss this passage as emblematic of Marie's poetic stance. For Robert Hanning, the scene underscores Marie's "agressively anti-Ovidian stance" throughout the *Lais*.[17] For Nancy Vine Durling, the painted chamber "serves as a metaphor for Marie's book, "with cover, written text and (female) author at the center."[18] The enclosure scene underscores Marie's desire, by revealing something about the lady, to make "a powerful statement about the externalization and symbolic representation of female experience."[19]

Yet if the symbolic force of this passage is undeniable, its precise argument—the nature of its "case" against Ovid—is not at all clear. For, as Marie emphasizes, the room in which the lady is enclosed has been constructed by the lady's husband, a jealous old man. If he has also supervised the painting of the murals, why does he elevate Venus, the love goddess, casting the master's work into the flames? If the husband is indeed the chamber's creator, which book of Ovid does Venus condemn—the *Ars amatoria*, in which adulterous love is celebrated? or does Venus burn the *Remedia amoris*, wherein love is rejected? Perhaps, as Hanning argues, Marie condemns the entire Ovidian tradition, in which love is calculated rather than spontaneous.[20] Yet if the painting expresses the husband's interests, why should it emblematize Marie's views? Perhaps we should not be too hasty to discount the possibility that the lady herself has painted the walls during her imprisonment—in the same way that Lancelot will depict love scenes on a wall during his captivity by Morgan in the thirteenth-century *Lancelot en prose*. As Herman Braet remarked some years ago, the painting's creator is left pointedly ambiguous, perhaps expressly so, by the author.[21]

By obscuring the identity of the painting's "author" and by declining to specify which of Ovid's books is thrown into the flames or to delineate his argument, Marie blurs the easy assignment of genders to polemical positions. Her generous deployment of Ovidian love conceits and love casuistry throughout the *lai* further complicates the author's case against Ovid, which is neither polemical nor confrontational. Marie names her opponent, but does not grant him the power of engagement in his arguments; she does not attack his misogyny or launch a formal "plait" [case] against the *magister*. Indeed, as critics have noted of *Guigemar*, Marie depicts characters who cast aside formal discussion or argument—described as their *plait*—in favor of an experience of love that springs from spontaneous emotion, as symbolized by

Guigemar's *plaie* [wound] and the *plait* [knot] that only the lovers can tie and untie.[22] As it replaces potential polemical disputation with a more complex scenario in which male and female agency and motives are obscured, the ekphrasis in the lady's chamber works like a textual *plait* or knot, an enigmatic moment in which the easy oppositions of male and female, author and text, argument and counterargument are all purposefully obfuscated.

In the first lines of *Guigemar's* prologue, the author "Marie" alludes to those who speak ill of "hume ne femme de grant pris" [men and women of valor]. By telling her story regardless of the threat of slander, the female author defends her right to speak; she implicitly validates female moral and intellectual authority. But she does not do so through a polemical vindication of female nature, neither here in *Guigemar* nor in the rest of the *Lais*. Rather she leaves her critics to their vindictive discourse ("ceo est lur dreiz de mesparler," it is their right to misspeak), and she asserts the worth of her own creative enterprise by allying herself with a male hero who is calumniated for his ambivalent sexuality and who is cured by the intervention of an androgynous stag-doe.[23]

Rather than invite her readers to take up a position for or against the *magister*, for or against a conception of male or female nature, Marie invites them to ponder the inscrutability of human motives and to explore the nature of sexual identity.[24] This enigmatic passage is emblematic of Marie's poetics in the *Lais*. While written from the position of one who does not shirk from claiming female authorship,[25] Marie moves well beyond *disputatio* and oppositional debate about gender. In *Guigemar* and in her other *lais*, Marie explores the complexities of social and sexual identities. Her aims in the *Lais* would seem to be strongly didactic, yet she confuses, rather than confirms, the association of superior moral worth with either women or men. As Pickens has noted, of the various characters in the *Lais*, "originateurs, transmetteurs, destinataires, récepteurs, régénérateurs, retransmetteurs, etc. masculins aussi bien que féminins participent à une entreprise mutuelle où les réussites et les échecs ne dépendent pas d'une identité sexuelle en particulier"[26] [originators, transmitters, those addressed, receivers, regenerators, retransmitters, etc., masculine as well as feminine participate in a mutual enterprise where the successes and failures do not depend upon any particular sexual identity].

Marie's general prologue to the *Lais* invokes the poetic practice of the ancients, who wrote "oscurement," so that those who came after them would "gloser la lettre" [gloss or interpret the writing], adding "de lur sen le surplus" [the supplement of their understanding; ll. 12, 15]. So, too, does Marie write "obscurely" about love so that her readers will be encouraged to "gloss" and add their own "sens." As it offers multiple perspectives on the nature of love between men and women, her collection of *Lais*—marvelous and enigmatic—invites reflection on the complex natures of women and men, bodies and gendered identities.

Comic Reversals in *Aucassin et Nicolette*

The complex relationship between gender and moral worth that Marie creates in the *Lais* is paradigmatic of many later courtly fictions, from the romances of Chrétien de Troyes, with its ambiguous presentation of Yvain, Guenevere, Lancelot, and Perceval, to the troubled world of the *Lancelot-Prose*. As these texts invite debate about issues relating to gender, they do so in ways that are usually far more complicated than a simple "us/them" opposition. Even romances that contain overtly antifeminist outbursts, as I have argued, often dramatize the insufficiencies and anxieties of the misogynist rather than the faults of "woman," his opponent.[27]

When the terms of the "formal debate" are explicitly incorporated into courtly fiction, they may be handled ironically, as in the thirteenth-century chantefable, *Aucassin et Nicolette*, where the hero, Aucassin, offers a fanciful definition of "woman's love" to the heroine, his beloved Nicolette:

> Avoi! fait Aucassin, bele douce amie, ce ne porroit estre que vos m'amissiés tant que je fac vos. Fenme ne puet tant amer l'oume con li hom fait le fenme; car li amors de le fenme est en son oeul et en son le cateron de sa mamele et en son l'orteil de pié, mais li amors de l'oume est en el cué plantee, don ele ne puet iscir.[28]

> [Not so! said Aucassin, dear sweet friend, it's not possible that you should love me as much as I love you. A woman cannot love a man as a man loves a woman, for a woman's love is in her eye, and in the tip of her breast, and in her toe, but a man's love is planted in his heart, from which it can not depart]

Locating the source of a woman's love in her body and that of a man in his heart, Aucassin recasts an Aristotelian conception of sexual difference, one that circulated widely in the Middle Ages: Corporality, the body, derives from and resides in females; spirituality, the soul, derives from and resides in males.[29] A man's love is superior to a woman's because it is grounded in the heart, rather than the tit and the toe. As an explanation of a woman's love, this head-to-foot description, which progresses in a neat downward triad from "oeul" to "mamele" to "orteil," is as implausible as it is laughable.[30] Aucassin's insistence on woman's physical attributes echoes the narrator's own fascination with Nicolette's body parts. These are described at rather regular intervals in the course of this short fiction—as, for example, when the narrator compares Nicolette's *mameletes dures* to "deus nois gauges" [two large walnuts; XII, p. 80].[31] Aucassin's definition reveals far more about the nature of male desire than about female psychology.

But the passage does more than poke gentle fun at Aucassin. This light-hearted spoof of an Aristotelian definition of woman as sensual and morally inferior to man works as a send-up of rhetorical categories and calls into question the construction of sexual difference. Furthermore, if we take into account the context of this statement, we can observe that Aucassin's misperception of woman underscores the ironic disjunction of social stereotypes, discourses, and identities that permeates this chantefable. Aucassin, Christian knight with a Saracen name who resists his destiny as a knight, speaks from a tower, within a prison where he has been locked up by his father, who wants to prevent his union with his beloved Nico-lette. The heroine, Saracen slave with a French name, for her part, has boldly escaped from her own prison to speak with her lover through a crack in the wall. As critics have repeatedly noted, Aucassin's passivity here and elsewhere in the romance, where he is frequently shown lamenting, contrasts with Nicolette's activity in many scenes where she plays the role of resourceful heroine, escaping from confinement, manipulating language and gesture, eventually disguising herself as a male *jongleur* to bring the story of star-crossed lovers to a happy conclusion.[32]

The extraordinary actions of a brave, resourceful woman thus counter the absurdity of Aucassin's claim that woman's love is lodged in her eye, nipple, and toe. Within the context of the lovers' adventures, Aucassin's foolish definition of woman's love points up the comic discrepancy between stereotypes about gender and the actions and behavior of men and women. Critics have disagreed, sometimes forcefully, about whether the fiction as a whole should be classified as a parody, a satire, a burlesque, or simply a gently comic *roman idyllique*.[33] For the purposes of our discussion, it matters little how we characterize this send-up of "the case against woman." It is more significant that this scene is one of many in the romance where the conventions of a discursive system—in this case, the clerical discourse that defines "woman"—are juxtaposed with an opposing discourse or set of actions that challenges the hegemony of each. Aucassin's "definition of woman" is a destabilizing moment amidst a succession of ironic reversals and discursive conflicts, which include the hero's praise of Hell over Heaven (VI) and the couple's discovery of the topsy-turvy world of Torelore, where a king lies in bed giving birth while his wife wages war on the battlefield with cheeses and vegetables (XXVIII-XXXII).

As critics have noted, the chantefable's many reversals and ironic juxtapositions serve a metacritical function in the text.[34] The fiction spoofs, in a variety of ways, the discourses of a sociopolitical system that categorizes identities and attempts to order social behavior. In so doing, it calls the audience's attention to the artificial nature of the social codes that govern gender, social class, religion, and modes of exchange. The text brings into play a number of what Eugene Vance has called "ideological polarities" (70); to those mentioned by Vance—which include knight/serf and wealth/poverty—we can add male/female and Christian/Saracen.[35] Within the frame of a hybrid text where conventions of lyric, narrative, romance, epic, and hagiography intersect in dynamic tension, the hierarchies upon which such distinctions are made are comically reversed or ironically undermined—at least temporarily. The text shows, repeatedly, how the actions and desires of human agents resist and disrupt their social constructions.

The hybrid nature of this chantefable brings modes of representation into conflict and brings social stereotypes under scrutiny—even as the narrative's "happy ending" reinforces sociopolitical norms. The sophisticated comedy of *Aucassin et Nicolette* suggests that medieval audiences possessed a high degree of self-consciousness about their social practices and that the differences in gender, language, economy, nation, and religion could be examined critically—not only through polemical debate, but also through the lens of comedy.

Performance and the Rhetoric of Gender in *Le Roman de Silence*

No discussion of gender debates in courtly fiction would be complete without Heldris de Cornuälle's *Roman de Silence*. As I have argued elsewhere, Heldris's profound investigation of the "nature de femme" is one of the central adventures of the romance.[36] The romance is remarkable not only for its extraordinary heroine, who cross-dresses as a knight in order to preserve her inheritance, but also for its exploration of linguistic and sexual ambiguities, and for the way it explicitly stages gender as performance.[37] Its provocative subject matter and rather testy narrator seem expressly poised to foster discussion and debate in the audience, and the romance has not failed to provoke debate about the author's and narrator's stance toward women: Is he a misogynist, a profeminist, or perhaps even a woman in narratorial drag?[38] If the truth about Heldris's affinities or identity will never be known, there can be no doubt that the romance exhibits a remarkable degree of self-consciousness about the way gender is constructed through language. This occurs both within the romance proper—in narrative presentation of the King's pronouncements on women's legal rights and moral value, and in the spirited debate between Nature and Nurture—and in the narrative interventions that punctuate and frame the romance.

The transvestite plot is set in motion by a powerful speech act: a royal pronouncement against female inheritance that results from King Ebain's faulty reasoning. Because a dispute over the inheritance of female twins caused the death of two knights, King Ebain decrees that *no* woman may inherit (ll. 309–318).[39] One idiosyncratic case is used to determine the lot of all women. Upon the birth of their only child, a daughter, the Duke and Duchess of Cornwall decide to raise her as a boy in order to preserve her birthright. Silence's gender identity is chosen as a matter of political expediency, dictated by a rather arbitrary, illogical interdiction. From the outset, Heldris develops the problem of gender within a tendentious rhetorical and political framework.

The high point of the narrator's presentation of gender as rhetorical construct occurs when the transvestite knight turns twelve, at puberty. The narrator stages this moment of sexual and social conflict as an allegorical debate among Nature, Nurture, and Reason (ll. 24967–2656). Nature, dismayed that her most beautiful creation has been debased by hunting and fighting, urges Silence to go back to her sewing, for such is nature's "custom": "Va en la chambre a la costure, Cho violt de nature li us" (ll. 2527–28). Nurture counters angrily, asserting her power to render Silence "desnaturee" and to make men "ovrer contre nature" [do things that are against nature; ll. 2592–2604]. Reason intervenes to convince Silence that a man's lot in life is more desirable than a woman's: Men live "deseure" [on top] and women "desos" [beneath] (ll. 2640–41). Silence finally reasons that to adopt women's ways would be to trade honor for shame: "Or sui jo moult vallans et pros./ Nel sui, par foi, ains sui honis/ quant as femes voel estre onis" (ll. 2642–44); she decides to continue living as a boy, concealing her "nature."

The scene is an impressive performance by a narrator who is skilled in rhetoric, observant of social practice, and familiar with scholastic dispute; the argument may well be inspired by medieval debates that cast sexual transgression as an affront against Nature, as in Alain de Lille's *De Planctu Naturae*.[40] Heldris's spirited treatment of the debate playfully opposes masculine and feminine stereotypes in broad strokes: Men hunt, own horses, and have "grant honor"; women sew, play games under the bedclothes, and are social underlings. In embodying Silence's identity crisis at puberty as a dispute between Nature, Nurture, and Reason, the narrator represents Silence's gender as a conscious choice of competing cultural models, which are quite explicitly played out before the heroine and the audience.

Despite the apparent division and oppositions of the debate, Heldris's presentation emphasizes the complementary nature of both positions. When Nature argues that her "custom" dictates that Silence sew and protests that the "us" at the end of her name, Silentius, runs counter to "us" [proper practice], Silence reflects that Nature has made her perceive a sophism: "Dont se porpense en lui meïsme/ Que Nature li fait *sofime*" (ll. 2539–40, emphasis mine). Her name, Silentius, enforces the impression that she is male, which runs counter to reality. The sophism, an argument that is false despite an appearance of truth, aptly describes the status of Nature's and Culture's arguments in the romance. On the one hand, both Nature's and Culture's propositions appear to be true. Silence's accomplishments as a knight demonstrate that education can prevail over anatomy (one point for Nurture), and her resumption of the feminine role of wife and queen in the end proves that the female body can not be diverted long from its "natural" function (one point for Nature). This means, of course, that both sides are also partially wrong. To Nature's dismay, Silence is able to perform splendidly as a knight. And Nurture's success is ultimately unmasked by Merlin, who reveals to all present at Ebain's court that Silence is female. The romance ends in a kind of draw, for clearly both Nature and Nurture have made Silence the success that she is.

In the end, the positions occupied by the allegorical figures operate less as polar opposites than as complementary forms of the same cultural construction of "nature de femme," which is produced by the dynamic *tençon* [dispute] between Nature and Nurture and deftly enacted by Silence in a variety of gender roles. What Heldris's staging of the debate about woman makes clear is that gender is "performed" within a highly contested discursive context and that its determinant linguistic and social codes may be manipulated by those like Silence who are clever with dress, gestures, and language.

If the body of the romance explores gender as a cultural and linguistic construct and as a variable performance, then its conclusion, the final revelation at Ebain's court, reveals the political forces that set the stage. As I have argued, the denouement and epilogue dramatize the power of two speakers who act to define "woman."[41] The first is King Ebain, who kills his evil wife and rewards Silence with his hand in marriage; the second is the narrator, who has overseen the representation of woman in the narrative and has the final word. Yet even as both speakers voice their opinions strongly and harshly, apparently upholding the traditional view of woman as subaltern and morally inferior, the text itself casts their "authoritative" pronouncements in a critical light. As in Marie de France and *Aucasssin et Nicolette*, a metacritical perspective on language, gender, and power emerges to replace an oppositional stance.

Antifeminism becomes more pronounced in the second half of the romance. It erupts in both the characters' and the narrator's interventions and culminates in Ebain's angry outburst at his wife, "Sens de feme gist en taisir" [A woman's meaning is to be silence] (l. 6398), which he repeats for good measure: "car femes n'ont sens que mais un/ c'est taisirs" [for women have only one meaning and that is to be silence; ll. 6401–20]. But this negative view of women is corrected once the "truth" of Silence's sex is revealed. Ebain realizes that Eufeme has betrayed him and that Silence is the most faithful of women. Revising his view of female nature, adopting a new tone, and reversing his interdiction, Ebain declares that a good woman is the world's most precious treasure and that, because of Silence, all women may inherit (ll. 6630–43).

In a final declamation of similar intensity, the narrator explains that good women are more to be praised than bad women condemned, for the former must work against their natural inclinations (ll. 6684–91). Heldris then excuses himself before his female readers for his harsh portrayal of Eufeme and urges them to strive to be like Silence, a "bone feme" (ll. 6696–6702).

Le Roman de Silence's conclusion thus highlights the King's and the narrator's speech acts as rhetorical pronouncements in which a certain conception of woman is expounded for political and authorial ends. After exploring the destabilization of normative categories in the adventures of his cross-dressed heroine, the narrator ultimately colludes with his fictional ruler to produce a cultural definition of woman that ensures legitimate succession and upholds the medieval hierarchies of gender and rank.[42]

But by portraying so explicitly the pronouncements in which Nature, Nurture, Reason, the King, and the narrator all seek to define woman and by locating the ultimate arbiter in the royal authority, who marries one woman and executes another, Heldris lays bare the political forces that shape the discourse of gender. The King's misogyny and his extravagant generosity toward Silence; the narrator's condemnation of Eufeme and his lavish praise for Silence—these bold moves dramatize the force with which words of praise and blame can transform social reality. These speech acts starkly reveal that what matters in this potentially deadly game is who has the final say—in this romance, the King and the clerk. The final words of both King and narrator are so emphatic and definitive that they call attention to their force as rhetorical acts. The romance's ending seems to anticipate, if not to provoke, a critical response from its readers and listeners and to invite reflection about the relationship between language, power, and gender.

In different ways, Marie de France's *Guigemar*, *Aucassin et Nicolette*, and Heldris de Cornuälle's *Silence* all incorporate elements of the debate about gender in their fictions. But all three transcend the binary opposition between male and female as absolutes, either by portraying the ambiguity of sexuality, by staging transgressive performances of gender, or by scrutinizing the relationship between language, gender, and power. Marie de France expressly confounds the easy association between gender and moral worth and posits sexuality and sexual difference as an enigma. The author of *Aucassin et Nicolette* scrutinizes sex roles and the linguistic and cultural codes that sustain them through a series of playful reversals and performances. In the arguments that punctuate the actions of his transgressive heroine, Heldris de Cornüälle reveals that the medieval conception of woman is a highly contested rhetorical construct produced by the collusion of clerical and aristocratic powers.

None of these texts permanently overturns the normative categories of gender. But each courtly fiction, in a different way, casts a critical eye on the ways in which the oppositions between men and women are produced and sustained in language and scrutinizes its own "performance" of gender. In so doing, these fictions move their audiences into a space beyond debate and invite them to participate in an interrogation of cultural conventions, codes, and norms. Such interrogation, prefatory to a more serious interruption, is one of the enduring legacies of courtly fictions, which not only transmitted the ideology of clerical and aristocratic culture, but also prompted its self-reflective scrutiny.

Notes

1. On medieval notions of sexual difference, see Joan Cadden, *Meanings of Sex Differences in the Middle Ages: Medicine, Science, and Culture* (Cambridge: Cambridge University Press, 1993).

2. On romance's literary complexity in its twelfth-century origins, see Matilda Bruckner, *Shaping Romance: Interpretation, Truth, and Closure in Twelfth-Century French Fictions* (Philadelphia: University of Pennyslvania Press, 1993).

3. See for example Kathryn Gravdal's study of the normalization and aestheticization of rape in French lyric and narrative, *Ravishing Maidens: Writing Rape in Medieval French Literature and Law* (Philadelphia: University of Pennsylvania Press, 1991).

4. Studies emphasizing the complexity and instability of gender roles in Old French narrative include E. Jane Burns, *Bodytalk: When Women Speak in Old French Literature* (Philadelphia: University of Pennsylvania Press, 1993); Burns, "Refashioning Courtly Love: Lancelot as Ladies' Man or as Lady/Man," in *Constructing Medieval Sexuality*, ed. Karma Lochrie, Peggy McCracken, and James A. Schultz (Minneapolis: University of Minnesota Press, 1997), pp. 111–34; my own "Questions of Gender in Old French Courtly Romance," in *The Cambridge Companion to Medieval Romance*, ed. Roberta L. Krueger (Cambridge: Cambridge University Press, 2000), pp. 132–49; Simon Gaunt, *Gender and Genre in Medieval French Literature* (Cambridge: Cambridge University Press, 1995); and the collection of essays edited by Karen J. Taylor, *Gender Transgressions:*

Crossing the Normative Barrier in Old French Literature (New York: Garland, 1998).

5. Judith Butler, *Gender Trouble: Feminism and the Subversion of Identity* (New York: Routledge, 1990).

6. The notion of performance is developed throughout her book; for a clear articulation, see Butler, *Gender Trouble*, pp. 135–37.

7. Studies of cross-dressing in Old French literature include Michèle Perret, "Travesties et transsexuelles: Ydes, Silence, Grisandole, Blanchandine," *Romance Notes* 25.3 (1985): 328–40; Valerie R. Hotchkiss, *Clothes Make the Man: Female Cross Dressing in Medieval Europe* (New York: Garland, 1996); Michelle Szkilnik, "The Grammar of the Sexes in Medieval French Romance," in *Gender Transgressions*, ed. Taylor, pp. 62–88; Keith Busby, "Plus acesmez qu'une popine: Male Cross-Dressing in Medieval French Narrative," in *Gender Transgressions*, ed. Taylor, pp. 46–59; and the articles cited below on the *Roman de Silence*.

8. See Catherine Brown, "*Muliebriter*: Doing Gender in the Letters of Heloise," in *Gender and Text in the Later Middle Ages*, ed. Jane Chance (Gainesville: University Press of Florida, 1996), p. 25–51. I use the example of Heloise advisedly, since the Latin text in which her letters appear is neither francophone nor courtly. But Heloise might arguably have been familiar with vernacular courtly traditions. The rhetorical sophistication and self-consciousness of her work find parallels in the writings of her successors, authors of courtly fictions.

9. As demonstrated by my *Women Readers and the Ideology of Gender in Old French Verse Romance* (Cambridge: Cambridge University Press, 1993).

10. For example, Robert de Blois's books of conduct for princes and ladies are compiled in the same manuscript as *Floris et Lyriopé*, a narrative in which a man cross-dresses as a woman to seduce his beloved, thereby explicitly bringing sexual difference into play, as I demonstrated in "Constructing Sexual Identities in Robert de Blois's Didactic Poetry," in *Women Readers and the Ideology of Gender in Old French Verse Romance*, pp. 156–182. The critical function of the literature of conduct is further examined in an anthology edited by Kathleen Ashley and Robert L. A. Clark, *Medieval Conduct: Texts, Theories, Practices* (Minneapolis: University of Minnesota Press, 2001).

11. See Burns, "Refashioning Courtly Love: Lancelot as Ladies' Man or as Lady/Man?" and Burns, "Speculum of the Courtly Lady: Women, Love, and Clothes," *Journal of Medieval and Early Modern Studies* 29:2 (1999): 253–92.

12. Helen Solterer, *The Master and Minerva: Disputing Women in French Medieval Culture* (Berkeley and Los Angeles: University of California Press, 1995); see especially chapter 4, pp. 97–130.

13. For editions and translations of selected texts that praise and blame women, see *Three Medieval Views of Women*, ed. and trans. Gloria K. Fiero, Wendy Pfeffer and Mathé Allain (New Haven, Conn.: Yale University Press, 1989), and *Woman Defamed and Woman Defended: An Anthology of Medieval Texts*, ed. Alcuin Blamires, Karen Pratt, and C. W. Marx (Oxford:

Clarendon Press, 1992). A critical study of profeminine arguments in formal "defense" texts and in other literary manifestations is Alcuin Blamires, *The Case for Women in Medieval Culture* (Oxford: Clarendon Press, 1997).

14. "The formal case has a quasi-judicial flavour and expressly sets out to promote women's cause and to exonerate them from slander. Its typical features are these: it questions the motives and morality of misogynists, who seem to forget that women brought them to life and that life without women would be difficult; it denounces antagonistic generalization; it asserts that God showed signs of special favour to women at creation and subsequently; it revises the culpability of Eve; it witnesses women's powerful interventions throughout history (from the Virgin Mary and scriptural heroines to Amazons and modern notables); and it argues that women's moral capacities expose the relative tawdriness of men's" (Blamires, *The Case for Women in Medieval Culture*, p. 9).

15. See Rupert T. Pickens, "The Poetics of Androgyny in the *Lais* of Marie de France: *Yonec, Milun*, and the General *Prologue*," in *Literary Aspects of Courtly Culture*, ed. Donald Maddox and Sara Sturm-Maddox (Cambridge: D. S. Brewer, 1994), pp. 211–19; and Matilda Bruckner, "Of Men and Beasts in *Bisclavret*," *Romanic Review* 82 (1991): 251–69.

16. "Guigemar," *Lais de Marie de France*, ed. Karl Warnke, tr. Laurence Harf-Lancner, Lettres Gothiques (Paris: Librairie Générale Française, 1990), ll. 229–45.

17. R. W. Hanning, "Courtly Contexts for Urban *Cultus*: Responses to Ovid in Chrétien's *Cligès* and Marie's *Guigemar*," *Symposium* 35.1 (1981): 35.

18. Nancy Vine Durling, "The Knot, the Belt, and the Making of *Guigemar*," *Assays: Critical Approaches to Medieval and Renaissance Texts* 6 (1991): 35.

19. Durling, "The Knot, the Belt, and the Making of *Guigemar*," 38.

20. Hanning, "Courtly Contexts for Urban *Cultus*," 45.

21. Herman Braet, "Note sur Marie de France et Ovide (Lai de *Guigemar*, vv. 233–244)," *Mélanges de Philologie et de Littératures romanes offertes à Jeanne Wathelet-Willen* (1978), p. 25.

22. Critics who have commented upon the symbolic importance of this word-play include Durling, "The Knot, the Belt, and the Making of *Guigemar*," 39–46; Milena Mikhaílova, *Le Présent de Marie* (Paris: Diderot, 1996), pp. 78–80; and R. Howard Bloch, "The Medieval Text—'Guigemar'—as a Provocation to the Discipline of Medieval Studies," *Romanic Review* 79.1 (1988): 72–73.

23. Marie's narrative affinity extends not only to the hero; for Rupert Pickens, it also includes the androgynous wounded deer who speaks proleptically about the course of love; Rupert T. Pickens, "Marie de France and the Body Poetic," in *Gender and Text*, ed. Jane Chance, p. 156.

24. The sexual ambiguity of Guigemar's story has been analyzed by Pickens, "Marie de France and the Body Poetic"; the story's inscrutability as a self-destructive fiction has been emphasized by Bloch, "The Medieval Text—'Guigemar'—as a Provocation"; its "extraordinary self-reflexiveness" by

Durling, "The Knot, the Belt, and the Making of Guigemar," 46; and its open-ended nature by Joan Brumlik, "Thematic Irony in Marie de France's *Guigemar*," *French Forum* 13.1 (1988): 5–16.

25. On Marie's stance as female author, see Michelle Freeman, "Marie de France's Poetics of Silence: The Implications for a Feminine *Translatio*," *PMLA* 99 (1984): 860–83; on Marie's affirmation of woman's moral authority in other work, see Sahar Amar, "Marie de France Rewrites Genesis: The Image of Woman in Marie de France's *Fables*," *Neophilologus* 81. 4 (1997): 489–99; and for a view on the gender of the author as expressly problematized, see Miranda Griffin, "Gender and Authority in the Medieval French *Lai*," *Forum for Modern Language Studies* 35, 1 (1999): 42–56.

26. Rupert Pickens, "Poétique et sexualité chez Marie de France," in *Et c'est la fin pour quoi sommes ensemble: hommage à Jean Dufournet: Littérature, histoire et langue du Moyen Age* (Paris: Champion, 1993), p. 1129.

27. See "Playing to the Ladies: Chivalry and Misogyny in *Ipomedon, Le Chevalier à l'épée*, and *La Vengeance Raguidel*," in Krueger, *Women Readers and the Ideology of Gender*, pp. 68–100.

28. *Aucassin et Nicolette*, ed. Jean Dufournet (Paris: Garnier-Flammarion), 1984, p. 84.

29. The locus classicus for this idea is Aristotle's *De Generatione Animalium*: "An animal is a living body, a body with Soul in it. The female always provides the material, the male provides that which fashions the material into shape; this, in our view, is the specific characteristic of each of the sexes: that is what it means to be male or female. Thus the physical part, the body, comes from the female, and the Soul from the male, since the Soul is the essence of a particular body" (7, 738b; cited and translated by Alcuin Blamires et al., *Woman Defamed and Woman Defended*, p. 40).

30. The passage is a pastiche of the formal courtly portrait analyzed by Alice M. Colby [Colby-Hall], *The Portrait in Twelfth-Century French: An Example of the Stylistic Originality of Chrétien de Troyes* (Geneva: Droz, 1965).

31. Nathaniel B. Smith notes the physicality of Nicolette's representation as an aspect of her "uncourtliness," which makes of her an "anti-heroine," in "The Uncourtliness of Nicolette," *Voices of Conscience: Essays on Medieval and Modern French Literature in Memory of James D. Powell and Rosemary Hodgins*, ed. Raymond J. Cormier (Philadelphia, Pa.: Temple University Press, 1977), pp. 169–82.

32. Critics who note the remarkable activities of the heroine include Smith, "The Uncourtliness of Nicolette"; Eugene Vance, "*Aucassin et Nicolette* as a Medieval Comedy of Signification and Exchange," in *The Nature of Medieval Narrative*, ed. Minnette Grunmann-Gaudet and Robin F. Jones (Lexington, Ky.: French Forum, 1980), pp. 57–76; and Kevin Brownlee, "Discourse as *Prouesces* in *Aucassin et Nicolette*," *Yale French Studies* 70 (1986): 167–92.

33. The long-held notion that *Aucassin et Nicolette* is a parody has been refuted by Tony Hunt; "La Parodie Médiévale: Le Cas d'*Aucassin et Nicolette*," *Romania*

100 (1979): 321–81. For an overview of the critical debate, see Rudy S. Spray-car, "Genre and Convention in *Aucassin et Nicolette*," *Romanic Review* 76 (1985): 94–115. For Spraycar, the text's "dominant mocking character" directs itself against "the abstract notion of *conventionality out of all measure*" (115).

34. In addition to Vance, Brownlee, and Spraycar, see R. Howard Bloch, "Money, Metaphor, and the Mediation of Social Difference in Old French Romance," *Symposium* 35 (1981): 18–33; more recently, Jane Gilbert, "The Practice of Gender in *Aucassin et Nicolette*," *Forum for Modern Language Studies* 33.3 (1997): 217–28; and the excellent article by Maria Rosa Menocal, "Signs of the Times: Self, Other and History in *Aucassin et Nicolette*," *Romanic Review* 80.4 (1989): 497–511.

35. On the French/Saracen dichotomy, see Menocal, "Signs of the Times."

36. See Krueger, "Women Readers and the Politics of Gender in *Le Roman de Silence*," in *Women Readers and the Ideology of Gender*, pp. 100–127.

37. Among the many studies that discuss the romance's textual ambiguities, its complex representation of sexuality, and its problematization of gender, we are particularly indebted to Michèle Perret, "Travesties et transsexuellles: Ydes, Silence, Grisandole, Blanchandine," op. cit.; Peter Allen, "The Ambiguity of Silence: Gender, Writing, and *Le Roman de Silence*," in *Signs, Sentence, Discourse: Language in Medieval Thought and Literature*, ed. Julian N. Wasserman and Lois Roney (Syracuse, N.Y.: Syracuse University Press, 1989), pp. 98–112; and Simon Gaunt, "The Significance of Silence," *Paragraph* 13.2 (1990): 202–16. For an astute reading of the romance's representation of gender in the light of Butler's theory of performance, see Peggy McCracken, "'The Boy Who Was a Girl': Reading Gender in the *Roman de Silence*," *Romanic Review* 85.4 (1994): 517–36.

38. For a spectrum of views on Heldris's authorial stance, see the collection of articles edited by F. Regina Psaki in *Arthuriana* 7.2 (1997).

39. *Le Roman de Silence: A Thirteenth-Century Arthurian Verse-Romance* by Heldris de Cornualle, ed. Lewis Thorpe (Cambridge: Heffer, 1972). An English translation (with facing-page edition) is *Silence: A Thirteenth-Century French Romance*, ed. and trans. Sarah Roche Mahdi. *Medieval Texts and Studies* 10 (East Lansing, Mich., 1992). See also Heldris de Cornualle, *Le Roman de Silence,* trans. Regina Psaki (New York: Garland, 1991). All translations within this article are my own.

40. See R. Howard Bloch, "Silence and Holes: The *Roman de Silence* and the Art of the Trouvère," *Yale French Studies* 10 (1986): 81–99. On the way that Heldris has feminized the portrayal of Nature, see Suzanne Conkin Akbari, "Nature's Forge Recast in the *Roman de Silence*," in *Literary Aspects of Courtly Culture; Selected Papers from the Seventh Triennial Congress of the International Courtly Literature Society*, ed. Donald Maddox and Sara Sturm-Maddox (Cambridge: D. S. Brewer, 1994), pp. 39–46.

41. See Krueger, *Women Readers and the Ideology of Gender*, pp. 122–27.

42. See Sharon Kinoshita, "Heldris de Cornuälle's *Roman de Silence* and the Feudal Politics of Lineage," *PMLA* 110 (1995): 397–409.

CHAPTER 5

THINKING THROUGH GENDER
IN LATE MEDIEVAL GERMAN LITERATURE

Ann Marie Rasmussen

The absence of modern scholarship on gender debates in late medieval German literature is due not to a lack of primary sources but rather to reliance on assumptions derived from the Old French querelle, *which are unproductive in the German context. Instead, a model combining codicology with gender analysis can more usefully explore the German debate. Key examples are drawn from the* Liederbuch der Clara Hatzlerin [Songbook of Clara Hätzerlin] *and from* Die Beichte einer Frau [A Woman's Confession].

If one's exploration of gender in late medieval German literature is guided by a definition of debate derived from the model of the *querelle des femmes*—a learned, self-reflexive academic debate, carried out by named authors (one of whom was a woman, Christine de Pizan), about gender, misogyny, language, and history—then there is no such debate in German medieval literature.[1] This assertion can be substantiated by reading any—indeed nearly all—of the standard literary histories of pre-Reformation German literature, which contain few references to gender and no discussions of any kind of late medieval German debate on the topic. If one's exploration of medieval and early modern German literature follows the *querelle* model, as most scholarship does, then the German *querelle* begins belatedly, in the seventeenth century, as a part of a pan-European discussion about learned women.[2] Yet how can there be a medieval European culture in which ideas about women, men, and gender are not the stuff of intellectual exchange and argument? In the case of late medieval German literature, we must look again, look elsewhere, and look otherwise.

This paper returns to a sample of late medieval, vernacular, German literary texts, specifically to examples from the largely anonymous, rhymed couplet genres of *Maeren* (comic tales or fabliaux), and *Minnereden* (discourses on love or *dits d'amour*), which discuss love in discursive-theoretical fashion, often by employing the rhetorical conventions of allegory and debate. It reconsiders their codicological contexts, that is to say, their place and order in late medieval compilation manuscripts. These manuscripts circulated at the courts of late medieval Germany and in cities among the urban elite—wealthy merchants, patricians, and educated professionals such as lawyers and doctors. A reexamination of this material reveals that it does indeed stage debates about women, men, and culture, but that it does so very differently from the model of a systematic, learned, academic debate arising from the Old French tradition. I argue that far from being absent from medieval German literature, debates about gender are omnipresent, so ubiquitous in fact that this small study can be but a prolegomenon to a history of late medieval German literature rewritten from the perspective of gender analysis.

How can we think about gender as a significant category of intellectual thought in the late medieval German world? How can we approach gender not as a common, unified set of universally held beliefs about masculinity and femininity preexisting their medieval textual representations, but as historically specific social knowledge; as a complex way of making sense of a complex world, which comes into being in texts? A useful analogy can be found in Gabrielle Spiegel's work on the emergence of the concept of genealogy as a mode of historical thinking and writing in thirteenth-century France. Seeking to understand the concept of genealogy as an intellectual category, she sums up its mode of functioning as a way of thinking and writing as follows: "There are two principal ways in which genealogy as a conceptual metaphor affected historical literature in thirteenth-century France: first, as form, by supplying a model for the disposition of narrative material (in other words, as a perceptual grid and narrative frame); second, as meaning, by reinterpreting historical events in accordance with the model of filiation suggested by genealogy."[3]

In the above citation, Spiegel contrasts form and meaning in order to capture the way in which genealogy can function as, first, a kind of conventional genre, that is to say, as a kind of formal template for organizing material, and second, as an intellectual concept that makes sense of the world. Spiegel's work reminds us that "thinking through genealogy" came into being at a specific time and place, and that genealogy need not have been the topic of learned, self-reflexive, academic debate in the medieval world for it to have been a functioning intellectual concept and a kind of genre scheme widely deployed to write, that is to say, to make narrative sense of, political and natural events. In thinking about gender in late medieval German literature, however, I wish to bypass the notion, suggested by the above quote, that form precedes meaning or has meaning impressed upon it, and instead stress the interdependence of form and meaning. I therefore propose not two but three principal ways in which the debate about gender is an organizing factor in the literature of fourteenth- and fifteenth-century Germany.

First, the medieval debate about gender in Germany exists as a set of themes, or—speaking formally—conventions, motifs, and images. We know this because generations of scholars, using the tools of poetics and thematic criticism and focusing on the interpretation of individual texts, have made this knowledge visible. However, scholarly debate continues about the status and meaning of these themes and conventions. Some scholarship suggests that literary conventions and images about gender mirror preexisting values, beliefs, and practices about gender in the medieval world. Other scholarship has rejected the idea that there is a simple, mimetic relationship between literature and the worlds out of which it emerges, arguing that fixed images do not have fixed meanings, and that representations of literary themes do not represent fixed and unified categories of meaning.

Thus the possibilities for achieving new understandings and new knowledge through the methods of poetics and thematic criticism are not exhausted. For example, much late medieval German literature holding promise for a study of gender is literature about courtly love, which has been studied primarily within the parameters of that august (and, by the 1400s, venerable) tradition. Such scholarly work, fine though much of it is, tends to obscure the multiple ways in which the late medieval texts about courtly love also enact and construct social knowledge of gender. I therefore propose that it is both feasible and necessary to think about late medieval German texts traditionally assigned to the category of courtly love from the perspective of gender criticism.

The second and third ways proposed in this paper to think about gender as an intellectual category focus increasingly on the manuscripts containing individual texts. They are based on the assumption that medieval compilation manuscripts, far from being "an arbitrary sum of their parts,"[4] reflect interpretive practices of editing, selecting, and ordering texts on the part of those who produced and owned them. Second, then, I propose that gender can also supply a model for the disposition of narrative material (in other words, it can function as "a perceptual grid and narrative frame"). This way of thinking about gender touches on narrative, but for the purposes of this paper I would like to think of it as a way to make sense of variation, here in the sense of different versions of the same text. Because medieval authors and scribes often freely adapted texts to the new interpretive communities represented by new manuscripts, variation is "one key to medieval literary aesthetics.[5] Attending to variation implies renewed attention to manuscripts by scholars carefully assessing as potentially meaningful the variations, or adaptations, of texts. Reexamining medieval German literature from the perspective of "gender as variation" suggests that debates about gender are discernable as an intellectual category guiding the production of variant versions of a text.

Third, I propose thinking about gender as a compilational practice.[6] Sarah Westphal shows the great care taken by medieval compilers in selecting texts and artfully arranging them around intellectual topics such as adventure, or estates, or love. These intellectual categories or issues function as linkages among individual stories, which are often relatively heterogeneous in tone and genre. Individual works are placed in dialogue with one another and so represent different, and often contradictory, positions, much as in a disputation or debate. Linking short texts into constellations in this fashion is the rule, not the exception, in late medieval compilation manuscripts of rhymed couplet texts. I propose that debates about men, women, and gender function as an intellectual category to create interpretive linkages among texts. Thinking about gender as a compilational practice implies, of course, readerly practice. It suggests that these debates functioned at the level of reception (in the highly elastic and productive medieval conception of literary reception), for the idea of constellations of texts linked by intellectual categories makes sense only if such constellations open up interpretive moments to scribes, compilers, authors, collectors, owners, and readers alike.

A few examples will, I hope, illustrate how gender as theme, gender as variation, and gender as a compilational principle can widen our range of vision and make visible the debate about men, women, and gender in the late medieval German world. Much of this literature takes up the pan-European themes of praising or blaming women, though these texts have received almost no attention in English-language scholarship.[7] Helmut de Boor's monumental anthology of medieval German texts includes many in the category *Lehre von Frauen und Minne* [Teachings about Women and Love].[8] The genre of the *Minnerede,* or discourse on love, also contains numerous texts praising or defaming women. Tilo Brandis's monumental compilation of all known *Minnereden* lists twenty-one works in the category *Lob der tugendhaften Frau* [Praise of the Virtuous Woman].[9] Six of these texts have author's names attached to them. The rest are anonymous, including the most widely copied text in this category, *Lob der Frauen* [Praise of Women] (Brandis 262), a piece of some 200-plus lines that appears fifteen times in thirteen manuscripts (one, Nuremberg, Germanisches Nationalmuseum, 966 Merkel, copies slightly different versions no less than three times). Like de Boor, Brandis offers no parallel category such as *Frauenschelte* [Blaming Women], but texts that scold and defame women are easily found in such categories as *Negative Minnelehre* [Negative Teachings about Love] and *Klage über Untugenden* [Laments about Vice] and the like.

The topoi of blaming or praising women appear of course in many other genres. There are simple texts, such as three short, anonymous works that are a part of a series of gnomic-type texts opening the fifteenth-century manuscript Prague, Knihovna Národního Musea, X A 12, known as the *Liederbuch der Clara Hätzlerin* [Songbook of Clara Hätzlerin] after the professional female scribe who compiled it in the prosperous town of Augsburg in 1474.[10] The texts, one in praise of women and two that defame them, are organized as ABC texts (in the same manner as children's books today). The ABC praising women begins "Allerliebsts / Beschaidens / Czuckersüsz" . . . [Most beloved / Modest / Sugar-sweet . . .],[11] while the two other ABC texts about women defame them with such phrases as "Abgerittene / Böszwichtin! . . ." [Worn out / Wicked woman . . .][12] or "Erenlose, / Falsche / Giftige / Hur!" [Dishonorable / false / venomous / whore].[13] Copied in immediate proximity of one another, all appear on the manuscript's opening folio. Surely the hypothesis merits further exploration that the "for and against" enacted by these brief and aesthetically unremarkable texts signals a preoccupation in the manuscript with debate literature about women more generally.[14]

It is perhaps methodologically a more interesting question to think about the ways in which debates about men, women, and gender might operate on the level of variation, that is to say, to show that adaptation, or variation, in different manuscript versions of a late medieval text produces different accounts of gender. Such is the case, I argue, in two versions of a widely copied *Minnerede* known as *Die Beichte einer Frau* [A Woman's Confession] (Brandis 340). In it an eavesdropping male narrator reports on a conversation he has overheard between a woman and her priest, in which the woman confesses to an illicit love affair and convinces the initially outraged priest that her behavior is entirely virtuous; the narrator then goes on to close the work with a long epilogue praising the female speaker. In Prague X A 12, *A Woman's Confession* is 558 verses long. It is the second lengthiest text to appear in Prague X A 12, following immediately after the previously mentioned *Praise of Women* (Brandis 262).[15] *A Woman's Confession* also appears in the enormous manuscript (498 folios) Heidelberg, Universitätsbibliothek, cpg 313, compiled sometime between 1470 and 1490, probably for someone in or close to the court of Count Palatine Philipp

IV.[16] This version is 200 lines shorter than the version in Prague X A 12. Gerhard Thiele, who edited the version from Heidelberg cpg 313, provided the following explanation for its decreased length: "This branch of the manuscript transmission skipped these verses out of laziness."[17] Yet this evaluation of the evidence does not tally well with Glier's finding that Heidelberg cpg 313 shows clear evidence of carefully planned organization.[18]

Thinking of gender as an intellectual category allows one to make better sense of the variation in these two versions of *A Woman's Confession*. Comparing the two manuscripts shows that in Heidelberg cpg 313, it is primarily the woman's speaking part that is shorter; she speaks only half as many lines as in Prague X A 12. Heidelberg cpg 313 does not contain lines in which the lady elaborates on the connection between the love affair and chivalry (Prague X A 12, lines 245–82). It also lacks a long dialogue, present in Prague X A 12 (lines 346–453) that takes place after the priest is won over, in which the female speaker admits her doubts and worries. These changes (and others) alter the characterization of the female speaker, specifically modifying her repeated claims that courtly love is virtuous and that she herself is an honorable woman. In lines 52–55 of Prague X A 12, the woman explicitly defines the love affair as a relationship that preserves her honor: "Nit anders er an mich muot / Dann das mir meret zucht vnd Er. / Dazu gibt er mir weis vnd ler, / Mein Er ist Im wol behuot" [He expects nothing from me / except that which increases my modesty and honor. / In such matters he teaches and instructs me. / He guards my honor well]. These lines are missing in Heidelberg cpg 313.

Thinking through gender allows an interpreter to discern in this example of variation not scribal error, but the production of differing notions of femininity. The key concept under debate is the construction of woman's honor, which in fifteenth-century Germany was conventionally understood to depend on women's sexual behavior: An honorable woman was chaste before marriage and sexually faithful after marriage. When the female speaker in Prague X A 12 explicitly links her amorous intrigue with her honor, she strongly suggests that her affair is chaste. She is therefore telling a story about her affair that conforms to conventional notions of women's honor, a story that strengthens the narrator's contention that women are virtuous and that such love affairs can educate men and women morally and ethically. Heidelberg cpg 313 leaves out the link with honor, thereby strongly suggesting that the love affair is sexual. It leaves out the female speaker's doubts and worries, and thereby presents her as more self-serving. Its version of the narrator's afterword is hyperbolic in its praise of women, thereby implying that the narrator is something of a fool. Heidelberg cpg 313 thus strongly suggests that both the priest and the narrator have been duped by persuasiveness of a beautiful woman, and that there is a correspondence between the woman's persuasive speech and her beautiful body (for both the priest and the eavesdropper look at her), both of which are dangerous. Both versions of *A Woman's Confession* do gender work. Prague X A 12 works to align the female speaker with traditional discourses of female virtue. Heidelberg cpg 313 undercuts the text's overt message that love service is ethically and socially valuable by implying that for women, beauty, persuasiveness, and deceit go together. Put another way: It links the praise of women with an enactment of highly questionable female virtue.

The above examples of "gender as theme" and "gender as variation" have already introduced examples of gender at work as a compilational principle. The opening folios of Prague X A 12 are dominated by texts about women's virtues and vices: The ABC texts on folio 2, the *Minnereden of Praise of Women* on folios 6–9, and *A Woman's Confession* on folios 9–17. Other brief, gnomic, and sometimes comic texts on folios 3–5 also treat gender, and on folio 6 an "ironic" praise of women begins, of which two lines are copied at the bottom of each page until folio 65, thus providing a kind of "counterpoint" to all the texts with which it shares a page. This opening constellation of texts signals, I submit, the manuscript's preoccupation with femininity as a topic of debate.

Can the compilational contexts in which *A Woman's Confession* is found tell us anything more about the meanings of gender produced in the two versions discussed above? In Heidelberg cpg 313, *A Woman's Confession* is separated by two hundred (!) folios from the constellation of serious *Minnereden* that open the manuscript, and is placed instead in a constellation of allegorical and comic texts. As we saw above, in Prague X A 12 *A Woman's Confession* directly follows *The Praise of Women*. *A Woman's Confession* is itself followed by a series of *Minnereden* about virtuous women (folios 18–37). Prague X A 12 thus creates a constellation of texts about female virtue that stabilizes the interpretation of the female speaker in *A Woman's Confession* as virtuous and chaste.

I offer a final example of a manuscript in which gender functions as a compilational principle.[19] Berlin, Staatsbibliothek zu Berlin Preussischer Kulturbesitz, mgo 186, was compiled in Baltic Livonia in 1431 (now part of Latvia and Estonia), which had been conquered in the thirteenth century by a branch of the Order of the Teutonic Knights and enjoyed a flourishing grain trade with the rest of Europe.[20] The manuscript records the date and provenance; its language, however, is lower Rhenish, a Low German dialect from the region immediately bordering Flanders. It has been suggested that it was compiled by or for a merchant; more plausible is an attribution of compilation or ownership to one of the many young Flemish noblemen who journeyed to Livonia to serve with the Teutonic Knights.[21] The manuscript contains one love lyric and five rhymed couplet texts (both *Minnereden* and

Maeren), and closes with a Low German adventure-romance, *Flos unde Blanke-flos,* belonging to the pan-European Floire and Blancheflor romance tradition.[22] Berlin mgo 186 is clearly a manuscript about love, yet its debates about love also represent debates about gender.

The rhymed couplet texts in this manuscript are a classic example of what Westphal has called a "*minne* constellation" (*minne* is the Middle High German term for sentimental and/or courtly love), a codicological formation found in numerous compilation manuscripts.[23] In Berlin mgo 186 the *minne* constellation of five texts fills 66 folios. The texts are: *Schule der Minne* [School of Love] (Brandis 433), an allegory of the virtues of love; *Streitgespräch zweier Frauen über die Minne* [Debate between Two Women about Love] (Brandis 401), in which a male narrator overhears two women debating whether happiness derives from the presence or absence of love and presenting examples of men's mistreatment of women; *Frauentreue* [The Fidelity of Women] (Fischer 38),[24] a tale of genuine female fidelity; *Die treue Magd* [The Faithful Maid] (Fischer 80), a comic tale or fabliaux that confirms women's mastery of erotic situations; and *Des Minners Anklagen* [The Lover's Lament] (Brandis 457), in which a disputation between love and beauty yields to a trial scene, wherein the Virtues pass judgment on the narrator's beloved. In this constellation, the tales of female virtues lead up to a tale of female promiscuity, and a tale in which the female beloved is tested and tried. Again the topics of female virtue and vice are contrastively linked to one another, while the trial poem closing the *minne* constellation points toward the potential of disputation and debate as a practice of reading and interpretation.

A number of topoi conventionally associated with the debate about gender are thematically represented in these texts: the praise and blame of women, a trial, disputation, and allegory. Further, the stories in this *minne* constellation debate with one another about what it means to be a woman: Are women capable of fidelity? Can women be trusted? Do virtuous, loving women exist? The constellation of stories also sets up conflicting notions of masculinity, from the eavesdropping narrator, whose implied position as a master of the intellectual and poetic conventions of writing contrasts with the oral performance staged by the female speakers,[25] to the cuckolded husband in *Die treue Magd,* the lamenting lover in *Des Minners Anklagen,* and the lover physically assaulted by a female personification in *Schule der Minne.* In the last three instances, the lover is an abject subject of female mastery. From the perspective of masculinity studies, this gender constellation, with its fantasies of what it means to be a man, warrants further study.

Thinking about gender as a theme, as a category at work in shaping textual variation, and as a compilational principle makes gender visible as a critically important intellectual and literary category of medieval German vernacular literature. Yet it also does more. Using gender as a category of scholarly analysis fruitfully complicates the conceptual frameworks traditionally employed in literary scholarship. For example, scholarship has conventionally dealt with the theme of courtly love in fifteenth-century German literature by examining it in relation to originary notions of courtly love developed in vernacular texts from the High Middle Ages. Thus late medieval literature on love is seen as having become a rarefied exercise in aesthetics and ethics: "Eroticism has become an ethical form of art with canonical values of its own that are rarely problematized."[26] Yet establishing historical continuity for medieval concepts of courtly love has precluded asking whether late medieval concepts of courtly love raise different issues; answer, as it were, different questions; or use notions of courtly love for different purposes. Using gender as a category of analysis encourages us to raise new kinds of questions about these texts, and to be historically specific about ideologies of courtly love.

Using gender as a category of analysis can also help us think further about concepts of authorship in the High Middle Ages. Albrecht Hausmann points out how medieval notions of authorship differ from modern notions of a "concept of authorship based on aesthetic production, in which the text always appears as a product that is secondary to its producer." Characteristic of the medieval text is instead the "melding together of reproduction and reception."[27] Needless to say, authorship is a highly complicated category for medieval literary scholarship, as is demonstrated by a simple list of the ways in which the author function is manifested in medieval texts: named authors, texts with false attributions to real or imagined authors, pictures of authors, communal authorship, author names without texts, pseudonyms, all of the above with—but usually without—extraliterary documentation of a life, and, of course, a wealth of anonymous texts.[28]

This complexity stands out as a particular problem for the late medieval period. Authorship clearly matters; more authors name themselves, and authorship can function as a compilational principle in late medieval manuscripts. Yet the very same manuscripts also brim over with anonymous texts. Using gender as a category of analysis supports the contention that medieval practices of copying, editing, and compiling involve, like authorship, intentional, interpretive action on the part of a now anonymous figure. "From a codicological perspective, the work of copying looks less like transcription and more like a creative process with strong, traditional underpinnings. The hierarchical distinctions among scribe, author, and compiler begin to vanish as the role of scribe is shown to include editing, merging, and breaking up of texts, as well as text selection and even composition."[29] The category of authorship in late medieval German literary culture appears to be both highly elastic, possibly including editing, selecting, ordering, and composing texts, and highly contingent, in the sense that naming practices operate only in particular circumstances for specific reasons.

I hope by now to have shown that the problem in identifying gender debates lies not in a lack of primary sources, but rather in the fact that the categories structuring much scholarship on this period render invisible the ubiquity of debates about gender in fifteenth-century Germany.

The absence of scholarly discussions of gender in this period arises from another problem as well. Older scholarship failed to find debates about gender in medieval German literature in part because it was guided by definitions strictly derived from the Old French model. The inexhaustibly rich Old French debates resonate powerfully with modern questions of agency and subjectivity, providing material for women's history and for gender studies, but their very exceptionality make them a poor model for studying debates about gender in other medieval European literatures and cultures. As feminist scholarship of the past twenty years and the essays in this volume make clear, academic, learned, self-reflexive debates are not the only medieval modes of intellectual thought and writing informed by debates about women, men, and gender.

Older scholarship's importation of definitions derived from the Old French *querelle* carried a number of assumptions about Old French high literary culture into the study of women and gender in late medieval German literature. I conclude this essay by offering some observations on ways in which medieval debates about gender differ in these two linguistically, politically, and socially distinct cultures.

First, the *querelle* debates are geographically localized and centralized in main centers of power such as Paris; German debates are diffused across the German-speaking territories, which are politically and socially highly heterogeneous. The *querelle* debates take place in a dense personal network characterized by overlapping social and political ties, networks whose emergence was probably facilitated by the early emergence of centralized political and cultural power in France. Likewise, the many different territories and structures of government in German-speaking lands tended to give rise to loose and fragmented debates about gender (and/or the evidence linking texts produced in one court or city with those produced in another has not survived). The Old French debates and the Spanish debates largely contain texts by named authors. In contrast, the German manuscripts and many, if not most, of the texts they contain are anonymous. Finally, the German debate diverges most markedly from the Old French material by the absence of a textual persona like "Christine" who could speak on behalf of "real" women with an authoritative voice. In Germany there is no advocate persona. Instead, the many functions of the advocate for women that Christine represents can be found in Germany divided among the many active literary women of the fifteenth century, for example, Elisabeth of Nassau-Saarbrücken and Eleonore of Austria, translators and adapters of romances; Clara Hätzlerin, the Augsburg scribe; or Mechthild of Rottenburg and Margarete of Savoy, patrons of literature.[30]

For all these reasons, the German debates represent a different kind of debate about the ideas that constitute social knowledge of women, men, and gender. This paper suggests that we think of these texts and these manuscripts as a polyphonic chorus representing a mode of knowledge deemed necessary if nobleman or noblewoman, courtier, patrician, or merchant, male or female, were to acquire the appearance of worldly success. Central to this worldly competence is knowledge of gender, staged in these manuscripts as a process in which what it means to be a woman or a man is constantly being defined and redefined. Far from being marginal, or nonexistent, this process of renegotiating the changing norms for gender in a changing world represents a central intellectual facet of the expanding world of secular, vernacular knowledge in fifteenth-century Germany.

Notes

1. See for example two otherwise excellent, largely descriptive discussions of medieval German literature, one in German and one in English: Joachim Bumke, *Geschichte der deutschen Literatur im späten Mittelalter,* vol. 3 of *Geschichte der deutschen Literatur im Mittelalter* (Munich: dtv, 1990); and chapters 2 and 3 of *The Cambridge History of German Literature,* ed. Helen Watanabe-O'Kelly (Cambridge: Cambridge University Press, 1997). See also vols. 2 and 3 of *Geschichte der deutschen Literatur von den Anfängen bis zur Gegenwart,* ed. Kurt Böttcher and Günther Albrecht (Berlin: Volk und Wissen, 1990), produced in the German Democratic Republic during its final years. Early feminist discussions of medieval German literature, which are primarily organized around the category of female authorship, are similarly silent on this topic, for example the now dated article by Ursula Liebertz-Grün, "Höfische Autorinnen: Von der karolingischen Kulturreform bis zum Humanismus," *Vom Mittelalter bis zum Ende des 18. Jahrhunderts,* vol. 1 of *Deutsche Literatur von Frauen,* edited by Gisela Brinker-Gabler (Munich: Beck, 1988), pp. 39–64. An exception is Irene Erfen, "Literaturbetrieb," *Von der Handschrift zum Buchdruck: Spätmittelalter, Reformation, Humanismus,* edited by Ingrid Bennewitz and Ulrich Müller, vol. 2 of *Deutsche Literatur: Eine Sozialgeschichte* (Reinbek bei Hamburg: Rowohlt, 1991), pp. 32–45. Erfen's article discusses women as active and educated participants in late medieval culture.

2. The standard work is Barbara Becker-Cantarino, *Der lange Weg zur Mündigkeit: Frau und Literatur (1500–1800)* (Stuttgart: Metzler, 1987). Useful is also Elisabeth Gössmann, "Für und wider die Frauengelehrsamkeit:

Eine europäische Diskussion im 17. Jahrhundert," *Deutsche Literatur von Frauen,* vol. 1, pp. 185–96. For newer work, see Cornelia Plume, *Heroinnen in der Geschlechterordnung: Weiblichkeitsprojektionen bei Daniel Casper Lohenstein und die Querelle des Femmes* (Berlin: Metzler, 1996).

3. Gabrielle M. Spiegel, "Genealogy: Form and Function in Medieval Historiography," *The Past as Text: The Theory and Practice of Medieval Historiography* (Baltimore: Johns Hopkins University Press, 1997), p. 105.

4. Hans Robert Jauss, "Literary History as a Challenge to Literary Theory," *Toward an Aesthetic of Reception,* trans. Timothy Bahti (Minneapolis: University of Minnesota Press, 1982), pp. 2–45, here p. 45.

5. Sarah Westphal, *Textual Poetics of German Manuscripts 1300–1500* (Columbia, S.C.: Camden House, 1993), p. 13.

6. Westphal, *Textual Poetics,* is the most significant contribution to scholarship on codicology as a way of understanding the medieval literature. On variation and compilation in *Maeren,* see Arend Mihm, *Überlieferung und Verbreitung der Märendichtung im Spätmittelalter* (Heidelberg: Winter, 1967). On variation in medieval German romances and epics, see Joachim Bumke, "Der unfeste Text: Überlegungen zur Überlieferungsgeschichte und Textkritik der höfischen Epik im 13. Jahrhundert," *'Aufführung' und 'Schrift' in Mittelalter und Früher Neuzeit,* edited by Jan-Dirk Müller (Stuttgart: Metzler, 1996), pp. 118–29. On variation in *Minnesong* (German courtly love poetry), see Albrecht Hausmann, *Reinmar der Alte als Autor: Untersuchungen zur Überlieferung und zur programmatischen Identität,* Bibliotheca Germanica, vol. 40 (Tübingen: Francke Verlag, 1999), pp. 13–50, which treat author function and manuscript variation.

7. One of the most prolific lyric poets of the later period, Heinrich of Meissen (d. 1318), was (and still is) best known by his moniker, Frauenlob (Praise of Women). This name may refer to the poems he wrote in praise of virtuous women, or to his songs in praise of the Virgin Mary, or of course, to both. On the topoi of blaming and praising women, see Helen Solterer, *The Master and Minerva: Disputing Women in Old French Literature* (Berkeley and Los Angeles: University of California Press, 1995); Alcuin Blamires, ed., *Woman Defamed and Woman Defended: An Anthology of Medieval Texts,* with Karen Pratt and C. W. Marx (Oxford: Clarendon Press, 1992); Alcuin Blamires, *The Case for Women in Medieval Culture* (Oxford: Clarendon Press, 1997). Blamires briefly mentions Gottfried von Strassburg's *Tristan,* which is usually the only German- language text to be discussed in this context.

8. Helmut de Boor, ed., *Mittelalter: Texte und Zeugnisse,* vol. 1, in 2 parts of *Die deutsche Literatur: Texte und Zeugnisse,* edited by Walther Killy (Munich: Beck, 1965), vol. 1, part 2, pp. 1775–1817. The anthology is thematically arranged, and many other texts about gender appear in other sections of the anthology.

9. *Mittelhochdeutsche, mittelniederdeutsche und mittelniederländische Minnereden: Verzeichnis der Handschriften und Drucke.* Münchener Texte und Unter-

suchungen, vol. 25 (Munich: Beck, 1968). Following scholarly practice, *Minnereden* are cited by the title assigned by Brandis (other titles may appear in the manuscripts) and by the number Brandis assigned. The standard study of *Minnereden* remains Ingeborg Glier, *Artes amandi: Untersuchung zu Geschichte, Ueberlieferung und Typologie der deutschen Minnereden,* Münchener Texte und Untersuchungen, vol. 34 (Munich: Beck, 1977).

10. Carl Ferdinand Haltaus, ed., *Liederbuch der Clara Hätzlerin.* Leipzig: 1840. Reprinted with an afterword by Hanns Fischer. Deutsche Neudrucke, Texte des Mittelalters, no. 85 (Berlin: de Gruyter, 1966). Hätzlerin was working in a time of great change; by 1474 the first printing presses were active in Augsburg. On Hätzlerin, see Burghart Wachinger, "Liebe und Literatur im spätmittelalterlichen Schwaben und Franken: Zur Augsburger Sammelhandschrift der Clara Hätzlerin," *Deutsche Vierteljahresschrift* 56 (1982): 386–406, and Sheila Edmonds, "Clara's Patron: The Identity of Jörg Roggenburg," *Beiträge zur deutschen Sprach- und Literaturgeschichte* 119 (1997): 261–7. Elvira Glaser has recently published three articles on the graphemic systems in manuscripts copied by Hätzlerin: "Zum Graphiesystem der Clara Hätzlerin: Portrait einer Lohnschreiberin in frühneuhochdeutscher Zeit," *Arbeiten zum Frühneuhochdeutschen: Gerhard Kettmann zum 65. Geburtstag,* edited by Rudolf Bentzinger and Norbert Richard Wolf (Würzburg: Königshausen & Neumann, 1993), pp. 53–73; "Das Beizbüchlein in der Abschrift der Clara Hätzlerin: Ein Zeugnis Augsburger Schreibsprache im 15. Jahrhundert (Tonvokalismus)," in *Sprachgeschichtliche Untersuchungen zum älteren und neueren Deutsch: Festschrift für Hans Wellmann,* edited by Werner König and Lorelies Ortner (Heidelberg: Winter, 1996), pp. 29–46; "Das Graphemsystem der Clara Hätzlerin im Kontext der Handschrift Heidelberg Cpg 677," in *Deutsche Sprache im Raum und Zeit: Festschrift für Peter Wiesinger,* edited by Peter Ernst and Franz Patocka (Vienna: Edition Praesens, 1998), pp. 479–94.

11. *Liederbuch der Clara Hätzlerin,* p. LXVII, no. 2. Spelling in this and the following citations from this manuscript have been slightly normalized.

12. *Liederbuch der Clara Hätzlerin,* p. LXVIII, no. 4.

13. *Liederbuch der Clara Hätzlerin,* p. LXVIII, no. 6.

14. My conclusion contrasts with that of Wachinger, who judges these "Kleinstdichtungen" to be of no thematic significance for the manuscript; see "Liebe und Literatur," 386–88.

15. In this paper I can treat only two of the seventeen manuscripts in which the text appears. In "Liebe und Literatur," 389–94, Wachinger discusses the complex manuscript filiations of Prague X A 12 with two other manuscripts, Bechstein's manuscript (now lost) and Berlin, Staatsbibliothek Preußischer Kulturbesitz, mgf 488, with which it shares a substantial number of texts, often in the same order. In all three of these manuscripts, *Lob der Frauen* and *Die Beichte einer Frau* are paired.

16. Wilhelm Brauns and Gerhard Thiele, eds., *Die Heidelberger Handschriften 313 und 355: Die Berliner Handschrift ms. germ. fol. 922,* Deutsche Texte des

Mittelalters, vol. 41. Berlin 1938. Vol. 2 of *Mittelhochdeutsche Minnereden.*
Reprinted with an afterword by Ingeborg Glier, 2 vols. in one (Zürich:
Weidman, 1967), pp. 33–42.

17. " . . . der Überlieferungsstrang des Cpg. 313 [hat] sich diese Verse aus Be-
quemlichkeit geschenkt," Thiele, *Heidelberger Handschriften,* pp. XVII-
XVIII.

18. Though of course the editor/compiler could have been copying a short
version. "Deutlicher als bei vielen anderen Handschriften aus diesem Bere-
ich lassen sich hier Überlieferungsgruppen greifen und Ansätze zu einem
planvollen Aufbau erkennen," Glier, "Nachwort," *Mittelhochdeutsche Minnereden,* p. 255.

19. Gender as a compilational practice can appear in other thematic contexts.
In Munich, Bayerische Staatsbibliothek, cgm 714, the debate about gender
appears in a political register. In a paired set of texts, part of a longer sequence of texts in the estates register, one poem asks why the noble class
is becoming ever feebler. The answer: Noblewomen sleep with their ser-
vants. The second poem asks why the strength and talent of the merchant
class is increasing. The answer: because the wives of merchants sleep with
noblemen. This example, while clearly misogynist, is interesting not just
because it brings in a political moment, but also because it is, however joc-
ularly, a historical explanation, one that attempts to establish a cause for
change over time. See Westphal, *Textual Poetics,* pp. 150–4.

20. For a sustained discussion of the compilational principles in this manuscript, see Westphal, *Textual Poetics,* pp. 120–5.

21. In defense of a holy cause, then, many a knight "journeyed forth," as they
euphemistically put it even then. The "journey" generally led to Prussia,
which bordered on lands inhabited by Lithuanian heathens. To win these
savage tribes to Christianity (together, of course, with their lands) was the
main objective of the Teutonic Order, which organized expeditions east
and north from its headquarters in Königsberg. The warriors were re-
cruited in the West (Chaucer's "gentil parfit knight" was one of them). "In
the late fourteenth century, it had become almost normal for a young man
of noble blood to make at least one such journey to Prussia as a part of his
education. Quite often such travelers turned into regular visitors, for instance the young master of Boucicaut who thrice made the journey because there happened to be no fighting going on in France, also because
of rumors of a *bel guerre* in Prussia *ceste saison.* Knights from the Low
Countries often joined in the bloody revels. Many of the warrior extolled
by Gelre (later Bavaria) Herald could boast of a glorious journey to Prussia—and the Herald knew what that meant, since he himself had been to
Prussia four times in eight years!" in Frits Pieter van Oostrom, *Court and
Culture: Dutch Literature, 1350–1450,* trans. Arnold J. Pomerans (Berkeley
and Los Angeles: University of California Press, 1992), pp. 164, 165. See
also Werner Paravicini, "Die Preussenreisen des europäischen Adels," *His-
torische Zeitschrift* 232 (1981): 25–28. On the Teutonic Order, see Erich

Maschke, *Domus hospitalis Theutonicorum. Europäische Verbindungslinien der Deutschordensgeschichte. Gesammelte Aufsätze aus den Jahren 1931–1963,* Quellen und Studien zur Geschichte des Deutschen Ordens, vol. 10 (Bonn: Verlag Wissenschaftliches Archiv, 1970).

22. *Flos unde Blankeflos,* ed. by Stephan Waetzoldt, Niederdeutsche Denkmäler, vol. 3 (Bremen: Kühtmann, 1880).

23. Westphal, *Textual Poetics,* pp. 104–108; 138–43.

24. These two texts are tales (*Maeren*). They can be found in Hanns Fischer, *Die deutsche Märendichtung des 15. Jahrhunderts,* Münchener Texte und Untersuchungen, vol. 12 (Munich: Beck, 1966).

25. On the motif of eavesdropping male narrators, see Ann Marie Rasmussen, "Gendered Knowledge in the Late Medieval German *Minnereden* on Eavesdropping," forthcoming in *Speculum*.

26. "Die Erotik ist zur sittlichen Kunst mit eigenem, kaum noch problematisiertem Wertekanon geworden," Wachinger, "Liebe und Literatur," 391.

27. " . . . ein produktionsästhetische[r] Autorbegriff, von dem aus der Text stets nur als ein seinem Produzenten nachgeordnetes Produkt erscheint," Hausmann, *Reinmar,* p. 18. "Verschmelzung von Reproduktion und Rezeption," Hausmann, *Reinmar,* p. 16.

28. The scholarship on medieval understandings of the "author function" is immense. I note two recent studies from the field of Old English: Fred C. Robinson, *The Editing of Old English* (Oxford: Blackwell, 1994), pp. 1–35, and Carol Braun Pasternack, *The Textuality of Old English Poetry,* Cambridge Studies in Anglo-Saxon England, vol. 13 (Cambridge, U.K.: Cambridge University Press, 1995). In addition, I note a few recent titles from German scholarship. Horst Wenzel, "Autorenbilder: Zur Ausdifferenzierung von Autorenfunktionen in mittelalterlichen Miniaturen," *Autor und Autorschaft im Mittelalter. Kolloquium Meissen,* edited by Elizabeth Anderson et al. (Tübingen: Niemeyer, 1998), pp. 1–28; in the same volume, Almut Suerbaum, "*Accessus ad auctores:* Autorkonzeptionen in mittelalterlichen Kommentartexten," *Autor und Autorschaft,* pp. 29–37; Burghart Wachinger, "Autorschaft und Überlieferung," *Autorentypen,* edited by Walter Haug and Burghart Wachinger (Tübingen: Niemeyer, 1991), pp. 1–28. On the codicological salience of authorship in compilation manuscripts, see Westphal, *Textual Poetics,* pp. 14–15; 143.

29. Westphal, *Textual Poetics,* p. 221.

30. On Mechthild of Rottenburg, also known as Mechthild von der Pfalz (her birth title), see Alfred Karnein, "Mechthild von der Pfalz as Patroness: Aspects of Female Patronage in the Early Renaissance," in *Medievalia et Humanistica,* New Series 22 (1995): 141–170.

CHAPTER 6

THE STRAINS OF DEFENSE: THE MANY VOICES
OF JEAN LEFÈVRE'S *LIVRE DE LEESCE*

Karen Pratt

Although in his Livre de Leesce *Jean LeFèvre enters the debate about women apparently supporting the female cause, his playful use of voice and intertextual allusion undermine the authority of his female advocate for women and reveal a tongue-in-cheek approach, no doubt designed to amuse a male audience rather than the ladies of Paris he invokes.*

When Christine de Pizan famously entered the *querelle de la Rose* at the turn of the fifteenth century, her main concern was to defend women against a tradition of clerical misogyny going back at least as far as Ovid.[1] Her woman's contribution to the gender debate, while significant and original, came after several centuries of male writing both for and against women.[2] Among the most influential medieval writers working in this field in the fourteenth century was Jean LeFèvre, a lawyer from Ressons-sur-le-Matz, who composed a defense known as the *Livre de Leesce*. Some modern critics, noting the important and persuasive arguments *Leesce* adduces in favor of the "weaker sex," consider it to be a serious defense of women (and perhaps because some of the same points can be found later in Christine's work).[3] In fact, however, the poem's ambiguities, competing voices, and intertextual dialogue allow for differing gendered readings and audience responses. Contrary to what is suggested by the female gender of the character Leesce, the work's lawyer for the defense, the authority of the women's case is undermined rather than furthered;

added to that is the ambiguity surrounding the exact nature of this person-ification. Moreover, Leesce is not only forced to debate with that garrulous proponent of misogamy, Matheolus or Matthew, but she also struggles to make herself heard over the voice of LeFèvre's male narrator, whose am-bivalence sheds doubt on his loyalty to the cause.[4] Thus the analysis of voice in the *Leesce* reveals it to be a complex work, creating for its readers many challenges of interpretation, not the least of which are those surrounding what happens when a *male* author chooses a *female* advocate for women. I shall argue that the *Livre de Leesce* was intended to be a playful, not serious, response to misogyny, containing a heavy dose of male irony. In accordance with that view, its primary audience was probably not the ladies addressed by LeFèvre, but men used to reading between the lines and appreciative of masculine innuendo: They would have understood that LeFèvre's defense of women was a literary game in which ambiguity and irony allowed an-tifeminist attitudes to be perpetuated with impunity. And while the *Livre de Leesce* is not the only medieval poem in which a male author deploys an ap-parently female narrator (I compare Leesce below with Jean Gerson's Elo-quance Theologienne), it certainly serves as a prominent example and reference point.

Jean LeFèvre practiced as a *procureur* at the royal parliament in Paris in the second half of the fourteenth century.[5] Most of his literary output consisted of translations of school texts in Latin and included the *Ecloga Theoduli,* the *Disticha Catonis,* and the pseudo-Ovidian *Vetula.*[6] In the 1380s he translated into French the *Lamentationes Matheoluli,* an anti-feminist and antimatrimonial poem in Latin by the self-proclaimed biga-mous cleric Matthew of Boulogne; shortly afterward LeFèvre countered it with the profeminist *Livre de Leesce.*[7] The latter is a debate poem of nearly 4,000 lines addressed to ladies and set in a courtroom, in which Matthew's misogyny is put on trial. It quotes at length the defamatory speech of the narrator of the *Lamentations,* whose arguments are then re-futed by a female personification called Leesce (Joy).

A tongue-in-cheek approach to the subject matter is already in evi-dence in LeFèvre's *Lamentations de Mathéolus,* where he expresses some un-ease with Matthew's criticisms of women by interrupting the misogamous treatise with apologies and with the authorial excuse that he was a mere translator (*Lamentations,* II, 1541–68). Close analysis of his practice as trans-lator does, however, suggest that these statements were not meant to be taken seriously, but with the same irony that is also identifiable in the *Leesce.*[8] Indeed, as Jill Mann demonstrates in her Cambridge inaugural lec-ture, responses to misogynist attacks constituted a popular literary subgenre in the Middle Ages, and were usually designed to publicize the controver-sial nature of the antifeminist works they appeared to be refuting, rather than to offer a serious and sincere reply to them.[9] LeFèvre's *Lamentations* and *Livre de Leesce* are therefore best seen as part of a long tradition of anti-feminist treatises and their (often humorous, even ironic) palinodes. Examples include *Le Blasme des fames,* or *Contenance des fames,* and *Le Bien des fames* (which sometimes appear as a diptych in manuscripts), Nicole Bozon's *Char d'Orgueil* and his *Bonté des Femmes,* Marbod of Rennes's *De meretrice* and *De matrona,* Machaut's *Jugement dou Roy de Behaigne* and *Jugement dou Roy de Navarre,* and several later works that may owe more to LeFèvre than used to be acknowledged.[10]

Some authors working in this tradition defend women in their own, masculine voice, yet are reluctant or incapable of completely expunging misogyny from their discourse. One such is Marbod of Rennes, whose criticisms in *De meretrice* are generalized to apply to woman as a whole species, while his praise for the good woman is reserved for a very narrow category, all the more laudable given her rarity and the difficulty the "weaker sex" has in avoiding sin.[11] Another is Boccaccio, who includes some very damning portraits of women in *De mulieribus claris* and then provides the lame explanation in his preface and dedication that it is his desire for accuracy that has led him to include these negative exempla. Other writers, however, create debates between male and female voices in which the women are given the better arguments. For example, Albertanus of Brescia, in his *Liber consolationis et consilii* (1246), allows Melibeus's wife Prudentia to plead convincingly, like a lawyer, for a woman's moral and social right to offer advice. Here though, the author's main concern in opposing Prudence and her husband is to encourage restraint rather than violent retaliation when dealing with offenders. Prudentia's literal gender is less important to Albertanus than her allegorical significance.[12] Yet Guillaume Alexis, in his *Débat de l'omme et de la femme* (fifteenth century), grants woman the last word, and with her plain speaking she wins the debate against masculine rhetorical sophistry and misogynist discourse.[13] This shows that in some texts, at least, the woman's speech is authoritative and not subverted.

The example of Albertanus's Prudentia shows that the personification of an abstract quality has the potential to create gender ambiguities between *signifiant* and *signifié,* the literal and the metaphorical, which, as we shall see, LeFèvre exploits deliberately so he can undermine Leesce's authority. In order to assess the effect of LeFèvre's main strategy for subtly weakening his case for women, that is, his choice of a female advocate, it is instructive to compare Leesce with an almost contemporary example of a female personification placed in a courtroom context: Eloquance Theologienne in a work written by Jean Gerson during the *querelle de la Rose.*[14] Gerson's dream-vision treatise is a serious attack against the immorality (as he saw it) of the *Roman de la Rose,* and he clearly set out to present Eloquance Theologienne as an authoritative, convincing speaker, pleading against Jean de Meun at the court of Christianity, presided over by Justice Canonique. The court is made up almost entirely of women, personifications of qualities such as Conscience, Mémoire, Providence, Raison, and various virtues. Their gender is at first marked by their feminine attributes: Chastity's beauty is commented upon ["Chasteté la tres belle"; l. 34] and she is called "vostre feable subjecte" [your loyal female subject; l. 39]. Moreover, in referring to these ladies, Gerson frequently prefixes their name with dame: "Il diffame dame Raison, ma bone maistresse" [He defames lady Reason, my good mistress; ll. 78–9]. Qualities whose grammatical gender is masculine, on the other hand, are presented as male figures; thus Dangier is "le bon portier" [the good porter; l. 46]. However, at the point in the debate when Eloquance rises to respond authoritatively to the defense of Jean de Meun's supporters, Gerson breaks his rule of retaining grammatical gender and treats Eloquance as a man:

> Eloquance Theologienne (qui est advocat de la court crestienne) . . . se leva en piés a belle contenance et maniere attrempee; et par grande auctorité et digne gravité, il, comme saige et bien apris depuis qu'il ot ung pou tenue sa face encline bas en guise d'ung home aucunement pansif, se sousleva meurement et seriement . . . (ll. 175–82).

> [Theological Eloquence (who is a lawyer at the Christian court) . . . rose to his/her feet with fine composure and a measured manner; and with great authority and suitable gravity, he, like a wise and experienced man, having bowed his head a little like a somewhat thoughtful man, stood up in a mature and calm way . . .]

Metaphorically, of course, Eloquance embodies a skill that Gerson, the chancellor of the University of Paris, felt that he himself possessed, namely, masculine eloquence. As we know, however, from allegorical representations in the Roman de la Rose and its manuscript illuminations, medieval allegory normally functioned on both the literal and metaphoric levels.[15] Clearly, to portray Eloquance as a literal female here, in accordance with her grammatical gender, was impossible for Gerson, since a woman pleading in a courtroom would not be a believable figure in late medieval France, but an amusing impossibility.[16] So, for her legal arguments to carry weight in a court of law, her creator has to change her sex.

From this point on there are no more indications of Eloquance's gender. However, her attack on the ending of the Roman de la Rose is a good example of misogyny insidiously creeping in, especially if a male author overlooks who is speaking. This oversight is ironic, since Gerson's Eloquance had earlier upbraided Jean de Meun for placing crude language in

Reason's mouth, language so inappropriate for the speaker and addressee that her authority is undermined:

> Et ycy garda mal l'acteur les riegles de mon escolle (les riegles de rethorique), qui sont de regarder cil qui parle et a qui on parle, et pour quel tamps on parle . . . je me dueil trop pour dame Raison et pour Chasteté de ce que il a fait dire par Raison la sage a ung fol amoureux teles gouliardies (ll. 641–4, 650–2).

> [And here the author did not keep to the rules I teach, i.e., the rules of rhetoric, which state that one should be mindful of who speaks, to whom and on what occasion one speaks. . . . I am really upset for Lady Reason and Chastity, for he made wise Reason utter such obscenities to a foolish lover.]

Despite Gerson's awareness of this rhetorical rule, he allows Eloquance, in claiming that the *Rose* has the proverbial sting in its tail ("En la fin gist le venin"; l. 481), to allude to the Horatian exemplum of the painter who produces a woman with a beautiful face but a fish's tail:

> La moquerie d'Orace a ycy lieu, du paintre qui fait une tres belle fame ou chief et fenist en poisson (on dit teles estre les Arpies, qui ont visaige vierge, mais ventre et autres parties tres ordes.) (ll. 481–4)

> [Horace's mocking anecdote is relevant here, about the painter who creates a beautiful woman's head but gives her a fish's tail. People say that the Harpies are like that, with their virginal faces but filthy bellies and other parts.]

It is doubtful that Gerson introduced this antifeminist exemplum and reference to the Harpies deliberately to undermine the authority of a female speaker by giving her inappropriate masculine language. Yet in attempting to create a female advocate, he fails to overcome his androcentrism and the clerical discourse he has inherited, with its ready-made *similitudines*. LeFèvre, however, as aware as Gerson of the importance of appropriate language, but also aware of the gender tensions created by female personification, deliberately exploits the cultural misogyny that Gerson fails completely to suppress.

Pierre Col's response to this treatise and to Christine de Pizan's letters attacking the *Rose* demonstrates how Gerson's choice of a female speaker is exploitable by his opponent.[17] Col refers constantly to Eloquance as Dame Eloquance, never allowing us to forget that she is a woman (e.g., ll. 125, 129, 188, 220, 225). He is thus able to lump Christine and Eloquance together as two misguided women readers ("je respons a dame Eloquance et a toy par ung meisme moyen" [I am replying to lady Eloquence and

yourself in the same way; l. 402]), who were accused by their male contemporaries of superficial, merely literal reading.[18] Col's virulent attack on
Christine is, because of the generalization implied by the phrase "woman's
mouth," equally applicable to Eloquance: "O tres fole oultrecuidance! O
parole trop tost yssue et sans avis de bouche de fame, qui condampne
home de si hault entendement . . ." [Oh outrageous arrogance. Oh words
uttered too quickly and without reflection from a woman's mouth in criticism of a man of such great intellect; ll. 388–90].

So, while Gerson, in his attempt to add weight to the arguments against
the *Rose,* allows Eloquance to adopt a masculine voice, Col is at pains to
underline her femaleness. He even distinguishes subtly between the male
author of the treatise, Gerson, and the female advocates Eloquance and
Christine by pointing out that Gerson himself had not been so rash as to
include the verdict to Jean de Meun's trial in his dream-vision narrative
("Vraiement celuy qui a compillee la plaidoierie dame Eloquance a esté
plus preudent et gracieux que tu [Christine de Pizan] n'as . . ." [Truly, he
who composed lady Eloquence's speech for the prosecution was wiser and
more gracious than you; p. 100, ll. 395–97]. This is a loophole that presumably Gerson did not anticipate.

Although the *querelle de la Rose* took place a few decades after the composition of the *Livre de Leesce,* the foregoing discussion demonstrates the
problems of authority that arise when a male author creates a female advocate. We find similar ambiguity in Machaut's *Jugement dou Roy de Navarre,*
the sequel to his *Jugement dou Roy de Behaigne.* Although by the end of the
trial Guillaume is found guilty of unfairness to women in his earlier judgment poem, the plaintiff Bonneürté and her female counsel (the twelve
Virtues) are not always treated seriously.[19] The Virtues can behave and speak
inappropriately: Mesure and Souffissance are rather long-winded (ll.
3221–310, 3502–724) and some lose their temper with Guillaume; their arguments are not always convincing or accurate: Prudence gets the details of
the Chastelaine de Vergi's story wrong;[20] and their authority is undermined
by being women: Guillaume has a complicitous laugh with the judge, the
King of Navarre, over the loquaciousness of his prosecutors (ll. 3141–60).

LeFèvre would have been familiar with Machaut's works, and although
his *Livre de Leesce* contains many serious arguments in defense of women,
contributing positively to the formal case as defined by Blamires (see Introduction), he also exploits the situation of the female advocate humorously. His approach, like Machaut's, is to create a courtroom atmosphere in
which an author and his misogyny are put on trial. Matthew's prosecutor,
Leesce, is introduced as an authoritative speaker, yet almost immediately
her voice becomes confused with that of LeFèvre's male profeminist narrator. Eventually both Leesce and the narrator become figures of fun.

Leesce's authority and credibility are undermined by several factors. First, her fictitious nature is emphasized by the fact that she represents an impossibility, since women were not allowed to practice law in Paris in the fourteenth century.[21] (The reason Matthew gives for this prohibition is that they were banned after a certain Calphurnia's crude behavior in court [*Lamentations,* II, 183–92]). Second, ambiguities of voice mean that she appears to be uttering language and arguments inappropriate to her nature. Third, she has difficulty making her voice heard over Matthew's misogynist carping. Fourth, LeFèvre blurs the distinction between her independent voice and the narrator's masculine viewpoint, so that ultimately she emerges as the personification of an aspect of the poet himself, namely, his desire for the solace that women provide.

Leesce is not the only character to be treated humorously in this work. The persona of the defender of women embodied by the narrator is also ironized and exaggerated for comic effect.[22] This is evident in the prologue, in which LeFèvre presents himself as a penitent sinner (ll. 1–5), asking the ladies in his audience for forgiveness in terms reminiscent of a courtly lover who has wronged his mistress. His crime was to *mesdire,* to slander women. However, he is quick to excuse himself as an innocent translator (ll. 6–11) (a strategy used by Jean de Meun in the middle of the *Rose*) and expresses the hope that he will atone for his sin by writing a defense of women.[23] From then on it is Maistre Mahieu, the author of the Latin *Lamentationes,* who is criticized as the slanderer of women, and toward the end LeFèvre turns the *Livre de Leesce* into a somewhat exaggerated sermon against *mesdisance* and *mesdisants* (ll. 3411–9), concluding (ironically, given his criticism of Mahieu) that "trop est fol qui d'autruy mesdit" [whoever slanders others is very foolish; l. 3831].

LeFèvre's apparently sincere apology in his prologue is soon undermined when he claims that there are always two sides to any question. His statement "Il n'est riens qui n'ait son contraire, / Qui en voulroit les preuves traire" [There is nothing that does not have its contrary, for those who wish to advance the arguments; ll. 21–2] reminds us that he was legally and rhetorically trained to argue two points of view and warns us against taking any of his arguments as deeply held convictions.[24] That the *Leesce* may have been for him and his copyists simply a rhetorical exercise is supported by the scribal rubric to MSV, "Cy commence leesce et le contraire de matheolore" [Here begins joy and the contrary argument to Matheolus]. Interestingly, though, the explicits, while still referring to the text as "le contre" or "contredit matheolus" add "contenant sexcusacion pour les dames leur honneur et leur prouesse" [containing his defense of women, their honor, and their virtue]. This reflects the fact that by the end of the work the emphasis has shifted from a point-by-point refutation of the bigamous cleric's misogyny to a more positive defense of women. However, as we shall see, the suggestive language and innuendo of the epilogue confirms the primarily comic intention of the *Leesce*.

To return to the prologue, LeFèvre illustrates his assertion that everything has its opposite with the stock example of a rose with its thorns and nettles lying amongst grass: "Les espines sont près des roses;/ Aussi est l'ortie poignant/ Jouste l'erbe souef joignant" [The thorns are close to the roses, just as the stinging nettle is next to the soft grass; ll. 24–6]. This is, of course, a commonplace, but it echoes two texts that LeFèvre probably knew. First, Ovid's *Remedia amoris,* in which Ovid, formerly Love's preceptor, is now administering its cure (to both men and women), comparing himself to the earth, which brings forth both sweet and harmful plants: "Terra salutares herbas, eademque nocentes/ Nutrit, et urticae proxima saepe rosa est" [The same earth fosters healing herbs and noxious, and oft is the nettle nearest to the rose; ll. 45–6].[25] If the source is the *Remedia,* the allusion is hardly designed to encourage men to love and admire women. Second, in his dedication to the Countess of Altavilla, Boccaccio advises her not to be shocked by the wantonness displayed in some of his stories, but to ignore offensive matters and concentrate on the laudable, just as when entering a garden she reaches for the flowers after brushing the thorns to one side. Again, the context and associations of this simile are not altogether flattering for LeFèvre's implied female audience, for Boccaccio is admitting that his *De mulieribus claris,* far from being a defense of women, offers both positive and negative exempla of the species. Throughout the *Leesce* intertextual dialogue with works such as these and especially the *Rose* tends to undermine the superficially profeminist tone of the palinode.

When LeFèvre comes to introduce the title of his book as the "Livre de Leesce" (l. 31) he gives the impression that he has written it out of love for Leesce, as if she were his lady, whom he is eager to please ["pour complaire"; l. 33]. There is a sudden change of viewpoint, however, as he adopts third-person pronouns instead of *vous* for the ladies he is addressing: "On les doit loer et amer . . . qui leur grace veult desservir" [Whoever wishes to merit their grace must praise and love them; ll. 38–40]. Now LeFèvre is aligning himself through the use of *on* with men, and in a move typical of misogynistic discourse, a more generalized concept of woman is conveyed. Moreover, the narrator's *causa scribendi* is revealed as a self-interested desire to win grace and (sexual) favors.[26] This interpretation is reinforced through the intertextual allusion to Deduit's *amie* in the *Roman de la rose,*[27] a work on which LeFèvre drew not only for the misogynist material he added to his source when translating the *Lamentationes,*[28] but also more surprisingly for material to be included in his palinode. In the *Rose* Leesce is characterized as beautiful, happy, and above all loving toward Deduit; she is flanked by her *ami* and the god of love. Her name also recalls ironically the last lines of the *Lamentations,* where LeFèvre claims that marriage puts an end to joy and leads only to sadness: "De leesce luy clos la sente/ Et luy doins les cles de tristesce" [I close off the path of happiness for him and give him the keys to sadness; IV, 812–13]. The implication of this allusion and of the *Rose* reference is that the lady who defends women in the *Leesce* is not a defender of marriage, but represents the pleasures of extramarital love. Besides, as a personification of *joie,* an emotion or state associated more with the male lover than with the female beloved in romance and lyric poetry, she is to be viewed not so much as a representative of women, but as an emotional state desired by the male speaker, and one that contrasts with the *tristece* produced by reading the *Lamentations* or any antifeminist work.[29] In other words, joy is a subjective emotion that can be produced in the narrator (or reader) by meditating on all that is good in women, not the defender of objective truths that LeFèvre maintains he can prove by marshaling arguments. Perhaps this is the reason why Leesce, who begins as a character in her own right—"Leesce respont en riant" [Leesce replies gaily; l. 823]—starts to lose her identity and even her name ("Joye respont incontinent" [Joyfulness replies immediately; l. 1925] and gradually becomes subsumed in the figure of "joyful" LeFèvre: "liement y responderay" [I shall reply joyfully; l. 1704]. She is even relegated to mere adviser to the author: "Je respons sans dueil et sans ire / Tout par le conseil de Leesce" [I reply without bitterness and anger on the advice of Leesce; ll. 2320–1]. Thus LeFèvre becomes the spokesman for Leesce's cause, "la partie de Leesce"(l. 2797, cf. ll. 2902–3), while her allegorical nature almost obliterates her literal function within the work.[30]

The second section of LeFèvre's prologue concentrates on the role of debate in arriving at the truth, which the author equates with joy (*leesce*), while lies are equated with sadness. In evoking the exemplum of the debate between Alithia and Pseustis from the *Ecloga Theoduli,* LeFèvre compares himself to the shepherdess, who refutes the pagan goatherd's mythological arguments with her biblical examples. This seems to prepare us for the authoritative and veracious arguments of another female figure, Leesce, though it also prepares us for LeFèvre's possibly humorous role as the new Alithia. Since LeFèvre had translated *Le Théodolet,* a school text, he was no doubt also aware that Alithia, in her zeal to beat her opponent, invokes misogynistic exempla from the Bible.[31] As we shall see, like her, LeFèvre, in his supposed dialectical quest for the truth, repeats a good deal of antifeminist material, only lightly disguised as the opinions of Matthew that have to be refuted. A further ambiguous allusion in the prologue is to the story of Zorobabel in the apocryphal Book of Esdras.[32] According to LeFèvre, when King Darius asked what was the most powerful thing in the world, three of his advisers answered: the king, wine, and women respectively. Zorobabel, however, gave the best response: the truth. Here again, an anecdote apparently designed to make a serious philosophical point barely disguises a joke against women (although the commonplace about women's supposed power could, of course, also be a joke about men's impotence—in all senses of the word).

Although exordial prayers for God's help are conventional, LeFèvre's concern that he should control his tongue so as not to be misunderstood or cause further annoyance, presumably to the ladies (ll. 75–80), is humorous. Through his exaggerated anticipation of difficulty and failure the male narrator is implying that to defend women is an impossible task. Moreover, his claim that he will summarize the contrary argument (ll. 87–89) and be brief can hardly be taken seriously in the light of the lengthy quotations that follow. The prologue therefore sets the mock-serious tone for the whole work.

LeFèvre commences his refutation of Matthew by quoting almost verbatim passages from the *Lamentations* and then responding to them, often apparently in the voice of Leesce. He thus sets up a dialogue between a man, whose opinions he has earlier identified with, and a woman, who is introduced at first as authoritative:

> Ad ce respont dame Leesce,
> pleine de sens et de noblesce,
> car elle est de meurs aornée,
> dont noblesce lui est donnée. (ll. 127–30)

> [To this Lady Leesce replies, / full of good sense and nobility, / for she is equipped with good manners, / which confer nobility on her]

Although one then expects a direct response from Leesce, her reply, like the arguments of Matthew that precede it, is reported indirectly by LeFèvre, in whose voice approval of *her* arguments is expressed: "Et monstre par argument fort" [and demonstrates with strong arguments; l. 131]; "Tels paroles sont bien au cas" [such words are very apposite; l. 140]. The use of the imperfect tense in line 132, "que maistre Mahieu avoit tort" [that Master Matthew was wrong], indicates that this is Leesce's opinion, although it may well be shared by the narrator. However, the direct speech in line 136, "Trespassés est, Dieux en ait l'ame!" [He is dead now, God rest his soul], appears to be an interjection by LeFèvre, referring not unsympathetically to the archmisogynist. Thus the following passage (ll. 136–51), describing Matthew's situation when he took a wife in full knowledge of the consequences, is difficult to ascribe to a particular speaker, apart from line 140 mentioned above. So when someone states, using legal terminology, "Et d'autre part je luy obice" [And on the other hand I can counter him; l. 152], it is unclear whether this is Leesce speaking directly in court or LeFèvre addressing his implied audience of females. The ambiguity created by this procedure means that we are unsure to whom to attribute crude expressions such as "Tart main a cul, quant pet est hors" [It's too late to put your hand over your bum when you've already farted; l. 161]. In fact, this is a quotation from the *Lamentations* and is followed in the *Leesce* by "Cils proverbes est assés ors" [This proverb is rather crude; l. 162], a comment that could be made by either LeFèvre or Leesce. However, the ambiguous context creates the humorous possibility that *she,* like Reason in the *Rose,* is speaking in an unladylike fashion. Similarly, the lengthy citation of Matthew's description of his wife's body prior to disillusionment would be incongruous in Leesce's mouth. Indeed, LeFèvre hints at his own pleasure in the retelling (from an obviously masculine viewpoint) when he claims that Matthew "au dire prenoit grant plaisance" [took great pleasure in the telling; l. 166].

Another strategy for undermining Leesce's cause is the citation of huge chunks of the *Lamentations* without removing those passages offensive to women.[33] LeFèvre barely summarizes Matthew's arguments. In fact, he retains much of the dialogue that enlivened the tales of adulterous or indiscreet women, and he seems to relish repeating exempla that support the antifeminist cause.[34] Lines 583–680 are based on *Lamentations,* I, 829–1196. LeFèvre interrupts in line 633 to distance himself from the misogynous viewpoint, and calls Matthew's exempla *truffes* in line 668.[35] However, he repeats without comment the master misogynist's assessment of a henpecked husband as "le bon homme" (*Leesce,* l. 678; *Lamentations,* I, l.1176), and after this lengthy tirade Leesce is given no opportunity to respond at line 681. Instead, we hear Matthew's views on woman's argumentativeness, which makes men weep and renders them impotent, and there follows more lascivious description using agricultural and hunting metaphors inappropriate for Leesce (ll. 720–32). Indeed, the reply, which follows LeFèvre's presentation of himself as defender of women against the likes of Matthew, Ovid, and Jean de Meun, appears to be in his voice, not Leesce's (ll. 775ff).

Eventually, Leesce laments the fact that she has been given limited scope to reply:

> Leesce dit: j'ay entendu
> Et petitement deffendu
> Jusques cy, mais ne vous desplaise,
> Preste suy que vous en rapaise. (ll. 981–4)

[Leesce says, I have listened / and defended myself briefly / thus far, but do not be dismayed / for I am ready to appease you]

It is not long, however, before another section of Matheolus is being paraphrased and quoted[36] (cf. *Leesce*, ll.1037–96, and *Lamentations*, II, 177–246; 313–52), and only in line 3488 is Matthew finally silenced by LeFèvre's announcement:

Vous orrés ja tost bonne gogue,
Et n'y a point de dialogue;
Leesce seule parlera
Et ses fais prouvés monstrera
Par exemples et par figures . . .
        Et pour les hommes faire taire,
Pour avoir droit a fin contraire,
Propose ma dame Leesce . . . (ll. 3488–92, 3496–8)

[You'll soon hear something to please you / and there won't be any more dialogue. / Leesce alone will speak / and will demonstrate the truth / of her facts through the use of exempla and figural language . . . / And to shut men up, / so that she might be allowed to arrive at the opposite conclusion, / my lady Leesce proposes . . .]

LeFèvre's expressed awareness that his apparently profeminist work has given ample voice to the antifeminist camp indicates that this strategy was deliberate. In compensation, Leesce has the last five hundred lines to herself, and it is here that she adduces some of her best arguments and examples of virtuous, strong, and clever women, some of which are to be found later in the works of Christine de Pizan. However, these may be being presented tongue-in-cheek, for *bonne gogue* in line 3488, quoted above, can mean "a joke" as well as a "source of pleasure." It is in this last section that Leesce succumbs to the fault criticized in Matthew: Untenable sexist generalization, which is exemplified by the use of the opposition *masles/femelles* rather than *hommes/femmes* (ll. 3530–2, 3610, 3648: "Vous, masles").[37] Moreover, her language is no less bawdy than Matthew's or LeFèvre's as she describes the gynaecological skills of Calabria de Paris (ll. 3778–85) or the root cause of misogyny: "Car nuls homs ne blasme leur gendre/ Tant que maistre jobart puist tendre" [For no man criticizes their sex as long as he can get his John Thomas up; ll. 3880–1].[38]

It is also striking that LeFèvre, having silenced Matthew, does not allow Leesce to speak alone, for he intervenes to answer on her behalf (ll. 3518–23), or challenges her himself, thus providing the competing voice of a devil's advocate:

Qui diroit que Leesce mente
Et qu'on ne doit masles blasmer,
Car il labourent en la mer
Et font des chasteaulx en ce monde,
Je suy tout prest que j'y responde . . . (ll. 3713–7)

[Should anyone say that Leesce is lying / and that one should not criticize males, / for they toil at sea / and build castles on this earth, / I am ready to reply . . .]

Et s'on opposoit le contraire,
Que Leesce, pour preuves faire,
Nomme les bonnes seulement
Et des mauvaises nullement
Ne fait aucune mencion,
Pour soustenir s'opinion,
Elle respont, pour soy deffendre

Et qui repliquer y vouldroit,
Je diroye, par sens contraire . . . (ll. 3794–3800, 3803–4)

[If one were to put the opposite argument, / that Leesce in providing evidence cites only good women / and makes no mention / of the evil ones, / in order to support her viewpoint, / she replies in her defense . . . And if one wished to respond, / I would say, by way of contradiction. . . .]

Here, as in the rest of the *Livre de Leesce,* the masculine voice cannot suppress ambivalence towards women. This ambivalence is reinforced by the blurring of the boundary between Matthew's expressed views and those of LeFèvre's narrator. When quoting a long passage from the *Lamentations,* in which Matthew had scorned women's contention that their work was more lucrative than men's, LeFèvre inserts a veracity claim into the text to support the female view, yet leaves in many of the verbs indicating that it is *women's opinion* he is reproducing:

Les femmes dient et maintiennent
Que les deffauls des hommes viennent;
Et s'il y a des biens assés,
Elles les dient amassés
Par elles, par leur diligence,
Par leur sens et par leur prudence.
Ainsi est il, en verité,
Tout vient de leur prosperité,
Bien fais *a elles attribuent.* (ll. 525–33, my emphases)

[Women say and maintain / that shortages are caused by men. / And if they are comfortably off, / they say that their goods have been amassed / by them, through their diligence, / good sense, and prudence. / Thus it is, truly, / everything comes from their prosperity, / they attribute all benefits to themselves.]

Readers are left to consider whether the claim that this is true (l. 531) is merely women's opinion too. And we ask where LeFèvre's allegiances lie— with the cause of Leesce or with that of her opponents? Ambiguity is again discernible in a passage that echoes the *Rose,* and in which LeFèvre laments the weight of tradition he is fighting against, while nevertheless identifying closely with Jean de Meun:

Mais j'ay sur moy maint adversaire
Et a forte partie a faire.
Maistre Mahieu a en aïde
Gallum, Juvenal et Ovide
Et maistre Jehan Clopinel,
Au cuer joli, au corps isnel,
Qui clochoit si comme je fais. (ll. 745–51)

[I have many an adversary against me / and must deal with a strong opposition. / Master Matthew has to help him / Gallus, Juvenal, and Ovid / and Master Jean Chopinel, / who had a pleasant wit and an agile body, / and limped as I do][39]

So LeFèvre seems to be undermining Leesce's position, either by challenging it or by creating an uncommitted, ambivalent, hence unconvincing, male champion of women to mediate her words.

The work ends as ambiguously as it began, with LeFèvre again ridiculing his own narratorial pose of defender of ladies. In emphasizing his inadequacy and asking his lady readers for their indulgence and support, he expresses more humility and envisages more opposition to their cause than is conventionally expressed in epilogues to other works (ll. 3948–54, cf. ll. 75–80). LeFèvre now abandons all confidence in the truth, which was the apparent subject of most of his prologue but which is now revealed to have been a false concern. In fact, he claims humorously that this *querelle* will never be properly decided, for there would be no judge rash enough to pronounce on it (ll. 3963–7).[40] There then follows a lighthearted coda, in which the author asks to be his ladies' protector, even advocate:

Vueilliés moy par grace advouer,
Ou je puis bien dire et vouer

Que jamais jour n'avray leesce;
Ainsi demourray en tristesce,
Qui de mon las corps fera proie,
S'il mestuet payer la lamproie. (ll. 3968–73)

[Please show pity on me and take me as your protector (give me your approval) / otherwise I can assert and vow / that I shall never be joyful; / so I
shall remain gripped by sadness, / which will prey on my weak body, / if I
have to foot the bill (pay costs)]

The term *advouer* is ambiguous, covering both a lover's desire to gain approval and continue to serve a lady (cf. prologue, ll. 32–33) and perhaps a
lawyer's desire to win further lady clients.[41] While the lover will never be
happy without his lady, the lawyer will be forever sad if he is out of pocket.
We may have here a novel version of the request for money or patronage
that ends some satirical, goliardic poetry.[42] LeFèvre may also be quoting
Machaut's *Jugement dou Roy de Navarre,* in which Largesse tells Guillaume
that because he has slandered women: "Vous n'estes pas avouez;/ Si devez
paier la lamproie." [You are not endorsed; thus you must pay the piper; ll.
3088–89][43] By employing economic terms, LeFèvre humorously debunks
the courtly pose adopted elsewhere and underlines the mercenary nature
of the defender of women he has created.

The epilogue continues with punning on LeFèvre's (the blacksmith's)
name, reminiscent of his earlier comic little ballad, with its obvious sexual
allusions and echoes of Jean de Meun's Nature in her forge:

Je forgeray toute ma vie
Pour plaire a ma dame Leesce,
Et en soustenant sa partie
Blasmeray courroux et tristesce. (ll. 3447–50)[44]

[I shall hammer away throughout my life / to please my lady Leesce / and
in supporting her cause / I shall criticize anger and sadness]

In the epilogue, LeFèvre, the worker in parchment (l. 3978),[45] not the
forger of iron, presents himself as dependent on the ladies' favor for his
leesce, and he makes it quite clear that his *causa scribendi* is to earn the
"soulas, joye et repos" [solace, joy, and contentment] that all healthy, libidi-
nous males with their "bourses et males" [purses and trunks; ll. 3980–82]
hope for from the female of the species.[46] Having identified male anger
over impotence as the source of misogyny, LeFèvre comically equates his
joyful defense of women with a healthy male libido. Ultimately, his response to Matthew's misogamy is not a work in praise of marriage, but in

praise of the joys of extramarital sex, as the intertextual dialogue with the *Rose* confirms.

Analysis of the use of voice and the function of the figure of Leesce in this work suggests that LeFèvre has not created an authoritative female advocate, but a personification of the joy and pleasures his narrator hopes to enjoy as a result of courting female favor. His aim is not, after all, to tell the truth about women, despite the protestations of his mock-serious prologue, but to entertain his (probably predominantly) male readers.

LeFèvre's enjoyment of linguistic play is obvious; the flawed courtroom debate is a game designed to further other, more venal (l. 3988) and venereal, ends. Unlike other medieval authors, who do not anticipate or welcome the addition of further words to their texts (see for example the ending of Chrétien's *Yvain* or of *La Mort le roi Artu*), LeFèvre implies that he has not had the last word, that the debate about women, being unresolvable, will be never-ending (ll. 3983–87). Comic closure is imposed on the text only when the narrator leaves the (court)room: "A Dieu vous commant, je m'en vois" [I commend you to God and I'm off; l. 3991].

The foregoing examination of voice and the nature and authority of both Leesce and the male narrator suggests that LeFèvre's *Livre de Leesce* is a deliberately ironic text, rich in ambiguity.[47] Its apologetic tone and presentation of valid arguments and strategies beneficial to the case for women explain why LeFèvre's palinode has been taken at face value. However, the *Leesce's* textual ambiguities and rhetorical sophistication (like that of the *Rose*) were no doubt designed as a smokescreen to enable LeFèvre to debate gender humorously, to create complicity with the male reader, and to perpetuate misogynistic discourse ironically. When Christine de Pizan mentions at the beginning of her *Cité des dames* that she had understood Matheolus to have written "a la reverence des femmes" [in admiration of women], but then found this to be untrue, it is quite likely that she was misled by LeFèvre's protestations that he had written a serious defense of women.[48] She was one reader, at least, who did not appreciate his joke.[49]

Notes

1. Apart from Christine's correspondence with the Col brothers and with Jean de Montreuil (see *Le Débat sur le "Roman de la Rose,"* ed. Eric Hicks [Paris: Champion, 1977]), her *Epistre au dieu d'Amours, Cité des dames,* and *Livre des trois vertus* may also be regarded as defenses of women; see Rosalind Brown-Grant, *Christine de Pizan and the Moral Defense of Women: Reading beyond Gender* (Cambridge: Cambridge University Press, 1999).

2. For a survey of relevant texts, see *Woman Defamed and Woman Defended: An Anthology of Medieval Texts,* ed. Alcuin Blamires with Karen Pratt and C.W.

Marx (Oxford: Clarendon Press, 1992), and Alcuin Blamires, *The Case for Women in Medieval Culture* (Oxford: Clarendon Press, 1997), chapter 1.

3. See Blamires, *The Case for Women,* pp. 36–7. See also Renate Blumenfeld-Kosinski, "Jean le Fèvre's *Livre de Leesce:* Praise or Blame of Women?" *Speculum* 69 (1994): 705–25 in which she states that LeFèvre "falls, perhaps despite himself, into the trap of misogynist stereotypes" (p. 724).

4. Although I refer to the authors and first-person narrators of the *Lamentations* and the *Leesce* as Matthew and LeFèvre respectively, one must always remember that the speakers are personae created by the writers, whose own views on women should not be confused with those of their fictional creations.

5. LeFèvre's importance has recently been shown by Blamires, *The Case for Women;* Blumenfeld-Kosinski, "Praise or Blame of Women?"; and Helen Solterer, *The Master and Minerva: Disputing Women in French Medieval Culture* (Berkeley and Los Angeles: University of California Press, 1995), chapter 5. In the late seventies his influence on Chaucer was discussed by Zacharias P. Thundy, "Matheolus, Chaucer, and the Wife of Bath," in *Chaucerian Problems and Perspectives,* ed. E. Vasta and Z. Thundy (Notre Dame, Ind.: University of Notre Dame Press, 1979), pp. 24–58.

6. For a discussion of LeFèvre's writings with proposed chronology, see *Le Respit de la mort par Jean Le Fèvre,* ed. Geneviève Hasenohr-Esnos (Paris: SATF, 1969), introduction. His *Théodolet* and *Vieille* both contain some antifeminist material.

7. See Jean LeFèvre, *Les Lamentations de Matheolus et le Livre de Leesce,* ed. A.-G. van Hamel, 2 vols. (Paris: Bouillon, 1892, 1905). According to the editor, the *Lamentations* has survived in eleven manuscripts, the *Leesce* in six (four of which contain both works), thus attesting to the popularity of LeFèvre's writings. Throughout this essay the terms "pro-" and "antifeminist," when applied to medieval authors, texts and audiences, denote attitudes for or against women, feminism being an anachronistic concept in the fourteenth century.

8. See my "Translating Misogamy: The Authority of the Intertext in the *Lamentationes Matheoluli* and its Middle French Translation by Jean LeFèvre," *Forum for Modern Language Studies* 35 (1999): 421–35, at pp. 424–5.

9. Jill Mann, *Apologies to Women* (Cambridge: Cambridge University Press, 1990).

10. In my "Analogy or Logic; Authority or Experience? Rhetorical Strategies for and against Women," in *Literary Aspects of Courtly Culture,* ed. Donald Maddox and Sara Sturm-Maddox (Cambridge: Brewer, 1994), pp. 57–66, at pp. 61–3, I suggest that Christine de Pizan drew on LeFèvre's work in composing her defenses of women. Although Thelma S. Fenster and Mary Carpenter Erler (*Poems of Cupid, God of Love* [Leiden: Brill, 1990], pp. 14–15) rightly state that ideas shared by LeFèvre and Christine were fairly commonplace at the time, Blamires, having surveyed the whole corpus of

defenses, concludes that Christine "absorbed ideas from *Leësce*" (*The Case for Women*, p. 44), and Blumenfeld-Kosinski ("Praise or Blame," p. 720) sees LeFèvre as a source for Christine's *Cité des dames.*

11. The rarity of the good woman is a commonplace of misogyny; see Blamires et al., *Woman Defamed*, p. 106 n. 31. On generalization as an antifeminist strategy, see R. Howard Bloch, *Medieval Misogyny* (Chicago: University of Chicago Press, 1991) and my "Analogy or Logic."

12. In fact she denies *being* prudence, but is instead *verba prudentiae*, thus rejecting the idea of gender specificity in her behavior. See Blamires's appreciation of Albertanus's defense in *The Case for Women*, pp. 22–6.

13. See Michel-André Bossy, "Woman's Plain Talk in *Le Débat de l'omme et de la femme* by Guillaume Alexis," *Fifteenth-Century Studies* 16 (1990): 23–41. Bossy notes interestingly that in Alexis's *Blason de faulses amours* the debating monk clinches the argument with a misogynistic diatribe. Thus Alexis was another writer who produced both a literary attack on and a defense of women.

14. See Jean Gerson, *Le Traictié d'une vision faite contre "Le Ronmant de la Rose" par le chancelier de Paris*, in Hicks, *Le Débat*, pp. 59–87.

15. See Jean Batany, *Approches du "Roman de la Rose"* (Montreal: Bordas, 1973), pp. 40–5; and Simon Gaunt, "Bel Acueil and the Improper Allegory of the *Romance of the Rose*," *New Medieval Literatures* 2 (1998): 65–93.

16. See Bossy, "Woman's Plain Talk," p. 32.

17. Col's reply is in Hicks, *Le Débat*, pp. 89–112.

18. See Solterer, *The Master and Minerva*, p. 4.

19. See Guillaume de Machaut, *The Judgement of the King of Navarre*, trans. and ed. R. Barton Palmer (New York: Garland, 1988), in which the editor argues that the Navarre "constructs the problems of Guillaume the protagonist for the purpose of generating a playful and entertaining text" (p. xxix).

20. Prudence claims erroneously that the knight revealed the chastelaine's secret to the duchess (ll. 2935–6). The arguments of both male and female characters in the poem are faulty and Machaut demonstrates amusingly how exempla can be interpreted in various ways according to the needs of the speaker. Consequently, the king's final judgment seems arbitrary in the absence of persuasive logic leading to an obvious conclusion. See Jean-Louis Picherit, "Les *Exemples* dans le *Jugement dou Roy de Navarre* de Guillaume de Machaut," *Lettres romanes* 36 (1982): 103–16.

21. Although earlier debate poems were set in ducal and royal courts, at which ladies would automatically be present, the increasingly frequent use of legal terminology meant that later poems such as LeFèvre's are to be located in the more masculine environment of a court of law. As we have seen, in this context a female advocate would be unthinkable.

22. Solterer is right to see a sycophantic response in the *Leesce*; see *The Master and Minerva*, pp. 131–50.

23. See note 8 on his *excusasions*. Solterer, *The Master and Minerva*, pp. 136–37, argues that when the author/translator excuses himself he is showing re-

morse. The passage in *Lamentations,* II, 1541–68, in which LeFèvre adopts the position of beaten wife (beating being the punishment for libel/slander at the time), expresses, according to Solterer, the wish to experience for himself the violence that he has inflicted on women through verbal defamation. While it is clear that LeFèvre betrays some anxiety about possible female responses to his writings, the humor and irony of these interventions are evident.

24. The juxtaposition of opposing views, a fundamental characteristic of debate poetry, is shown by Catherine Brown to be fundamental to medieval heuristic practice. LeFèvre's assertion, however, that he will use the dialectical method (universally practiced in medieval schools) to arrive at the truth about women is mere pretense. Although he may share Andreas Capellanus's message (as defined by Brown) that "one who knows cannot be deceived" (p. 112), LeFèvre's ultimate aim is ludic rather than didactic, and his desire is to entertain rather than enlighten. See Catherine Brown, *Contrary Things: Exegesis, Dialectic, and the Poetics of Didacticism* (Stanford, Calif.: University of Stanford Press, 1998).

25. Ovid, *The Art of Love, and Other Poems,* ed. and trans. J. H. Mozley (London: Heinemann, 1947).

26. This attitude on the part of LeFèvre's narrator was shared by Robert de Blois, who, in his *L'Honneur des dames,* returns "to the clubbishness of the first-person plural generalization: 'we' have no joy or pleasure without women," according to Blamires (*The Case for Women,* p. 26).

27. Guillaume de Lorris and Jean de Meun, *Le Roman de la Rose,* ed. Félix Lecoy, 3 vols. (Paris: Champion, 1965–70), ll. 829–33.

28. See my "Translating Misogamy."

29. Although LeFèvre associates sadness and anger with the *source* of antifeminism—the motivation for Matthew's vituperation (*Leesce,* ll. 2662–73)—most of his references to the joy/sadness binary relate to the *effect* on the male poet/reader of good/bad relations with women; see *Leesce,* ll. 53–4, 84, 360–4, 1263–4, etc.

30. Jill Mann complains of a similar approach in Machaut's *Jugement dou Roy de Navarre,* in which the poet is accused of misogyny by an allegorical personification, "Bonneurté, meaning Happiness or Good Fortune (3851)," not by a "real woman" (*Apologies to Women,* p. 27). Machaut agrees with LeFèvre that by pleasing his lady the poet will acquire the quality she represents (*Jugement dou Roy de Navarre,* ll. 3805–3924).

31. See Bossy, "Woman's Plain Talk," p. 27.

32. For the background to this anecdote, see Blamires, *The Case for Women,* pp. 50–61.

33. See Blumenfeld-Kosinski, "Praise or Blame," p. 723.

34. The story of the Widow of Ephesus (ll. 1347–1408) illustrates well the relish with which antifeminist exempla are retold in the *Leesce.* Typically, LeFèvre retains much dialogue and even comments made by Matthew, some in the first person, thus merging their voices (see ll. 1357, 1402).

35. Yet in ll. 633–4, "Je croy bien que ce fu a tort,/ Et toutesvoies l'asne en fu mort" [I really think wrongfully so, yet the donkey did die because of this], the *reponse* to Matthew's anecdote may well be humorous and deliberately lame. So what if the donkey died?

36. As elsewhere in the *Leesce,* this passage reproduces Matthew's opinions and crude language unaltered; hence the reference to Calphurnia's *cul* (line 1040) and the misogynist comment "par droit, si com j'ay entendu" (*Lamentations*, II, 197) [rightly, as I understood/heard it], which, thanks to the ironic ambiguities of voice cultivated by LeFèvre, sound as if they may have been spoken by a defender of women.

37. See my "Analogy or Logic," p. 64.

38. Of course, this unladylike language reminds us of what Leesce really represents for LeFèvre, who here forgets that he is meant to be addressing the ladies of Paris.

39. In this same speech LeFèvre acknowledges the pleasures for the male of speaking about women (cf. ll. 166–7, quoted above) when he implies that Matthew, like the devil, has the best tunes: "J'ay contre moy bourdes et fables/ Et poëtries delitables" [I have against me jokes and stories and entertaining poetry; ll. 753–4].

40. It seems to be in the nature of these gender debates that judgment is either postponed or hastily pronounced in an arbitrary manner. This underlines the mock seriousness of male-authored texts that put misogynists on trial in a lame attempt to appease women.

41. Solterer mentions that LeFèvre frequently acted for female clients (*The Master and Minerva,* pp. 133–4 and p. 245, note 5).

42. The later reference to the author's thirst (ll. 3974–6) also recalls the drinking songs of the goliard poets and anticipates Villon's joke in the *Testament* (ll. 817–24) concerning Lazarus, the rich man, and the lack of alcoholic beverages in Hell.

43. Text and translation are taken from the edition by R. Barton Palmer.

44. Like Machaut's Guillaume, whose punishment for maligning women is to write a *lai,* a dance song, and a ballad, it seems that LeFèvre's atonement for translating the *Lamentationes* is to write the *Leesce.* However, the ballad it contains in lines 3447–67 is comic, with its sexual metaphor (l. 3447) and its reminder of potential opposition in "quoy que l'on die" (l. 3454) [whatever one might say].

45. The proliferation of puns continues in the word *cure,* meaning "care," but alluding also to the curing of skins.

46. The allusion here is to the ending of Jean de Meun's *Rose,* when the lover becomes a pilgrim equipped with staff and a pouch containing two hammers provided by Nature "con cele qui forgier savoit" [like one who knew how to work in a forge; ll. 21316–7] for procreative purposes.

47. Although I am reading LeFèvre's humor as a joke against women, this does not exclude the possibility that comedy masks a deep-seated anxiety about the power woman wields over the desiring male.

48. I have argued this point more fully in my "Analogy or Logic," p. 62.
49. I should like to thank Alcuin Blamires for introducing me to LeFèvre, and Jeanette Beer for her continued support.

CHAPTER 7

THE FREEDOMS OF FICTION
FOR GENDER IN PREMODERN FRANCE

Helen Solterer

A major shift in meaning in the word "franchise" can be traced through French and English literary and political writing. Assessing the change within the framework of the fifteenth-century controversy over Alain Chartier's "Belle Dame sans merci," we see that the various fictive forms of the "Belle Dame" enabled readers to imagine women's public and emotional states as provocatively free.

With this essay, I want to introduce a notion of freedom into our explorations of gender in late medieval European culture. It is certainly a charged notion. We have been taught by many revolutions to understand it as something distinctively modern—a condition that differentiates our lives from those of the distant past. Wasn't freedom one of modernity's rallying cries? When we focus on the case of women, this idea carries a further burden. Since it continues to be fought over today, in Europe as around the globe, freedom in earlier centuries looks especially dubious.

Against these odds, I shall pursue it because there are signs that it played a role in some of the first extended debates over women's public status. I'll begin with one example from around 1424: an uncompromising statement voiced by a persona whom everybody loved to hate. As Alain Chartier introduced the "belle dame sans merci," she was notorious for laying claim to her autonomy in love. Faced with a pressing suitor, she asserts:

D'amours ne quier courroux n'aysance, Ne grant espoir ne grant desir;
Et si n'ay de voz maulz plaisance Ne regart a voustre plaisir. Choisisse qui
vouldra choisir. Je suis france et france vueil estre, Sans moy de mon cuer
dessaisir Pour en faire un autre le maistre.[1]

[I'm not looking for trouble or delight from love; that is not what I hope
for or greatly desire. I get no pleasure from your suffering, nor does your enjoyment concern me. Between the two, let her choose what she wishes. I
am free and wish to remain free. I don't want my heart taken from me, making someone else master.]

This declaration of *franchise* rang familiar to its initial audiences in fifteenth-century France. The woman's claim on her freedom of maneuver
was a form of resistance in love banter required by courtly codes. It rever-
berated with the wary voices of many earlier personae. Like that of the noblewoman in Andreas Capellanus's *De amore,* it was double-edged:
"Cuicunque sub amoris clipeo ipsa videatur militare libertas et res appre-
hendenda, mihi tamen deterrima videtur servitus et res per omnia
fugienda" [Let any man who so desires regard campaigning under Love's
shield as the essence of freedom and a course worth adopting, but to me
it appears the worst possible slavery, and a course to be avoided in all cir-
cumstances].[2] One lover's exhilaration was another's bondage. In this setup,
what a man professed as love was tantamount to slavery for a woman; she
could always be counted on to object. Yet generations of courtiers had
learned to recognize the noblewoman's objection as one block that eventually gave way. The woman's turnaround—from refusal to final acceptance
of his profession of love—was the *sine qua non* of good courtship.

The "belle dame" seemed to reinforce all the commonplaces of premodern love literature. Partisans of Paris's Court of Love then and critics
now have both typecast Chartier's persona nostalgically, framing her in a
scenario from the good old days when a lover's free love took precedence
over a woman's desire.[3] Was her declaration just another rendition of this
ancien régime of courtly love?

Judging from the quick, sharp response in the French courts to the
poem *La Belle Dame sans merci,* something had changed. Chartier's work
touched off a scandal.[4] Courts' attention across the north of France was
galvanized; all across Europe too, as translations spread, people took no-
tice.[5] Over the decade of the 1430s, the controversy gained momentum as
numerous French poems were composed about the "belle dame" persona.
They volleyed back and forth, attacking and defending her. In these
poems' scenes of interrogation and judgment, the sore point was her *franchise.* They circle around it again and again.

The first charge in the first attacking poem, called *Les Accusations contre la Belle Dame sans merci* (c. 1425?), went after her capacity to speak freely. The allegorical figure "Franc Vouloir" (Free Will) announces: "Ce fut tres horrible parole dicte de bouche feminine qui doit estre selon lescole damours humble douce et benigne" [This was despicable talk coming from a woman's mouth, which is supposed to be humble, gentle, and sweet according to the school of love].[6] Even before opposing what women's freedom might add up to, the poem attacks her free speech. Along with this battle comes the fundamental one over desire: Once a woman articulates hers, it must be challenged by Franc Vouloir, the familiar, powerful symbol of his.

Why did the "belle dame's" claim on *franchise* trigger such conflicted responses? How could a notion that seemed so conventional, so timeworn by courtly rituals, start a fuss all over again? What exactly does this *franchise* entail?

One clue lies in the English translation of Chartier's poem done by Richard Ros in the 1450s. He rendered the woman's declaration this way:

> Of love I seke neither plesaunce nor ese,
> Nor greet desyr, nor right gret affyaunce;
> Though ye be seke, it doth me nothing plese;
> Also, I take no hede to your plesaunce.
> Chese who-so wil, their hertes to avaunce,
> Free am I now, and free wil I endure;
> To be ruled by mannes governaunce
> For erthely good, nay! That I you ensure![7]

Ros translated *franc* as "free." He left behind the commonplaces of courtly liberality or magnanimity—translations that English and French courtiers of the day might well have expected. Are we reckoning with a mistranslation? I am not persuaded, mostly because Ros's version of the full stanza of Chartier's narrative suggests that he understood the ramifications of the woman's *franchise*. Ros's English structures her desires as a matter of governance. When he translated *maistrise* as "ruled by mannes governaunce," he gave it political clout. He was building on Chartier's pairing of *maistrise* with *franc seigneuriage* in the stanza that follows in the *Belle Dame*. This combination placed the woman's declaration of free desire in a wider, civic context.

Following Ros's lead in translation, I shall investigate the reasons why in the early fifteenth century the link *franchise*/freedom touched an old nerve in a new way. By going in this direction, I am weighing a case for a value not ordinarily attributed to women in courtly texts. I am breaking through the expectations of premodern audiences and contemporary critics alike that *franchise* would remain the traditional courtly virtue of liberality. The

case for freedom is a gamble. Yet I shall take it, because there is evidence that
freedom's changing significance was already recognizable to audiences of
the *Belle Dame* and of the ensuing controversy.

In doing this, I find it is also important to reckon with the difficulties
involved on the other end of the timeline. Part of the problem, as we have
already noted, is our tendency to confuse the premodern *franchise* with its
modern sibling; and in the French context, with the republican virtue of
freedom. It is rousing to find in the "belle dame" a revolutionary woman
avant la lettre. Burkhardt may have suffered from the same temptation when
he trumpeted a notion of women's "perfect equality with men," as a singular trait of the European Renaissance.[8] *Liberté, egalité*—the French revolutionary slogan echoes in both these accounts of the public status of
premodern women. However tempting, the parallel with their eighteenth-
century *consoeurs* does not hold. We cannot put their cases on a par. But admitting this should not prevent us from determining whether there is any
relation between their assertions of *franchise*.

The *Belle Dame* controversy can serve as a laboratory of sorts for my investigation. Since the controversy entertained *franchise* for women, we can
test for its implications here. This experiment may help to highlight a cri-
terion for the ongoing debate over gender in these premodern centuries.

I

Let's look first at *franchise* on its home ground: the court. In this arena reserved for one social estate alone, *franchise* defines nobility of character for
men and women.[9] Allegories and romances in the High Middle Ages promoted it as an exclusively aristocratic attribute and bolstered it with a
strong sense of entitlement. Such a definition makes clear the political hierarchy that is at stake, and the process by which it is legitimized. Nobles
must be identified as *francs:* it is their badge of class. That's why in the
twelfth-century chivalric romance *Ipomédon,* the young bachelor protagonist will not forfeit his own *franchise* lightly: "Ne perdrai pur vos en nule
guise honur ne franchisese murir dei, meulz voil murir ke vif remeindre e
mei hunir" [Never for any reason will I lose my honor or my *franchise;* if I
must die, it would be better to die than to remain living dishonored].[10]
Franchise is an ultimate test of character for the aristocracy, as the pairing
with honor underscores. Without it, the class would be seriously diminished socially. It involves a fundamental dignity underlying courtly groom-
ing, authenticating it. It is not only an externally visible trait, worn like
insignia, but it inheres within individuals. *Franchise* is characteriological. It
shows one way to track how cultural distinctions of the upper classes are
internalized. In that old face-off between Culture and Nature, *franchise*

functions as basic human integrity for both sexes, as if it is natural, as if it is an intrinsic, indispensable state on a par with honor.[11]

In large part, the nobility was inculcated with this rule through courtly literature. Young bachelors were trained in the values of *franchise,* and those qualities had a direct bearing on matters of love as well. The narrator of *Ipomédon* asks the protagonist: "Quidez-vous, garcon, pur beauté pussez par amur estre amé, pur franchise ne pur largesce?" [Do you believe, boy, that you can be loved for love's sake, for your beauty, your largesse, your *franchise?*].[12] Whatever the right answer is to this rhetorical question, love is linked to *franchise. Franchise* emerges as a prerequisite for erotic desire. Coupled this time with physical attractiveness and generosity, *franchise* makes high-class loving possible. So it is that the exemplary regal figure Conrad in Jean Renart's thirteenth-century *Roman de la rose (Guillaume de Dole)* is portrayed as "li bons rois, li frans debonere, il savoit toz les tors d'amors" [the good king, the noble gentleman, (who) knew all the tricks of love].[13] The tautology is simple: He is king because he is *franc,* and *franc* because he is noble. Furthermore, the political value of his *franchise* conditions his desires. It follows that he will prove an exemplary lover. In this world, as far as men go, the arena of love is reserved for the upper class.

This tautological definition seems to hold true for women too. In Marie de France's *Guigemar* we find "une dame de haut parage, franche, curteise, bele e sage" [a lady of high standing, noble in spirit, courtly, beautiful, and wise].[14] *Franchise* takes its place in the catalogue of her virtues that distinguish her class and mark her as worthy of love. Even in the overdetermined case of the lady that the Virgin Mary represented, *franchise* remains a crucial attribute. In the *Miracles de Nostre Dame,* she is thus portrayed by the narrator-supplicant: "car renom, bontez, et simplesce, courtoisie, doulceur, largesce, honneste, maintien, avenance, franchise, attraient contenance dont elles est dame est tresoriere ont mon cuer en telle maniere" [a lady of fine reputation, goodness and simplicity, courtesy and gentility; she is the treasurer of honesty, composure, comeliness, nobility of spirit *(franchise)*, and attractive demeanor, and in this way she has my heart].[15] For the saintly figure to appear human, to take her place among the *grandes dames,* she is invariably endowed with *franchise.* Whenever medieval writers set out to create characters worth emulating, worth loving, from ground level at court to the hereafter, *franchise* was routinely one of the chief properties to include.

When it came to parodying these characters, turning their worlds upside down through farce and social satire, *franchise* was just as visible. In the thirteenth-century *Aucassin et Nicolette,* the lovable outsider Nicolette is stamped with *franchise.* The bachelor Aucassin protests to his judgmental king of a father: "S'ele estoit enpereris de Constentinoble u d'Alemaigne,

u roine de France u d'Engletere, si aroit il assés peu en li, tant est france et
cortoise et de bon aire et entecie de toutes bones teces" [If she (Nicolette)
were the empress of Constantinople or Germany, or the queen of France
or England, she couldn't have greater nobility of spirit, or be more courtly,
gracious, or possessed of any greater qualities].[16] That the foreign and socially ambiguous figure of Nicolette is "france" signals how valuable her
franchise is. The sharpest satire targets what is supposed to be taken for
granted.

What happens to *franchise* when noblemen and -women meet during
courting rituals? In the artful game of move and countermove that Andreas
Capellanus sketches out, we find this encounter:

> Mulier ait: Si amori vacare eligerem, indubitanter scias quod pro posse stud-
> erem potioris mihi solatia quaerere. Homo ait: Liberum tibi eligendi amoris
> esse non dubitatur arbitrium. Ego tamen tibi nunquam servire cessabo . . .
> corde tamen vobis colligatus exsisto.

> [The woman says: Were I to decide to concentrate on love, you can take it
> as certain that to the best of my ability I should seek for myself the conso-
> lations of the better suitor. The man says: Your freedom to choose love is not
> in dispute. But I shall never cease to serve you. . . . I remain closely bound
> to you in heart] (Walsh, pp. 95–97)

The woman's freedom to choose a lover is a trap here. Since the man confirms her right conditionally, that right becomes a way to exert pressure,
and he uses it to contain her. In his hands, her *franchise* becomes a double
bind. While she may be able to assert her freedom, the relentless comebacks
of the lover effectively undercut its value. For her, the real benefits of freedom are jeopardized. Since this dialogue ends with the woman's turnaround and change of heart, as in many of Capellanus's scenarios, the
apparent equilibrium of *franchise* between the sexes is broken. Even when
we listen in to the woman's own voice as this particular encounter plays
out, the imbalance becomes obvious.

> Mulier ait: Illud quod tibi possum praestare suffragium libera tibi voce
> promisi. . . . Nam quod postulas, nullis posses precibus vel laboribus impe-
> trare; firmum etenim est et totius meae mentis propositum Veneris me nun-
> quam supponere servituti.

> [The woman says: I have freely promised you the boon that I can grant
> you . . . As for your demand, you could not obtain that by any prayers or
> toils, for it is the unshakable resolve of my whole mind never to subject my-
> self to the slavery of Venus] (Walsh, p. 101)

This emphatic statement turns out to be the woman's last-ditch effort. In the dialectics of these dialogues, her "No" comes to mean "Yes." Asserting the freedom of her promises and repudiating servitude paves the way for her to capitulate in the end.

Far from a common attribute for the nobility in the twelfth and thirteenth centuries, *franchise* was a selective virtue coded according to gender. For women, it represented the necessary attribute that explained their free choice to satisfy their lovers. Their freedom functioned in a hierarchical social system that curbed their autonomy. It catered to the aristocratic fantasy that a male lover got what he wanted when a woman was free and ready to give herself over.

It is proverbial to analyze this uneven relation at the heart of courtly cultures of friendship and love in terms of a feudal gift-giving system. As is well known, such exchange bound a superior and an inferior party together, a lord to a vassal. In the transfer of feudal roles onto the rapport between lover and lady, the noble lover starts by offering his services to the *franchise* of the woman he is pursuing. Guillaume de Lorris's *Roman de la rose,* for example, clearly presents such a scene when Bel Acueil (Fair Welcome) initiates the bachelor into the courtly company in the garden:

> Sire, fis je, a bel acueil, Ceste promesse en gre recueil. Si vos gran graces et merites De la bonte que vos me dites, Car mout vos muet de grant franchise; Quant vos plera, vostre service Sui prez de penre volentiers. (ll. 2805–2811)[17]

> [Sire, I said to Bel Acueil, I accept this promise gladly. I will offer you grace and I am grateful for the goodwill that you show to me. Clearly it comes from your great nobility of spirit *(franchise)*; whenever it is pleasing to you, I will be ready to enter into your service]

As the allegorical stand-in for the lady, Bel Acueil is defined by *franchise,* and this sets the stage for the lover's service. In exchange, the lady is expected to give freely of herself. The problem is that in doing so, she is progressively divested of the lord's role initially projected onto her. The implicit bargain here ties the woman to the lover. Her *franchise,* like the lord's, demands unlimited generosity. But it does not involve the same authority or superiority.

Jean de Meun's *Rose* illustrates in starker, more pragmatic terms the limits of *franchise* for women. The scene shifts socially, and moves from the action of courtship to that of marriage with all its legal regulations. One episode related by the character Ami (Friend) to the debutant lover involves a bourgeois husband whose jealousy explodes in violence against his wife. Part of the commentary drawn from the husband's rage involves *franchise:*

> Por ce, compainz, li ancien, Sanz servitude et sanz lien, Paisiblement, sanz vilonnie, S'entreportoient compaingnie, N'il ne donnassent pas franchise Por l'or d'arrabie ne de frise; Car qui tout l'or en porroit prendre, Ne la porroit il pas bien vendre. (ll. 9497–9504)

> [It is for this reason, my friend, that the ancients kept company together, peacefully, and without malice, with no slavery or bond tying them. They would never give away their freedom for all the gold in Arabia or Friesland, for even if they could get all that gold for it, it wouldn't be worth selling it for that price]

Ami turns to the Greek past to seek evidence for the *franchise* of this married man as a fundamental personal freedom. His conclusion: Giving it away to anyone is a dangerous affair that the ancients would never have entertained. For Jean de Meun, *franchise* is an exceptional virtue that can never be considered a gift. It cannot enter into the usual trading between peers. Nor can it be bought and sold. It is priceless, even in a world that sanctions slavery. Not even the prized currency of Arabian or Frisian gold adds up. Pulled out of circulation from both feudal gift and bourgeois barter economies, *franchise* is invested with political value. It is set in opposition to the worst state of slavery. The whole commentary hangs on this distinction. *Franchise* is to be defended absolutely. Among men. Following Aristotle, the condition of *franchise*/freedom is available theoretically to everyone, but is reserved in practice for men.[18] Political *franchise* is particularly important in the context of marriage because, as Aristotle's *Politics* lays it out, it represents the city-state in miniature. It is the smallest political unit. And here we can see the crossover between the political and emotional states of *franchise*. If the married man is to be free in his desires, he must be free to exercise his prerogatives as head of the household—political head. His *franchise* must be doubly potent.

Since de Meun's married man takes to wife beating, the irony is glaring. His *franchise* is advanced as a cover-all explanation of his abuse. Once marriage to a woman is seen to deprive him of his freedom—political, emotional, even economic—she is necessarily cast as scapegoat. She bears the blame for the bondage in marriage that he finds intolerable, and must bear too the blows for his loss of freedom. Her freedom is nowhere to be found in Jean de Meun's scene.

For de Meun, *franchise* involves a connection made willingly among people, i.e., men, without any double-binding conditions. Yet if we take de Meun's writing as a whole, a discrepancy comes to light. In his translation of the letters of Heloise and Abelard, this is the sense of *franchise* voiced by Heloise herself. But de Meun's Heloise capitalizes on that notion of a freely chosen, nonbinding commitment and does not hesitate to apply such an understanding brazenly to her own condition.[19] It makes her defense of free love bolder: "Sed plerisque tacitis quibus amorem conjugio, libertatem vinculo preferebam . . . ;/ Par quoy je priseroie mielx amour que mariage et franchise que len" [I would cherish love far more than marriage, freedom more than any bond; ed. Hicks, pp. 48–49].[20] Her claim on freedom is powerful because the audience for de Meun's translation knew that scholastic reasoning legitimized it, at least in principle.

Heloise's claim recalls the Thomist premise concerning the unattached woman.[21] When Aquinas put the notion of woman to the test, analyzing its essences, such a woman looked dangerous; she was hard to grasp. She was not placeable socially. Without attachments, she stood in ambiguous relation to the law. In scholastic Latin, she is literally undetermined—neither legally defined nor located. As Alain de Libera suggests, this is tantamount to contending that a woman acting as a lover outside the bounds of family and marriage is "more than free" (p. 208).

Chaucer's *Franklin's Tale* includes just such a principle articulated by a woman. In a conventional scenario of a knight in hot pursuit, the woman says:

> Love wol nat been constreyned by maistrye.
> Whan maistrie comth, the God of Love anon
> Beteth his wynges, and farewel, he is gon!
> Love is a thyng as any spirit free.
> Wommen, of kynde, desiren libertee
> And nat to been constreyned as a thral;
> And so doon men, if I sooth seyen shal. (vv. 763–770)[22]

The language has changed, but the claim remains the same. Women's desire for liberty in Chaucer dovetails with Heloise's assertion of *franchise*. Whether the context is one of love or marriage, liberty/*franchise*/freedom retains its political punch. The opposing vocabulary of constraint, mastery, and thralldom makes this clear. It sets into relief the unspoken threat that is particularly strong for women: servitude and emotional subjugation.

This dialectic between freedom and slavery was reinforced when Nicole Oresme translated Aristotle's *Politics* into French in the late fourteenth century. Oresme launched another sustained vernacular reflection on what he labeled "liberté ou franchise" [liberty or freedom]—its conditions and opposing forces.[23] Both text and gloss take it up in relation to women. Oresme argues through Aristotle, "Et donques estre femme et estre serf sont choses distinguees, separees et differentes par nature" [And therefore being a woman and being a slave are distinct and separate things according to nature; Menut 46]. Oresme was intent on maintaining this distinction, no matter how women appear in their situations as daughter, wife, housekeeper. He implies that woman is naturally free. Yet it does not take long for his inspiring axiom to be eroded. Daily life shows how it is routinely compromised. Oresme has to admit:

> Toutesvoies, ceulz qui sunt frans de nature se pevent faire serfs et mescheans par malvese acoustumance; et au contraire, les serfs se pevent faire frans pource que tous ont liberté et franchise de volenté. (Menut, p. 54)

> [Nevertheless, those who are free by nature can become serfs through misfortune and bad customs; yet serfs cannot become free since everyone possesses liberty and free will]

Clearly women could be and were enslaved. Oresme was caught between principle and practice. In Charles V's Paris, there was no less friction than in Aristotle's Athens. Women's condition hung in the balance, between the ideal of realizing the principle of *franchise* universally and the many political limits constraining it.

Returning to our case of the "belle dame," what is shocking about her declaration of freedom is that it takes Oresme's universal principle seriously. *Franchise* belongs to the "belle dame." The woman is not predicating her condition on anything or anyone; nor does she presuppose any effect. Saying that she is free does not obligate her. Yet it does commit her to what Georges Duby calls "a hierarchical notion of liberty."[24] The highly regulated caste society of a French court placed Chartier's "belle dame" inevitably in relation to many lords as well as to many underlings. The difference was: In such rarefied classes, could she use her *franchise* to assume those relations willingly?

The statement "je suis france" is her first major subjective speech act. At the least, Chartier's persona begins to realize her freedom through language. Earlier in Chartier's poem, she comments on the exaggerated distress of the lover; she rebuffs his advances and makes clear her lack of interest. But the first time she describes herself, she makes that radical and fundamental declaration. Declaring her freedom is the first instance of attaining it. As Jacques Derrida has said about declarative acts of independence, "the self surges up here . . . in a single coup de force."[25]

We have here a clear-cut example of performative language, in which an utterance enacts its meaning. The "belle dame's" declaration of freedom also illustrates a late medieval conception of such language, what Oresme dubbed *mos actisans* [activating words], which were themselves an event.[26] They extend beyond the single subjective act to build a test case.

The declaring, surging self of a "belle dame" in Chartier's work also speaks in the name of women in general. When the lover counters her claim on *franchise* by complaining that women already possess "lordship and rule of every maner age" (Ros translation, v. 320; *maistrise et franc seigneuriage,* Laidlaw, v. 292), she retorts:

> Dames ne sont mye si lourdes,
> Si mal entendans ne si foles
> Que, pou un peu de plaisans bourdes
> Confites en belles parolles,
> Dont vous autres tenés escoles
> Pour leur faire croire merveille. (*La Belle Dame sans merci,* vv. 297–302)

> Ladies be nat so simple, thus I mene,
> So dul of wit, so sotted of foly,
> That for wordes which sayd ben of the splene,
> In fayre langage, paynted ful plesauntly
> Which ye and no holde scoles of dayly,
> To make hem of gret wonders to suppose. (Richard Ros, tr., vv. 325–330)

A declaration of individual freedom confronts the pretty talk surrounding women. Its hallmark frankness calls to task amorous rhetoric and its logic. It helps to puncture the lover's angry pretension that mastery and "lordship" have always been available to women in matters of love. It exposes the fundamental contradiction that undergirds the practices of *franchise* between men and women. Chartier's poem bears on women's lot as a whole. Enacting her own *franchise,* the "belle dame" can become a spokesperson for others.

The one-two punch of such assertions of autonomy posed a precise threat. They disrupted the bonds of indebtedness that justified the inequities of a courtly society running along feudal lines. They smacked of a political challenge. Further, they risked destroying the trappings of love service, with all their metaphors of gift exchange.

When we take account of the different resonances and circumstances of *franchise* that grew throughout the premodern period, it becomes clear that *franchise* was bursting out of the mold of a courtly virtue to signify a liberating process. No certain entitlement, it designated more and more a fundamental and open-ended experience. Despite the exclusionary force of patriarchal thinking that limited discussions of *franchise*/freedom to men, by the fourteenth and fifteenth centuries courtly writing did not corroborate that restriction uniformly. Judging from the "belle dame," a woman's *franchise* represented a challenge to the double standard that the idea of *franchise* had implicitly signified earlier.

II

I want to consider the contexts for weighing this challenge by turning now to the *Belle Dame* controversy. This debate, like many before and after it, uses figurative terms of law to tackle the question of the character's *franchise*. There was nothing surprising about this framework. The relish for dialectical reasoning was strong in the premodern period; it fed into the legal mode of interrogation.[27] The poems that make up our controversy capitalize on the standard juridical metaphors of courtly writing: The writer is charged with the crime of treason; various advocates are named: Truth and Justice on one side, Desire and Hope on the other; the lady is put in the box to testify.[28] As a whole the woman's *franchise* is framed as a matter to be disputed and judged.

This figurative framework is all the more striking to me because it suggests something that this early phase of debating gender shares with our debates today. We are accustomed to nodding in recognition at the premodern taste for allegories of law. Our own critical rhetoric, I would hazard to say, shows a similar bent. We would be hard-pressed to find work in contemporary gender theory that has not been marked by what is, fundamentally, a figurative way of proceeding legally, and this without accounting for the writing that takes law and gender as its explicit subject. All of us who mount cases, even those between scare quotes, are up to much the same thing. The difference is that the premodern habit of arguing figuratively and legally defied closure. The scholastic tradition of disputes as well as those traditions involving courtly writing were notorious for their inconclusive form. Today's debates, more blunt and more speedily accomplished, are driven by a desire for resolution: A political end must be in sight. In this small parenthesis, I want to point out the enduring pattern in gender debates over the centuries to mount cases; despite the different tendencies to foreclose, the habit of mimicking litigation remains constant. This habit comes to the fore when we are reckoning with an issue as protean and as precious as freedom.

In the case of our premodern debate, on the one side, the "belle dame's" freedom is defended as the privilege of any honorable lover. The *Dame leale en amours,* a polemical poem advocating for the woman (c. 1425–29?), makes the argument:

> Elle puet choisir l'un d'iceulx Qui sera mieulx a son talent, Selonc vostre loy proprement, Car la liberté qu'elle a Peut retenir tout franchement Serviteur tel qu'il lui plaira. (ed. Piaget, ll. 361–66)

[And if several lovers seek her out, she can choose any lover who can appeal best to her desire, according to your own law, because the liberty that she has permits her to retain freely whatever servant is pleasing to her]

The woman's desire is presented here as legitimate. The anonymous poet bolsters this case by attributing it to the allegorical figure of Truth, the woman's counsel. And by definition, Truth acts in keeping with the law, understood here figuratively as the law of love. In fact, the woman's desire is vindicated. Her choice is judged favorably. Furthermore, freedom and the strictures of retainership are judged compatible. From an implicit position of master, the "belle dame" can exercise her choice of lover-servant and operate impeccably within the code of love service.

The strategy of this position is shrewd: It takes the universal courtly virtue of *franchise* at face value. In other words, if the "belle dame" has been given her freedom in name by the courtly system, then that name will be activated for her. The discrepancy of *franchise* is overturned: She will speak and behave so as to make her freedom stick. The *Dame leale* cultivates the liberating irony of respecting the courtly convention. In the words of the allegorical defense lawyer, Truth:

Que, selonc droit, poons prouver Tantost que la dame a bon cuer A vous servir et honnourer. Vous lui avez volu donner Franchise, tout a son vouloir, Pour a son plaisir en user, Qui qui s'en puist plaindre ou doloir. (Piaget, ll. 367–76)

[And according to the law, we can prove that the lady has a good heart with which to serve and honor you. You wanted to bestow on her freedom, as she wished, freedom that she can enjoy to her own benefit. Who could complain or be sorry about that?]

The radical prospect of taking the woman's *franchise* seriously is cast ironically as abiding by the figurative law. No contest. In this way, the *Dame leale* exposes the fundamental gendered contradiction in the courtly system that has sapped the issue of freedom. The upshot is to make sure that women's freedom stays prominently at the center of the debate.

On the other polemical side, in Achille Caulier's caustic poem *La Cruelle Femme en amour* (c. 1430), every effort is made to return to the courtly status quo, that is, to squash the notion of women's freedom and to stigmatize it. The "belle dame" is accused of taking liberties. In the complex allegorical configuration, the judge Love reminds the lawyer Truth:

Vous sçavez, mon tresredoubté, comment, selon l'acteur premier, la damme horrible sans pité Se monstra pleine de dangier, Non pas tant seulement au mort, Mais a tous, quant elle disoit: Choisisse qui vouldra. Au fort, Franche vers tous estre vouloit, Et dist que telle demourroit Sans se dessaisir de son cuer, Car ja ne s'en dessaisiroit Pour en faire un aultre seigneur. (ll. 349–367)[29]

[You know, my esteemed sir, how according to the first author (Alain Chartier), the horrible, pitiless lady showed herself to be fully dangerous, not only to her dead lover but to everyone when she said: Let her choose whomsoever she wishes. In fact, she wanted to be free toward everyone and she said she would remain so, without having her heart taken from her, making someone else master]

Repeating the "belle dame's" declaration from Chartier's work, making a slogan of it, accentuates the threat that it represents. The danger lies in the woman's wanting it all: Not only does she seek freedom for herself by articulating it forthrightly, she advocates it for everyone. Consequently, she is menacing to everyone. The *Cruelle Femme* thus upped the ante in the controversy: It cast the woman's claim as breaking even the structure of "hierarchical liberty." It combated the universal principle.

Putting side by side the opposing views of the *Dame leale* and the *Cruelle Femme* sets into relief the problem posed by a woman's emotional *franchise*. Both views assess it according to the same metaphoric legal standards; they follow traditionally in the long line of courtly writing that grappled with desire by using the figures of judgments in law. Yet the *Belle Dame* controversy also showed up the contradictions surrounding *franchise* in courtly writing, contradictions that no longer seemed tenable. By fixing on the woman's desire for freedom, the controversy seemed to demonstrate the exhaustion of one aspect of courtly life as against the challenging prospect of another, newer principle.

This discrepancy is worth considering. It makes me wonder: Did the focus on women's emotional *franchise* in this controversy point to other preoccupations at the time? Did it, for example, bear any relation to the mounting debate on liberty and political sovereignty in a France caught in the throes of the Hundred Years' War? Chartier's *femme franc(h)e* encourages me to follow this line of thinking, since her name echoed her country's. It evoked the plight of the French kingdom at the time. In order to find out, we need to tune into still more resonances linking *franc(h)e* to *franchise*.

III

The trick of conflating the notion "franc" with the name "France" has a long history. Marc Bloch put it succinctly: "That the *populus Francorum* was composed only of free men, independently of any ethnic distinction, is proved by the fact that the national name and the legal status came to be synonymous. *Libre* or *franc*—the two words became interchangeable."[30] From the time of Charlemagne on, this interchangeability was a source of political propaganda and great literary play. During the heyday of vernacular historiography, from the thirteenth through the fifteenth centuries, it was richly exploited: A ploy used by several noble lineages to justify their dynastic ambitions.[31] By Chartier's era, it was still visible, further heightened by the events of English invasion and occupation.[32] It carried on well into the sixteenth century: The *rhétoriqueur* Jean Lemaire de Belges typified the play with his famous "F" refrain: "The French people, well formed, free, fierce, firm . . . Your names match your effect" [François, faictiz, francz, fortz, fermes au fait . . . Telz sont vos noms, concordans à l'affect].[33] Even the epoch-making event of the French Revolution did much to exploit this association between *franchise* and France, and to parade it publicly. From then on in nineteenth-century Europe, the republican virtue of liberty was commonly attributed to the French nation. Modern French dictionaries continued to make it a national property:

> Franchise: derived from the Celtic *frank* (free, unencumbered, independent), like the words *France* and *French*. This word belongs specifically to our language. The quality that it designates in its most recent usage is one of the distinctive qualities of our race. To ask someone if s/he is *franc* is to ask everything. *Franchise* and the other virtues proceed directly from liberty, just as lying and all other vices come from servitude. Despite all the hardships that France has suffered, our origin, our past, our national character and our language place us at the head of a humanitarian movement toward liberty and toward *franchise*. (*Grand Dictionnaire universel du XIXe siècle*)[34]

This canonical dictionary definition gathers together all the past associations of *franchise* that I have surveyed in rapid-fire style. With an imagined etymology, it authorizes a sense of French superiority that mixes race, language, and nation, all wrapped up in *franchise*.[35] What a concept.

It was Chartier's generation of writers that first gave the notion of France/*franchise* a feminine face. They invented a dignified and free woman who also represented France through this wordplay. Long before there was a republican Marianne, before even the feisty Joan of Arc, there was a lady dressed in a fleur-de-lys gown.[36] Portrayed increasingly in the arts, she emerged at a moment in the royal and national imaginary when the issue of political freedom was under severe pressure.

Christine de Pizan was a major player in devising the lady's features. In her autobiographical allegory *L'Advision Cristine* (1405), she built an account of French history around "a crowned lady."[37] This figure begins a lamentation about her own dire state by explaining her name:"ycelle plante parcruit tant que de la beauté d'elle je pris mon nom et fus "Libera" appellé" [I took my name from the beauty of this plant that grew so well, and was called *Libera* (Reno and Dulac 17–18)]. *Liber* was also interchangeable with *franc* in the fifteenth century; Christine used the wordplay to present the woman France, and to introduce her question of freedom in undeniable terms:"Le renom de ma franchise ja espandus en toutes places" (Reno and Dulac, p. 18) [The renown of my *franchise* spread everywhere].[38]

Chartier capitalized on Christine's figure of an outspoken, free-talking woman when he shaped his own France in the *Quadrilogue Invectif* (1422) as "contrainte par besoing" [a woman constrayned].[39] She was more overwrought than Christine's figure, tearing her hair out over "les naturelz ennemis quierent moy oster liberté pour tenir en leur miserable subjection" [the naturall enemyes (who) seek and laboure to take my libertee for to kepe me in thaie miserable subieccion; Droz, p. 12, Blayney, p. 153]. In her distress she was certainly responding to the violent attacks that Paris endured in the intervening years: royal assassination, civil war, an English takeover.[40] Chartier confronted this state of emergency with the language of blame. His figure of France castigates the citizens for their infighting and negligence:"Vous cognoistrez que les pluseurs de vous laissent la seigneurie dont vous estes subgiez sans defense exposee a tote fortune" [And ye shall knowe that many of yow leuyth the seigneurie to whom ye be subgittes withoute defence, exposid to all fortunes; Droz, p. 13, Blayney, p. 155]. She rails against the third estate, "le peuple veult estre en sceurté gardé et tenu franc et si est inpacient de souffrir subgection de seigneurie" [the people wolde lyve in fredom and suerte, and yet ben thei impacient to suffre the subiection of lordship; Droz, p. 14, Blayney, p. 154]. True to her name, Chartier's France was also a stern advocate for political *franchise*.[41]

In focusing on Chartier's rendition of the woman France under duress, I shall turn her around. Instead of inquiring why the kingdom and nation France was typed perennially in feminine terms, I ask: Does this royal French symbol pertain at all to the issue of women's *franchise?* Picking apart this symbol, can we find any link with the *Belle Dame*'s declaration several years later? Or any hint of other debates involving the situations of French noblewomen?

In pursuing these questions, we have to continue to account for the hierarchies of social estate. Any notion of liberty and sovereignty was reserved for a tiny segment of the population in any premodern kingdom such as France.[42] So too were debates about it. It is also important to reckon with the qualm that *la femme franc(h)e* is little more than a decorous front. Wasn't this symbol projected to sort out political issues pertaining to ruling classes composed of men alone? Clearly there are reasons why we expect this traf-

fic in feminine symbols. Marchello-Nizia's and Duby's theories about the
dame being used to attract young men to court service have trained us to
be wary of taking such symbols at face value.[43] Yet that does not discount
the possibility that the symbol was deployed otherwise. Malleable, multivalent, conflicted, *la femme franc(h)e* could also signify differently regarding
women. It is still worth considering whether the notion of a freestanding,
noncommittal state, however aristocratic, could be tested in some small
measure in relation to women's status. Was it available in contemporaneous
arguments about their empowerment or disenfranchisement?

IV

It is helpful to recognize that this was the period in the fifteenth century
when several royal propagandists in Paris were investigating the alleged *lex
salica*. The research into it was single-minded. It involved coming up with
evidence that legitimated the exclusion of women from political rule in
France. The Salic law was the statute produced to disenfranchise them from
succession and governance. As the chief commentator, Jean de Montreuil,
summed it up:

> Qui exclut et forclot femmes de tout en tout de pouoir succeder a la
> couronne de France, comme icelle loy et decret die absolument que femme
> n'ait quelconque portion dou royaume (c'est a entendre a la couronne de
> France).

> [This law and decree excludes and prevents women from any and all ability
> to succeed to the crown of France, just as it says absolutely that no part in
> the realm may pass to a woman (meaning the crown of France)][44]

For Montreuil, the determining phrase was "no part in the realm may pass
to a woman" because it authorized the barring of women from the highest form of political power.[45]

Sarah Hanley has proved that the Salic law was a complex tissue of invented and established material that took shape over the course of centuries.[46] In the early fifteenth century, its fabrication took a decisive turn.
The issue of women on the throne came to the fore again when the in-
vading English staked their claim to the French kingdom based on Salic law.
Paranoia over English designs was widespread. It fed into a flurry of forged
texts and commentaries meant to rebuff the claim, such as Montreuil's.

The question of women's rule was also caught up in arguments building between Montreuil and Christine de Pizan. Here is where we can detect a significant overlap with issues pursued by allegories in the literary

controversies of the day. As Hanley argued, Montreuil had seen his rival Christine marshal compelling evidence in her *Cité des dames* that France could boast a tradition of women rulers—queens regent, counselors. Far from being disenfranchised, Christine outlined how they intervened effectively in politics: They were "well informed in government" (II.68.3, Richards, p. 213; *avisee en gouvernement* [Curnow, vol. 2, p. 968]). History was Christine's proof. History, too, had to be Montreuil's revenge, and he went to great lengths—all the way to forgery—to prove Christine wrong in the matter of women's rule. His trumped-up version of the Salic law was intended to establish once and for all a rationale for women's political disenfranchisement.

This small connection between literary and political treatments of women's status is telling. In the contentious inner circles of Parisian intellectuals, the ongoing debates converged: What was being thrashed out in the chancellery among the king's administrators turned up in the humanist quarrels over literature. Or, the well-known debates over allegories became the testing ground for political concerns. The boundaries of the two spheres were not sacrosanct, and the players were often the same.

This convergence did not stop with Montreuil, Christine de Pizan, and their struggle over women's political status. The controversy over Alain Chartier's courtly writing was also perceived by his contemporaries as an arena in which problems of sovereignty were disputed. His name came to be associated with the phrase epitomizing the Salic prohibition of women's political authority. It cropped up in the major compilation of statutes used in early modern France, the *Institutes coustumieres:*

> Maistre Alain Chartier dict que par usage et coustume gardee de tout temps en ce royaume, toutesfois et quantes que femme est deboutee d'aucune succession, comme de fief noble, les fils qui en viennent et descendent en sont aussi forclos.

> [Master Alain Chartier decrees according to custom and common practice that are always upheld in this kingdom, that women are deprived of rights of succession, as well as rights to feudal property; their sons and all other descendants in this line are also excluded.][47]

There may be little explicit evidence in Chartier's writing that justifies attributing this decree to him.[48] But the furor over the "belle dame" helps to explain why his name carried over into the sphere of legal statutes. The woman's declaration goes to the core of the issue about autonomy. It contradicts the terms of the fraudulent Salic law. It can be seen to represent her as a worthy and rightful holder of "a part . . . in the kingdom." The controversy around the "belle dame" continued to test the force of her declaration in the *Dame leale* and the *Cruelle Femme*. These mock legalistic poems zeroed in on her public authority as a major point of contention.

What is missing in Chartier's spurious decree and in the alleged Salic law is the vocabulary of *franchise*. It does not occur. Its absence, however, does not discount its relevance. In the century-long debate over noblewomen's political disenfranchisement, *franchise* was implicit. The chain of inferences around political authority confirms this: In order to be sovereign, one must be free, and as we found in the earliest understandings of *franchise,* being free also depended largely on being noble. In early-fifteenth-century France this privileged vicious circle still held, linking sovereignty, aristocracy, and freedom.[49]

For noblewomen at court, it raised an additional problem. The fight over their sovereignty, intensified by the Salic fabrications, impinged on their political freedom. If the legitimacy of women's sovereignty was attacked, then their basic *franchise* was in jeopardy. As Montreuil and later royal propagandists such as Jean Juvenal des Ursins would have it, women were not fit for being sovereign.[50] As Christine would counter with historical arguments, they were certainly sovereign rulers.[51] Around 1425, the *Belle Dame's* declaration of *franchise* sounded politically poignant.

V

I see one way that premodern explorations of gender dealt with this barrier of disenfranchisement for noblewomen—*fiction*. It may seem banal to introduce the category of fiction at this late stage when we are working with allegories such as Chartier's *Belle Dame*. Its intricate configurations beg the question. Yet we often lose sight of the particular historical circumstances of fiction. The concept that we take for granted, the fashionable topic of humanist inquiry imported from Italy, was reintroduced into France at just this moment.[52] Parisian intellectuals were especially fascinated with fiction's transformational properties: its power to recast and change something that already exists. When I bring up fiction now, like them I am less interested in the form of fiction than in what that form enables. Here is a medium whose inventions can comment on the existing, disabling states of people. And, as we assume too, fiction invites us to speculate, what if those states were otherwise?

Because of this rediscovery of fiction, I am prompted to think through its powers in relation to noblewomen at the time. It is important to remember that both controversies around the *Rose* and the *Belle Dame* were triggered by works of fiction. Both developed in part through fiction. In the case of the *Rose* polemic, Christine de Pizan began with her *Epistre au*

dieu d'Amours and the *Dit de la rose,* where she first tried out fictively her
analysis of courtly and clerical habits of badmouthing women.[53] This allegorical letter and *dit* enabled her to critique safely a practice of defaming
women before a public of likely offenders. And this before taking to the
forum of humanist controversy. The *Belle Dame* controversy evolved *entirely*
through fiction, from Chartier's text to the later poems. In keeping with
the contemporaneous rumination over fiction, the controversy made the
particular powers of fiction explicit when it created an allegorical figure by
that name. Even more radically than in the *Rose* polemic, it directed those
powers to critiquing the conditions of women.

In a scene from the *Cruelle Femme,* the persona Fiction enters the proceedings: Truth, the counsel defending the "belle dame," complains to the
judge, the God of Love, that she has been supplanted by Fiction, who tried
to talk in her name. Faced with this imposter, the judge demands that
Truth clarify what falsehoods Fiction has committed. She reminds us how
Fiction has represented the woman who endangers everyone with her
claim: "Je suis france." (Once again, the egregious slogan is repeated.) Truth
also points out:

> Fiction dedans son procès Dist que c'estoit un decepveur, Faisant de ses yeux
> entregès, Et l'appelle faulx enformeur; C'est trop parlé a la faveur De celle
> ou n'a que cruaulté. (*Cruelle Femme,* ll. 473–78)

> [In the affair, Fiction said that the lover was a trickster, who looked daggers
> at her, and called him a false informer. That is saying too much in favor of
> that woman who is so cruel]

What is striking here is the way Fiction is aligned with the "belle dame":
With her declaration of emotional liberty, as much as with her freedom to
look at whomsoever she likes. Fiction stands as her major defender—even
when stigmatized. This scene plays one property of fiction against another.[54] On the one hand, fiction is implicated in the smear campaign
against the *femme franche.* It has to be attacked just as vehemently as does
this image of women because it is false. In other words, it is contrary to
fact. On the other hand, fiction is itself responsible for this image. It enables it authoritatively. Here is fiction's second distinctive property of
make-believe—the potential to invent compelling alternatives.

The controversy around the *Belle Dame sans merci* highlights this specific
promise of fiction. It provides a tool for surpassing limits set for women by
metaphors for law in courtly writing and by invented yet enforced statutes.
From within the framework of a trial, it responded to the quandary of political formulations that did not address women's conditions equitably.

There it could expose the limiting, damaging aspects of courtly life with impunity. It allowed for various qualities and social roles to be tried on for size. What if a woman acted on her *franchise* in public? For those debating gender, the promise offered by fiction lay in converting a "what if" hypothetical into an "as if" proposition.

This promise was already tantalizingly evident. We found it in the casuistry of Capellanus's *De amore*. There too a completely other state was projected through its double-edged talk, as if it existed in people's thoughts and emotions already. In the dialogue between nobles, for example, the woman makes clear to her male interlocutor that her free will must be respected:

> J'aim meux dont demorer em France Ou ma petite souffissance Et avoir franche volenté Qu'avoir argent a grant plenté Et demurer en Honguerie Por a autrui estre sougie. (French translation of Capellanus, Drouart La Vache, *Li Livres d'amours*)[55]

> [I prefer to remain content within France and to keep free discretion to journey at will rather than to be laden with Hungarian silver but subject to the control of another, because to have much on such terms is to have nothing; Walsh, p. 101].

The woman's *franchise* is defended masterfully. It rejects the authority of any other over it: What is coded here symbolically as any foreign power. This *franchise* is also defended playfully through the wordplay linking the woman's freedom to France. It matters. A Frenchwoman's freedom represents the kind of substantial object of make-believe that is associated with fiction.

Fiction's promise about *franchise* is significantly strengthened through the controversy around the *Belle Dame*. Not only is it reinforced through the allegorical figure that defends a woman's *franchise,* it is also realized through the landscape where that defense takes place. Most of the poems put in layers one new world upon another. In the *Cruelle Femme,* we enter first into a "fantastical state" [fantasieux estat, l. 73], which in turn provokes *ymagination* (l. 78). Then we travel to "this place of diverse thoughts made by fantasy and care" [ce lieu de diverses pensees firent fantasie et soussy, ll. 135–36]. By invoking such interlocking places, the *Belle Dame* controversy as a whole was pioneering imaginary worlds where desires for women's *franchise* could develop.

The *Belle Dame* controversy has been dismissed routinely as a literary game: amusing, absorbing, ultimately inconsequential.[56] I see this assessment as the flipside of my argument about the promise of fiction for questions of gender. What looked frivolous also offered a means by which

people could envisage themselves differently. Fiction can act as a transforming instrument. In Christine de Pizan's words, fiction transmutates.[57]
It changes the ways of evaluating people symbolically. It spurred French-
speaking audiences on to entertain the desires and social chances of
women in different and possible ways. It added impetus to the ongoing
mutation of a principle of freedom by making it imaginatively theirs. If the
concept of a free woman was ever formulated—and a French one at that—
these premodern controversies played an early part in the process.[58]

Generations later, other writers carried on the experiment with fiction's shape-changing power in relation to gender. In Bertrand de la Borderie's *L'Amye de Court* (1541), a text traditionally seen to launch the early
modern *querelle des femmes,* fiction was brought to bear again on the question of women's freedom. The court woman contends:

> La liberté estre present célestre, Que Dieu voulut esgallement offrir A tous
> vivants dont ne pouvons souffrir Qu'elle nous soit usurpée des hommes Qui
> ne sont dieux, ny riens plus que nous sommes: Car de tollir ce qu'ilz n'ont
> point donné Seroit statut assex mal ordonné Plus procedant d'injuste tyran-
> nie Que d'equité.[59]

> [Liberty is a heavenly gift that God wanted to offer to all the living equally.
> We cannot abide that it was snatched from us by men who are no more gods
> than we are. Stealing something that was never given is a statute that is badly
> established. It is unjust, tyrannical. It is hardly equitable]

Like the "belle dame," this persona argues against the double standard of
freedom in her world. Her fictive voice upholds her liberty implicitly as a
form of natural law. In so doing, it defies the validity of existing statutes.
Fiction can realize the most potent attack against inequities that are
propped up and explained away by political formulations and legal codes
of the time. It is liberating.

In ancien régime France, the dictionary of the Académie Française in
1694 cross-referenced its definition of *liberté* with that of *franchise;* this reference was intended to alert readers not only to the common understanding of the two words, but to their shared background.[60] The two "came
out of old poetry that talked about love." Fictions of premodern courtly
literature were identified as one site where an idea of freedom was entertained seriously.

Today, Drucilla Cornell continues to remind us of the strategic importance of fiction for our work in gender when she says: "There is a necessary aesthetic dimension to a feminist practice of freedom."[61] Following in
the line of Christine de Pizan and of the *Belle Dame* controversy, Cornell
understands that to embrace aesthetics, to dare to play symbolically with

what it means to be free, provides one vital way of putting freedom into action. Cornell also advocates such fictive play as an alternative to legal assurances of freedom.[62] She does not make the choice simply out of exasperation with the law or the political process in general, but out of the realization that they can never fully accommodate our ever-changing experiences of freedom. Experimenting with fiction can help.

Fictionalizing struggles around gender is not a sign of weakness. Nor is it an entertaining pastime, then or now. It is a compelling draft of what has still to be imagined and transformed about our living.

Notes

This essay has developed through the inquiring questions of participants at the Fordham Conference on the Debate on Women, Men, and Gender in March 1999. I have also benefited from the challenges of the North Carolina Research Group on Medieval and Early Modern Women; thanks go especially to Jane Burns, Meg Greer, and Ann Marie Rasmussen. When it comes to my historical thinking, I am grateful to Sarah Hanley, who is always a generous reader.

1. Alain Chartier, "La Belle Dame sans merci," *Poèmes,* ed. James Laidlaw (Paris: Union Générale d'Editions, 1988), p. 167. All translations are mine unless otherwise noted.

2. *Andreas Capellanus on Love,* ed. and tr. P. G. Walsh (London: Duckworth, 1982), pp. 102–3.

3. On the retro vision of Paris's Court of Love, see Jacqueline Cerquiglini-Toulet, *La Couleur de la mélancholie : la fréquentation des livres au XIVe siècle, 1300–1415* (Paris: Hatier, 1993), pp. 55–6. On the typecasting of the "belle dame," see Anne Berthelot, "*Le Dit de la panthère d'amour* ou la courtoisie menacée," *Francographies* 1 (1995): 251–63, and Berthelot, "*La Belle Dame sans mercy,* ou la dame qui ne voulait pas jouer," in *La Fin'amor dans la culture féodale : Actes du colloque du Centre d'Etudes Médiévales de l'Université de Picardie Jules Verne* (Greifswald: Reineke, 1994), pp. 13–21; see also William Kibler, "The Narrator as Key to Alain Chartier's *La Belle Dame sans Merci,*" *The French Review* 52.5 (April 1979): 714–23; Giuseppe E. Sansone, "*La Belle Dame sans Merci* et le langage courtois," *Le Moyen Français* 39–40–41 (1997): 513–26.

4. On this controversy, see my *Master and Minerva: Disputing Women in French Medieval Culture* (Berkeley and Los Angeles: University of California Press, 1995), pp. 176–99.

5. The number of translations proves that Chartier's *Belle Dame* quickly became a European work. The key passage in Italian runs as follows: "Ché io son franca e franca esser intendo, né del mio cuor mi vo' dispposseder" (Carlo del Nero, *La Dame sanza merzede,* ed. Giuseppe E. Sansone [Rome: Zauli Editore, 1997], ll. 291–2); and in Catalan: "Yo francha són e francha vull estar, sens lo meu cor depertir d'una fulla per fer a mi altri senyorejar"

(Francesc Oliver, ed. Martí de Riquer [Barcelona: Quaderns Crema, 1983], ll. 286–88).

6. Baudet Herenc, "Le Parlement d'amours fut tenu au jardin de plaisance contre la Belle Dame sans mercy," in *Le Jardin de Plaisance et fleur de rethorique,* facsimile of the edition published by Antoine Vérard, vers 1501 (Paris: Firmin-Didot, 1910), vol. 1, fol. 141. The poem goes under several titles, including *Les Accusations, Le Jugement,* and *Le Procès de la Belle Dame sans merci.*

7. Sir Richard Ros, "La Belle Dame sans mercy," *Chaucerian and Other Pieces,* ed. Walter W. Skeat (Oxford: Clarendon Press, 1907), p. 309. Despite an attribution in the manuscript to Ros, this translation was usually attributed to Chaucer.

8. *The Civilization of the Renaissance in Italy* (1860), authorized translation from the 15th edition, S. G. C. Middlemore (New York: Albert and Charles Boni, 1935), p. 389. This is the point of departure for the volume *Rewriting the Renaissance: The Discourses of Sexual Difference in Early Modern Europe,* eds. Margaret W. Ferguson, Maureen Quilligan, and Nancy J. Vickers (Chicago: University of Chicago Press, 1986), p. xv. The editors put it briskly into question, looking at a Venetian nun's experience and the way it illustrates "precisely women's lack of freedom" (p. xv). Equality and freedom are cited together—a sign of our revolutionary heritage, even when it comes to the case of women.

9. See Glyn Burgess's review of *franc* and *franchise* in his *Contribution à l'étude du vocabulaire pré-courtois* (Geneva: Droz, 1970), pp. 65–7.

10. *Ipomédon: poème de Hue de Rotelande,* ed. A. J. Holden (Paris: Klincksieck, 1970), p. 103.

11. See Thelma Fenster, "La *Fama,* la femme, et la dame de la Tour : Christine de Pizan et la médisance," in *Au Champs des escriptures,* ed. Eric Hicks (Paris: Champion, 2000), pp. 461–77; and Kristen Neuschel, *Word of Honor: Interpreting Noble Culture in Sixteenth-Century France* (Ithaca, N.Y.: Cornell University Press, 1989).

12. In surveying medieval texts for instances of *franchise,* I have drawn on databases of ARTFL, the University of Chicago [www.lib.chicago.edu/efts/ARTFL], as well as that of "Moyen français" at the Institut National de la Langue Française [www.inalf.cnrs.fr].

13. Jean Renart, *Le Roman de la rose ou de Guillaume de Dole,* ed. Félix Lecoy (Paris: Champion, 1977), vv. 160–1. See also *The Romance of the Rose or of Guillaume de Dole,* ed. and trans. Regina Psaki (New York: Garland Press, 1995).

14. "Guigemar," *Les Lais de Marie de France,* ed. Jean Rychner (Paris: Champion, 1966), vv. 211–12.

15. *Les Miracles de Nostre Dame par personnages,* eds. Gaston Paris and Ulysse Robert, 8 vols., SATF (Paris: Firmin-Didot, 1876–93), vol. 4 (1879), p. 254.

16. *Aucassin et Nicolette, chantefable du XIIIe siècle,* ed. Mario Roques (Paris: Champion, 1954), II, 38–41.

17. All quotations from Guillaume de Lorris and Jean de Meun, *Le Roman de la Rose,* ed. Armand Strubel (Paris: Librairie Générale Française, 1992).

18. Elizabeth Spelman, *Inessential Women: Problems of Exclusion in Feminist Thought* (Boston: Beacon Press, 1988).

19. See Catherine Brown, "*Muliebriter:* Doing Gender in the Letters of Heloise," in *Gender and Text in the Later Middle Ages,* ed. Jane Chance (Gainesville: University Press of Florida, 1996), pp. 25–51.

20. *La Vie et les epistres: Pierres Abaelart et Heloys sa fame: Traduction du XIIIe siecle* attribuee a *Jean de Meun,* ed. Eric Hicks (Paris: Champion-Slatkine, 1991), pp. 48–49. Freedom, as an absolute value for Heloise, stands in stark contrast to Christine de Pizan's notion of it. Christine remains a conservative marriage counselor. "Et entre vos, dames, qui estes mariees, n'ayés point a despit d'estre tant subgiettes a voz maris: car n'est pas aucunesfoiz le meilleur a creature d'estre franche. Et ce tesmonigne ce que l'ange de Dieu a Edras: Ceux, dist il, qui userent de leur franche voulenté churent en pechié et despirent Nostre Seigneur et deffollerent les justes; et pour ce furent peris (Christine de Pizan, *Le Livre de la Cité des dames,* ed. Maureen Cheney Curnow, Ph.D diss., Vanderbilt University, 1975, vol. 3, p. 1032) [And you ladies who are married, do not scorn being subject to your husbands, for sometimes it is not the best thing for a creature to be independent. This is attested by what the angel said to Ezra: Those, he said, who take advantage of their free will can fall into sin and despise our Lord and deceive the just, and for this perish; *The Book of the City of Women,* trans. Earl Jeffrey Richards (New York: Persea Books, 1982, p. 255)]. See also *La città delle dame,* trans. Patrizia Caraffi, ed. E. Jeffrey Richards (Milan: Luni Editrice, 1997). Even in her most gynocentric work, Christine places freedom for women within the confines of marital responsibilities and underscores women's necessary deference to their husbands as their overlords. Politically, Christine is in Aristotle's camp.

21. *Quaestiones disputatae.* De malo, q. 15, a. 3, in *Opera omnia,* ed. Vernon J. Bourke (New York: Musurgia, 1949), vol. 8, p. 387. See also Alain de Libera's discussion, *Penser au moyen âge* (Paris: Seuil, 1991), p. 208.

22. *The Riverside Chaucer,* ed. Larry D. Benson (Boston: Houghton Mifflin, 1987). This passage is reminiscent of one on de Meun's *Rose,* ll. 9407–10: "Ja de sa fame n'iert amez qui sires veust estre clamez; Car il covient amors morir quant amant veulent seignorir" [He who wants to be acclaimed sire will not be loved by his wife; When a lover wants to rule the roost, it is the death of love]. The key term again is *seignorir.*

23. *Maistre Nicole Oresme: Le Livre de Politiques d'Aristote,* ed. Albert Douglas Menut (Philadelphia, Pa.: Transactions of the American Philosophical Society 60, part 6, 1970), p. 257. Oresme also defines freedom as "la supposition de policie democratique"[the given of democratic politics], p. 257.

24. Georges Duby, "The Nobility in Medieval France," in *The Chivalrous Society,* trans. Cynthia Postan (Berkeley and Los Angeles: University of California Press, 1977), p. 96.

25. Derrida is referring here to the American Declaration of Independence, analyzing what was at stake in the act of making it and signing it. Yet he associates "this surge of self" with any founding declarative act. "Declarations of Independence," *New Political Science* 15 [1986]: 10.

26. See my commentary on Oresme's *mos actisans:* "Flaming Words: Verbal Violence and Gender in Premodern Paris," *Romanic Review* 86.2 (March 1995): 355–78; at pp. 365–66.

27. Karen Sullivan, "The Inquisitorial Origins of Literary Debate," *Romanic Review* 3 (1997): 27–51.

28. See Patricia McCune, "The Ideology of Mercy in English Literature and Law, 1200–1600," Ph.D. thesis, University of Michigan, 1989.

29. "La Cruelle Femme en Amour," ed. Arthur Piaget in "La Belle Dame et ses imitations," *Romania* 31 (1902): 322–409.

30. Marc Bloch, *Feudal Society,* vol. 1, trans. L. A. Manyon (London: Routledge & Kegan Paul, 1962), p. 255.

31. Gabrielle M. Spiegel demonstrates how the *Fais des Romains,* what she calls "a basic manual of lay culture," uses ancient Rome as a way to narrate the story of aristocratic autonomy and the history of French liberty. See *Romancing the Past: The Rise of Vernacular Historiography in Thirteenth-Century France* (Berkeley and Los Angeles: University of California Press, 1993), pp. 120, 144.

32. See Colette Beaune's review of *franc*/France in "La France et les Français," *Naissance de la nation France* (Paris: Gallimard, 1985), pp. 417–53, esp. pp. 418–29. See also *The Birth of an Ideology: Myths and Symbols of Nation in Late-Medieval France,* trans. Susan Ross Huston, ed. Fredric L. Cheyette (Berkeley and Los Angeles: University of California Press, 1991), pp. 284–92. Beaune does not consider Christine de Pizan's writing.

33. Jean Lemaire de Belges, *La Concorde des deux langages* (1510), ed. Jean Frappier (Geneva: Droz, 1947), v. 583, p. 31.

34. *Grand Dictionnaire universel du XIXe siècle (*Paris: Larousse, 1872), vol. 8, pt. 1, p. 755.

35. The turn of phrase is Beaune's, in *Naissance de la nation France,* pp. 423, 285.

36. Beaune, *Naissance de la nation France,* pp. 424–29 [*Birth of an Ideology,* pp. 288–92]; Michel Winock, "Joan of Arc," *Lieux de Mémoire,* ed. Pierre Nora (Paris: Gallimard, 1992), vol. 3, 3:675–730.

37. *Le Livre de l'Advision Cristine,* ed. Christine Reno and Liliane Dulac (Paris: Honoré Champion, 2000). There is also the edition of Mary Louis Towner (Washington, D.C.: Catholic University of America, 1932), p. 79.

38. Benjamin M. Semple points out Christine's inquiry in the *Advision* into "the liberty of thought" ("The Critique of Knowledge as Power: The Limits of Philosophy and Theology in Christine de Pizan," in *Christine de Pizan and the Categories of Difference,* ed. Marilynn Desmond [Minneapolis: University of Minnesota Press, 1998], p. 112). See also Rosalind Brown-Grant, *Christine de Pizan and the Moral Defence of Women: Reading beyond Gender* (Cambridge: Cambridge University Press, 1999), pp. 101–2.

39. Alain Chartier, *Le Quadrilogue Invectif*, ed. Eugénie Droz (Paris: Honoré Champion, 1950), p. 9; *Fifteenth-Century English Translations of Alain Chartier's Le Traité de l'Esperance and Le Quadrilogue Invectif,* ed. Margaret S. Blayney (Oxford: Oxford University Press, 1980), p. 148.

40. See Bernard Guenée, *Un Meurtre, Une Société: l'Assassinat du duc d'Orléans. 23 novembre 1407* (Paris: Gallimard, 1992).

41. Joël Blanchard, "L'Entrée du poète dans le champ politique au XVe siècle," *Annales E.S.C.* 41, no. 1 (January–February 1986), 43–61; Claude Gauvard, "Christine de Pizan et ses contemporains: L'Engagement politique des écrivains dans le royaume de France aux XIVe et XVe siècles," in *Une Femme de lettres au Moyen Age: Etudes autour de Christine de Pizan,* eds. Liliane Dulac and Bernard Ribémont (Orléans: Paradigme, 1995), pp. 105–28.

42. See the issue on sovereignty, *Annales* 51, no. 2 (March–April 1996), pp. 275–354.

43. Christiane Marchello-Nizia, "Amour courtois, société masculine et figures du pouvoir,"*Annales E.S.C.* 36 (1981): 969–82. Georges Duby, *Mâle moyen âge: de l'amour et autres essais* (Paris: Flammarion, 1988).

44. Jean de Montreuil, "Traité contre les Anglais" (ca. 1409–13), *Opera: L'Oeuvre historique et polémique,* eds. Ezio Ornato, Nicole Grévy, and Gilbery Ouy, vol. 2 (Turin: G. Giappichelli, 1975), p. 168.

45. Jean de Montreuil, "A Toute la Chevalerie" (ca. 1409–13), *Opera,* p. 132.

46. "La loi salique," *Encyclopédie politique et historique des femmes,* ed. Christine Fauré (Paris: Presses Universitaires de France, 1997), 11–30, esp. 18–20; and Sarah Hanley, "Identity Politics and Rulership in France: Female Political Place and the Fraudulent Salic Law in Christine de Pizan and Jean de Montreuil," in *Changing Identities in Early Modern France,* ed. Michael Wolfe (Durham, N. C.: Duke University Press, 1996), pp. 78–94. Hanley shows how Montreuil, working with a late-fourteenth-century manuscript of legal commentary referring to the Salic law, introduced the key phrase "Mulier vero nullam in regno habeat portionem," p. 81. See also Fanny Cosandey, *La Reine de France: Symbole et pouvoir* (Paris: Gallimard, 2000), pp. 19–54. Since Cosandey refers to the Salic law as a bona fide law, she does not fully benefit from Hanley's argument about its fabrications. Implicitly, she considers it a legal precept.

47. Antoine Loisel, *Institutes coustumieres* (Paris: Abel L'Angelier, 1611, third edition, transcription, facsimile [Mayenne: Floch, 1935], #310), p. 54.

48. Hanley argues that this is wrong: "In error Alain Chartier said that feudal law prevented women from succeeding" ("Identity Politics," p. 90).

49. See Albert Rigaudière, "L'Invention de la souveraineté," *Pouvoirs* 67 (1993).

50. "A law called the Salic law . . . and furthermore it is true according to custom and common usage maintained and observed in this realm that a woman is deprived of the right of succession, as of the right to feudal property; her sons and descendents are also deprived and prevented from succeeding; this is publicly upheld" [Une loy nomme la loy sallicque . . . et si est vray en oultre que par la coustume et usaige notoirement gardees et

observees en ce royaulme, toutesfoys que une femme est deboutee d'une succession, comme d'aucun fief, les filx qui descenent d'elle sont forcloz et deboutés; et ainsi en use l'en publicquement notoirement]; Jean Juvenal des Ursins, "Audite celi" (1435), in *Ecrits politiques de Jean Juvenal des Ursins,* ed. P. S. Lewis, vol. 1 (Paris: Klincksieck, 1978), pp. 156, 158.

51. "Parquoy, se tu veulz prendre le loysir de concorder les histoires enssemble et carculer le temps et le nombre, tu trouveras par moult long espace avoir duré royaume et la signeurie des femmes et puez notter qu'en toutes les seigneuries qui ont eu monde esté qui par l'espace d'autant de temps aient dure on ne retrouvera point plus de notables princes ne ou plus grant quentité, ne qui plus de nottables faiz ayent fait, que furent et que firent des roynes et des dames d'icelluy royaume" (*Cité des dames,* ed. Curnow, p. 700) [Therefore, if you wish to take the occasion to synchronize different historical accounts and calculate the periods and epochs, you will find this kingdom and dominion of women lasted for quite a long time (Troy), and you will be able to note that, in all the dominions which have existed in the world and which have lasted as long, one will not find more notable princes in greater numbers nor as many people who accomplished such noteworthy deeds than among the queens and ladies of this kingdom; *City of Ladies,* trans. Richards, p. 51).

52. See my discussion in "Fiction versus Defamation: The Quarrel over the *Romance of the Rose,*" *The Medieval History Journal,* 2.1 (1999): 132–39. See also Giorgio Ronconi, *Le origini delle dispute umanistiche sulla poesia (Mussato e Petrarca)* (Rome: Bulzoni, 1976).

53. See the remarks by Thelma Fenster and Mary Carpenter Erler in their edition *Poems of Cupid, God of Love: Christine de Pizan's* Epistre au dieu d'Amours *and* Dit de la Rose; *Thomas Hoccleve's* "The Letter of Cupid" (Leiden: E. J. Brill, 1990), pp. 4–5.

54. Ann Rigney, "Semantic Slides: History and the Concept of Fiction," in *The Past of History,* forthcoming. See also her *Imperfect Histories,* forthcoming from Cornell University Press. Thanks to Rigney for sharing her work with me before publication, and for stimulating discussions about it.

55. Ed. Robert Bossuat (Paris: Champion, 1926), ll. 2779–84.

56. Leonard Johnson, *Poets as Players: Theme and Variation in Late Medieval French Poetry* (Stanford, Calif.: Stanford University Press, 1990).

57. "Mais, je diray, par ficcion, le fait de la mutacion comment de femme devins homme" [I shall say, through fiction, the fact of this transformation/mutation, how it was I become a man from a woman]. *Le Livre de la Mutacion de Fortune,* ed. Suzanne Solente (Paris: A. & J. Picard, 1959), vol. 1, ll. 150–53.

58. Simone de Beauvoir, *The Second Sex,* trans. H. M. Parshley (New York: Vintage Books, 1989), pp. 714–15. Toril Moi identifies Beauvoir's thinking with freedom: "Since her most fundamental social and individual value is freedom, Beauvoir's feminism should rightly be referred to as a 'feminism

of freedom.'" *What Is a Woman? And Other Essays* (Oxford: Oxford University Press, 1999), p. 388.

59. Bertrand de la Borderie, *L'Amye de Court,* in *Le Miroir des femmes,* vol. 1, *Moralistes polémistes au XVIe siècle,* eds. Luce Guillerm, Jean-Pierre Guillerm, Laurence Hordoir, Marie-Françoise Piéjus (Lille: Presses Universitaires de Lille, 1983), p. 205.

60. For discussion of seventeenth- and eighteenth-century notions of liberty in relation to the condition of women, see Joan Wallach Scott, *Only Paradoxes to Offer: French Feminism and the Rights of Man* (Cambridge: Harvard University Press, 1996).

61. *At the Heart of Freedom: Feminism, Sex, and Equality* (Princeton, N.J.: Princeton University Press, 1998), p. 24.

62. Catharine MacKinnon is commonly seen as blind to or critical of this fictive play. Critics in the humanities often call her feminist legal theory to task for believing literally in what the law can accomplish for women. Consider this MacKinnon statement: "Given the pervasiveness of inequality, imagination is the faculty required to think in sex equality terms" ("Reflections on Sex Equality Under Law," *American Feminist Thought at Century's End,* ed. Linda S. Kauffman [Oxford: Blackwell, 1993], p. 398). In this regard, she is in agreement with Cornell, who asserts: "A sense of freedom is intimately tied to the renewal of the imagination as we come to terms with who we are and who we wish to be as sexuate beings" (*The Imaginary Domain: Abortion, Pornography and Sexual Harassment* [New York: Routledge, 1995], p. 8)

CHAPTER 8

DEBATE ABOUT WOMEN
IN TRECENTO FLORENCE

Pamela Benson

Formal defenses of woman during the Middle Ages and Renaissance were not uniform throughout Europe. Republican Florentines, reacting to courtly defenses that advanced woman's capacity to play a political role, advocated improving the practical circumstances of women's lives but did not provide the grounds for any political reform that might undermine the institution of the family.

In Florence in the Middle Ages, making the case for women in the vernacular meant entering into a debate.[1] Whereas the case *against* women often stood on its own, as in Boccaccio's notorious *Corbaccio,* the case *for* women always was presented in company with its opposite. Misogynist texts did not attempt to persuade. They presented extremes of accepted notions about women's minds and bodies, and represented common male anxieties about their own authority and dignity as female attacks on that authority and dignity; theirs was often a comic mode of exaggeration. By contrast, texts that made the case for women attempted to persuade by refuting the case against, which was always either formally present in the text or implied. Seeming to address a court disposed to regard the defendant as guilty until proven innocent, such texts offered alternate ways of reading the evidence about women and attacked the motives of the men who scorned them. This strategy offered opportunities for radical challenges to fundamental beliefs about women and thus to the organization of society based on those beliefs, but these were never realized. Woman could be proven innocent of the crimes attributed to her by misogynists when the charges themselves were shown to be false, or when her accusers could be proven to be so guilty themselves that their case deserved to be thrown out of court; both strategies only resulted in a reaffirmation of the social status quo.

The fact is that the case for women in the Florentine vernacular shifted from potentially radical to practical and conservative in the course of the fourteenth century. The case first moved from Latin into Florentine in the early days of vernacular literature in two works more or less contemporary with Dante's *Commedia*. These two early texts present arguments that have the potential to challenge woman's political inferiority. In both the anonymous *Fiore di virtù* [Flowers of Virtue], a compilation of wisdom about the practice of virtue, and Francesco da Barberino's *Reggimento e costumi di donna* [The Government and Conduct of Women], an advice book directed to parents and to women themselves, the case for women appears as part of a formal debate about womankind's essential nature and moral and social capacities. In both, the case for women undermines the notion that women are by nature men's political inferiors, although neither text is so radical as to argue that society should be made to conform to women's natural capacities. Despite the wide diffusion of the *Fiore* (the *Reggimento* seems to have circulated in a very narrow circle), no vernacular Florentine authors followed its method of defense.[2] The next author to present a formal case for women, Antonio Pucci, Florentine town crier and prolific author, transformed the defense from a theoretical one about abstract womankind to a practical one concerned in large part with the oppression of women, especially women in late Trecento Florence. His *Libro di varie storie* [Book of Various Narratives, 1362), a commonplace book, and his *Contrasto delle donne* [Dispute about Women], a freestanding debate, do not discover new capacities in women but rather urge the reform of male conduct toward women.[3] After Pucci, no Florentines contributed in Italian to the formal debate about women for another one hundred years.

This move from potentially radical to conservative to silence is surprising because it occurred at a time when the rest of Europe, or at least Latin-language Italian culture and texts in French, especially those associated with Christine de Pizan, seemed to be moving in the other direction. I suggest that the reasons for this contrary current in Florence are, first, political, attributable to Florence's intensely republican ideology; and, second, literary, for the vernacular moved away from the decorated courtly style frequent early in the century to a more popular style, and Latin saw the advent of humanism.

That women had the potential to participate effectively in social and political life beyond the boundaries of the home was not a view to appeal to late-fourteenth-century Florentines. Neither their government nor their domestic arrangements had room for female authority, perhaps because their communal government had been consciously and painfully formed in opposition to the power and the practices of local feudal noble families in which women could have considerable authority. The commune was republican and offered increasingly wide opportunities for citizen participation, but participation was exclusively male.[4] There was no way that a woman could come to power or participate in civic government, whereas under feudalism and in the court societies of northern Italy, of course, women could and did inherit power. Sentiment against the nobility strengthened in Florence in the 1370s by the commune's active engagement in an ideological and practical struggle against the increasingly powerful authoritarian single-family rule of the Visconti family of Milan, which dominated the states of northern Italy. As one scholar has said, "Florence practised government through a regime that celebrated merchant capital, banned magnates from office, and justified itself through an ideology of *libertas* and all-inclusive association. Milan subordinated all aspects of commercial, cultural, and religious life to the will of a single, military-minded ruler. . . ."[5] The classic case for women was therefore inappropriate to the concerns of mercantile, republican Florence, whereas Pucci's innovations to the strategies of defense are in keeping with the values of the city.

Anticourtly feeling in Florence is also evident in the rough, even slangy style and realistic representation of urban everyday life in much of the verse and prose written in Florence in the later Trecento. Even literature meant for the high bourgeoisie mixed elegant refinement of style with realistic detail.[6] Since the case for women was associated with the court both as a topos and in the elegant manner in which it was propounded—this courtliness is quite evident in both the *Fiore* and the *Reggimento*—it was out of step with contemporary literary life. The new literary climate accounts for Pucci's concrete style and content, but it also may account in part for the absence of successors to him; there were better ways to talk about domestic life and civic values.[7] Literary taste and pride in the republic work together to shape Pucci's conduct of the case for women and then to motivate its abandonment by vernacular writers.

At the same time that vernacular literature abandoned the case for women, Florentine humanists took it up in Latin works. Petrarch and Boccaccio introduced new genres for discourse about the role of women that made Pucci's Italian language and genres seem old-fashioned and inadequate vehicles for argument. Boccaccio invented the collection of female biographies, his *De mulieribus claris,* and Petrarch wrote a much circulated letter to the empress Anna, wife of Charles IV, in praise of women's capacity to rule. Boccaccio's substantial book had a marked effect on the manner and terms of the case for women throughout Europe, but for the reasons discussed above, his text did not stimulate Florentine Latinists, let alone vernacular writers, to develop its radical political potential. Rather, Vespasiano da Bisticci, the first author of women's biographies in Florence, adapted Boccaccio's form to Pucci's mercantile values. His *Libro delle lodi delle donne* [Book of the Praise of Women, ca. 1480) is both innovative and conservative: innovative in that it includes the lives of several living Florentine women, and conservative in that Vespasiano's praise of these women reinforces the city's traditional domestic and pious ideal of women's conduct.

The First Wave:
Barberino's *Reggimento* and the Anonymous *Fiore*

Both the *Fiore* and the *Reggimento,* the two works from the first part of the Trecento that include formal debates about women, rehearse matched pairs of arguments that had become conventional in Latin texts on the subject, and both conclude that men are superior but that both sexes are necessary. (This latter conclusion is not as self-evident as it seems, since the misogynist case frequently includes the exclamation that life would be better if men could generate young without women.) Both set the discussion of woman in the larger context of discussions of how to be virtuous; in doing so, they look forward to Renaissance defenses of women such as Castiglione's.[8] Unlike Renaissance authors, however, neither grounds his discussion of women in the actual, material world of his time. All the evidence and examples cited are drawn from biblical sources, the fathers of the church, and medieval compendia of classical authors; none come from experience or contemporary life, and no contemporary women are praised.

In the *Fiore,* defense of women is put in the context of love but in a broader context of a discussion of virtues and vices. After treating various kinds of love, such as love of God, family, friendship, passion, and brotherhood, the author includes a section defending women as objects of love:

> Perché dalle donne discende lo informamento d'amore, sono fermo d'essere loro difenditore a ciascuno che dice di loro, per ordine. E imprimamente arrecherò certe autorità di savi che hanno detto bene delle femine, e poi dirò l'autorità di coloro che n'hanno detto male; e alla fine concorderò queste autoritadi insieme e darò verace soluzione, volendo tagliare le lingue a'malvagi dicitori.[9]

> [Because the infamous reputation of this noble virtue stems in great part from women, I am determined to defend them against anyone who wants to speak badly of them. I shall therefore proceed as follows: First I shall quote the authority of certain wise men who speak kindly of women, then the au-

thority of those who speak ill. And finally I want to compare these sayings, giving a truthful declaration and absolution, cutting the vile tongue of the perverse talkers as they deserve it][10]

The wisdom in favor of women and the attack that follows are almost entirely timeless; both sides argue by assertion, simply making a claim about women and, often, citing an authority who made the assertion; they make no coherent argument and cite no examples. Both rely substantially on Solomon, though the far longer attack also cites Marsillius, Avicenna, and Socrates. The assertions in favor speak to only two topics, woman as wife and woman's *sottigliezza* [subtlety]. The case against answers without introducing any new topics. The debate about woman as wife does not offer fundamentally different views; it simply counters the good wife with the bad wife. Thus the benefits that good women bring to a marriage—happiness, honor, and offspring ("se le femine non fossono, gli uomini invecchierebbono, e perirebbe il mondo" [if there were no women, all men would grow old and the world would perish])[11]—are balanced by the disadvantages and discomforts of marriage to a bad woman: anger, untrustworthiness, iniquity.

While the topic of marriage does not challenge traditional definitions of woman and her role in any way, the second topic, woman's subtlety, has politically explosive potential. The pro-woman section asserts that women are intellectually capable: "E se le femine si dessino alle scienze e alle usanze del mondo come fanno gli uomini, s'alluminerebbono per la loro sottigliezza" [And if the women were to occupy themselves with the arts and sciences of the world as men do, they would achieve great things because of the natural subtleness of their intellect].[12] The text does not draw the logical conclusion that follows from this radical claim, namely, that culture, not woman's essential nature, has defined women's roles; if this is true, then culture can also *re*-define women's roles. The anti-woman section does not deny that women have intellectual capacity equal to men's; rather it responds with assertions that women's moral weakness makes their intellect dangerous. Women are responsible for the Fall; they use their subtlety to tempt men and will use learning to achieve bad ends. Sallust said of a woman who learned to read: "Là ov'è lo veleno del serpente s'aggiunge lo veleno dello scorpione" [The venom of the serpent is united with the venom of the scorpion].[13] This is an effective attack because it renders absurd and even dangerous the implication that woman's role ought to be reshaped to match her intellectual capacity. The radical potential that lies in asserting woman's intellectual capacity can be realized only if it is developed in company with an argument for woman's moral capacity, as later it would be in many Renaissance treatises. Since the *Fiore* puts woman's moral capacity at odds with her intellect, the political potential of the argument is not released.

These matched cases effectively neutralize each other. Some wives are good and some wives are bad; women have a quick intelligence but do not apply it for the good. The third section of the debate does not dispute this conclusion but rather presents a case against men and evokes pity for women, the mens' victims: It attacks Solomon's authority because he was seduced and acted against his own faith, and it contrasts the petty evils of women with the enormities committed by men, especially against women. The end result of confronting cases for and against women is stasis. The timeless oppression of women by men is acknowledged, but no foundation for changing the situation is developed. It seems inevitable . . .

Unless love intervenes to defend women. That is the moral of the tale concluding this section of the *Fiore*. The tale is an adaptation of the Damon and Pithias story, in which the role of Pithias is played by a woman called Pitia. Condemned to death, she asks permission to go home to settle her affairs. Her lover gives himself as a hostage to guarantee her return; against expectation, she does return, and the king, seeing their perfect love, pardons her so that such loyal lovers might not be parted. Finally, according to the reasoning of the *Fiore,* both sexes are deeply and irremediably flawed, and love is the only solution.

The *Reggimento,* by contrast, is an advice book on the education and conduct of women. It is organized as a series of solutions to problems that parents and women have, such as how much education to give a daughter, or how a woman who has passed the age appropriate for marriage and suddenly is to be married should conduct herself in the period of time before the marriage. Different solutions to the problems are offered for the different social classes; all the solutions are associated with a particular virtue, and often a novella is told to illustrate the positive results of following the author's recommendations. The book is thus seriously engaged with the topic of the moral and intellectual capacities of women, but what these are is never in doubt; throughout his discussion of the problems, the author assumes that women are capable of learning from his advice and of being good but in need of authoritative male direction.

In the *Reggimento,* furthermore, the formal debate about the nature of womankind is structurally disconnected from the serious discussion of virtue and conduct, but it supports the assumption that women can learn and be good. The debate appears late in the book following a chapter devoted to *questioni d'amore* [love debates], and is itself a courtly dialogue of the love debate type. It is presented as a display of wit, a courtly entertainment in which the "contenzioni e mottetti" spoken by a knight and his male friend on one side and a lady on the other are judged by a female character called Justice, who determines "chi netto parla e chi non sa parlare" [who speaks clearly and who does not know how to speak].[14] The dialogue illustrates how a well brought up woman should conduct herself in conversation and what opinion of her sex it is proper for her to hold; essentially, the lady asserts that women are morally superior to men but inferior to them in political and domestic hierarchies.

The dialogue has four parts. The lady opens by citing the privileges granted to women by Eve's creation inside Paradise (whereas Adam was created outside) and from the bone of man (whereas man was made from mud) and by reaffirming the reciprocal domestic and social responsibilities of the sexes.[15] The men answer by presenting a very condensed version of the conventional case against women. Their topics are: Eve as cause of the Fall; the false etymology of the word *fenmina*—"fe-men-ha" [has done less], because woman does less than any other animal; woman's need of the rule of man; and woman as deceiver of great men such as Solomon, Aristotle, Samson, David, and Absalom. The lady answers these attacks with a quibbling and confusing, though witty, discussion of woman's *sottigliezza*. She further asserts that accusations of vice are more appropriate to men than to women, but her defense depends for its success on woman's inferior social position. Women do not need strength, for they are subtle; thus lack of strength in them cannot be called a vice. But Adam, who was less subtle, is more to be blamed for listening to Eve than Eve is for listening to the serpent because he was her governor; she did less evil and so lived up to her name, *fenmina,* or "fe-men-ha." The same argument holds for all the great men deceived by women: They should have remained true to their position in the social hierarchy, for woman's subtlety is a threat only to those who fail to do so. Thus woman's subtlety, well governed by herself or by her male head, is not bad. Justice then concludes with her verdict. She rejects the misogyny of the men's attacks and the misanthropy of the woman's defense, but she confirms the hierarchy of vice that is implied by the lady's defense: Men are more full of vice than women, but women, except for Mary, are nearly as bad as men; both sexes are necessary to the world.[16] Justice's judgment underlies the careful rules of conduct for women that Barberino had developed in the earlier part of the book. Finally, like the author of the *Fiore,* he finds a way of admitting woman's intelligence and moral capacity without challenging the hierarchy of the sexes in the civic or domestic world; nor does he assert that women should have the opportunity to participate in society beyond the domestic sphere, as many Renaissance texts later claim. Nonetheless, because woman's intelligence and moral capacity are acknowledged, the potential for the radical argument is present in his text.

Pucci's Innovations:
Il Libro di varie storie and *Il Contrasto delle donne*

The potential for radical redefinition of women's political role disappears when we turn to the debates that appear in Pucci's two texts. Neither prompts readers to consider the essential moral and intellectual capacities of women nor suggests, even faintly, what they might do if given the opportunity to act in the larger world. Rather, in these two as throughout his works, Pucci "is the poet of the sobriety of family life governed by the wife," as Alberto Varvaro, modern editor of the *Libro di varie storie,* describes him, and the texts provoke discussion of domestic life as it ought to be and was at that particular moment in Florence.[17] In them Pucci defends women by evoking the indignities that they suffer at the hands of men and by praising the way women respond to their husbands' mistreatment; he represents some women as civic-minded, but this civic-mindedness takes the form of commitment to traditional Florentine domestic life. Pucci's arguments and examples suggest that the mistreatment of women harms the institution of the family, and thus harms the commune, which is founded on the family.

Pucci's *Libro di varie storie* is a commonplace book that manuscript evidence suggests was intended for public circulation;[18] in it Pucci juxtaposes an exhaustive collection of conventional anti-woman material with an equally comprehensive collection of pro-woman material. Pseudo-Theophrastus is answered by the privileges; Solomon's wisdom is attacked by ad hominem slander; Phaedra, Silla, Bathsheba, and others are matched by Judith, Mary Magdalene, Lucretia, and others; attacks on women's faithfulness are countered by examples of male guardians' pandering; and a poem against women is offset by a poem in their favor. The *Contrasto delle donne* is a long debate poem in octaves spoken alternately by two speakers, one against and one for women. Most of it is devoted to discussion of famous women, but the last few sets of stanzas discuss religious devotion, marriage, and jealousy. Three major differences set these works off from the *Fiore* and the *Reggimento* and give the debate contemporary urgency: First, the author aligns himself with the pro-woman side; second, rather than concentrating on the relative capacity for virtue of the two sexes, the debate provokes thought about social rights and the domestic situation of women; and third, whereas all the examples in the earlier texts are biblical and classical, some of the authorities, examples, and instances of customs prejudicial to women's welfare that Pucci cites are Florentine.

Both the *Libro* and the *Contrasto* at first seem to be neutral in the debate because each includes only the anti-woman case and the pro-woman case without a third, mediating voice to resolve the conflict. By way of contrast, at the end of the *Fiore* the author tells his reader to pity women but does not advise him to reformulate his notion of women's nature, and in the *Reggimento,* Justice's authoritative conclusion weighted the dialogue in favor of a middle position. Such resolutions are not necessary in Pucci's texts, however, because, despite their debate form, they both favor women.[19]

In both of Pucci's texts, the order of statements for and against makes the difference. The pro-woman case has the advantage because it comes second: In the *Libro,* the entire anti-woman side is followed by the pro-woman side, while in the *Contrasto* the voices speak alternately—the voice against begins and the voice for answers—but in both structures the speaker for woman has the last word in each phase of the debate. In the *Libro,* the case for woman is also strengthened by the insertion of the narrator's "I" only in the pro-woman section. This "I" identifies Pucci, the author, with the pro-woman position and makes it seem that gathering the anti-woman material and pondering it has led him to take up their defense; this does not, of course, necessarily mean that Pucci, the man, favored women (although the genre of commonplace book does favor the identification of the "I" with Pucci himself), but it does weight the discussion in this particular text in woman's favor. In the *Contrasto,* neither speaker can be identified with the author, since both use the first person; this text moves its reader toward sympathy with women by the way each side argues. The anti-woman case is weak—its exponent speaks nothing but clichés—and the pro-woman case is strong, as its speaker reveals the "truth" behind the anti-woman stories: Men abuse women, either violently through rape or less obviously but equally effectively through slander; women respond to the abuse with dignity, although they need a defender who will undo the effects of slander. By writing the *Contrasto* as he did, Pucci accomplished this defense.

In expressing the attitudes in the anti-woman section of the *Libro,* Pucci consistently attributes them to others or to common opinion. He represents the very long analysis of the difficulties of marriage as quoted verbatim: "Teofrasto, essendo domandato da un suo amico s'egli il consigliava ch'egli togliesse moglie o no, cosi rispuose . . ."[20] [Theophrastus, being asked by a friend if he advised him to marry or not, answered (as taken verbatim)]. Every negative platitude is assigned to another author; for example, "Terenzo disse: La femina non sa né ragione né bene né quello ch'è meglio o peggio" [Terence said: Woman knows neither reason nor good nor that which is better or worse],[21] and the numerous examples of bad women interspersed throughout the section are simply listed without comment or are attributed to unidentified sources, i.e., "Silla fu figliuola del re Niso, al quale tagliò la testa e portolla al nemico suo, di cui ella era vaga, come dett'è" [Silla was the daughter of King Niso, whose head she cut off and carried to his enemy, of whom she was enamored, as it is said].[22] The section ends with the quotation of a poem *contra le femine* that Pucci says his contemporary Buto Giovannini sent to him.

Pucci's procedure in the negative section hardly seems surprising, given that the debate about women traditionally consisted of an exchange of authorities and that commonplace books usually simply recorded material that the author found interesting. The pro-woman section, however, does away with any sense of neutrality. It begins with Pucci's own response to Buto Giovannini, in Pucci's (?) poem "La femina fa l'uom viver contento" [Woman makes man live happily], and the following prose section opens: "Non so vedere per che cagione i filosofi e gl'altri uomini si dilettano di dispregiare tanto le femine" [I do not see why philosophers and other men delight in scorning women so much].[23] Even though this pro-woman "I" also relies on "philosophers and other men" (he opens his case with the privileges), Pucci does not present the authorities dogmatically as he did in the anti-woman section but rather appeals to the reader's reason. Most of his speech is made up of examples rather than other people's assertions, and he begins almost all with an invitation to the reader to join him in reconsidering the justice of anti-woman claims. The passion of Pucci's "I" is a persuasive tool. For example, in presenting the case of Lucretia, for which he refers the reader to Livy, "I" begins, "Se vogliamo dire d'adulterio, chi'l commette più che gl'uomini? e quante donne hanno portata corona di castità?" [If we wish to speak of adultery, who commits it more than men? and how many women have worn the crown of chastity?][24] By phrasing these standard arguments in favor of women as questions rather than assertions, Pucci gives the reader the sense that the pro-woman case is obvious and that the reader himself is helping to build the case through his answers.[25]

In urging his reader to side with women, Pucci is not, however, suggesting that his reader revise his notion of what women ought to be or the roles they ought to play. Despite the reference to Livy, the above example of Lucretia does not speak of her desire that her husband take vengeance, nor does it imply that she had any political wisdom; rather Pucci stresses her modesty when she committed suicide—"imaginando il dibattersi si mise i panni tra' gambe per onestade" [anticipating her death throes, out of modesty she tucked her clothes between her legs].[26] Similarly, in citing Judith, an example that later makers of the case for women in the humanist tradition would cite as evidence of women's capacity to govern, Pucci describes her as "più forte e gagliarda che niuno uomo" [stronger and more vigorous than any man],[27] and he tells how she gave her people renewed courage when she returned with Holofernes's head, but he does not direct the reader's attention to any particular conclusion to be drawn from the example. Her story merely illustrates the claim that there have been many good women and many bad men, and this is finally the conclusion that the *Libro* urges: Pucci asks his reader to join him in holding a positive opinion of women and a more temperate one of men.

In the *Contrasto,* on the other hand, Pucci does not obviously take sides, since it is not possible to associate his own voice more with one of the dialogue's two speakers than with the other. The poem opens with the anti-woman speaker vowing to offer proof of women's *malizia* [malice] if only someone will come forward in their defense.[28] The second speaker volunteers to defend not women, but the truth. Each speaker has exactly the same number of lines as the other; the final stanza is shared between the two of them and is inconclusive; neither gives in and they go off for a glass of wine.

The two "I"s in the *Contrasto* alternately vie for the reader's assent to their arguments. In the first sixty-two stanzas, they offer different interpretations of the actions of famous women. Whereas the traditional way of arguing for women by example was to counter a list of men deceived by women with an attack against male foolishness, a defense of woman's subtlety, or an alternative list of women, all of them good (we saw some of these strategies at work in the *Reggimento*), in the *Contrasto* the speaker for women offers no new examples; rather, he responds to each example of a woman's bad behavior with a reinterpretation, finding positive motives in even the worst conduct.

This strategy is not consistently persuasive. Sometimes the "anti" speaker seems foolish and the "pro" one wise, as when Judith is condemned because she did the "devilish" deed of betraying Holofernes by cutting off his head while he slept, and she is defended on the grounds that she did it to put an end to the war and made it possible for her people to rout the enemy (stanzas 11, 12). Sometimes the anti speaker makes a good point and is answered with short-sighted ingenuity by the pro speaker, as when Salome is condemned for having the Baptist's head cut off and is defended as simply having been obedient to her mother (shifting the blame to the mother hardly works as a defense of women) and as having acted against an enemy of her faith—Christian readers did not usually side with Jews against Christians (stanzas 15, 16). Sometimes the pro speaker challenges the status quo quite radically, as when he answers the attack against Livia for leaving her husband Nero in order to marry Octavian by arguing that, according to the Old Testament, men were free to leave their wives and the same standard ought to be applied to Livia's case. Sometimes the anti case is quite strong and the pro defense only strengthens it, as when the attack on Phaedra is answered by the assertion that she acted out of passion. Given the mixed strength and weakness of arguments on both sides, it is quite possible that a reader could have finished reading the famous-woman section of the *Contrasto* without being filled with admiration for women. The likely conclusion at this point in the dialogue is that of the *Fiore,* the *Reggimento,* and Pucci's own *Libro:* Women are neither all good nor all bad. This very moderately positive view of women is not accompanied by any praise of woman's subtlety (or intelligence) or of their capacity for political virtue, so that as in the *Libro,* there is no implication that the reader should revise his notion of women's essential nature. Even the example of Judith does not show women's capacity to govern, but merely their ability to act unselfishly for the civic good in a crisis, and most of the exemplary women are used to frame the defense in domestic and sexual terms: Livia should have been granted the right to divorce; Salome was obedient to her mother; Lucretia was raped. This pro-woman strategy focuses discussion on domestic life and on women's suffering at the hands of men; it constitutes the second major difference between Pucci's two contributions to the debate and the *Fiore* and *Reggimento.*

The domestic topic is developed explicitly in the final section of the *Contrasto.* After a brief debate in which the privileges of woman are invoked, the speakers present opposing views of women's and men's conduct in church and in the home. They each sketch tiny dramatic vignettes of typical scenes from everyday life and analyze the causes of domestic strife. Many of the topics are derived from the passages in Pseudo-Theophrastus that Pucci translated in the *Libro,* but both speakers use details that make even perennial topics, such as women's more frequent attendance at church, their gossiping in church, and husbands' lack of control of their wives seem contemporary and local. The pro-woman voice's objections bring up two issues that were of special concern in Florence in the second half of the fourteenth century, namely, sumptuary laws and domestic slavery, making the *Contrasto* particularly relevant to a Florentine audience.

None of the anti speaker's attacks arouse the pro speaker to defend women by assigning new rights or capacities to them. Most often the attacks on women lead to criticism of men for having behaved in a way that leads to female misconduct and endangers the institution of the family. For example, a comical depiction of women in church, complete with a few scraps of overheard conversation, provides the pro speaker with the opportunity to criticize husbands for laxity:

> Elle van ben co'paternostri in mano
> E fanno d'adorar molti sembianti,
> Ma quando in chiesa si trovan di piano
> Poco ragionan di Dio e di santi;
> Ma: "le galline mie non beccan grano":
> Dolgonsi delle balie e delle fanti,
> E qual dice: "così mi fe' la gatta:
> E quest'è l'orazion ch'è da lor fatta.[29]

[Indeed, they go there with their prayer books in hand / And make the appearance of praying, / But when they find themselves in church by plan / They talk little of God and the saints; / But: "My hens are not pecking the grain": / They complain about nurses and servant boys, / And one says: "Look what the cat did to me": / And this is the prayer that they recite]

Just as he did not deny that the famous women did what the anti speaker said they did, here the pro speaker does not refute the verisimilitude of the anti speaker's scene painting; rather, he rejects the notion that women's bad or ungoverned behavior results from their corrupt nature. In his stanza, he blames it instead on husbands' failure to play their traditional roles properly:

Che maraviglia è questa, che ciascuno
Par che diletti le donne spregiare,
E quasi poi non si truova nïuno
Ch'a la sua non si lasci cavalcare?[30]

[What marvel is this, since everyone / Appears to delight in disdaining women, / Yet one finds almost no one / Who doesn't let his wife ride him?]

This defense by assertion of male domestic authority delegates the responsibility for women's behavior to men, who ought to be able to govern them better. Similarly, in the next set of stanzas, in answer to the anti speaker's traditional Pseudo-Theophrastan assertion that husbands have to buy their wives' obedience with money, i.e., material goods that please them, the pro speaker again turns the tables on men by discovering a contradiction in male behavior. He asserts that wives want to dress in a way that will raise their social status, and men like to have their wives look beautiful for this purpose, but then beat them if their beauty turns heads.

In both of these examples, the speaker for women attacks men for behavior that damages the institution of the family. If husbands kept control in their households, women would not waste their time gossiping in church. If husbands valued their wives' efforts to advance them by dressing well, they would not make their homes miserable by physically abusing their wives and turning them into enemies. The kind of reform that he is urging with these criticisms of men would benefit women only by making their lives peaceful; they would not in any way prepare for a change in women's social role.

The failure to properly govern the home, wife beating, and jealousy were by no means solely Florentine issues—any sensible late medieval man living in a commune would have been sensitive to the paramount importance of the home to his economic as well as his emotional well-being—but Pucci's use of the Florentine vernacular in the poem makes it seem that he is talking about Florence in particular; he speaks quite literally in the voice of a Florentine. The late-fourteenth-century Florentine character of the dialogue becomes even clearer when the topics of women's clothing (in the stanza just discussed) and slavery (in a later stanza) arise. Pucci's handling of these issues is exemplary of the way the *Contrasto* localizes the debate about women, the third difference between Pucci's works and those of the beginning of the century.

The moral complaint about women's finery goes back to Theophrastus, but in Trecento Florence objections were also made to it on economic grounds (competition among women wasted money), and sumptuary laws were repeatedly passed.[31] In stanza 72, Pucci's pro-woman speaker calls attention to the hypocrisy of blaming this extravagance of dress on women alone. He attributes women's desire for fine clothes to social ambition ("per esser il messere"[to be a fine lady]) but he also claims that husbands' social and economic ambitions make them desire fine clothes for their wives: "Ognun mercenaio/Vuol bella donna" [Every man involved with goods for sale/Wants a beautiful woman]. He points out the self-defeating foolishness of the husband who gets the desired attention for his wife and then reacts with jealousy: "Poi s'ell'è guatata/ Per gelosia la batte ogni fiata" [And then if she is looked at/He beats her out of jealousy every time].[32] The word *mercenaio* calls attention to the husband's errors. Though it may merely mean "merchant," it is not the customary word for merchant, and its unusualness calls attention to its root—*merce* [merchandise]. It suggests that this man thinks of his wife as merely a neutral counter in an economic game; he can use her to display his wealth and, thought wealthy by others, he can perhaps accumulate even more. These lines may also suggest the husband's similarity to a pimp: He dresses his wife in a way that he thinks advertises his wealth, but when her finery is read as advertising a kind of commerce in which he does not want to engage, he beats her instead of dressing her more modestly.

Like women's clothing, domestic slavery, the pro-woman speaker's final example of the abuse of wives, was a topic of particular relevance in Florence at the very time Pucci wrote. The holding of non-Christian slaves became widespread throughout the Italian peninsula during the second half of the fourteenth century, and the slave trade was legalized in Florence in 1363.[33] Domestic slavery benefited the Florentine merchant classes, who were Pucci's audience, by permitting them to circumvent the problem of the high wages caused by the Black Death and to trim their household budgets, though the illegitimate children it produced led to economic strain.[34] Pucci's pro-woman speaker represents this as a short-sighted economy because it wastes the most valuable resource of the family, the husband and wife's fertility.

The pro speaker raises the issue of slavery in answer to the anti speaker's assertion that an unfaithful wife deserves to be beaten about the head by her husband. In stanza 74 he says:

Che dirà tu, di chi l'à buona e bella
E tienla a capital men d'una fava?
Anzi la tratta siccome fancella,
E giacesi da parte con la schiava?

[What will you say of the man / Who has a good and beautiful wife / And supports her with capital worth less than a bean? / Rather, he treats her like a servant girl, / And lies apart with the slave girl?]

These lines cut against the husband in two ways: By sleeping with his slave he drives his wife to turn to other men for sexual satisfaction and thus makes it likely that the child of another man will be born into his family; and by sleeping with his slave, he wastes his own seed, which should be used for producing a legitimate heir.

The use of the words *capital* [capital] and *fava* [bean] are particularly telling in the Florentine merchant context. The economic term "capital" evokes the economic basis of the married sexual relationship: The wife should be a good that is used to produce other goods, that is, children. The bean, *fava,* was (and is) a staple of the Florentine diet, cheap and available to all social classes. It was not a commodity with which to feed the woman on whom a secure economic future for the family depended. The reference to capital may also bring up thoughts of the dowry that the wife brought to the marriage; this dowry was supposed to be used to support her, and the husband's stinginess was depriving her of what was rightfully hers. The marriage alliance itself was an investment—a wasted investment in the case of the man who dallied with his slave because his mistreatment of his wife, both the beating about the head and the neglect of her body, would raise the resentment of her natal family and negate the positive economic and social effects of a marriage alliance. The husband who sleeps with his slave is no wiser financially than the husband who dolls his wife up in order to advance himself and then gets jealous when she attracts attention.[35]

Although it does not mention slavery, the *Libro* also evokes contemporary Florentine social debate. The poem that begins the pro-woman section, the poem that Pucci attributes to himself, praises women by praising wives and criticizing husbands who abuse them. In it, Pucci stirs up sympathy for women by representing the difficulties that their subservient position in married life creates for them, and antipathy for men by

representing the ways in which their mistreatment of their wives undermines the values of family and commune. But the poem never questions
the rightness of the wife's subservient position; women's right to decent
treatment, not women's right to new status, is the topic of the poem.

> La femina fa l'uom viver contento;
> gl'uomini senza lor niente sanno.
> Trista la casa dove non ne stanno,
> però che senza lor vi si fa stento.
> Per ognuna ch'è rea ne son cento
> che con gran pregio di virtude vanno;
> e quando son vestite di bel panno
> nostr'è l'onore e lor l'addornamento.
>
> Ma gl'uomini le tengon pur con busse,
> e senza colpa ognun par che si muova
> a bestemmiar chi 'n casa gliel condusse.
>
> Tal vuol gran dota che non val tre uova,
> e po' si pente ch'a ciò si ridusse
> e tanto le vuol ben quant'ell'è nuova.
> Perché di lor mi giova,
> Contr'a chi mal ne dice, senza fallo,
> difender vo'le a piede e a cavallo.[36]

[Woman makes man live happily; / men without them know nothing
(pleasant). / The house where there are no women is sad, / since without
them there they suffer economic difficulties. / For every bad one there are
one hundred good ones / who go about highly esteemed for virtue; /and
when they are dressed in beautiful clothes / ours is the honor and theirs the
adornment

But yet men keep them with blows / and without guilt everyone seems moved
/ to curse whoever brought her into his house. / That one wants a huge dowry
who isn't worth three eggs, / and then regrets that he reduced himself to accepting that / and loves her only in proportion to her newness to him

This is why it pleases me, / against whoever speaks badly of them, without
their fault / to defend them on foot and on horseback]

Topics familiar from the *Contrasto* are the role wives play in preventing the
extinction of families (3–4), the injustice of wife beating (9), the bad citi-
zenship of male dissatisfaction (here Pucci says it divides them from their
own family and its allies by making them ungrateful to those who

arranged their marriages [10–11]), and women's wearing of fine clothing (7–8). Unlike the *Contrasto,* however, in this poem the issue of fine clothing is presented from an unambiguously positive viewpoint. Worn by a good woman, finery could have a positive effect on that quality most essential to Florentine merchant well-being, *onore* (honor).[37] The use of the word *onore* here suggests that the woman gains prestige for her husband and does not awaken in him the anxiety that he will be made a cuckold that Pucci attributes to the jealous, mercenary husband in the *Contrasto.* Correctly used by both wife and husband, female adornment is a good thing. A good husband, Pucci suggests, can recognize the contributions that a wife makes to the continuance and reputation of his family, but men generally are incapable of appreciating their wives.

While an intelligent husband gains honor by the way he governs his wife's dress, Pucci suggests that most men lose it in their marriages by not maintaining supremacy, by beating their wives, by cursing those who arranged the marriage, and especially by demanding a dowry out of proportion to their deserts and then not valuing the wife who brought it. The dowry was deeply connected with the notion of honor in late Trecento Florence. It was considered essential that the money and goods a father gave with his daughter be adequate to the prestige of the house she was entering. A good dowry was expected to have a positive effect on the woman's future, since a "handsome dowry enhanced the wife's position in the house of her husband and in-laws."[38] Pucci mocks men who are overly ambitious in their pursuit of large dowries and do not appreciate what they get and the obligations it puts them under ("That one wants a huge dowry who isn't worth three eggs himself, / and then regrets that he reduced himself to accepting that / and loves her only in proportion to her newness to him"). This husband is guilty both of overreaching and of dishonoring his wife. His behavior is deeply antisocial.

By announcing himself as women's champion at the end of this poem— he will defend women on foot and horseback—Pucci makes the Florentine married woman the particular object of his protection. The rest of the defense in the *Libro* does not address issues of particular relevance to Florence, but the poem would probably have prepared a Florentine reader to apply its lessons to his own situation, and this inclination would have been increased by Pucci's frequent use of Florentine authors in both the anti and the pro sections; not only does the poem by the Florentine Buto Giovannini end the anti section, but the pro section includes evidence from "il sommo poeta Dante."

Alternatives to the Vernacular Case for Women

Although Pucci's citation of contemporary authors who were identified with Florence and who were familiar to his readers may suggest that the debate about women had been taken over by Florentines and become local, Pucci was the only fourteenth-century vernacular Florentine writer after the *Fiore* and the *Reggimento* to write a case for women. This is not to say that praise of women was neglected in the period, but it was presented either in genres distinct from the debate or in Latin. The vernacular genres were used to flatter important merchant and banking families by means of the praise of named, living female members of their families, and the Latin ones flattered important noblewomen by means of dedications and compliments within the texts. The former shared the mercantile values of Pucci's debates without their critique of merchant practices; the latter shared the courtly values of the *Fiore* and *Reggimento*.

Pucci himself wrote an excellent example of a vernacular encomium of Florentine women, his sirventese (a poetic composition of four-line interlinked stanzas, frequently a list) "in memory of the beautiful women who were in Florence in 1335."[39] This list of twenty-eight living women of the best families identifies them by their given names and their houses (Peruzi, Albizi, Medici, Altoviti, etc.), notes their husbands' admiration and loyalty to them, and praises them in flowery terms for their beauty, refinement and "French manners" (ll. 46–7), honor, etc. For example:

> Degli Ubaldin monna Giovanna è fiume
> D'ogni bellezza e d'ogni bel costume:
> Con Cambio Bonamichi in un volume
> Fa dimora.[40]

> [Mistress Giovanna of the Ubaldin is a stream / Of every beauty and of all lovely behavior: / With Cambio Bonamichi in a single volume / She makes her residence]

Although this list could be analyzed to discover the qualities attributed to good women, a task always undertaken by literature in the debate tradition, this sirventese does not present such an analysis. Similarly, Franco Sacchetti's *Battaglia delle belle donne di Firenze con le vecchie* [Battle between the Beautiful and the Old Ladies of Florence] uses jeweled language to describe the beauty and virtue of the young women. Their fathers' and husbands' names are included, represented as at war with a group of allegorically named old women. Further, novella 137 in Sacchetti's collection *Il Trecentonovelle* [The Three Hundred Tales] describes the clever ways that particular Florentine women evaded the sumptuary laws.[41] These texts confirm mercantile values as did Pucci's two debate texts and they also offer their own novelty in their use of the names of living women, but none of them engages in the theorizing that characterizes the debate more formally.

By contrast, Petrarch's and Boccaccio's contributions to the discussion of women, written at just the time Pucci was writing his *Libro* and *Contrasto,* make major contributions to theory. They develop the potential of the case for women to challenge traditional notions of women's inferior intelligence and capacity for political action that was nascent in the *Reggimento* and the *Fiore,* and they also develop the association of the case with court culture. Quickly imitated in Latin and in vernaculars outside Florence, they were ignored in Florence for a century.

Petrarch's letter to "Ad Annam imperatricem" [To the empress Anna] and Andrea da Pisa's close imitation of it (1425), addressed to Filippo Maria Visconti, duke of Milan, were both written to console rulers when their first-born child was a girl rather than a boy.[42] Both begin with a brief general defense of women. They cite the arguments that Christ was born of a woman and that all men, among them kings, are born of woman; then they provide a list of women whose wit, wisdom, valor, deeds, and knowledge of how to govern show the nobility and fame of the female sex, to paraphrase Petrarch.[43] Both briefly celebrate the deeds of women such as Minerva, Sappho, Camilla, and even Semiramis (for dominating much of Asia). Petrarch also praises the eleventh-century Countess Matilda of Tuscany.

In their praise of women's wit these two letters present a notion of woman that can be said to derive from potential present in the *Reggimento* and the *Fiore,* in which woman's subtlety is defended to a very limited extent. But these epistles' celebration of women for their literary works, their military triumphs, and their government of states goes far beyond any conception of woman's role accepted in the *Reggimento* or *Fiore,* and the entire notion of women expressed in the letters is alien to Pucci's text and to his Florentine mercantile audience. This new attitude formed the basis of Renaissance court profeminism, and it encouraged the provision of education to women.

Boccaccio's *De mulieribus claris* was also dedicated to a courtly patron, Andrea Acciaiuoli, who, though a Florentine, married into Neapolitan nobility. The book does not so clearly offer a defense of women, of course. Not only does Boccaccio make no formal arguments in favor of women, but he is ambivalent on the subject of women's goodness and natural potential for wit, wisdom, valor, and so forth. Yet Boccaccio's doubts do not prevent him from demonstrating, through example after example, that women can play the political and social roles of the kind that Petrarch forecast for Anna's baby girl.

The book's form and ideas were quickly influential in France in the works of Christine de Pizan and, from the mid-fifteenth century onward, in the courts of northern Italy; but Boccaccio's first follower in the Florentine vernacular, Vespasiano da Bisticci in his *Il Libro delle lodi delle donne* (ca. 1480), remained in the tradition established by Pucci. Vespasiano borrowed Boccaccio's form without Boccaccio's ideas. After a brief defense of Eve and women in general and a great many biographical sketches of women from the Old and New Testaments and of Christian saints, Vespasiano briefly sketches the lives of a number of Italian women worthy of praise, including several living Florentine women from merchant and banking families. They are praised for the Florentine virtues of thrift, loyalty to family interests, and educating their children in religion, but not for the learning or even for the management of family business interests that other sources tell us characterized some of them. Vespasiano's book does not challenge the traditional gendering of activities as did the *Fiore, Reggimento, De mulieribus claris,* and "Ad Annam imperatricem." Rather, Vespasiano follows the line laid out by Pucci. Just as Pucci employed the mode of defense to express a mercantile perspective on women's social role and virtues, Vespasiano's book employs the genre of biography to express the same ethos. The *Libro delle lodi delle donne* demonstrates that the mercantile and still-republican audience of late Quattrocento Florence remained true to the notion of woman and her role that Pucci defended a century earlier, even when directly exposed to a radical alternative. This fidelity suggests that in the late Middle Ages and early Renaissance, the mode of defense of women had more to do with the place in which the defense was written, the audience to which it was directed, and the preexisting roles that women played than with a politically motivated desire to advance the cause of women or reform political structures.

Notes

1. I have taken the term "the case for women" from Alcuin Blamires, *The Case for Women in Medieval Culture* (for reference, see Introduction to this volume). He defines the 'case' as "a corpus of ideas about how to fashion a commendation of women explicitly or implicitly retaliating against misogyny" and as "an affirmative profile of women." He often uses the term to avoid the modern feminist connotations of such terms as "profeminist" and "protofeminist," and I have adopted it for that reason. I am not sure whether Blamires would agree with my sense that the ideas from the "corpus" could be deployed selectively to shape very different individual cases that would still be recognizable as part of the larger topos because of their conventionality.

2. On the wide diffusion of the *Fiore,* see Nicholas Fersin, trans., *The Florentine Fior di Virtu of 1491* (Library of Congress, 1953), p. vii. The case for women was probably widely known throughout the century through its inclusion in sermons, written along the lines laid out by Humbert de Romans, master general of the Dominican order, 1254–63. In "Ad Omnes

Mulieres" [To Women in General], sermon xciv, Humbert cites the privileges and says: "Haec autem omnia movere debent mulieres ad Dei dilectionem, qui haec contulit eis, et retrahere ab eis quae mala sunt, et ad sectandum, quae bona sunt in muliere, et ejus amore" (Carla Casagrande, ed., *Prediche alle donne del secolo XIII: Testi di Umberto da Romans, Gilberto da Tournai, Stefano di Borbone* [Milan: Bompiani, 1997], p. 44) [All of this ought to encourage women to love the God who gave them all this, and to pursue for love of him all that is good in a woman; it should also deter them from all that is evil *(Early Dominicans: Selected Writings,* ed. Simon Tugwell, O.P., Classics of Western Spirituality [New York: Paulist Press, 1982], p. 330).

3. For the date of the *Libro,* see Antonio Pucci, *Libro di varie storie,* ed. Alberto Varvaro, Atti della Accademia di scienze, lettere e arti di Palermo, 4th series 16.2 (1957), pp. 54–5.

4. On the "democratization of the polis" in the second half of the fourteenth century, see Marvin Becker, *Florence in Transition,* vol. 2, *Studies in the Rise of the Territorial State* (Baltimore, Md.: Johns Hopkins, 1968), p. 49; for the association of this greater democratization with a movement away from aristocratic forms and concerns in literature, see pp. 49–55.

5. David Wallace, *Chaucerian Polity: Absolutist Lineages and Associational Forms in England and Italy* (Stanford, Calif.: Stanford University Press, 1997), p. 10. For a useful explanation of the Florentine/Milanese competition in the latter fourteenth century, see pp. 9–65. On Florentine republicanism, anti-magnate feeling, the importance of civic commitment, and the concept of liberty, see also Becker pp. 55–61.

6. On these aspects of the style of Pucci's younger contemporary Sacchetti, see Antonio Lanza, *Primi secoli: saggi di letteratura italiana antica* (Rome: Archivio Guido Izzi, 1991), pp. 139–72.

7. An extended examination of Boccaccio's *Corbaccio* is beyond the scope of this paper, but it seems to me that it could be very profitably considered in this context. It not only excoriates women primarily through calling attention to their physicality and materialism but it also attacks the literary elevation of them in courtly literature. It is surprising that the *Corbaccio,* which seems to have been widely circulated, did not stimulate defenses of women as did the similar *Araignment of Lewde, idle, froward, and unconstant Women* did in the early seventeenth century in England; on the Swetnam controversy, see Linda Woodbridge, *Women and the English Renaissance* (Urbana: University of Illinois Press, 1984).

8. On the Renaissance case for women, see my *The Invention of the Renaissance Woman: The Challenge of Female Independence in the Literature and Thought of Italy and England* (University Park: Pennsylvania State University Press, 1992), and Constance Jordan, *Renaissance Feminism: Literary Texts and Political Models* (Ithaca, N.Y.: Cornell University Press, 1990).

9. Agenore Gelli, *Fiore di virtù, testo di lingua ridotto a corretta lezione,* 2nd ed. (Florence: Le Monnier, 1856), p. 18.

10. Fersin, *The Florentine Fior di Virtu of 1491,* p. 15. Although the printed text that Fersin translated differs at some places from the printed transcription of the manuscript that I used, it does not differ significantly in any of the passages I have quoted.

11. *Fior,* p. 16; and *Fiore,* p. 19.

12. *Fior,* p. 16; *Fiore,* p. 19.

13. *Fior,* p. 16–17; *Fiore,* p. 20.

14. Francesco da Barberino, *Reggimento e costumi di donna,* 2nd ed. rev., ed. Giuseppe E. Sansone (Rome: Zauli, 1995), p. 213.

15. For the privileges, see Blamires, pp. 96–112.

16. Barberino, pp. 213–14.

17. Antonio Pucci, *Libro di varie storie,* p. 64.

18. Pucci, *Libro,* pp. 55–58.

19. Here I differ with Varvaro, editor of the *Libro.* He sees "open juxtapositions" that refer the decision to the reader, but he does not support this assertion with analysis; p. 62.

20. Antonio Pucci, *Libro di varie storie,* p. 298. All translations from the *Libro* are mine.

21. *Libro,* p. 214.

22. *Libro,* p. 213.

23. *Libro,* p. 218.

24. Pucci, *Libro,* p. 219.

25. I take Pucci's intended reader to be male because all the antifeminist authorities being refuted are male and because woman is always referred to as "lei" [she] or "la femina" [woman]. Nothing invites a woman's point of view.

26. *Libro,* p. 220.

27. *Libro,* p. 219.

28. Antonio Pucci, *Il contrasto delle donne,* ed. Antonio Pace (Menasha, Wis.: George Banta, 1944), 1.3. All translations are mine.

29. Pucci, *Contrasto,* stanza 69.

30. Pucci, *Contrasto,* stanza 70.

31. For the text of sumptuary statutes passed in Florence in 1355 and 1356, around the time of the *Contrasto,* see the appendix to Giovanni Boccaccio, *The Corbaccio,* ed. and trans. Anthony K. Cassell (Urbana: University of Illinois Press, 1975), pp. 153–64.

32. *Contrasto,* stanza 72.

33. For a brief account of slavery in Florence, see John Larner, *Italy in the Age of Dante and Petrarch, 1216–1380* (London and New York: Longman, 1980), pp. 199–200; for an extended account, see Iris Origo, "The Domestic Enemy: Eastern Slaves in Tuscany in the 14th and 15th Centuries," *Speculum* 30 (1955): 321–66.

34. The former interpretation is Larner's; for the latter, see Christiane Klapisch-Zuber, *Women, Family, and Ritual in Renaissance Italy,* trans. Lydia G. Cochrane (Chicago and London: University of Chicago Press, 1987), p. 104.

35. Pucci seems to have been especially interested in the challenge female domestic slaves posed to Florentine values and institutions. His poem "Le schiave hanno vantaggio in ciascun atto" [Slaves have the advantage in every act] argues that slave women have the advantage over married women because married women have to buy their husbands (by giving them a dowry), yet slaves satisfy their own sexual appetites better than wives do; though slaves work harder, they eat better; if slaves break something, they are scolded less than "una fiorentina." The poem ends, "Uccida la contina/que' che 'n Firenze prima le condusse,/ché si può dir che la città distrusse" [May continual fever kill/ whoever first brought slavewomen to Florence,/because it can be said that he destroyed the city]; see G. Corsi, ed., *Rimatori del Trecento* (Turin: UTET, 1969), p. 812.

36. *Libro,* pp. 217–18.

37. For a definintion of "honor" and its role in Florentine marriage, see Julius Kirshner, *Pursuing Honor While Avoiding Sin: The Monte delle Doti of Florence* (Milan: Dott. A. Giuffre: 1978), pp. 5–7.

38. Ibid., p. 15.

39. Antonio Pucci, "Per ricordo de le bele done ch'erano in Firenze nel MCCCXXXV," in *La poesia popolare in Antonio Pucci,* ed. Ferruccio Ferri (Bologna: Libreria L. Beltrami, 1909), pp. 255–60.

40. Lines 81–84.

41. Franco Sacchetti, *La Battaglia delle belle donne di Firenze,* ed. Sara Esposito (Rome: Zauli, 1996), and Franco Sacchetti, *Le Trecentonovelle,* ed. Emilio Faccioli (Turin: Einaudi, 1970).

42. Francesco Petrarca, *Le Familiari,* 21.8, ed. Vittorio Rossi, vol. 4, ed. Umberto Bosco (Florence: Edizione Nazionale delle opere di Francesco Petrarca, 1942), pp. 61–8, and Francesco Flamini, "Due Canzoni di Andrea da Pisa d'argomento storico," *Giornale storico della letteratura italiana* 15 (1890): 238–50.

43. "Adde quod nec partu tantum, sed ingenio et virtute multiplici et rebus gestis et regni gloria sexus est nobilis" (Petrarca, *Le Familiari,* p. 62).

CHAPTER 9

A WOMAN'S PLACE: VISUALIZING THE FEMININE IDEAL IN THE COURTS AND COMMUNES OF RENAISSANCE ITALY

Margaret Franklin

In fifteenth-century Italy, at a time when secular and ecclesiastical authorities saw women only as virgins, wives, and mothers, certain visual representations celebrated women's heroism, leadership, and even military prowess. Two cycles that include donne illustri *[famous women]—that by Andrea del Castagno for a politically prominent Tuscan patron, and the other by Ercole de'Roberti for Eleonora d'Este, duchess of Ferrara—depict idealized femininity in dramatically divergent ways.*

In the fifteenth century, representations of female worthies from classical and biblical lore began to appear in the visual art of Italy. These legendary women were celebrated for possessing such virtues as patriotic heroism, the capacity for shrewd leadership, and even military prowess.[1] Yet their presence in Renaissance art remains problematic and even paradoxical, as they were created in an age when many secular and ecclesiastical authorities defined the roles of women strictly in terms of their obligations as virgin, wife, and mother. Two cycles in particular of *uomini famosi/donne illustri* [famous men and women], one painted by Andrea del Castagno for a politically prominent Tuscan patron and the other by Ercole de'Roberti for Eleonora d'Este, duchess of Ferrara, diverge dramatically in their manner of depicting idealized femininity. Their differences are evidence of a significant mismatch between the political systems under which they were produced and the role played by women in those systems. They are also important reminders that the debate regarding female virtue was not confined to the written word but was manifested visually by prominent Quattrocento artists and patrons.

The destinies of women in Quattrocento Italy were largely determined by the social milieu into which they were born. From the sermons of popular ecclesiastics and the treatises of secular moralists to the preserved letters of scarcely literate wives communicating with the aid of scribes, it becomes clear that in fifteenth-century Tuscan republics, a woman's responsibilities included not only the management of her husband's home but also the upholding of personal characteristics traditionally valued in females. Contemporary humanists drew heavily on the Aristotelian model of fundamental differences between the sexes, which translated into prescribed and essentially immutable differences in the virtues, conduct, and lifestyles of men and women.[2] In his *Trattato del governo della famiglia,* written in the early Quattrocento, the Florentine scholar D'Agnolo Pandolfini includes in his index of wifely duties the observation of decorum, modesty, and silence.[3] Francesco Barbaro, writing in Florence in 1416, advanced similar views in his *De re uxoria,* where he too related the crucial feminine virtue of modesty to the necessity for domestic seclusion, and considered that a woman's inborn deficiencies rendered her capable only of looking after her husband's possessions.[4] The notion that women "are almost all timid by nature, soft, and slow" led Leon Battista Alberti to continue to promulgate the view that a woman's sphere was properly "in the house, among the women," where they were "more useful when they sit still and watch over our things."[5]

While the autonomy of women living in Italian republics was negligible, those who were born into the ruling families of the northern Italian courts enjoyed an independence that allowed them to participate substantially in the *vita activa.* The position of female consorts in these courts seems to have undergone a perceptible evolution as these fledgling principalities coalesced throughout the fifteenth century into dynastic strongholds.[6] Having adopted a strategy of equating the right to rule with prescribed bloodlines, daughters born into the ruling families of Quattrocento courts usually married into other princely families and were provided with both an education and the expectation that they would use that education to promote the interests of their dynasties.[7] Whereas women living in Tuscan republics were denied legal involvement in the governance of their communes, a duchess or marchesa was expected to act as an ambassador for her husband and assume his authority when he was indisposed or unavailable.

Images of Famous Women
in a Tuscan Portrait Cycle

One extant mid-Quattrocento Italian *uomini famosi/donne illustri* cycle of near-life-size portraits was painted by Andrea Castagno for the Villa Carducci in Legnaia, just outside Florence (fig. 1). The purpose of *uomini famosi* cycles in the Renaissance was to create a bond between viewer and image in order that those representatives of humanity who were acknowledged to possess qualities worthy of emulation might exert a lasting influence on those who lived and worked in their presence.[8] Castagno's cycle was painted on the long wall of a rectangular hall that faced an open loggia where families and their guests could linger while enjoying companionship, conversation, and fresh air.[9] This would also have been the setting for gatherings of the Florentine elite, including intellectuals who would have been familiar with the worthies chosen for inclusion in this cycle.

The figures painted for the Villa Carducci include three Italian poets (Boccaccio, Dante, and Petrarch) in the company of three Florentine military leaders (Pippo Spano, Farinata degli Uberti, and Niccolò Acciaiuoli) and three women: the Cumaean sibyl, Esther, and Tomyris. The *tituli* painted beneath the poets simply identify them by name; those accompanying the military men and the women are more descriptive. The men, all of Florentine origin, appear to have been selected in accordance with the tradition of glorifying the commune through the celebration of native sons noted for their accomplishments in *scienza e armi*: Pippo Spano is identified as *relator victorie theutocarum* [conqueror of the Turks], Farinata as *suae patrie liberator* [liberator of his country], and Niccolò Acciaiuoli as *neapoletani regni dispensator* [administrator for the Neapolitan kings]. The Cumaean sibyl, secondarily famous for defending her virginity against all suitors, is identified by an inscription that reads *Sibilla Cumana que prophetavit adventum Christi* [the one who prophesied the coming of Christ]; Esther, the biblical heroine who married King Ahasuerus of Persia and successfully foiled a scheme to eradicate the Jews in his kingdom, is the *gentis sue liberatrix* [liberator of her people]; and Tomyris, the queen of Scythia who defeated the Persian army of King Cyrus, has a *titulus* that reads *vindicavit se de filio et patriam liberavit suam* [revenged herself in relation to her son and freed her country]. Many scholars have noted that the figures represented in the Villa Carducci cycle support an overriding theme of civic responsibility; each can be viewed as an example of one who employed either might or wit to champion the cause of the people.[10]

A clue to the role played by Castagno's women in the Villa Carducci cycle may lie in the manner in which they are represented relative to their male counterparts. The descriptive *tituli* seem to suggest that the actions

1. Andrea del Castagno, *Uomini famosi/donne illustri* cycle from the Villa Carducci, 1449–51, Galleria degli Uffizi, Florence

performed by the nine illustrious exemplars were not governed by gender-specific restrictions; however, the body language of these figures tells a different story. In this context the Renaissance concepts of *gagliardia* and *leggiadrìa* become relevant. The term *gagliardo* relates to actions that, according to Renaissance conduct manuals, are appropriately performed only by men; *leggiadrìa,* as defined by the mid-Cinquecento writer Agnolo Firenzuola, is suitable for ladies and characterized by "grace, modesty, gentleness, measure, and elegance in such a way that no movement, no action, shall be without moderation . . . but ordered, composed, regulated, gracious . . ."[11] In constructing the ideal *donna di palazzo* [female courtier], Castiglione emphasizes that

> . . . a woman should in no way resemble a man as regards her ways, manners, words, gestures and bearing. Thus just as it is very fitting that a man should display a certain robust and sturdy manliness, so it is well for a woman to have a certain soft and delicate tenderness . . . [which] always makes her appear a woman, without any resemblance to a man.[12]

When confronted with the military figures included in the Villa Carducci cycle, the viewer is immediately struck by the way the men appear to move

RA VINDICAVIT SE DEFILIO ETPATRIAM LIBERAVIT SVAM

2. Andrea del Castagno, *Queen Tomyris*, 1449–51, Galleria degli Uffizi, Florence

outward from their niches into the real space of the room. The stance Pippo Spano assumes is aggressively *gagliardo;* firmly planted with legs widespread, his challenging expression unites with his uncompromising stance to exude an impression of raw masculinity. His chest, arms, legs, and feet clearly project forward of the pilasters that delineate the width of his fictive space, as do the hands that grip both ends of his sword. Farinata degli Uberti's manner is also *gagliardo;* although he appears less combative, his elbow pierces the picture plane to protrude decisively into the viewer's space. Farinata leans his sheathed sword outward so that it partially obscures a painted pilaster, and, indeed, his tall hat precludes all possibility of his ever having been confined in his allotted space. Even Niccolò Acciaiuoli thrusts his baton into the room, again protruding in front of the illusionist architecture that ostensibly delimits his section of the wall and casting a shadow with a foot that barely rests on the ledge. The perceived impossibility of restraining these men corporally enhances the impression of their zealous heroism.

Turning to Tomyris, the presumed female equivalent of these bold men, we see that the *titulus,* which conjures up images no less virile than "conqueror of the Turks" or "liberator of his country" is confounded by Castagno's graceful image (fig. 2). Although she is clad in armor, Tomyris's sleeveless dress obscures all but the elaborate mail on her arms. Her regal bearing is softened by the way in which she catches up her skirt below the hip, revealing a petticoat that falls to her ankles. The Scythian queen, who not only decapitated her dead enemy but had his head submerged in the blood of her fallen son and soldiers, gently holds a spear by the end of its wooden shaft; the one finger crooked over the tip renders her grasp impotent and nonthreatening. The point of her lance is grounded on the ledge in an exhibition of pacific intent. Except for two points of her golden crown and the toes of one foot, Tomyris remains placidly confined with the architectural framework of her niche. Had *each* figure thus conformed to his or her circumscribed area, it may rightly have been assumed that the relationship between figure and allotted space was neither a reflection of character nor an agent of differentiation. As it is, the need to break free of their boundaries is clearly a component of the virtue for which the men are being honored; we must therefore assume that Tomyris's willingness to be confined is no less an aspect of what makes her both admirable and capable of being imitated.

While the figures of the poets are markedly less *gagliardo* than those of their military compatriots, they too gesture in such a way as to negate the boundary between fictive and real space. Dante breaks the picture plane with a decisively extended arm, while Petrarch's hand and cloak and Boccaccio's ample sleeve project forward of their painted marble frames. Petrarch's left

3. Andrea del Castagno, *The Cumaean Sibyl*, 1449–51, Galleria degli Uffizi, Florence

heel is lifted well off the ground, as if he were preparing to take a step forward. Comparing these figures with their female counterpart, who also holds a book, we find that the Cumaean sibyl betrays neither the preoccupation nor the frenzy that had characteristically been employed to identify this pagan seer as a conduit of divine revelation in the Middle Ages (fig. 3). This is not the aged, wily prophetess who confronted a Roman tyrant, but a woman whose extraordinary beauty belies the legend that she lived to be centuries old. In pointing heavenward, her arm not only bends in correspondence with her painted border but stays close to her body, effectively avoiding a motion that might correspond in assertiveness to those made by the other writers. Like Tomyris, she is restricted to the space within the architectural perimeter of her niche, with only the hint of a forearm, the toes of one foot and the small gold ball of her crown projecting from her designated space. Finally, while Esther's arms move more freely as her right hand reaches out over the ledge, the effect of cutting off her portrait just below the waist in this *sopraporta* painting is to visually entrap her in a small area from which she is powerless to emerge.[13]

The most parsimonious explanation for the inclusion of women in the Villa Carducci cycle is that portraits of notable women served essentially the same function as that of notable men: as paragons of virtues that their viewers would find personally desirable. As wife, widow, and virgin, respectively, the "masculine" deeds accomplished by these three women were underpinned by their adherence to the sexual behavior appropriate to their status. Even as Esther came to Ahasuerus a pure maiden, she remained a faithful wife; Tomyris never remarried after the death of her husband, letting her actions be guided both by maternal devotion and the desire to safeguard his interests; and the Cumaean sibyl spurned even the advances of Apollo in order to protect her virginity. Each of these heroines is portrayed in Castagno's cycle as appealingly feminine and decorous, in the manner required of honorable Tuscan women.

It is clearly for the qualities with which men could identify and to which men should aspire, however, that these three women were integrated into the Villa Carducci program. Castagno's *tituli* make no reference to their chastity, but focus instead on those achievements that equate their actions with those of the illustrious men. Although these heroines meet the requirements of sexual propriety necessary for representation in a family home prepared to cater to female guests, it is their deeds accomplished in spheres of traditionally masculine endeavor that are immortalized in the writing beneath their images. By draining the assertiveness and cunning from the Cumaean sibyl, the daring and shrewdness from Esther, and the aggression and vindictiveness from Tomyris, Castagno has succeeded in dividing their lives into that which is masculine and therefore rightly emulated by men, and that which is feminine and therefore imitable by women. These figures are mannequins whose inclusion in a man's world required the same superficially decorous facade demanded of contemporary women. Chosen because of their enterprising engagement in political affairs, these heroines are nonetheless as confined to their painted niches as Tuscan patrician women were to their homes. Ideological notions about equality of virtue that may be suggested by their *tituli* are not supported by their images.

Eleonora d'Este's *donne illustri*

In 1473 Eleonora, daughter of King Ferdinand of Naples, arrived in Ferrara to marry the duke, Ercole d'Este. Along with her substantial dowry, Eleonora brought to Ferrara a prestigious link with a prominent ruling family that served to elevate the smaller principality's diplomatic position with respect to other political powers. The woman who was a princess before she became a duchess relinquished neither the air nor the trappings of authority.[14] Eleonora remained, throughout her twenty years as duchess, one of the duke's closest advisers, and as the wife of the acknowledged incumbent of a hereditary rulership, the power she assumed when ruling in his stead became as absolute as the power he himself enjoyed. According to Jacopo Foresti, a contemporary compiler of the biographies of *donne illustri,* "her husband recognized the intelligence and wondrous prudence of his young wife and soon entrusted her with most of the administrative duties of the country, especially because he was often gone from home on military campaigns; she assumed these duties until her death."[15]

A *donne illustri* cycle that Eleonora commissioned ca. 1486–90 has been convincingly attributed to Ercole de'Roberti, the official Ferrarese court painter from the mid-1480s until his death in 1496.[16] The manner in which these wooden panels were originally meant to be displayed is uncertain, but the argument that they were commissioned by and executed for the Este family is supported by a 1624 inventory in which one of the paintings is documented as being in the collection of Cardinal Alessandro d'Este.[17] Although markedly smaller than those portraits painted by Castagno for the Villa Carducci cycle, the shallow-stage format employed by Ercole resembles that commonly utilized in *uomini famosi* cycles.

The women depicted in this series include, first, Portia, the wife of Junius Brutus, who was famed for wounding herself in order to demonstrate her support for her husband's plot against the life of Julius Caesar and for ultimately committing suicide upon hearing of her husband's death (fig. 4); second, Lucretia, whose suicide following sexual violation at the hands of Sextus Tarquinius led to restoration of republican rule in Rome (fig. 5); and, finally, the unnamed wife of Hasdrubal, who plunged with her children into the fiery ruins of Carthage in order to escape the indignities they would be likely to suffer at the hands of Scipio Aemilianus and his conquering Romans (fig. 6). The Ferrarese paintings incorporate more narrative elements than do portraits deriving from series of famous men—most notably the inclusion of key witnesses to the message of heroism being delivered: Brutus, mouth turned down in a solemn frown, listens to Portia's explanation for the bloody gash on her foot. Junius Brutus and Collatinus both gaze mournfully but impotently at Lucretia as she calmly raises a dagger toward her breast. The wife of Hasdrubal is frozen in the act of running over fragments of ruined architecture, apparently shouting at the two children who resist her attempts to drag them into the flames.

The episode chosen from the life of Portia is not that of her suicide, which hinged on the slaying of a ruler. Rather, she is celebrated for displaying a determination and strength of character comparable to Brutus's own; she has made a statement in support both of her husband *and* his political agenda. Visually, the figure of Portia defies the many standards of acceptable female decorum elegantly illustrated by Castagno at the Villa Carducci; her pose is strikingly *gagliardo* in its unguarded assertiveness. She stands in a fully frontal contrapposto pose with her arms to the side and outstretched toward the viewer. Her hands are held open, her palms almost breaking through the picture plane into the beholder's space. With this gesture Portia invites the spectator to gaze at her body, most particularly the slightly raised and bared foot, with its bloody wound. Further, her mouth is open; she is not only revealing her actions in a remarkably forthright manner, she has broken a decorous silence, so valued in fifteenth-century women, in order to explain her actions to her husband. The decisive nature of Portia's actions is emphasized by contrast with the lugubrious and apparently immobilized Brutus.

Ercole's depiction of the wife of Hasdrubal is also markedly lacking in decorum: Shown in the act of fleeing, she thrusts her elbows out in an attempt to control her small children. Her manner is aggressive: She grips the unwilling infants (one is actually attempting to push her hand away while the other staggers backward) and opens her mouth wide in exhortation. Ignoring the dictates of Castiglione and his fellow prescribers of female conduct who insisted that aristocratic women were not to engage in vigorous activity, the wife of Hasdrubal rushes forward, legs apart, her drapery fluttering and raised well above the ankle. She has sacrificed what was surely her customary stateliness in order to escape a far more dishonorable indignity. In creating "masculinized" portrayals of Portia and the wife of Hasdrubal, Ercole has shunned the strategy employed by Castagno of dividing masculine and feminine attributes. His women instead convey

4. Ercole de'Roberti (c. 1456–1496), *Portia and Brutus*, c. 1490 (19–3/16" x 13–1/2"). Courtesy of the Kimbell Art Museum, Fort Worth, Texas

5. Ercole de'Roberti, *Lucretia, Brutus and Collatinus*, c. 1486–90, Galleria Estense, Modena, Italy.

6. Ercole de'Roberti, *The Wife of Hasdrubal and Her Children*, c. 1486–90 (18–1/2"
x 12"). Alisa Mellon Bruce Fund. Photograph © Board of Trustees, National
Gallery of Art, Washington

courage, loyalty, daring, and indifference to physical harm in depictions that call attention to these very characteristics; to an unprecedented extent, these representations are freed from more conventional gender-based restrictions. The elimination of this type of visual incongruity evident in Castagno appears to challenge the very notion of natural distinctions between the virtues of men and women.

Although representations centering on the fomenting of plebeian revolt would have been anathema in the court of the Este dukes, by capturing Lucretia in the instant before she has actually committed her violent deed, Ercole has redirected the emphasis away from the subsequent actions of others and also from her own weakened condition, to focus instead on the strength of her determination. Lucretia stands erect and motionless, and although her relative calm appears somewhat incongruous with the animated appearance of both Portia and the wife of Hasdrubal, her staid demeanor is perhaps dictated by the circumstances under which her heroism was demonstrated; as one who had already been sexually violated, it would have been important to quell any suggestion that a lack of decorum was in any way responsible.

In Ercole's work we witness the visual manifestation of a late-fifteenth-century ideology propounded by a handful of writers in the northern Italian courts that argued for the equality and even superiority of females.[18] His women were conceptualized, by both patron and artist, as paragons of *virtù*—indistinguishable in type between the sexes—with which a woman dedicated to being an honorable wife and mother and a just and pious leader could identify. The conjoining of personal integrity and political loyalty renders images of Portia, Lucretia, and the wife of Hasdrubal singularly apt models for the consort of a ruling prince.[19] In identifying herself with these women, Eleonora could acknowledge visually her obligation to maintain the trust and respect of both her husband and his people; she adheres to conventional dictates of female morality and takes active measures to prove her allegiance, even in adversity, to the realm she helped to govern.

Evidence provided in this study suggests that in fifteenth-century Italy the functional significance and manner of representing women celebrated primarily for their participation in the public arena were tied to the extent to which women participated in the *vita activa*. The task of assimilating unconventional but exemplary women into a genre depicting illustrious role models appears to have been substantially guided by an imperative to support the established social order. In the Tuscan republics, this necessitated dichotomizing representations of women famous for their embodiment of both masculine and feminine virtue such that those virtues "rightfully" belonging to each gender could be distinguished. In the Villa Carducci cycle, where heroic women are represented in the company of men who share their celebrated attributes, the solution to visually differentiating between the sexes in a way that would conform to traditional gender expectations lay in creating a conventionally decorous female image and surrounding her with the trappings of masculine virtue. The incorporation of certain antique heroines as visual exemplars in Quattrocento Tuscan art was not likely to compromise the established social order as long as they upheld those virtues expected of contemporary women and were represented in ways that essentially conformed to prevailing notions of female decorum. In Ferrara, paintings of women whose heroism was associated with both personal valor and political allegiance were executed in the circle of a duchess who, due to her position as both wife and daughter of ruling princes, could identify with the necessity of exhibiting virtues for whom the distinction between masculine and feminine was irrelevant. A court artist such as Ercole de'Roberti was therefore able to conjoin the bodies, minds, and spirits of assertively honorable women to create rational images that were free to talk, scream, run, and bleed.

Notes

1. In most cases heroines depicted in Renaissance art were selected independently of the medieval literary tradition of the *Neufs Preuses* [Nine Worthy Women] that developed in the interest of preserving the memory of pre-Christian luminaries. For the only known cycle that did come from this tradition, see Paolo D'Ancona, "Gli Affreschi del Castello di Manta nel Saluzzese," *L'Arte* 8 (1905): 94–106, 183–98.

2. Aristotle's assertions that the male is "better and more divine in [his] nature than the material on which he works [the female]" and that "the woman is as it were an impotent male" led him to postulate fundamental differences in character and fueled the late medieval and Renaissance notion that the unequal distribution of familial, social, and political authority between men and women was the logical consequence of inborn differences. For Aristotle, see for example *Generation of Animals,* 4.1, 765b1 and 1.20, 728a1; and *Politics* 1.13, 1260a1 in *The Complete Works of Aristotle: The Revised Oxford Translation,* ed. Jonathan Barnes, Bollingen Series 71 (Princeton, N.J.: Princeton University Press, 1984), pp. 1184, 1130, and 1999. For Aristotle's influence on thinking about women in the Middle Ages and Renaissance, see for example Joan Cadden, *The Meanings of Sex Difference in the Middle Ages: Medicine, Science, and Culture* (Cambridge: Cambridge University Press, 1993), and Ian Maclean, *The Renaissance Notion of Woman* (Cambridge: Cambridge University Press, 1980).

3. D'Agnolo Pandolfini, *Trattato del governo della famiglia colla vita del medesimo scritta da Vespasiano da Bisticci* (Milan: Società tipografica de'classici italiani, 1802).

4. Francesco Barbaro, *De re uxoria,* in *La letteratura italiana: storia e testi* 13 (1952); for English translation, see Barbaro, *De re uxoria* (London: John Leigh and Thomas Burrell, 1677).

5. See for example Book Three of Leon Battista Alberti's *I libri della famiglia,* ed. Ruggiero Romano and Alberto Tenenti (Turin: Giulio Einaudi, 1969).

6. For an overview of the princely courts in Quattrocento Italy, see Sergio Bertelli, Franco Cardini, and Elvira Garbero Zorzi, *The Courts of the Italian Renaissance* (New York: Facts on File, 1986), p. 66; see also Bram Kempers, *Painting, Power and Patronage,* trans. Beverley Jackson (New York: Penguin Books USA, 1992), pp. 219–41; and Lauro Martines, *Power and Imagination* (New York: Knopf, 1976), pp. 218–40.

7. For several documented examples see Cecil H. Clough, "Wives and Daughters of the Montefeltro: Outstanding Bluestockings of the Quattrocento," *Renaissance Studies* 10.1 (March 1966): 31–55; at pp. 39–44.

8. Portrait cycles representing both historical and contemporary luminaries enhanced facades and chambers of both public and private buildings in the fifteenth century; see for example Maria Monica Donato, "Famosi cives: testi, frammenti e cicli perduti a Firenze fra tre e quattrocento," *Ricerche di storia dell'arte* 30 (1986): 27–42

9. The nine frescoes were transferred to plaster ground in 1954 and are now in the Uffizi, Florence.

10. For a different interpretation that links this cycle to a fourteenth-century preaching treatise, see Josephine Dunn, "Andrea del Castagno's Famous Women: One Sibyl and Two Queens," *Zeitschrift für Kunstgeschichte* 58.3 (1995): 359–80.

11. As defined by the mid-Cinquecento writer Agnolo Firenzuola, *Dialogo delle bellezze delle donne* in *Opera scelte,* ed. Giuseppe Fatini (Turin: Giulio Einaudi, 1957, rpt. 1966), pp. 509–10. For a discussion of *gagliardia* and *leggiadrìa* as they relate to Renaissance portraiture, see Rona Goffen, "Lotto's Lucretia," *Renaissance Quarterly* 52.3 (autumn 1999): 742–81; see also Sharon Fermor, "Movement and Gender in Sixteenth-Century Painting," in *The Body Imaged: The Human Form and Visual Culture Since the Renaissance,* ed. Kathleen Adler and Marcia Pointon (Cambridge: Cambridge University Press, 1993), pp. 129–45.

12. " . . . ma sopra tutto parmi che nei modi, manieré, parole, gesti e portamenti suoi, debba la donna essere molto dissimile dall'omo; perché come ad esso conviene mostrar una certa virilità soda e ferma, cosí alla donna sta ben aver una tenerezza molle e delicata . . . che nell'andar e stare e dir ciò che si voglia sempre la faccia parer donna, senza similitudine alcuna d'omo." Baldesar Castiglione, *Il libro del cortegiano,* ed. Giulio Preti (Turin: Giulio Einaudi, 1969), p. 251. For translation, see *The Book of the Courtier,* ed. George Bull (London: Penguin, 1976), p. 211.

13. For Renaissance iconography of Esther, see Cristelle L. Baskins, "Typology, Sexuality, and the Renaissance Esther," in *Sexuality and Gender in Early*

Modern Europe, ed. James Grantham Turner (Cambridge: Cambridge University Press, 1993), pp. 31–55.

14. See Werner L. Gundersheimer, "Women, Learning, and Power: Eleonora of Aragon and the Court of Ferrara," in *Beyond Their Sex: Learned Women of the European Past,* ed. Patricia H. Labalme (New York: New York University Press, 1980), pp. 43–65.

15. Jacopo Filippo Foresti da Bergamo, *De plurimis claris selectisque mulieribus* (Ferrara, 1497), CLXXVII.

16. For this series, see Denise Allen and Luke Syson, "Ercole de'Roberti. The Renaissance in Ferrara," in *The Burlington Magazine* 141 (April 1999): xxxii–xxxv; Ruth Wilkins Sullivan, "Three Ferrarese Panels on the Theme of 'Death Rather than Dishonour' and the Neapolitan Connection," *Zeitschrift für Kunstgeschichte* 57 (1994): 601–25; and Joseph Manca, *The Art of Ercole de'Roberti* (Cambridge: Cambridge University Press, 1992), pp. 133–39. For earlier attributions, see Manca, *Ercole de'Roberti,* pp. 132–36.

17. See Manca, *Ercole de'Roberti,* p. 135. The three paintings each measure approximately 47 x 35 cm.

18. For an analysis of these attitudes, which represent a striking deviation from the traditional assessment of female virtue, see Pamela Benson, *The Invention of the Renaissance Woman* (University Park: Pennsylvania State University Press, 1992).

19. Sullivan, "Three Ferrarese Panels," has suggested that the theme of this *donne illustri* series is "death over dishonor," deriving from the *imprese* of Eleonora's father, King Ferrante of Naples. In 1465 Ferrante created the Order of the Ermine, which incorporated his personal motto, *malo mori, quam foedari* [I prefer to die rather than to be defiled].

CHAPTER 10

"DECEITFUL SECTS":
THE DEBATE ABOUT WOMEN
IN THE AGE OF ISABEL THE CATHOLIC

Barbara F. Weissberger

In the debate about women during the reign of Isabel the Catholic of Spain
(1475–1504), queenship shaped the debate as much as cultural circumstances
did. Isabel's unprecedented female sovereignty complicated the ways in which
her queenly power used, and was used by, religious, ethnic, and sexual discourses of the time. The often intertwined antisemitic, misogynist, and homo-
phobic discourses of debate literature patronized by or addressed to Isabel
articulate anxieties about the queen's profoundly patriarchal agenda.

Female monarchs have been influential in promoting and shaping the
Iberian debate about women from its inception. In Spain,[1] one of the
debate's foundational works is *Coplas de las calidades de las donas,* composed
in the middle of the fifteenth century by the Aragonese courtier Pere Torrellas.[2] The *Maldezir de mugeres,* as it came to be called, had an immediate
impact in the court of Juan II and his consort Queen María of Aragón.[3]
Torrellas's truculently misogynist poem elicited rebuttals and endorsements
from dozens of Castilian and Aragonese court poets for well over half a
century. Tradition has it that the anti-Torrellas poets, the defenders of
women, were responding to a call from Queen María herself.[4] Although
there seems to be no documentary evidence for the claim other than relevant works dedicated to her, the very fact that queenship and gender issues are linked in this way in fifteenth-century Spain bears a closer look,

especially since there are no debate texts in Spain known to have been written by women. As Louise Fradenburg has observed, sovereignty does not exist apart from constructions of gender; rather it is a means of perpetuating and transforming those constructions: "Sovereignty is a site of gender-transgression and crossover, although it does not necessarily follow that sovereignty has revolutionary designs on gender constructs."[5] In fact, as we shall see, the opposite can be true, with a queen promoting "reactionary" or traditional gender constructs even as she violates gender roles.

I am concerned here with this paradoxical phenomenon and with its effects on the gender-debate tradition in the reign of a far more powerful sovereign than María of Aragón: Queen Isabel I of Castile, known as Isabel the Catholic. Isabel acceded to the disputed throne of Castile in 1474 upon the death of her half-brother Enrique IV; she ruled until 1504. In my regicentric approach to the debate in late medieval Spain I shall maintain that the presence of a powerful female sovereign shapes the conventions of the debate and complicates its production of a seamless gender ideology. In the case of a queen regnant like Isabel (in contrast to a queen consort), the most fundamental site of gender-transgression, to use Fradenburg's term, is the gender of the monarch herself. The rule of a woman inevitably created anxiety, confusion, and resistance in a patriarchal society grounded in the theological subordination of women to men. As we shall see, the form and function of the debate about gender in Isabelline Spain responds to the anomalous power of a female sovereign.

In my forthcoming book I analyze in depth the various ways in which Isabel's complex and contradictory fashioning by writers associated directly or indirectly with her court helped to allay her subjects' fears of being dominated by a woman, especially by one whose political agenda was so intensely masculinist.[6] The construction of "Isabel" by her subjects illustrates another of Fradenburg's observations on the "plasticity of gender in the field of sovereignty." In other words, the enactment of multiple, transgressive gender roles paradoxically combined with the exemplification of a perfectly ordered "masculinity" or "femininity" allows the sovereign's subjects to negotiate apparently contradictory needs. The requirement that the sovereign be different from her/his subjects, "extraordinary, excessive, dangerous," coexists and conflicts with the need that she/he be the same, "ordinary, proper, law-abiding."[7] Representations of queenship in texts written during her reign—whether directly or indirectly associated with Isabel herself—frequently transgress the borders of the feminine within the traditional binary opposition of "feminine" and "masculine," but they just as frequently police that border. Thus when Isabel appears in the chronicles, courtly lyrics, political treatises, and satirical verse written by her male subjects she is alternately and sometimes simultaneously (as in the poem by

Antón de Montoro discussed below) portrayed as both active and passive, dominant and submissive, harsh and forgiving, feared and loved. Ultimately, however, the contradictory aspects of Isabel's discursive fashioning serve a profoundly patriarchal program of political and social reform grounded in hierarchical, heteronormative gender roles and relations, as well as in the exclusion of religious and racial minorities.

Increasing concern for religious, racial, and sexual "purity" in the Isabelline period affects the debate about gender in Spain in ways that set it apart from its manifestations in northern Europe. Many believed that Isabel had undertaken a providential mission to restore a society that was chaotic, decadent, feminized, and orientalized to its former ordered, masculine, Christian/European vigor before the Muslim conquest of the peninsula in 711. Because the program of nation-building in the Isabelline period involved the increasing marginalization or exclusion of Jews, Muslims, and the converts from those religions to Catholicism, a fully historicized regicentric analysis of the gender debate must take into account the intersection of gender with categories of race, ethnicity, and religion. This interrelationship holds particular relevance for Iberian society, shaped as it was by eight centuries of coexistence and conflict among three cultures: Muslim, Jewish, and Christian. For reasons too complicated to recount here, the question of the place of Jews and *conversos* (Jewish converts to Catholicism) in the nascent Spanish identity became one of the most pressing of Isabel's reign. The "black legend" about Spain, propagated by the northern European Protestant countries that competed with Iberia in the age of expansion, singled out the Inquisition as the shameful institution responsible for the surveillance and prosecution of real or invented crypto-Judaism. In this essay, however, I am more concerned with discursive anti-Semitism, and in particular, the wide variety of late-fifteenth-century texts that demonize through feminization.[8] In Spain as in the rest of early modern Europe, the body and blood of the Jews (and of *conversos,* since they were believed to bear still the taint of their ethnicity) were considered both polluted and polluting.[9] Because the misogynists represent women in similar fashion, the discourse of anti-Semitism and the discourse of misogyny are often conjoined and mutually reinforcing.[10] As we shall see, the conjunction plays a central role in the articulation of and resistance to the absolute power of the woman who furthered the idea of a nation purified by the exclusion of contaminating others.

This complex intersection of queenship, gender, sexuality, race, and genre will be analyzed here by focusing on three very different Isabelline texts that have direct or indirect ties to the debate about women. The first is a verse panegyric (ca. 1474) addressed directly to Isabel by Antón de Montoro, a clothier who depended for his livelihood on the ostentation of the queen's courtiers, and who accrued status (and ridicule) among them for his poetry. The second is a prose romance by Juan de Flores, one of Isabel's official chroniclers and trusted administrators. Flores's *Grisel y Mirabella* (published in 1495) contains a dramatization of a gender debate featuring the archmisogynist Torrellas himself and a powerful queen who takes revenge on him for his crimes against women. The third text is an anonymous pornographic poem (published in 1514) that stages a mock-debate between male and female genitalia and relates the outcome to the excessive power of female sovereigns. All three illustrate the impact of Isabel's gender and patriarchal politics on the binary opposition that structures the debate genre and that the debate also articulates and contains. One could in fact argue that the very structure of the debate form, with its comfortingly clear binary opposition of man versus woman, attracted Isabelline male writers seeking to contain the "ideological dissonance"[11] generated by their monarch, or, conversely, to exploit that dissonance for their own purposes. In the three specific cases studied here, the purpose is to resist the female sovereign's "masculine" power.

A brief overview of the historical context is necessary to situate the texts I will discuss. The circumstances surrounding the succession to the Castilian throne in 1474 meant that Isabel had to marry early.[12] A dynastic crisis caused by the putative illegitimacy of her predecessor's heir, Juana de Castilla, made it imperative for Isabel to produce a legitimate, preferably male, heir. She promptly did so, choosing Fernando V of Aragón while she was still a princess, marrying him in 1469, against King Enrique IV's mandate, and producing five heirs, a male (Juan, b. 1478) among them. Marriage and motherhood helped to alleviate the disturbance in the cultural field caused by her power. Nevertheless, many of her subjects fully expected her to function as consort to Fernando. They were sorely disappointed.[13] From the moment of her crowning Isabel ensured that Fernando's rights of governance over Castile would be restricted, and that continued to be the case even after Fernando inherited the kingdom of Aragón in 1479.

The twenty-five years of Isabel's joint rule with Fernando of Aragón constitute a critical moment in Iberian history, for her rule laid the foundations for the world empire that Spain would acquire under the queen's grandson, Charles V. During their reign Isabel and Fernando forged a delicate but lasting union between their two proprietary kingdoms and then supported that union with a series of bold political measures that had a profound and lasting effect on Spanish society. In their program of centralization and expansion of monarchic authority, Isabel's Castile, demographically and economically stronger than Aragón, led the way. Within the span of seventeen years, from 1475 to the *annus mirabilus* of 1492, Isabel dramatically transformed the contractual and pluralistic government maintained by her predecessors, her father Juan II (1406–1454) and her half-brother Enrique IV (1454–1474). She first defeated Enrique's daughter Juana de Castilla, her rival for the throne, who was militarily backed by the Portuguese. With peace established, the queen turned her full attention to domestic matters, reining in the political power of the nobility, which had grown unchecked throughout the fifteenth century. She reclaimed many of the lands and privileges ceded to the nobility by her predecessors, and she addressed the prevailing lawlessness by creating a national militia. She ordered a broad-based monastic reform and instituted the Office of the Inquisition to guard the orthodoxy of the many Jews who had converted to Catholicism since the pogroms of 1391. Her attempt to impose religious homogeneity culminated in the expulsion of the Jewish population in 1492, the completion in the same year of the eight-centuries-long Reconquest with the military defeat of the last Muslim kingdom of Granada, and the choice given Muslims in 1502 to either convert or leave.[14] Remarkably, she accomplished all of this as a female sovereign in a profoundly patriarchal society.

Finally, a few words about Isabel's own role in fashioning her complex public image.[15] There is no doubt that she promoted and institutionally enforced values of unity, authority, heteronormativity, religious orthodoxy, and ethnic/racial purity in order to impose her absolute power on the culturally diverse and politically fractious Castilian subjects.[16] Her awareness of the role of historical writing in the legitimation of monarchic succession and authority shows in her active supervision of the official chronicles of her predecessors' reigns that she commissioned shortly after her rise to the throne. It is no coincidence, for example, that almost all the official chronicles produced at that time paint an extremely negative portrait of her predecessor Enrique IV, called "el Impotente," and of his heir Juana, the putative offspring of her mother's affair with Enrique's favorite, Beltrán de la Cueva. If Isabel had found the works of the royal historians detrimental to her authority and her policies, she could easily have prevented their free circulation at court.[17] On the other hand, she might have tolerated the accounts that did criticize her because of their value as safety valves for the many dissenting views and practices among her subjects.

The most fruitful way of looking at the fashioning of Isabelline power and gender is through the Foucauldian lens adopted by British cultural materialists and some new historicists, that is, as inherently unstable.[18] In this view the discourses of royal power, including that of gender, are reciprocally productive—shaped by and also shaping "Isabel"—and the contradictory gender roles and attributes contained in those discourses both enable and resist subjection to that power. Louis Montrose observes about Elizabeth I of England that:

The historical subject, Elizabeth Tudor, was no more than a privileged agent in the production of the royal image. At a fundamental level, all Elizabethan subjects may be said to have participated in a ceaseless and casual process of producing and reproducing 'The Queen' in their daily practices . . . But she was also rather more systematically and consciously fashioned by those Elizabethan subjects who were specifically engaged in production of the texts, icons, and performances in which the queen was variously represented to her people, to her court, to foreign powers, and (of course) to Elizabeth herself.[19]

As we shall see in the debate texts examined below, that idea of a multiply fashioned "Queen" applies equally well to Isabel.

Three changes occurring in the Castilian debate tradition during the Isabelline period suggest that the anxieties attending the profound transformations in Spanish society wrought by an all-powerful woman affected the cultivation of the genre. One is the proliferation of texts that fit the category Alcuin Blamires calls the "incidental" case for/against women: that is, its appearance in a wide variety of texts not specifically or entirely dedicated to the debate.[20] These incidental occurrences range from medical treatises on coitus to bawdy satirical verse to courtly lyrics and romances.[21] A second change pertains to the misogynist side of the debate, which becomes preoccupied with the material woman. Among the detractors of women there is a greater emphasis on fear and loathing of the female body, and they frequently construct women not merely as weak, fickle, or mendacious, but as violent, devouring, or demonic.[22] A third, related change is the increasing imbrication of gender-based invective with defamation based on sexuality, race, ethnicity, and religion. Particularly significant, as I suggested above, is the cultivation of a mutually constructing discourse of misogyny and anti-Semitism, which is also frequently entangled with homophobia.[23] All of the works that I discuss here display the interaction of these discourses to a greater or lesser degree, further complicating the effects of queenship on the debate and of the debate on queenship.

Torrellas's *Coplas de las calidades de las donas*

Isabel's powerful presence cannot alone explain all of the aforementioned developments. The interrelationship of the categories of gender and religion, for example, is already evident at midcentury in Torrellas's *Coplas de las calidades de las donas*. Toward the end of his diatribe, the poet identifies the source of female mendacity and treachery:

> . . . Por gana de ser loadas
> qualquier alabança cogen . . .

Sintiendo que son subjectas
e sin nengún poderío,
a fin de aver señorío
tienen engañosas sectas.[24]

[Desiring to be lauded, / they accept any praise . . . / Knowing themselves to be subordinated / and powerless, / In order to have seignory / they form deceitful sects]

The reason Torrellas gives for the founding of the sects of women is resentment over their subordination in the God-given patriarchal sex/gender system and their subversive desire to overthrow it. These lines are especially interesting for my purposes, since they tacitly acknowledge the inequities inherent in the traditional gender hierarchy and express fear that the subjected gender may seek to correct them.

Torrellas's reference to women's "deceitful sects," like so much in this influential work, continued to resonate with participants on both sides of the debate for many years. Diego de Valera, for example, opens his *Tratado en defensa de las virtuosas mujeres* [Treatise in Defense of Virtuous Women] (before 1445), dedicated to Queen María of Aragón, with a call to his fellow courtiers to refute Torrellas and his "nueva secta" [new sect]. Valera thus turns Torrellas's attack on women back against him, making the misogynist himself the leader of a new sect, one that threatens the "true faith" that worships women.[25]

Over fifty years later, the same religious image resurfaces in a poem by Pedro Manuel de Urrea. In his "Coplas en alabança de las mujeres," Urrea attacks Torrellas and his fellow misogynist, Hernán Mexía, by deepening the heretical implications of Valera's image of Torrellas as leader of a heretical sect:

Vuestro pecado y desuío
no se absuelue yendo a Roma
soys los dos un desuarío
soys el frayle y el judío
que hizieron ley de Mahoma . . . [26]

[Your sin and deviance / cannot be absolved by going to Rome; / you are both mad, / you are the friar and the Jew / who made the law of Mohammed]

Urrea identifies the "deceitful sect" as Islam, whose founding the poet attributes in a bizarre conflation to a friar and a Jew. The religious language, further developed in the succeeding stanzas, culminates in the following lines:

Decreto es determinado
juzgado por buena suerte
que qualquiere deslenguado
que de dama mal a hablado
meresce pena de muerte.
Que niega la obligación
y quiebra la ley deuida
aborrece la razón
y para perder la vida
el mismo ordena el pregón. (ed. Dutton, p. 263; vv. 140–49)

[The decree has been issued / and fairly determined / that any foulmouthed
man / who has spoken ill of a lady / deserves the death sentence. / For he
denies his obligation, / breaks the just law, / and despises reason, / and he
himself composes / the proclamation of his crime]

It is hard not to read Inquisitional connotations into the "decree" that imposes the death sentence on those who sin by failing to live by the laws of
the "religion of love." The comparison of the poet himself with the town
crier who calls out the offenses of the guilty man on his way to be executed is highly suggestive of the very public humiliation and punishment
to which those condemned by the Holy Office were subjected.

I shall return to Torrellas's warning about the "dangerous sects" of
women as I examine expressions of masculine anxiety over feminine
power in the three Isabelline texts mentioned above: Antón de Montoro's
panegyric to Isabel, "¡Oh, Ropero, amargo, triste"; the romance *Grisel y
Mirabella* by Juan de Flores; and "Pleyto del manto," an anonymous pornographic satire published after Isabel's death.[27] As will become clear, compared with Montoro's direct address to his queen, the impact of female
sovereignty is more indirectly felt in the romances composed and printed
during Isabel's reign, several of which hold the distinction of becoming
European best-sellers.[28] Flores's *Grisel y Mirabella* engages the issue of the
limits of monarchic authority and the interrelationship of domestic and
political power relations. Most indirect of all is the obscene "Pleyto del
manto," where the attack on the queen's misappropriation of power is un-
derstandably launched from behind the screen of anonymity and humor.

Antón de Montoro's
"¡Oh Ropero, amargo, triste!"

Montoro has attracted renewed critical attention as part of a general
reevaluation of *converso* identities in medieval Spain.[29] E. Michael Gerli
has shown how Montoro rose to prominence at court through the indis-

pensable sartorial services that he provided as tailor to an ostentatious aristocracy, as well as through his considerable literary talents and his self-dramatization as a poor and despised *converso,* which contradicted the real circumstances of his life.[30]

Montoro's poetry contains excellent examples of the recurrent Marian metaphorization of Isabel, the assimilation of the earthly queen of Castile to the Virgin Mary, Queen of Heaven. This common element in the construction of Isabel's femininity illustrates the messianic fervor surrounding her assumption of power.[31] The nobles and clerics closest to the monarch extol her for changing darkness to light, chaos to order, and depravity to morality. In their letters, poems, official chronicles, and treatises, Gómez Manrique and Iñigo de Mendoza—both of whom wrote formal debate texts as well[32]—construct her power and the *stabilitas* it enables as masculine and set it against the "feminine" *instabilitas* of the recent past, specifically that caused by her immediate predecessor and half-brother, Enrique IV.[33] With her encouragement, Isabel's supporters implicate her predecessor in a synecdochic chain of sexual and political transgressions.[34] Enrique's presumed impotent and sodomitical nature is related to his preferment of Jews, Moors, and *conversos,* and his inability to control his adulterous queen is linked to the dynastic crisis resulting from the putative illegitimacy of his heir Juana. Valera for one relates Enrique's weakness as king directly to his maurophilia, his unseemly appreciation for the "pérfida mahomética seta" [perfidious Mohammedan sect] that in 711 overthrew the virile Christian kingdom of the Visigoths.[35] Isabel's God-given mission is to undo the catastrophe and to reverse the Iberian Christians' fall from Paradise, just as Mary undid the fall of Adam brought about by Eve.

In a poem composed somewhat before the one I will analyze at some length, Montoro divinizes his "alta reina soberana" [noble sovereign queen] by declaring that

> si fuérades antes vos
> que la hija de Santana
> de vos el hijo de Dios
> recibiera carne humana.[36]

[if you had lived before / the daughter of St. Anne, / the son of God / would have taken form from your flesh]

Montoro's blasphemous adulation of the queen is particularly striking because it uses two elements of Catholic doctrine that Jewish converts found especially difficult to accept: the Immaculate Conception of Mary and the Virgin Birth of Christ.[37]

Montoro's sacrilegious flattery of his monarch becomes more nuanced in his best-known poem, a eulogistic lyric that also flaunts the poet's stigmatized identity as a *converso*. This metrically sophisticated eight-stanza poem is divided into two distinct and seemingly unrelated halves. Montoro's ambivalent attitude toward the queen becomes apparent only when we compare these two sections.[38]

In the first section, Montoro speaks bitterly of his lifelong profession of Christianity. Here he makes explicit what was implicit in the earlier lyric:

¡Oh Ropero, amargo, triste,
que no sientes tu dolor!
Setenta años que naciste
y en todos siempre dijiste:
"inviolata permansiste,"
y nunca juré al Criador.
Hice el Credo y adorar
ollas de tocino grueso,
torreznos a medio asar
oir misas y rezar,
santiguar y persinar;
y nunca pude matar
este rastro de confeso.[39]

[Oh, sad and bitter Clothier, / you who cannot feel your own pain! / For all of your seventy years / you prayed: / "inviolata permansiste" / and never took the Creator's name in vain. / I said the Credo and adored / dishes full of fat bacon, / half-cooked rashers. / I heard masses and prayed / and made the sign of the cross, / but I could never kill off / the mark of the convert]

Here again, but more poignantly, Montoro refers to the Virgin Birth of Mary, a doctrine that troubled many *conversos*. All of his efforts to live the life of a good Christian, seventy long years of adoring the Trinity, espousing Mary's virginity, and pretending to enjoy the pork forbidden in Judaism have been useless, Montoro complains, because "no pude perder el nombre/de viejo, puto, judío" [I could never lose the name of old Jewish faggot].[40] To understand the force of the last two epithets, we must keep in mind the traditional Christian stereotypes of the male Jew's body as sexually defective or diseased.[41] The body of the male Jew, and specifically its circumcised penis, was considered an ineradicable corporeal stigma that set Jews apart. Among the Jews, too, as Daniel Boyarin explains, circumcision was understood as feminizing the male.[42] This belief may have facilitated the anti-Semitic perception of the *converso* as the passive partner in an imagined sodomitical couple, hence "puto." The stigma of circumcision also applied to the *conversos,* even to those whose families had been practicing Christians for generations (as was the case of Montoro)[43] and were therefore almost certainly uncircumcised.

Montoro's self-abjection as an old Jewish faggot is certainly jarring in a poem ostensibly praising one's queen. It becomes even more so when we realize that the line in which it appears falls at the poem's exact structural center, and that Montoro's lament thus introduces the encomium proper of the queen:

> Pues, alta reina sin par,
> en cuyo mando consiste,
> gran razón es de loar
> y ensalzar
> la muy sancta fe de Criste.
> Pues, reina de gran valor,
> que la santa fee crecienta,
> no quiere nuestro Señor,
> con furor,
> la muerte del pecador,
> mas que viva y se arrepienta.[44]

[So, noble queen without equal, / whose rule consists / of praising and increasing / Christ's faith. So, most worthy queen / who promotes the holy faith, / our Lord does not wish / the sinner to die violently, / rather to live and repent]

As Marithelma Costa shows, the reiterated interpellation of Isabel as all-powerful and courageous and the reminders of Christ's forgiveness of sinners prepare for the courtly petition the poet makes in the last two stanzas. Here Montoro again uses the sacrilegious association of Isabel and the Virgin Mary, as he addresses Isabel as "hija de angélica madre" [daughter of an angelic mother], a reference to Isabel's literal, biological mother, but also to St. Anne and the Immaculate Conception. It immediately becomes apparent, however, that Montoro's praise of his queen is far from disinterested. The final stanza reveals the point of the extravagant *captatio benevolentiae* that preceded:

> Pues, reina de gran estado,
> hija de angélica madre,
> aquel dios crucificado,
> muy abierto su costado,
> con vituperios bordado
> e inclinado,

dijo: "Perdónalos, Padre."
Pues, reina de auctoridad,
esta muerte sin sosiego
cese ya, por tu piedad
y bondad,
hasta allá por Navidad,
cuando sabe bien el fuego.[45]

[So, queen of high rank, / daughter of an angelic mother, / that crucified God, / his side pierced, / covered with insults / and bent down, / said: "Forgive them, Father." / So, powerful queen, / stop this endless death, / for your pity and goodness's sake, / until Christmas, / when fire feels good]

Montoro's panegyric is an urgent plea for the queen to stop the persecution and murder of *conversos*. This may be a reference to the *auto-da-fes* of the Inquisition that began in 1480, but is more likely a response to the riots and massacres of the mid-1470s that formed part of the war of succession between Isabel and her rival Juana de Castilla.[46]

Montoro's stark poem constructs Isabel as Mary, the better to exhort her forgiveness for the *converso* "sinners" (whether the victims of the pogroms or those accused of Judaizing is unclear), just as Jesus forgave his persecutors. The sacrilegious metaphor shifts the gender identification of the queen from the feminine Mary to the masculine Christ. In this way Montoro casts doubt upon Isabel's possession of that most naturalized of feminine virtues, compassion. Complicating the image further is the fact that the poet is apparently drawing on the feminized Christ of late medieval devotion, whom Carolyn Bynum designates "Jesus as Mother."[47] The double transgendering of Jesus as forgiving mother and Isabel as punishing father is a bold one. Even more daring is the conflation of the previously mentioned sexual and ethnic slurs suffered personally by Montoro and the vituperation of Christ at the Passion. In this light, the panegyrist's goal becomes nothing less than an effort to rewrite biblical history. He does so by drawing a blasphemous comparison between Montoro the faggot Jew and Jesus the maligned but admirably feminized son of God, whose sacrifice the chaste, compassionate, and all-powerful Marian queen—"reina de auctoridad"—has the power to prevent.

In Montoro's panegyric, then, praise of Isabel for possessing the desirable feminine condition of sexual purity turns into blame because she lacks feminine compassion for her maligned and persecuted subjects. What begins as an exercise in self-abasement ends up as a theological lesson and moral admonition. While declaring himself abject and powerless, Montoro appropriates the discourse of power to preach to one *not yet converted* to the belief that all Christians are equal before God. While not a debate text proper, the poem uses the profeminine glorification of women to fashion a queen for all her people.[48]

Juan de Flores's *Grisel y Mirabella*

One important text weaves the incidental case against women into a formal gender debate so that it may comment on the threat posed by female sovereignty to the so-called Law of the Father. The romance *Grisel y Mirabella* was composed by the prolific Juan de Flores, who served Isabel in various official capacities as chronicler, magistrate, administrator, and member of the royal council.[49] Probably written in the 1470s at the height of the war of succession for the Castilian throne, it was printed for the first time in 1495. It was soon translated into several languages and became a European best-seller.[50]

The structural and thematic center of this tale of tragic lovers set in a mythical Escocia [Scotland] is the judicial debate ordered by the King of Scotland when his daughter Mirabella, whom he has locked in a tower to prevent her marriage, is discovered *in flagrante delicto* with her suitor Grisel. The King, whom the narrator calls "el más justificado príncipe que a la sazón se fallase en el mundo . . ."(ed. Lopez and Nuñez, p. 58) [the most just prince in the world at that time], is ostensibly upholding the law of the land that states: "El que más causa fuese al otro de haver amado que padesciese muerte y el otro, destierro por toda su vida. Y como acaesce cuando dos personas se aman, el uno tener más culpa que el otro en la recuesta: por esto las leyes no disponían que las penas fuesen iguales" (58) [The one who bore greater responsibility for causing the other to love should be put to death and the other one exiled for life. And as it happens when two people love each other that one is more culpable than the other in the affair, the laws did not mandate that the punishments be equal].[51]

The lawyer that the King invites to argue the case against women is none other than Torrellas. This fictionalization of Castile's archetypal womanhater is clear evidence that by the end of the fifteenth century Torrellas had achieved the status of a cultural icon. His worthy opponent in the trial debate is the equally surprising metafictional character Breçayda [Criseyde] of Trojan legend fame, represented by dozens of medieval writers as the archetypal inconstant woman.[52] Despite Breçayda's impassioned defense of women, the all-male jury finds against Mirabella. Outraged, her female defender accuses the jury and the male-authored laws that they uphold as being inevitably self-interested. She acknowledges that women lack debating skills, but she attributes this handicap to men's ownership of the pen and their consequent unhindered liberty to do all the writing, as had Chaucer's Wife of Bath and Christine de Pizan earlier: "Vosotros, que tenéis la pluma en la mano, pintáis como queréis; por donde no es mengua . . . que si con vosotros iguales nos hiciera [Dios] en el saber, estaba dudoso el debate" (p. 72) [You who hold the pen in your hand, can depict us however you wish, for which reason it is not shameful (to have lost), for if God had made us equal in learning, the outcome would have been in doubt]. The reference to God's ultimate responsibility for denying women access to learning is an interesting one. Is it intended as a softening of the criticism of men, as a blasphemous indictment of divine wisdom, or both?

The gender debate in *Grisel* is followed by another gender competition, a "combat of generosity" that dramatizes the loyalty of the lovers (and refutes one of Torrellas's arguments about women) as each lover proclaims her or his inability to live without the other. The dramatic double suicide that follows—the princess Mirabella throws herself into her father's lion pit—does not, however, lead to the kind of ending that romance readers might expect.

Distraught by her daughter's death, the Queen of Scotland seeks revenge on Torrellas. Fortune smiles on her when the misogynist falls in love with his erstwhile opponent Breçayda. With Breçayda's help and that of her ladies-in-waiting, the Queen concocts an elaborate plot to lure Torrellas to his death. Breçayda writes to Torrellas feigning interest in his proposal in order to lure him to a secret rendezvous. He responds cynically, playing the role of the courtly lover in hopes of seducing her while at the same time boasting to the other courtiers of his imminent conquest. When Torrellas appears for the tryst, Breçayda's women proceed to strip, bind, gag, flay, and burn him at the stake, all the while enjoying a lavish banquet. The next day they place his ashes in reliquaries to wear around their necks "porque trayendo más a memoria su venganza, mayor placer hobiesen" (p. 930) [so that by better recalling their revenge, they would feel greater pleasure].

Critics have been unable to agree on Juan de Flores's position in the debate about women and more specifically about the sense of this bizarre and ambiguous epilogue.[53] Are we to read Torrellas's torture-murder as a Bakhtinian women-on-top subversion of the oppressive, perhaps incestuous patriarchal "law of Scotland"?[54] as an exposure of the subjectivity of misogynist *auctoritas* through Torrellas's abrupt and cynical transformation into Breçayda's pursuer, which thus proves false the findings of the trial? or as a grotesque portrayal of female deviancy that upholds those findings? In support of the latter view, Lillian von der Walde has uncovered a demonic subtext to the epilogue, showing the similarities between the enraged mob of animalistic noblewomen and the ritual murders ascribed to witches.[55] While the motif of female revenge on misogynists is not uncommon in the European debate, the historical context of Flores's version of this motif suggests that he is drawing on Torrellas's own image of the "deceitful sect" of women, infusing it with sinister allusions to the heresies and apostasies (i.e., the reliquaries made of Torrellas's ashes) that led to the real tortures and burnings of the Inquisition.[56] In this phobic masculine fantasy, the Queen uses her power to wreak havoc on the gender hierarchy that maintains and reproduces patriarchal society. While it can certainly be argued that the King is also criticized for his legalistic and harsh application of Scotland's laws, he at least is represented as a rational being. The Queen, on the other hand, is in the final scene of the romance portrayed as a rabid beast intent on tearing apart its prey, a grotesque inversion of the predators who devour Mirabella's body when she throws herself into her father's lion pit.

"Pleyto del manto"

The confrontation between patriarchal law and female outlaws that Flores stages in *Grisel y Mirabella* is also the subject of the last text I want to discuss, the pornographic poem "Pleyto del Manto" [Lawsuit over the Cloak].[57] First appearing in the 1514 edition of the massive poetic anthology entitled *Cancionero general,* the anonymous work was probably composed during Isabel's lifetime.[58] "Pleyto del manto" is both a mock-debate to decide the superiority of men or women and an accomplished parody of fifteenth-century legal language and procedures. This makes it likely that it was written either by a nobleman (possibly even García de Astorga, who contributed a verse and prose epilogue to the poem ["Pleyto," pp. 62–65]) or a *letrado,* one of the university-trained men on whom the Catholic Monarchs increasingly relied to administer their growing administrative and judicial bureaucracy.

The excuse for the lawsuit is the disputed ownership of a black velvet cloak that a nobleman throws over a prostitute and her client when he encounters them copulating in a garden. The cloak's owner generously but ambiguously bequeaths it to "el que lo tiene dentro" [the one who holds it inside]. This is the question that the lawyers for the two parties, the metonymic *coño* [cunt] and *carajo* [prick], argue before the judge. The consideration during the trial of the relative "holding" power of the penis or the vagina clearly travesties the prevailing Aristotelian theory of male and female roles in reproduction. In *Generation of Animals,* Aristotle had insisted on the superiority of the active, formative virtue of the male over the matter passively provided by the female. The influence of this generative hierarchy throughout the Middle Ages cannot be overemphasized.[59] In the festive court of "Pleyto del manto," however, the material basis of the hierarchy is allowed free rein: the *carajo* repeatedly expresses his fear of engulfment and castration by the *coño*. The cluster of metaphors he applies to his female opponent make this anxiety clear: She is a "muy hondo mar" [very deep sea], "hondura" [deep pit], "osario" [ossary], "luzillo" [tomb], "tinieblas" [(infernal) darkness].[60] "Pleyto del manto" thus vividly exemplifies for Spain the grounding of the Western discourse of misogyny in the destructiveness to men of women's sexual voraciousness.[61]

Like the Queen of Scotland and her accomplices in *Grisel,* the dangerous *coño* prevails in "Pleyto" through deceit and through the subverison of the law of the land, in this case by bribing the judge. The mock-Draconian punishment the judge decrees is that the *carajo* be imprisoned in the *coño* until it pays the court costs, i.e., ejaculates. What is most pertinent to my argument, however, is the judge's defensive justification for his severe ruling:

> Y si algunos juzgaran
> mal de aquesto que leyeren,
> respondo que "leyes van
> allí donde coños quieren." (p. 58, vv. 15–18)

[And to those readers who may judge / these proceedings harshly, / I respond that "as cunts wish, / so go the laws"]

The judge, in washing his hands of the whole dirty business, "por no quedar enconado [sic]" ["so as to avoid a fight," but the punning "to avoid tangling with the cunt" is inescapable] justifies his finding for the *coño* with a travestied reference to the common Spanish proverb "Allá van leyes donde reyes quieren" [As monarchs wish, so go the laws], itself a popular rendering of the legal maxim "Quod principi placuit legibus solutus" [The prince is above the law]. During the second half of the fifteenth century Castilian monarchs frequently invoked that dictum in order to strengthen royal absolutism.[62] The beleaguered judge's obscene take on "might makes right" is, in this most material of debates about women, a clear reference to the uncontrollable power of female sexuality. But it is also a reference to the female sovereign who corrupts the law of the land and destroys masculine property rights.[63]

To grasp the historical significance of the misogynist humor of "Pleyto del manto" we must recall that one of Isabel's primary goals, and one that had to be implemented with great care, was the curtailment of the political power of the nobility. The queen accomplished this in part by codifying Castile's laws and by centralizing its justice system. Just a year after her coronation at the Cortes of 1474, she instituted the Santa Hermandad [Holy Brotherhood], a combination of national police force and rudimentary national army.[64] The *alcaldes* [sheriffs] of the Hermandad were supported by local taxes, possessed greater jurisdiction than local justices, and were firmly controlled by a national general assembly. Even more radical changes were effected at the Cortes of 1480, on the heels of the victory in

the war of succession. Of signal importance was the diminution of the nobility's representation on the royal council, the highest court in the realm,
and a corresponding increase in the participation of the *letrados,* chosen by
the monarchs. Liss summarizes the impact of the 1480 Cortes as follows:
"For Castile, the ordinances of the Cortes of Toledo were in effect the
constitution of an emerging nation-state that was also a near-absolute
monarchy, and they were the work of royal lawyers experienced in promoting royal interests." One of these lawyers, Alonso Díaz de Montalvo,
was ordered to prepare a single compendium of Castilian law. Completed
in 1484 and printed the following year, the regalist code provided a body
of precedent designed to obviate the promulgation of laws by the Cortes
and to elevate reliance upon royal decree. The code became the basis of juridical action for over fifty years (p. 184).

An initiative that went hand in hand with Isabel's legal reversal of the
devolution of power onto the aristocracy was her reclaiming of the royal
patrimony, the monies and territories that her predecessor Enrique IV and
her brother Alfonso XII had dispensed as *mercedes* [privileges] to the nobility in the usually vain attempt to secure their loyalty. Isabel rescinded all
the privileges that she deemed coerced from Enrique by the nobles. As Liss
notes (p. 185), the rescission reflected Isabel's view of Castile's recent past,
specifically, the belief that the source of the civil war had been the nobility's assault on monarchy: "The *mercedes* reform was in fact the reversal of
this injustice, and, in signalling a low opinion of the validity of either Enrique's or Alfonso's reign, it buoyed the idea of Isabel's own reign as the
one most validly stemming from that of her father [Juan II]."

With this in mind, we can consider the brief but richly suggestive reference to Torrellas's "deceitful sects" that occurs at a strategic moment in
"Pleyto." After the judge issues his biased ruling, the *carajo* makes a formal
appeal:

> Ante Torrellas apelo,
> que merece mil renombres,
> porque sostuvo sin velo
> mientras estuvo en este suelo
> el partido de los hombres. ("Pleyto," p. 60)

[I appeal before Torrellas, / who deserves a thousand praises, / because while
he was on this earth / he openly took the side of men]

Not only does the judge deny the appeal, he takes the opportunity to admonish the losing side about the dangers of their antifemale bias. As he
does so, he raises the debate to a more abstract level, from the specific

"querellas" [complaints] men have about material women to the "natural" law of love:

> Y esta nuestra nación
> si no bastan mis poderes,
> digo a vuestra inclinación,
> que va errada el afición
> cuando sale de mujeres.
> Y la passión que os guía
> no ciega el camino llano.
> Devéis tener otra vía,
> que no seguir herejía,
> muy peor que de Arriano. (p. 62, vv. 5–15)

[And for this our nation, / if my power fails (to stop you?), / I say about your inclinations / that your affection goes awry / if it is taken away from women. / And the passion that guides you / does not blind you to the open road. / You must take a different path / rather than follow a heresy / much worse than Arian's][65]

In other words, if men allow their affections to go astray, they may find themselves becoming a "heretical sect" and practicing a heresy worse than the Arianism of the Visigoths, the Germanic people who ruled in Spain from the fall of Rome until they were overthrown in the eighth century by the Moors: the heresy of sodomy. The judge reads the appeal in the name of Torrellas as a dangerous sign: He counters by advocating a pro-feminine stance, not to be fair or gracious to women, but rather to safe-guard masculinity from the threat of homosexuality.

Two aspects of the judge's criticism of Arian Christianity suggest that it also contains anti-Semitic overtones. The first lies in his use of the term "nación," on one level simply a synonym for "group," in this case, males. But Benzion Netanyahu has shown that the term also had both national-ist and racist connotations, since it was often used to identify the *conversos* as a people, a distinct nationality that was related in many ways to the Jews. Netanyahu explains that "the *otherness* of the *converso,* which was reflected by the *non*-religious side of his being, soon stamped him not only as 'dif-ferent' from the Old Christians but also as a 'foreigner' and, as such, as an intruder. This brought out the Jewishness of the Marranos [*conversos*] from another standpoint—that of the relations between an alien minority and the majority within which it lives."[66] He gives the example of Alfonso de Palencia, who served, like Juan de Flores, as official chronicler of Isabel's reign. In the *Crónica de Enrique IV* that Palencia wrote at Isabel's behest, the chronicler calls the *conversos* a "nación aparte."[67]

As I have discussed elsewhere, however, Palencia pursues his primary goal of legitimizing Isabel's claim to the throne of Castile by crafting a "discourse of effeminacy" that stigmatizes her predecessor Enrique IV and his court favorites and advisers, many of them *conversos*. In fact, more than one Isabelline writer blames the Jews for introducing the "disease" of sodomy into Iberia.[68] The *Libro del Alborayque,* for example, an anti-Semitic tract written toward 1490, concocts an entire epidemiological chart for sodomy and authorizes it with biblical references: "La sodomía es venida de judíos . . . Esayas primo cap:'audite berbum Domini principes sodomorum.' De los judíos vino a los moros, a los malos christianos, como Diego Arias [treasurer of Castile under Juan II], el qual fue principio y causa de la perdición que será fecha en España"[69] [Sodomy comes from the Jews. Isaiah, Chapter One:"audite berbum Domini principes sodomorum."The Jews passed it on to the Moors and to the bad Christians like Diego Arias, who was the beginning and cause of the damnation that will come to Spain]. The heresy that the judge in "Pleyto" deems worse than Arianism ultimately conjoins sexual deviance, racial pollution, and religious heresy.[70] Torrellas, archetypal enemy of women, thereby emerges as a friend to sodomites and Jews.

In studying the European gender debates we must recognize that they are shaped by particular sociopolitical circumstances. In late-fifteenth-century Spain those circumstances have to do with the presence on the throne of Isabel the Catholic. As a powerful female sovereign ruling in her own right, Isabel embodies a threat to the patriarchal status quo and to the subjectivity of her male subjects. At the same time, the goals of unity, hierarchy, and order that she upheld appealed to many of those subjects, who were weary of the decades-long struggle for power between the nobility and the monarchy, and the perceived decadence and corruption of both. But Isabel's political goals were grounded in the ethnic/racial, religious, and sexual "purification" of Spanish society of its corrupting Others. My tracing of the role of the "heretical sects" of women, misogynists, Jews, *conversos,* sodomites, and Arian Christians in the Isabelline gender debate tradition has shown how all of these issues—of queenship, gender, power, sexuality, ethnicity, and religion—intersect with issues of genre in complex ways. For Antón de Montoro, Juan de Flores, and the anonymous author of "Pleyto del manto," the debate genre provides a means of articulating and containing the anxiety produced by the disturbing intersection of the queen's feminine gender, absolute power, and patriarchal politics. Finally, out of the debate emerges the archmisogynist Pere Torrellas, Spain's earliest icon of secular masculinity, the symbol of everything that "Isabel" paradoxically threatens (e.g., the patriarchal law of the land in *Grisel y Mirabella* and "Pleyto del manto") and upholds (e.g., the religious homogeneity and heteronormativity that the Inquisition enforces).

The discursive net Torrellas casts at midcentury in his *Coplas de las calidades de las donas* widens in the Isabelline period to trap other "feminine" sects that are perceived to pose a danger to the "masculine" nation. Of the three works I have examined, the panegyric to Isabel by the *converso* Antón de Montoro is the most moving in its reference to the real violence enacted upon one of those sects and his poignant manipulation of profeminine discourse to fashion his queen as truly Christian, that is, merciful. The overlapping construction of queens, women, religious, racial, and sexual outsiders examined here show that late medieval Spain offers a particularly fertile and poignant ground for understanding the political relevance of medieval gender debates.

Notes

1. Although "Spain" is a convenient way to refer to the kingdoms of Castile and Aragón, which were precariously joined in 1479, one should bear in mind that it is, strictly speaking, an anachronism. The term implies a national identity that was beginning to be constructed in Isabel's reign.

2. On the life and work of Torrellas, see Pedro Bach y Rita, ed., *The Works of Pere Torroella, a Catalan Writer of the Fifteenth Century* (New York: Instituto de las Españas, 1930). He wrote *Coplas* sometime between 1440 and 1460. The "debate about women" can be said to actually begin with a prose treatise written by a member of the Castilian monarch Juan II's court, the royal chaplain Alfonso Martínez de Toledo. His *Arcipreste de Talavera o Corbacho*, completed in 1438, was published three times during the reign of Isabel the Catholic. See the edition by E. Michael Gerli (Madrid: Cátedra, 1992). For elucidation of aspects of Martínez de Toledo's gender ideology, see the recent studies by Catherine Brown, "Queer Representation in the *Arcipreste de Talavera,* or *The Maldezir de mugeres* Is a Drag," in *Queer Iberia: Sexualities, Cultures, and Crossings from the Middle Ages to the Renaissance,* eds. Josiah Blackmore and Gregory S. Hutcheson (Durham, N.C.: Duke University Press, 1999), pp. 73–103, and Michael Solomon, *The Literature of Misogyny in Medieval Spain: The "Arcipreste de Talavera" and the "Spill."* Cambridge Studies in Latin American and Iberian Literature 10 (Cambridge: Cambridge University Press, 1997).

3. For a bibliography of selected debate texts in fifteenth-century Spain and of scholarship about the debate, see Julian Weiss's essay in this collection. The "classic" studies are by Barbara Matulka, *The Novels of Juan de Flores and Their European Diffusion: A Study in Comparative Literature* (1931; repr. Geneva: Slatkine, 1974); Jacob Ornstein, "La misoginia y el profeminismo en la literatura castellana," *Revista de Filología Hispánica* 3 (1941): 219–32; and the survey by María Pilar de Oñate, *El feminismo en la literatura española* (Madrid: Espasa-Calpe, 1938). For more recent approaches to the misogynist discourse, see María Jesús Lacarra, "Algunos datos para la historia de la misoginia en la Edad Media," *Studia in honorem Profesor Martín de Riquer,* 2

vols., ed. Carlos Alvar (Barcelona: Quaderns Crema, 1986), vol. 1, pp. 339–61; Harriet Goldberg, "Sexual Humor in Misogynist Medieval Exempla," *Women in Hispanic Literature: Icons and Fallen Idols,* ed. Beth Miller (Berkeley and Los Angeles: University of California Press, 1983), pp. 67–83; and María-Milagros Rivera, "El cuerpo femenino y la querella de las mujeres (corona de Aragón, siglo XV)," in *Historia de las mujeres en Occidente,* 2 vols., eds. Georges Duby and Michelle Perrot, trans. Marco Aurelio Galmarini and Cristina García Ohlrich (Madrid: Taurus, 1992) vol. II, pp. 593–605.

4. For a summary of participants in the poetic debate in Castile and Aragón, and in Naples, see Miguel Angel Pérez Priego, ed., *Poesía femenina en los cancioneros* (Madrid: Castalia, 1989), pp. 33–36.

5. Introduction to Louise Fradenburg, *Women and Sovereignty* (Edinburgh: Edinburgh University Press, 1992), p. 1.

6. See also my "'¡A tierra, puto!': Alfonso de Palencia's Discourse of Effeminacy," in *Queer Iberia,* pp. 291–324, and "Male Sexual Anxieties in *Carajicomedia:* A Response to Female Sovereignty," in *Poetry at Court in Trastamaran Spain: From the Cancionero de Baena to the Cancionero General,* eds. E. Michael Gerli and Julian Weiss (Tempe, Ariz.: Medieval and Renaissance Texts and Studies, 1998), pp. 221–34. The latter represents female sexual power in misogynist tones quite similar to those of "Pleyto del manto," one of the works I treat in this essay. I develop the arguments of both of these essays and extend them to a wide range of texts, from the mid-fifteenth-century *Laberinto de Fortuna* (1445) by Juan de Mena to its obscene anonymous parody *Carajicomedia* (1519), in my forthcoming book, *Spain's Broken Body: Gender Ideology in the Age of Isabel the Catholic.*

7. Fradenburg, *Women and Sovereignty,* p. 3.

8. Although he does not deal with gender, Julio Rodríguez-Puértolas provides a concise overview of anti-Semitism in fifteenth-century Spain in "Jews and Conversos in Fifteenth-Century Castilian *Cancioneros:* Texts and Contexts," in *Poetry at Court,* eds. Gerli and Weiss, pp. 187–97. The literature on the Jews and *conversos* in medieval Spain is vast. For a brief introduction, see Scarlett Freund and Teófilo F. Ruiz, "Jews, Conversos, and the Inquisition in Spain, 1301–1492: The Ambiguities of History," in *Jewish-Christian Encounters over the Centuries,* eds. Marvin Perry and Frederick Schweitzer (New York: Peter Lang, 1994), pp. 169–95. Essential recent studies include: Henry Kamen, *The Spanish Inquistition: A Historical Revision* (New Haven, Conn.: Yale University Press, 1981), B. Netanyahu, *The Origins of the Inquisition in Fifteenth Century Spain* (New York: Random House, 1995), and Norman Roth, *Conversos, Inquisition and the Expulsion of the Jews from Spain* (Madison: University of Wisconsin Press, 1995).

9. An essential book for the conflation of various stigmatizing discourses in medieval Iberia (although its focus is fourteenth-century Aragon rather than fifteenth-century Castile) is David Nirenberg, *Communities of Violence:*

Persecution of Minorities in the Middle Ages (Princeton, N.J.: Princeton University Press, 1996). See especially the discussion of the linkages made among, lepers, Muslims, Jews, and sodomites, and of town ordinances aimed at preventing contagion by Jews in chapter 4.

10. See Nirenberg, *Communities of Violence,* chapter 5. Also useful is Louise Mirrer's study of the feminization and devaluation of racial otherness in medieval Iberia, *Women, Jews, and Muslims in the Texts of Reconquest Castile* (Ann Arbor: University of Michigan Press, 1996). For a broad European overview of the conflation of sexuality, race, and religion in the represention of those who pollute the body politic, see Dyan Elliott, *Fallen Bodies: Pollution, Sexuality, and Demonology in the Middle Ages* (Philadelphia: University of Pennsylvania Press, 1999), and Miri Rubin, *Gentile Tales:The Narrative Assault on Late Medieval Jews* (New Haven, Conn.: Yale University Press, 1999).

11. Louis Adrian Montrose, "The Elizabethan Subject and the Spenserian Text," *Literary Theory / Renaissance Texts,* eds. Patricia Parker and David Quint (Baltimore, Md.: Johns Hopkins Press, 1986), p. 309. See also his important "'Shaping Fantasies': Figurations of Gender and Power in Elizabethan Culture," *Representations* 1.2 (1981): 61–93.

12. By way of comparison, we might consider the well-studied case of Elizabeth I of England. Although she ascended the throne of England eighty-three years after Isabel was crowned queen of Castile, the resistance to Elizabeth's rule was even more pronounced than in Spain. As Montrose has noted: "As the anomalous ruler of a society that was pervasively patriarchal in its organization and distribution of authority, the unmarried woman at the society's symbolic center embodied a challenge to the homology between hierarchies of rule and of gender" ("The Elizabethan Subject," p. 309). Leah Marcus notes that "further weakening her claim was the fact that her father HenryVIII had declared her a bastard.To counter all of this Elizabeth and her male writing subjects fostered what one scholar calls 'the myth of her own androgyny,' variously representing her as man and woman, queen and king, mother and firstborn son" (see Marcus, "Shakespeare's Comic Heroines, Elizabeth I, and the Political Uses of Androgeny," in *Women in the Middle Ages and the Renaissance: Literary and Historical Perspectives,* ed. Mary Beth Rose (Syracuse, N.Y.: Syracuse University Press, 1986), p. 137. Almost immediately upon her coronation, she began to formulate strategies to resist her subjects' pressure that she fulfill her destiny of marrying and bearing an heir. For example, before Parliament in 1559 she claimed that she was already married: "I am already bounde unto an Husband, which is the Kingdom of England."To the urging that she produce an heir, she replied in the same speech that she already had children, namely "every one of you, and as many as are English" (qtd. in Montrose,"The Elizabethan Subject," p. 309). For analyses of several other royal speeches, see Allison Heisch,"Queen Elizabeth I and the Persistence of Patriarchy," *Feminist Review* 4 (1980): 45–56. Her best-known self-representation and one of the

most effective in affirming her absolute authority over her subjects while diffusing male anxieties about female power was as the "virgin queen." Thus, by transferring her wifely and maternal duties from her natural to her political body, she manipulated traditional gender roles to her advantage; by promoting a cult of virginity, she transvalued her failure to ensure dynastic continuity (as well as countering the Catholic cult of the Virgin Mary). As this essay shows, Isabel followed a different path to affirm her absolute power.

13. For a gender analysis of the shape that disappointment took in one of her royal chroniclers, Alfonso de Palencia, see my "Discourse of Effeminacy." I have drawn on that essay for some of the background material provided here.

14. Isabel's policies were never totally successful, since many *conversos* and *moriscos* (Muslims who chose to convert to Catholicism after the 1502 edict) continued to practice their own customs throughout the sixteenth century. Nevertheless, homogeneity became an increasingly important element in the discourse of nationhood throughout Isabel's reign and beyond.

15. By comparison, most critics ascribe considerable agency to Elizabeth I in the fashioning of her image. See, for example, Marcus's "Shakespeare's Comic Heroines"; Philippa Berry, *Of Chastity and Power: Elizabethan Literature and the Unmarried Queen* (London: Routledge, 1994); and Carole Levin, *The Heart and Stomach of a King: Elizabeth I and the Politics of Sex and Power* (Philadelphia: University of Pennsylvania Press, 1994).

16. Histories of Isabel's life and reign throughout the five hundred years since her death have often been hagiographical, perpetuating one of the modes of her contemporary fashioning that I discuss in this essay. By far the best modern biography of Isabel is by Tarsicio de Azcona, *Isabel la Católica: Estudio crítico de su vida y su reinado,* 3rd ed. (Madrid: Biblioteca de Autores Cristianos, 1993). In English, the 1992 biography by Peggy Liss, *Isabel, the Queen: Life and Times* (Oxford: Oxford University Press, 1992), is useful, although it is overly reliant on the highly partisan chronicles that the queen herself commissioned.

17. She dismissed one of her chroniclers, Hernando del Pulgar, presumably over his reluctance to have his work censored. See my "Discourse of Effeminacy" for more details. I also provide examples there of the gendered imagery of chaos and degeneracy that pervades Isabelline official chronicles of her father Juan II and her half-brother Enrique IV's reigns. Gregory S. Hutcheson's essay on Juan II's court, "Desperately Seeking Sodom," in *Queer Iberia,* treats similar rhetoric in the court of Isabel's father.

18. Michel Foucault, *The History of Sexuality,* vol. 1: *An Introduction,* trans. Robert Hurley (New York: Vintage Books, 1990).

19. Montrose, "The Elizabethan Subject," pp. 317–18.

20. Alcuin Blamires, *The Case for Women in Medieval Culture* (Oxford: Clarendon Press, 1997).

21. For relevant works, consult Julian Weiss's bibliography in this collection. On the medicalization of misogyny in medieval Iberia, see Solomon, *The Literature of Misogyny*. I deal with the other three genres mentioned below.

22. This more material form of misogyny is detectable in works like *Grisel y Mirabella* by Juan de Flores and the anonymous "Pleyto del manto," both of which I discuss below (see notes 49 and 57 for editions of these works). It is also evident in *Carajicomedia*, ed. Alvaro Alonso (Archidona, Málaga: Ediciones Aljibe, 1995), and in Fernando de Rojas's *La Celestina*, ed. Dorothy S. Severin (Madrid: Cátedra, 1988); in the latter, see especially the servant's description of their highborn mistress Melibea in act 9. At the same time, when dividing participants in the debate about women in Spain into pro and anti camps, it is important to keep in mind that in Spain as in the rest of Europe, contributors to the debate exulted in their ability to argue both sides of the 'woman' question. Part of the popularity of the debate was due to the opportunity it gave participants to display their command of the rhetorical techniques of argumentation, e.g., appeals to authority, the use of exempla and anecdote, analogy, invective, and puns (Katherine Usher Henderson and Barbara F. McManus, *Half Humankind: Contexts and Texts of the Controversy about Women in England, 1540–1640* [Urbana and Chicago: University of Illinois Press, 1985], pp. 32–39). This helps explain the frequent retractions by late medieval Castilian antifeminist writers (Torrellas produced two). The best-known of these is the palinode at the end of the printed versions of Martínez de Toledo's *Arcipreste de Talavera o Corbacho,* which appeared, significantly, in 1498, 1499, and 1500, that is, in the final years of Isabel's reign. In his 1970 edition of the work, Gonzalez Muela was still puzzled by the retraction (see the edition cited in note 2 above, pp. 10–11). More directly relevant to my discussion are two palinodes, one in prose and one in verse, by Torrellas himself. Such seeming about-faces are properly understood in the context of a court culture that encouraged display, competition, wordplay, and irony. For an interpretation of Martínez de Toledo's retraction along these lines, see Marina Scordilis Brownlee, "Hermeneutics of Reading in the *Corbacho,*" in *Medieval Texts and Contemporary Readers* (Ithaca, N.Y.: Cornell University Press, 1987), pp. 216–33. See Catherine Brown, *Contrary Things: Exegesis, Dialectic, and the Poetics of Didacticism* (Stanford, Calif.: Stanford University Press, 1998) for an important recent study of Martínez de Toledo.

23. Susan Schibanoff points out the similar overlap among racial, gender, and religious discourses in Chaucer's "Man of Law's Tale" in "Worlds Apart: Orientalism, Antifeminism, and Heresy in Chaucer's 'Man of Law's Tale'," *Exemplaria* 8.1 (1996): 59–96. For medieval Spain, in addition to Mirrer, *Women, Jews, and Muslims,* see Rodríguez-Puértolas, ed., *Poesía crítica y satírica del siglo XV* (Madrid: Castalia, 1981), which focuses specifically on anti-Semitism in fifteenth-century satirical verse. For a broader European view, see Rubin, *Gentile Tales*.

24. Pérez Priego, *Poesía femenina,* pp. 137–8; vv. 68–76. I have chosen to quote Torrellas from this accessible edition of medieval Spanish verse debate texts. The most complete and careful edition of the fifteenth-century *cancioneros* that gathered together the work of Torrellas, Montoro, and some seven hundred other court poets of the second half of the fifteenth century is that of Brian Dutton and Jineen Krogstad, eds., *El cancionero del siglo XV, c. 1360–1520,* Biblioteca del Siglo XV, Maior, vol. 6 (Salamanca: Universidad de Salamanca, 1990–91). All translations of Spanish poetry into English are my own.

25. Diego de Valera, *Tratado en defensa de las virtuosas mujeres,* vol. 1 of *Prosistas castellanos del siglo XV,* ed. Mario Penna (Madrid: Atlas, 1955), pp. 55–76. The quotation is on p. 55.

26. Dutton and Krogstad, *El cancionero,* p. 262; vv. 31–35. I have modernized punctuation and capitalization in Urrea's poem.

27. For purposes of this discussion, I count the authors of panegyrics to the queen as participants in the gender debate since one of their favorite strategies is the comparison of Isabel to the Virgin Mary, the same exemplar of womanly goodness who is so often cited by the profeminine side of the debate.

28. No texts overtly criticizing Isabel directly survive. At least two bawdy texts, both anonymous, aim ironic barbs at the queen: "Pleyto del manto," discussed below, and *Carajicomedia* (see my essay cited in note 6). Both were probably written (and very likely circulated) during Isabel's reign, but they remained unpublished until well after her death. For a comparison with the Elizabethan case, see Julia M. Walker, ed., *Dissing Elizabeth: Negative Representations of Gloriana* (Durham, N.C.: Duke University Press, 1998).

29. For an overview of the scholarly reevaluation, see Seidenspinner-Núñez, "Inflecting the *Converso* Voice: A Commentary on Recent Theories," *La Corónica* 25.1 (1996): 6–18.

30. See E. Michael Gerli, "Antón de Montoro and the Wages of Eloquence: Poverty, Patronage, and Poetry in Fifteenth-Century Castile," *Romance Philology* 48 (1994–95): 1–13. Also useful on Montoro and the self-denigration of *converso* courtiers is Francisco Márquez Villanueva, "Jewish 'Fools' of the Spanish Fifteenth Century," *Hispanic Review* 50 (1982): 385–409.

31. On the ubiquity of sacrilegious language in the poetry of Isabel's reign, see María Rosa Lida de Malkiel, "La hipérbole sagrada en la poesía castellana del siglo XV," *Estudios sobre la literatura española del siglo XV* (Madrid: José Porrúa Turanzas, 1977), pp. 291–309.

32. For Gómez Manrique's anti-Torrellas poem, see Pérez Priego, *Poesía femenina,* pp. 147–51; the same collection includes Iñigo de Mendoza's contribution to the debate (pp. 191–201), which vituperatively attacks "las malas" and praises "las buenas."

33. I examine these texts and issues in my forthcoming book.

34. See my "Discourse of Effeminacy" for a description of this stigmatizing discourse in the works of various Isabelline chroniclers.

35. Diego de Valera, *Tratado de las epístolas,* in *Prosistas castellanos,* ed. Mario Penna, pp. 3–51 (quotation at p. 31).

36. For Montoro's poetry I have used the edition by Marithelma Costa, *Poesía completa* (Cleveland, Ohio: Cleveland State University Press, 1990). For the quotation, see p. 333.

37. It is interesting that Montoro's poem elicited irate refutations from several fellow poets, including a long attack from the Portuguese poet Franciso Vaca (*Cancionero general,* lxxv-lxxvii).Vaca calls him *traydor* [traitor], *omicido* [murderer], and *loco* [crazy] for comparing the earthly queen to the Queen of Heaven and denounces his sacrilege in apocalyptic terms: "Pues como osastes hablar/tal motivo sin recelos/que solo de lo pensar/la tierra deue temblar/y derrocarse los cielos" [How did you dare to speak this way without fear, when merely thinking it causes the earth to shake and the sky to fall; lxxvi]. The two poems in effect constitute a mini-debate about women. The strength of Vaca's attack on Montoro on theological grounds is another indication of the interweaving of misogyny, anti-Semitism, and sovereignty that I trace here.

38. Marithelma Costa analyzes how the formal and rhetorical virtuosity of the poem contributes to the authority of Montoro's protest in "Discurso de la fiesta y protesta política en la producción poética de Antón de Montoro," *Estudios en homenaje a Enrique Ruiz-Fornells,* eds. Juan Fernández Jiménez, José Labrador Herraiz, and L. Teresa Valdivieso (Erie, Penn.: Associación de licenciados y Doctores Españoles en los Estados Unidos, 1990), pp. 115–22.

39. Costa, *Poesía completa,* p. 202; st. 1–2.

40. Costa, *Poesía completa,* p. 203; vv. 23–24. I am grateful to Julian Weiss for his suggestions on translating Montoro.

41. Montoro repeats the insult, applying it collectively to the *conversos* in a poem written on the occasion of the pogroms that occurred in Córdoba in 1473 (Costa, *Poesía completa,* p. 29, v. 188: "pobres, cornudos y putos" [poor, cuckolded, and faggots]). Costa believes that Montoro wrote the panegyric I am discussing here around the same time (p. 391). See Joshua Trachtenberg, *The Devil and the Jews: The Medieval Conception of the Jew and Its Relation to Modern Antisemitism* (Philadelphia, Pa.: Jewish Publication Society of America, 1983), and Rubin, *Gentile Tales.*

42. Daniel Boyarin, "'This We Know to Be the Carnal Israel': Circumcision and the Erotic Life of God and Israel," *Critical Inquiry* 18.3 (1992): 474–505. Boyarin cites midrashic and rabbinic texts to support his gendered interpretation of circumcision. According to midrash, circumcision makes the male Jew open to receive the divine speech and vision of God (one text calls circumcised men "daughters"). As Boyarin points out, such a gender paradox is not unusual "for the mystical experience au fond, when experienced erotically, often involves (perhaps only in the West) gender paradox. The mystical experience is interpreted as a penetration by the divine word or spirit into the body and soul of the adept . . . an image of sexuality in which the mystic is figured as the female partner" (pp. 494–5).

43. According to Costa (*Poesía completa,* xii), Montoro's ancestors probably converted to Christianity shortly after the pogroms of 1391; Montoro died sometime around 1477. There is no evidence to suggest the sincerity of his faith.

44. Costa, *Poesía completa,* pp. 203–4, st. 5–6.

45. Costa, *Poesía completa,* p. 204; st. 7–8.

46. Rodríguez-Puértolas, following Kenneth Scholberg in *Sátira e invectiva en la España medieval* (Madrid: Gredos, 1971), links the fires of Christmas in Montoro's poem and the fires of the Inquisition, but Costa (*Poesía completa,* pp. 202–4) places the poem a few years before the institution of the Inquisition. She deems it a response to the Andalusian pogroms of 1473–4.

47. Carolyn Bynum, *Jesus as Mother: Studies in the Spirituality of the High Middle Ages* (Berkeley and Los Angeles: University of California Press, 1982).

48. Montoro did in fact contribute directly to the debate about women with a very brief poem attacking Torrellas. He insults the poet's parentage by declaring him the product of a masturbating shepherd and the earth that absorbed his spilled semen: "Mas algund pastor de sierra,/mientra su ganado pace, vos dio por madre la tierra/y sacó vos una perra/segund mandrágala nace" (Costa, *Poesía completa,* pp. 138–9; vv. 14–18) [Rather some mountain shepherd, while his flock grazed, made the earth your mother, and you were born, as the mandrake is, pulled out of her (the earth) by some dog]. According to Costa (p. 139, n. 10), the root of the mandrake was believed to have a human shape and since it could not be readily uprooted, it was tied to the tail of a dog. Made to run, the dog would pull the plant out of the ground.

49. Juan de Flores, *Grisel y Mirabella,* ed. Pablo Alcázar López and José A. González Nuñez (Granada: Editorial Don Quixote, 1983). For biographical information on Flores, see Joseph Gwara, "The Identity of Juan de Flores: The Evidence of the *Crónica incompleta de los Reyes Católicos,*" *Journal of Hispanic Philology* 11 (1987): 103–30, 205–22; Carmen Parrilla, "Un cronista olvidado: Juan de Flores, autor de la *Crónica incompleta de los Reyes Católicos,*" in *The Age of the Catholic Monarchs, 1474–1516: Literary Studies in Memory of Keith Whinnom,* eds. Alan Deyermond and Ian Macpherson (Liverpool: Liverpool University Press, 1989), pp. 123–33; see also Lillian von der Walde Moheno, *Amor e ilegalidad: 'Grisel y Mirabella', de Juan de Flores* (Mexico: Universidad Nacional Autónoma de Mexico, 1996) for a summary of the recent findings about Flores's life and works. According to Parrilla, Flores was also for a time rector of Spain's most prestigious university, at Salamanca. The theories of love taught at Salamanca have been shown to have been influential on many Isabelline works (see Pedro Cátedra, *Amor y pedagogía en la Edad Media (Estudios de doctrina amorosa y práctica literaria)* [Salamanca: Universidad de Salamanca, 1989]).

50. See Matulka, *The Novels of Juan de Flores,* for more information.

51. For the view that Flores uses the rigidity and harshness of the King toward his only daughter and heir to comment on Isabel's harsh punishment of

her rebellious subjects, see Patricia E. Grieve, *Desire and Death in Spanish Sentimental Romance (1440–1550),* (Newark, Del.: Juan de la Cuesta, 1987); von der Walde, *Amor e ilegalidad;* and Marina Brownlee, *The Severed Word: Ovid's "Heroides" and the "Novela sentimental"* (Princeton: Princeton University Press, 1990). Given the plasticity of gender that marks sovereignty, it is entirely possible that both the King and Queen of Scotland are used to represent aspects of Flores's royal employer. The more literal possibility, that the King of Scotland is a counterpart of Fernando, is less likely, since Flores intentionally marginalizes the king in his chronicle of the Catholic Monarchs' reign. In treating *Grisel,* I have chosen to focus on Flores's less conventionalized, more complex characterization of the queen.

52. For fine feminist analyses of this archetypal character, see chapter 3 on Chaucer's *Troilus and Criseyde* of David Aers's *Community, Gender, and Individual Identity: English Writing, 1360–1430* (London and New York: Routledge, 1988), and Roberta Krueger on Benoît de Sainte-Maure's highly influential *Le Roman de Troie* in *Women Readers and the Ideology of Gender in Old French Verse Romance* (Cambridge: Cambridge University Press, 1997), pp. 4–7.

53. Matulka, *The Novels of Juan de Flores,* defends Flores as staunchly profeminine, and her view prevailed until fairly recently. Cf. Antony van Beysterveldt, "Revisión de los debates feministas del siglo XV y las novelas de Juan de Flores," *Hispania* 64 (1981): 1–13; Barbara F. Weissberger, "Authority Figures in *Siervo libre de Amor* and *Grisel y Mirabella,*" in *"Revista de estudios hispánicos* [Puerto Rico] 9 (1982 [1984]): 255–62; and von der Walde, *Amor e ilegalidad.*

54. I offer this type of reading in "Role-Reversal and Festivity in the Romances of Juan de Flores," *Journal of Hispanic Philology* 13.3 (1989): 197–213.

55. *Amor e ilegalidad,* especially, pp. 213–44.

56. In the ironic retraction appended to the printed versions of *Arcipreste de Talavera o Corbacho,* Martínez de Toledo uses similar Inquisitional language: "Pero si auer quisiere su amor e querencia, conviene que al huego e biuas llamas ponga el libro que compuse de aquel breue tractado de la reprobación del loco amor" (Gerli, p. 304) [But if the reader desires to have his love and desire, he had better consign to the fire and open flames that brief treatise I composed reproving passionate love]. He then recounts a dream highly reminiscent of the final scenes of *Grisel y Mirabella.* In it he is attacked by more than a thousand famous women from around the world who "traían esecuciones a manera de martirio, dando los golpes tales de ruecas e chapines, puños e remesones, qual sea en penitencia de los males que hize e aun de mis pecados" (p. 305) [brought the means to martyr me, hitting me hard with their distaffs, slippers, fists, and yanking my hair out, so that I made penance for the harm I did and even for my sins].

57. "Pleyto del Manto," *Cancionero de obras de burlas provocantes a risa,* eds. Pablo Jauralde Pou and Juan Alfredo Bellón Cazabán (Madrid: Akal, 1974), pp. 47–67.

58. Marcial Rubio Arquez, "El 'Pleito del manto': un caso de parodia en el *Cancionero General*," in *Actas del IX Simposio de la Sociedad Española de Literatura General y Comparada* (18–20 November 1992), 2 vols., vol. 2 (Zaragoza: University of Zaragoza, 1992), pp. 237–50.

59. On Aristotelian reproductive theory, see Danielle Jacquart and Claude Thomasset, *Sexuality and Medicine in the Middle Ages,* trans. Matthew Adamson (Princeton: Princeton University Press, 1988 [1985]), esp. p. 59.

60. "Pleyto," pp. 47, 48–9, 54, 58–9.

61. See Louise O. Vasvari, "El hijo del molinero: para la polisemia popular del Libro del Arcipreste," in *Erotismo en las letras hispánicas,* eds. Luce López-Baralt and Francisco Márquez Villanueva (Mexico: Colegio de México, 1995), pp. 461–77, for the Spanish context, specifically the *Libro de Buen Amor.*

62. On the growth of royal absolutism in the fifteenth century and the strategies used to justify it, see José Manuel Nieto Soria, *Fundamentos ideológicos del poder real en Castilla* (s. XIII–XVI) (Madrid: Eudema, 1988), pp. 135–36 and passim.

63. On the litigious atmosphere of early modern Spain, see Richard L. Kagan, *Lawsuits and Litigants in Castile, 1500–1700* (Chapel Hill: University of North Carolina Press, 1981).

64. See Liss, *Isabel, the Queen,* p. 130.

65. The syntax in the modern edition of these verses is rather unclear; I have been unable to consult any manuscript versions. Louise Vasvari clarifies the vaginal vs. anal connotations of the "open road" imagery in medieval bawdy verse in "Peregrinaciones por topografías pornográficas en el *Libro de Buen Amor,*" in *Actas del VI Congreso de la Asociación Hispánica de Literatura Medieval* (Alcalá: Universidad de Alcalá, 1997), pp. 1563–72.

66. Netanyahu, *The Origins of the Inquisition,* p. 995.

67. The original Latin of Palencia's history reads "tamquam segregata natio" (qtd. in Netanyahu, p. 1306, n. 27).

68. Palencia singles out the powerful *converso* Álvaro de Luna, Juan II's favorite, as the one who introduced "el vicio nefando" [the nefarious vice] into Castile (Weissberger, "Discourse of Effeminacy," p. 304). For the discourses of sodomy and anti-Semitism in Juan II's chroniclers, see Hutcheson, "Desperately Seeking Sodom." On the Inquisition's persecution of sodomites, see Rafael Carrasco, *Inquisición y represión sexual en Valencia: Historia de los sodomitas (1565–1785)* (Barcelona: Laertes S.A. de Ediciones, 1985).

69. *Libro llamado El Alboraique,* in Nicolás López Martínez, *Los judaizantes castellanos y la Inquisición en tiempo de Isabel la Católica* (Burgos: Seminario Metropolitano de Burgos, 1954), pp. 391–404.

70. It is interesting to recall that Arianism taught that Christ the Son was not consubstantial with God the Father, a doctrine that holds parallels with the Jewish denial that Christ was the Messiah.

CHAPTER 11

"¿QUÉ DEMANDAMOS DE LAS MUGERES?": FORMING THE DEBATE ABOUT WOMEN IN LATE MEDIEVAL SPAIN (WITH A BAROQUE RESPONSE)

Julian Weiss

This study explores the debate over women in Spain during the later Middle Ages and Early Modern period by drawing on the insights of Pierre Bourdieu. It analyzes the ideological process whereby noblemen defined, accumulated, and fought over their cultural and symbolic capital as courtiers and men of letters. While marginalizing women, the debate also recognized them as essential to the production of masculine courtly identity and culture. An appendix offers a bibliography of primary texts from Castile and Aragon.

Al muy prepotente don Juan el segundo,
aquel con quien Júpiter tovo tal zelo,
que tanta de parte le haze del mundo
quanta a sí mesmo se haze en el cielo.

[To the most prepotent Juan II, / for whom Jupiter had so much love, / that he bestows on him such dominions on earth / as he himself possesses in heaven]

These are the opening lines of Juan de Mena's famous *Laberinto de Fortuna* (1444), an epic allegory that occupies a privileged place in the Spanish literary canon. Notorious for its relentlessly classicizing style, the poem is at once a plea for Castile's moral and political regeneration and a self-conscious manifesto for the aspirations of vernacular literature as it strove to emulate the cultural authority of antiquity. It is dedicated to a king whose majesty—at this juncture at least—seems conjured more out of the pulsing rhythms of Mena's *arte mayor* meter than out of political reality (in 1444 Juan II was being held hostage by rebellious barons). Over fifty years later, after the fall of Granada, the expulsion of the Jews, the voyages to the New World, the pacification of the aristocracy, and the unification of Castile and Aragón under the powerful monarchs Ferdinand and Isabel, Mena's vision seemed to have been fulfilled. At this time, a young humanist scholar, Hernán Núñez de Toledo, edited the poem and published it along with his own vast commentary. First printed in 1499, then revised in 1505, the poem and commentary became one of the best-selling texts of the Spanish Renaissance, a nationalist classic that embodied the political and cultural aspirations of the new imperial age. As he glossed the poem's opening lines, Hernán Núñez pondered the precise boundaries of the world over which Juan II had exercised his dominion. Among the possible meanings of the term *mundo* Núñez included the following definition, endorsed by the classical authority of the great Varro: "Y 'mundo' en latín significa el atavío con que las mugeres se componen: auctor es Marco Varrón en el libro primero de la *Lingua latina*" [And *mundus* in Latin means the cosmetics with which women make themselves up; the authority is Marcus Varro in book 1 of *Lingua latina*].[1]

For a number of reasons, this gloss and the lines it elucidates combine to form a convenient text for my own gloss on the debate over women in Spain during the transition from the late Middle Ages to early modernity, when so many cultural as well as political boundaries were being reconfigured. This particular definition of *mundus* is certainly an incidental detail in Núñez's encyclopedic commentary. The commentator merely doffs his hat at a scholarly curiosity and passes on to explain what was already pretty obvious in Mena's text: that *mundo*, "earth," is to be understood in opposition to *cielo*, "heavens," and that the king holds sway over the former, not the latter. But the detail gives us pause. To what extent did Núñez and his readers reflect upon the unspoken assumptions that might form an ideological nexus between the notions of 'world' and 'female cosmetics'? According to Ernout and Meillet, the only documented author to link explicitly the two meanings was the late-second-century grammarian Festus, who did so on the grounds that they are connected by the idea of motion or change: "Mundus appellatur caelum, terra, mare et aer. Mundus etiam dicitur ornatus mulieris, quia non alius est quam quod moueri potest" [*Mundus* means the heavens, the earth, the sea, and the air. *Mundus* also means the ornaments of woman, since it is nothing other than that which can be moved].[2] Like female cosmetics, which purify and embellish, but which are also mutable and hence untrustworthy, so the world is understood as a contradictory site of order and deceit, a move that rationalizes into moral terms the ineluctable fact of historical change. Certainly, the gendering of this contradiction as female will not surprise anyone familiar with the history of Western misogyny. R. Howard Bloch, for example, discusses the "cosmetic theology" of early Christian writers whose fascinated loathing for female cosmetics "is of a piece with the patristic devaluation of the material world, which comes to be seen as a mask, a mere cosmetic reproduction."[3] In Núñez's commentary, however, the issue is not misogynist asceticism but secular power, not escape from the world but active engagement with it. His text invites speculation on the corollary to this association between the world and female cosmetics: namely, that women are "made up," or constituted as social beings, *by* and *in* the world, and that one way in which the world reproduces itself—culturally, politically, economically—is through the regulation of women and, in the symbolic domain, through the "fashioning" of woman. In this paper, therefore, I argue that the debate about woman that flourished (if that's the right word) in Spain between ca. 1430–1520 has to be set in the context of the hegemonic process. We would be wrong to pigeonhole it as a mere courtly entertainment or literary game, or to classify it as yet another instance of misogynist discourse caught in its own self-repeating, transhistorical loop.[4] We need to investigate how the debate's formalized reification of woman—whether defended as a manifestation of providential order or attacked as the ultimate sign of instability—is implicated in the political, economic, and cultural changes of the period. The debate over the mutability (or otherwise) of women mediates a debate over the mutability of culture.

Recent research has shown how central questions of sexuality and gender were to the changes and conflicts that characterized late medieval and early modern Spain. Although this is not the place to summarize the work done on such issues as the construction of gender categories, misogyny, the representation of women, and women writers and mystics, it is clear that sexual politics is a key feature of the three reigns that structure the fifteenth century.[5] According to the grand narrative of Castilian historiography, the chaos created by the reign of two "weak" male monarchs, Juan II (1406–54) and Enrique IV (1454–74), was resolved by a powerful queen, Isabel la Católica, whose "virile" reign (1474–1504) laid the basis for national redemption, orthodoxy, and empire. As Barbara Weissberger has shown, the ideological contradiction between the dominant patriarchal values and the actually existing political power of a real woman produced substantial fears and anxieties in the cultural sphere.[6] But Isabel was not the only powerful queen during this period. During the minority of her father, Juan II, one of the co-regents of Castile was Isabel's English grandmother, Catherine of Lancaster (1368–1413), who was described by contemporary historians as possessing a "mannish" appearance and a predilection for intrigue with a cabal of female consorts.[7] From the care and tutelage of his mother, Juan II passed into the hands (some say literally) of his male protégé, Álvaro de Luna, whose power over the monarch was epitomized by the rumor that he regulated even the king's sexual encounters with his wife.[8] (So Mena's comparison between the "prepotent" Juan II and that priapic shape-shifter Jupiter may well have raised a laugh or two.) In the wars of succession that brought Isabel to the throne, the political enemies of Enrique IV employed what Weissberger has called "a discourse of effeminacy" in their successful attempt to discredit him, his policies, and his daughter, Juana, Isabel's rival. Ritual dethronement, accusations of maurophilia and religious heterodoxy, rumors of homosexuality and the inability to procreate (in part because of an allegedly odd-shaped penis—not the last time, of course, that the "guilt" of a political leader was to be determined by the shape of his genitalia) all lend an air of inevitability to his sobriquet "el Impotente."[9]

Waging political battles on the ideological terrain of sexuality and gender is not the only context in which to situate the courtly debate over woman. The fact that Woman was put into question so frequently and with such virulence at this time is also an index of conflicts and changes that were taking place in the very structure and definition of the nobility at a crucial moment in its long transformation from a warrior to a courtier caste. The creation of new noble families, changes in property rights and patterns of inheritance, new interpretations of knighthood and gentility, the spread of lay literacy and the debate between the relative worth of arms and letters—all these factors come into play. Exactly how they come into play is in part a matter for empirical research and close readings of specific texts, many of which have scarcely been studied at all, and some of which lack modern editions. I append a bibliography of primary texts, therefore, that revises the corpus established over fifty years ago by Jacob Ornstein, in the hope that this revision will lead to broader and more detailed treatments than are possible here.[10] But, equally importantly, reading the *querelle* is also a matter for theoretical reflection. For this reason, the first of the following five sections outlines the conceptual issues that underpin my analysis of selected aspects of the debate. Sections two and three address in turn the cultural categories of the masculine courtly subject and the emergent notion of the "literary." After this, in section four, I consider some paradoxes inherent in the ideological relation between the dominant and the dominated, specifically, men's anxiety that their identity rests on the shaky foundations of a female Other who, by their own definition, is mutable and beyond absolute control. The fifth and final section jumps to the Baroque, and shows how the misogynist argument of mutability is appropriated as the central trope in one woman's critique of patriarchal discourse.

Questions of Method:
Hegemony, Form, and the Sociology of Culture

How we mark the formal boundaries of ideological "debate" depends in large measure upon our theoretical assumptions about historical change. For historical materialists, debate lies at the very heart of history, when understood in Antonio Gramsci's terms as a hegemonic process. According to this, the dominant maintains its supremacy by acknowledging oppositional or alternative discourses and practices, only to negate them outright, assimilate them, or concede to them a modicum of legitimacy. Similarly, the threatening potential of subaltern groups often derives its strength from dominant ideologies. In this way, as Raymond Williams emphasizes, hegemony "has continually to be renewed, recreated, defended, and modified."[11] Viewed thus, moments when "debate" becomes explicit, or formalized, take on special relevance, indicating instances of particular conflict or contradiction within the hegemonic process. As we study what Alcuin Blamires has called "the formal case" for women, I argue that we need to make a much greater case for form.[12] I should like to go beyond taxonomy and give center stage to the ideological analysis of forms and conventions—at all levels, from the macro level of oral and literate modes of thought and expression, through courtly and clerical, prose and verse, right down to the micro level of syntax, versification, and meter—because that can help us to restore a sense of conflict, and hence of history, to what often seems a highly conventionalized and settled rehearsal of ideas about gender and the relationship between the sexes.[13]

Methodologically, to understand the hegemonic power of the formal debate about gender, we must do more than abstract the ideas from their contexts and construct a metadebate, which is the emphasis of most scholars who have reviewed the Spanish texts.[14] To avoid reading the works as merely a reflex of their historical circumstances, we need to adopt an ideological approach to their esthetic forms, styles, and conventions. These formal aspects of the debate texts should not be discarded as merely the esthetic husk of misogyny, for the esthetic is also what Raymond Williams calls an ideological "situation." The esthetic situates us in relation to meanings, values, and social practices in the very process of representing them, and can naturalize as beautiful and fitting their material conditions of existence. The esthetic, of course, is not just a decorum of vested interests: As the Russian Formalists would have it, it can also "make strange" our perceptions of the world, and unmask their arbitrariness.[15] Close textual analysis of literary forms—in combination, as I shall explain, with Pierre Bourdieu's concepts of field, habitus, and symbolic power—helps us to read particular instances of the debate as moments in the continual renegotiation of the hegemonic.

Paying attention to form also entails the basic distinction made by feminist linguists between "naming and representation." According to Deborah Cameron, the complexity of getting to grips with sexist language is that it "cannot be regarded as simply the 'naming' of the world from one, masculinist perspective; it is better conceptualized as a multifaceted phenomenon occurring in a number of quite complex systems of representation, all with their places in historical traditions."[16] Indeed, when we peruse the relevant texts from fifteenth-century Castile, we soon see that although the debate over gender is most explicitly a debate over 'woman,' it is never exclusively so. Occurring in a variety of discursive situations (within the court; within the medical and academic professions; in sermons, and so forth), the praise and blame of woman is often a way of rationalizing or naturalizing hierarchies within a particular "field" (on which term, see below). The debate over woman certainly does enact patriarchal ideologies of gender, and no feminist will underestimate its debilitating effects upon the lives of real women. But the debate is also inextricably intertwined with a range of other ideologies that structure social castes and classes, notions of race, morality or medicine, or such practices as courtliness and the literary, which are the two activities that interest me most in this essay.[17] It is this complex interweaving of ideologies that makes misogyny so powerful and pervasive, such a towering, yet also such an elusive target: Like the 'woman' it despises, "la misoginia è movile." Woman hating did not formally acquire the independent label of "misogyny" until later, when our modern taxonomies of hatred began to take shape.[18] It is not, of course, that misogyny did not exist, but rather that it was conceptually subsumed into other (often overlapping) categories. It is only in the course of the early modern period that the term "misogyny" emerged, unevenly, from the darkness of doxa—those realms of thought and social practice that, according to Bourdieu, are so taken for granted that they require no name.[19] For the texts discussed in this paper, the word employed is "maldezir" [invective, or personal slander], which belongs to the field of court society and to the habitus of courtliness.

Field, habitus, doxa. These terms come from the noted sociologist of culture Pierre Bourdieu, whose theoretical writings have had such an impact on cultural theory in recent years.[20] I have already said something about doxa, and before continuing I need to explain the other terms that I shall be using in this paper. Amongst other things, Bourdieu helps us to explore the relation between language use and the reproduction of "culture," understood both in its broad anthropological sense as the complete set of practices, beliefs, and values that structure a whole society, and in more specialized senses such as "high art" or "working-class culture." Language is never just a communicative act undertaken at an interpersonal level, but every act is marked by the larger social and ideological settings in which it takes place and that it helps to reproduce. In other words, linguistic interaction is never entirely interest free; knowingly or not, it is profit oriented. It takes place within "fields," also often called "markets" (the political, the literary, the religious, and so forth), in which agents occupy particular positions and exchange (besides information) different forms of "capital" that constitute the basic resources of that field or market. Besides economic capital—wealth, property—there is, for instance, cultural capital (the knowledge, skills, and qualifications that characterize the field) and symbolic capital (the stock of honor and status the agents can draw on), both of which can provide agents with the legitimacy to act and speak in a particular situation.

Crucial here is the notion of "habitus." This is a set of dispositions that incline agents to think, act, and speak in a certain way appropriate to a particular field. These dispositions, which can be abstracted for analysis as the "rules of the game," endow the agents with a practical sense (*le sens pratique*) of the field, its generative principles: They are learned but deeply internalized, and are often incorporated bodily as particular ways of speaking, holding the body, eating, etc. They provide the agent with a sense of controlled improvisation, of freedom within limits, of good (and bad) taste.

Finally, symbolic violence and power: Bourdieu is concerned to break away from a mechanistic approach to understanding the ways in which a culture reproduces itself, one that reduces human actions to the simple application of explicitly articulated rules. His interest in the play of freedom and necessity (hardly an original interest, to be sure) leads him to explore the various ways in which power relations are internalized and sustained. Like others (such as Antonio Gramsci), Bourdieu attaches importance to the fact that hierarchies are not just imposed from above but are also held in place from below. There is a willing, often preconscious, complicity between the dominant and dominated, which can operate in symbolic or euphemized ways as part of the "natural" order of things. To understand its operation and its effects, the exercise of symbolic power has to be set in the interstices between the field and the habitus. In the case of this essay, this means asking, how does that "controlled improvisation" performed in the debate over women connect with the field of court culture? what resources of cultural and symbolic capital are mobilized in the process? and what forms of violence are naturalized and—if at all—secure the complicity of the oppressed?

Courtliness in Question

In an important essay, E. Michael Gerli has argued that the misogynist *Arcipreste de Talavera* by Alfonso Martínez de Toledo (1438), which along with Pere Torrellas's *Coplas de las calidades de las donas* was one of the works that sparked the debate in Castile, constituted a moral response to the excesses of courtly love, feared as a new aristocratic "religion."[21] This insight needs to be developed by viewing the debate as part of a more general pattern of realignments taking place both *between* and *within* the fields of clerical and lay culture. Though Martínez de Toledo's moral and intellectual legitimacy derives from his ecclesiastical position and his clerical learning, he was by no means an outsider in court circles. As chaplain to Juan II, he wrote, like generations of clerics before him, as a member of court society. His treatise, in four parts plus ironic retraction, offers not only a vicious satire of women and the effects of love, but also instruction on physiology, astrology, and fortune. In this respect, the book covers a similar thematic range to the earliest known anthology of Castilian court verse, the *Cancionero de Juan Alfonso de Baena,* which had been compiled just a few years before by the eponymous cleric. As one of the many *letrados* (clerics) on the royal staff, Baena dedicated his anthology not only to Juan II, his first wife María, and the noblemen and -women at court, but also to the many "perlados" and "priores" [prelates and priors] connected to the royal household.[22] Indeed, the *Cancionero* contains a high proportion of verse written by ecclesiastical figures, often in debate with courtiers over such theological and astrological topics as the Holy Trinity, free will, and predestination. These poetic altercations, known as *preguntas y respuestas* [questions and answers], debate more than their ostensible themes. Also at stake, and perhaps more significantly so, is the question of who has the right to speak on such weighty issues.[23] Martínez de Toledo's assault on women, with its sermonizing style and its philosophical disquisitions on humoral theory and on the influence of the stars, needs to be seen in this context: As an intervention in the continuing and open-ended redefinition of what constituted cultural and symbolic capital at court, and its redistribution both horizontally (between the clerical and warrior castes, between men and women) and vertically (among the different ranks or economic classes within each group). For all his reliance on Andreas Capellanus, Martínez de Toledo realized that the clerical monopoly of *curialitas*—always in contention—was a thing of the past.[24]

The Spanish debate over woman has often been called a courtly entertainment, or a literary "game." Certainly, it can be viewed as a game (another term, like "market," that Bourdieu uses to describe the concept of field), but it was one played seriously and with serious consequences. The composition of poetry was part of the cut and thrust of court life, with its constant struggle over rank and status. In his discussion of power, ideology, and subjectification in the *cancionero* lyric, Mark Johnston starts from the premise that "the composition of courtly lyric involved competition for a status above and beyond the benefits gained from the exercise of literacy alone," and that we need to explore—among other things—how such verse "positions a subject to advantage."[25] So it is worth asking just what kind of advantage—indeed what kind of subject position—Pere Torrellas thought he was establishing when he wrote his infamous diatribe on the deceits and mutability of women.

It is possible that Pere Torrellas (ca. 1410–1486) wrote his *Coplas de las calidades de las donas,* also called *Coplas de maldezir de mugeres* [Stanzas on the Qualities of Women, or Stanzas Cursing Women] as a young man, sometime before 1435.[26] The poem is structured around a paradoxical double move: The opening lines declare that the courtly lover destroys himself in pursuit of his lady ("Quien bien persigue/ dona, a sí mesmo destruye") because women are. . . . There then follow twelve stanzas of diatribe, much of it Aristotelian in origin, which lists a number of well-known misogynist claims about women's inconstancy, secrecy, and so forth. The final stanza is a palinode of sorts, in which Torrellas claims not only that his lady is an exception to the rule, but that the rule itself is open to question:

> Entre las otras sois vos
> dama d'aquesta mi vida,
> [. . .]
> Vos sois la que desfazéis
> lo que contienen mis *versos;*
> vos sois la que mereçéis
> renombre, y lahor cobréis
> entre *las otras diversos.* (emphasis mine)

[You are among the others (i.e., virtuous women)/ lady of my life, / [. . .] / you are the one who belies / what is contained in my verse; / you are the one who deserves / renown, and you will gain praise / (that is) different among other women].[27]

On one level, Torrellas clearly intended to limit the generality of his earlier invective by stating that his beloved belongs "entre las otras" [among the others], thus implying that there does in fact exist a category of "good" woman. But a more challenging intellectual conceit is forged in the hyperbaton of the final four lines, with its discordant juxtaposition of a feminine pronominal phrase, "las otras [mujeres]," and the masculine adjective "diversos." Although "diversos" qualifies "renombre, y lahor" and rhymes with "versos," it is also, so to speak, pulled into the semantic orbit of "las otras" ("other different women"). The poem thus concludes with a formal ploy that highlights lack of agreement between masculine and feminine, and the role language plays in creating this dissonance. Torrellas's conceit seems to have been lost on several scribes and sixteenth-century editors, who plainly felt a need to resolve his apparent grammatical crux, either by writing "los otros diversos" or by jettisoning the rhyme scheme and writing "las otras diversas." Without trying to read too much into this, these variants eloquently symbolize the urge to force the social category of "woman" into inherited and fixed patterns of discourse, and the disjunctions that could result.

However much Torrellas hedged his bets in the final stanza, the poem as a whole was a bold gesture: It was the first time that noblewomen had been insulted in this particular courtly form, in the relatively recent lyric language of Castilian; and whether it was intended as such or not, the poem was read as a heterodoxical assault on women and an intolerable transgression of courtly conduct. Many of the poems in response are either dedicated principally to the theme of masculine gentility or include gentility alongside their counterclaims for female virtue (see appended bibliography). Though not the longest, the rebuke by Antón de Montoro is the sharpest and most brutal, not least because Montoro was a *converso* of nonnoble origins: "Yo non sé quién sois, Torrellas" [I do not know who you are, Torrellas], and he then proceeds to describe him as the product of a masturbating shepherd, born from the earth like a mandrake; in short a "nobody," who, like the mandrake, is brought into the world shrieking, spewing lust and poison in equal measure. At this distance, such responses seem predictable, and make us wonder what Torrellas felt he had to gain by insulting women in this way. To answer the question, we cannot rely simply on internal textual analysis; we need to situate the poem in a larger literary and social context.

Torrellas's poem, structured around a paradox and with the built-in ambiguities of the final stanza, was designed to set his lady—and hence himself—over and above the common undifferentiated mass of noblewomen and their courtiers. Within the courtly market of exchange, he seeks the profit of distinction. But his strategy entailed a serious misjudgment. His error did not derive from any failure on his part to have internalized the correct courtly habitus—respect for virtuous women, verbal ingenuity, being in love, being able to rhyme, etc.—but from the disjunction between habitus and field. As John B. Thompson put it in his summary of Bourdieu's theories, "particular practices or perceptions should be seen, not as the product of the habitus as such, but as the product of the *relation between* the habitus, on the one hand, and the specific social contexts or 'fields' within which individuals act, on the other" (*Language and Symbolic Power*, p. 14; emphasis in original). Put simply, Torrellas misread the field, and his own position within it.

In the earlier lyric tradition of Galician-Portuguese, which had lost ground as a literary language to Castilian and Catalan during the later fourteenth century, the composition of *cantigas de escarnio e maldezir* [poems of personal invective and slander] was a legitimate part of courtliness. The often highly scurrilous and personal insults were regarded as a display of courtly *facetia* or wit, so long as certain proprieties were maintained (at least on a theoretical level). The participants frequently abused each other's nobility, but their abusive language did not seem to call into serious question their own gentility. Verbal duels were analogous to, and perhaps a substitute for, armed duels. There was a substantial vogue for invective against women, but with a fundamental class distinction, for the women in question were *soldadeiras,* or lower-class female minstrels.[28] Torrellas misappropriated this tradition.

He also lacked legitimacy. For Bourdieu, legitimacy comes not just from words alone; one needs the delegated authority that comes from an institutional position, or that is endowed by the accumulation of sufficient cultural and symbolic capital. It is hard to say whether the negative Castilian response was at some level conditioned by cultural rivalries with Aragón (both Castilian and Catalan were emergent lyric languages); there is no sign of rivalry in, for example, the friendship between the marqués de Santillana and Jordi de Sant Jordi, both contemporaries of the Catalan Torrellas. But there were definite cultural differences, specifically with regard to the literature on women. As a Catalan, Torrellas came from the same literary environment that had in previous generations produced a substantial corpus of material concerning female virtue and vice: translations of Andreas Capellanus and Boccaccio, Bernard Metge's *Lo somni,* and Friar Francesc Eiximenis's *Llibre de les dones* (for details, see the appended bibliography). Torrellas may have believed that his poem displayed an impressive cultural competence with these texts and that this endowed him with sufficient legitimacy to indulge in a daring act of controlled improvisation. As Rosanna Cantavella has suggested, if Torrellas had written his poem in Catalan, it would have offered nothing new.[29]

Torrellas's *Coplas* not only includes one retraction, it is also followed by several others, and the phenomenon is not unique to him. I have already mentioned Martínez de Toledo's ironic inversion of Andreas Capellanus, but several other participants chose to play both sides in the debate: Fernando de la Torre, Hernán Mexía, Antón de Montoro, Fray Íñigo de Mendoza, and (for reasons I shall explain) Juan de Tapia. In one respect, this can be seen as the desire to display one's mastery of the cultural capital available in the field. But in some cases—in that of Torrellas, for example—it also needs to be read as part of a deeper process of the courtier's subjectification. The courtier's identity is fashioned through the acquisition of the shared conventions of the group; these provide him with that sense of controlled improvisation (or *sens pratique,* practical sense) that gives his actions meaning and value in a particular field. Controlled improvisation implies difference, not total consensus and homogeneity. Within consensus one needs distinction. This can be created not just by mastering the rules and displaying that mastery (which after all is open to anyone else in a similar position within the field), but also by hinting that there lies something outside the game, hidden and inaccessible to others. In the early fifteenth century, the perfect embodiment of a Castilian troubadour was widely held to be Alfonso Álvarez de Villasandino, who concealed the source of his distinction within an "arte secreta."[30]

The masculine courtly subject is structured by a rhetoric of display and dissimulation that euphemizes his objective conditions within court society. The court was a place of artifice, intrigue, and uncertainty, and the successful courtier was by necessity a *vir geminus,* striving to exert control over an identity that was by definition at the service of others. As Aldo Scaglione put it, courtiers were "constantly operating under the creative stress of a need to justify their social function by serving the power structures at the same time that they were seeking their own personal ennoblement by rising to a privileged status of free, refined agents."[31] In one of his retractions, Torrellas hints that there was a true meaning hidden to all but the most insightful:

> A quien basta el conocer
> de bien ver
> lo que en mis coplas se dize,
> verá que no contradice
> ni desdize
> bien de ninguna muger.[32]

> [Whoever has sufficient knowledge/ to perceive clearly/ what is said in my verses,/ will see that it does not contradict/ nor belittle/ the virtue of any woman]

But in yet another short misogynist poem, "Yerra con poco saber" (ed. Bach y Rita, p. 270), he claims that the ignorant are those who believe that there is such a thing as a constant woman. A further and potentially astonishing volte-face is the retraction included as a gloss on the final stanza of his first antifeminine poem, in which he eulogizes Juana de Aragón (whom Dutton identifies as Giovanna II d'Angiò Durazzo, queen of Naples, 1419–35; a poem so far unnoticed, since it is not included in the edition by Bach y Rita). Besides being the adoptive mother of Alfonso V "the Magnanimous," she was—at least according to popular tradition—a promiscuous woman ["una donna lussuriosa"].[33] Far from bringing closure, then, this "retraction" would put Torrellas's "secret core" beyond reach, on an endlessly receding horizon of irony.

One final reason why Torrellas became such a scandalous figure, fictionalized in later literature as the archmisogynist, is something over which the author could exert no control. Although the poem survives in textual form, and thus was made known to subsequent generations, the debate it provoked is situated within a particular conjunction of oral and textual modes of perceiving and transmitting knowledge, what Walter Ong has called the "psychodynamics of orality and textuality." As part of a publicly performed debate, the verse debate is heavily influenced by oral modes of thought.[34] In orality, knowledge is reproduced through antagonism and "heroic figures" (or in this case an antihero, whose counterpart was Macías, a real poet later fictionalized as a tragic lover). The debate is therefore also structured by the materiality of the communicative forms with which the culture reproduces and transmits its own self-knowledge.

Writing Women out of "Literature"

Following the misogynist *Coplas de las calidades de las donas,* by Pere Torrellas, and Martínez de Toledo's *Arcipreste de Talavera,* the defense opens with a triad of texts: Diego de Valera's *Tratado en defensa de las virtuosas mujeres,* Juan Rodríguez del Padrón's *Triunfo de las donas,* and Álvaro de Luna's *Libro de las claras e virtuosas mujeres.* They cannot be dated with precision, but the first two were dedicated to Queen María (died 1445), and the third was composed by the royal favorite, who was beheaded in 1453. Although there is no space to discuss the differences among the texts, they share the changing literary horizons of the reign of Juan II, with its aspirations to vernacular humanism.

I shall focus upon Diego de Valera's *Tratado en defensa de las virtuosas mujeres,* which was written in reply to the "nueva seta" (p. 50), or "new sect" of slanderers, and which draws on a corpus of conventional arguments and historical examples of virtuous women.[35] It is not so much the content as the form of these arguments that interests me here, however. Valera was a member of the minor nobility, one of the most prominent diplomats and courtiers of his day, a man at the center of the movement to redefine knighthood. Indeed, the work survives in four manuscripts copied alongside his other treatises on the duties and definitions of the military and courtier caste. The *Tratado* is an important instance of the desire to combine arms and letters, since it is an ostentatiously learned treatise, equipped with a pseudo-academic apparatus of *accessus* and gloss.[36] Imitating the so-called "sublime" style, Valera attacks not just the malice (p. 62) of those who slander woman, but more importantly their "ignorance," and he thus enters into one of the great cultural battles of late medieval Europe: The struggle over lay literacy.

As they wrested the power of the written word from the clerical caste, the nobility had to ward off arguments that learning compromised their ability as warriors, whose traditional raison d'être, according to the conventions of the three-estates theory, was to fight in defense of the realm. Modern scholarship has labeled this the "arms v. letters" debate and shown that what was at stake was not so much lay literacy as such, but the particular forms and domains of knowledge that the ability to read and write enabled. In other words, in reaching their compromise with the clerical estate over the right to literacy, the noble laity also had to carve out a legitimate space within the division of intellectual labor.[37] The debate over woman allowed them to intrude into otherwise forbidden areas, like theology or natural philosophy, since clerics and theologians could hardly argue that woman was not part of the nobility's legitimate domain; in other words, a reified woman constituted a "saber" that was no longer simply confined to the arena of courtliness but also encompassed more literate endeavors. As such, she became another resource in the struggle for cultural capital within the redrawn boundaries that defined the field of vernacular literacy, as it forged a relative (though never absolute) autonomy from clerical culture.

If the treatises by Diego de Valera, Álvaro de Luna, and Rodríguez del Padrón illustrate the point that knowledge of woman was an essential component in a peculiarly aristocratic cultural field, and a means of demonstrating their intellectual mastery of new learned forms of writing, this was done not just to affirm their autonomy from the clerical domain. There are other gender and class hierarchies involved, as well as the desire to assert dominance over other players in the field. Luna's class position, for example, is clearly articulated. His defense of female virtue is based upon a rejection of "popular" wisdom about women, the inferiority of which is demonstrated by his learned parade of classical and biblical exempla. The use of popular sayings (*refranes*) was common on both sides of the debate as a means of ideologically grounding arguments in the proverbial realm of "tradition," but it was also part of a broader interest in oral literary forms (such as the ballad [*romancero*]) that evolved during this century. Luna's strategy helps to structure an emergent hierarchy between "high" and "low" culture that in turn enables him to accumulate more symbolic capital than those other participants in the debate who resorted to what, in another context, the marqués de Santillana called the culture of "las gentes de baxa e servil condición" [people of low and servile condition].[38]

The cultural capital of literacy operates in particularly interesting ways in Valera's *Tratado*. Formally speaking, this is a didactic treatise in which the author instructs an imaginary male friend. In the preface, he explains that he uses writing because verbal debate lends itself to "muchas cavilaciones e engaños" [doubt and deception; p. 61], and he addresses a single individual because "como son muchas las imaginaciones, así son muchos los juizios" [as there are many minds, so there are many opinions; p. 61]. Moreover, his accumulation of historical examples also corrects the misconceptions of the "new sect." Form, therefore, provides a sense of security, stability, and reflective reason rooted in a transhistorical understanding of the present. Unlike the publicly performed debate carried on in the lyrics, Valera's choice of form privileges the individual private reader, who engages the material in a distanced, meditative, and rational manner, in contrast to those whose illiteracy renders them gullible and inconstant, "ligeros como las foias de los árboles que todo viento las mueve" [fluttering like the leaves on the trees blown to and fro by every wind; p. 50].[39] This learned work illustrates how the emerging vernacular field of the "literary" constructs a subject who is a reflective "individual," as in the binarism "individual v. society," with society being the inconstant, undiscriminating, and above all anonymous mass (what would later in the Renaissance be labeled the "vulgo"). Again, a contrast with the verse debate is instructive. The inherited conventions of this mode allowed, indeed encouraged, direct and personal engagement between the contenders. In the prose treatises by Luna, Rodríguez del Padrón, and Valera, no attack is made upon a specific contemporary. None of the "new sect" to which Valera gestures in his prologue is identified, but rather he chooses to dismantle the contradictions and self-interest of Seneca, Ovid, and Boccaccio, three authorities not only of misogyny, but also (in Castilian translations and adaptations) of the new vernacular literary canon. Put simply, the center of gravity of the debate is relocated into the past.

This move illustrates one aspect of the habitus—a set of cognitive and motivating practices—that typifies the emergent field of vernacular "literature." The reading subject, now in critical dialogue primarily with the past, looks down upon the present from a transhistorical vantage point. Although the engagement with history provides tremendous opportunities for empowerment, for dominated as well as dominant groups, there is nothing *inherently* empowering about it. Its political and social efficacy depends upon the way it is appropriated and put into action. In the case of the three prose treatises under discussion here, the reader's stance seems contemplative rather than active, and the engagement seems primarily with the eternal verities enshrined in the philosophical arguments and copious accumulation of historical exempla rather than with solving the problems of the here and now. Certainly, at the end of his treatise, Valera does urge his imaginary male friend—the inscribed reader—to act in the further defense of women (p. 60). But this is to be done not through direct action, but by emending and improving upon his text, righting the wrongs not of misogynists, but of his own literary style and knowledge. This return to the text is an entirely conventional plea for emendation, but it is a convention that has a very particular ideological effect upon the reading subject. The reader seems suspended in limbo by the centripetal force that turns his thoughts back upon the text, and by the centrifugal force that turns his gaze—both physical and mental—outward into the wider reaches of erudition encompassed by the marginal glosses that surround the text on the manuscript page (and these glosses are almost twice as long as the treatise itself). The form of the work structures a reading practice that has more to do with men acquiring a greater share of the cultural capital provided by literacy than with empowering actual women. This is hardly surprising when one considers that although Valera argues strenuously for the moral equality of the sexes, he maintains the divinely ordained principle that man stands in relation to woman as master to disciple (p. 78).

Valera's defense illustrates one way in which the "woman question" is implicated in the emergent field of the literary in the Castilian vernacular. Another crucial element in this new literary field—another aspect of its habitus—is the allocation to women of an appropriate role or space.[40] As Valera put it, "¿Qué demandamos de las mugeres?" [What do we expect from women? p. 55]. Although his treatise is dedicated to Queen María as the paradigm of virtuous womanhood, she is not the author's direct interlocutor; rather she stands on the sidelines as both authority for and proof of Valera's knowledge of female virtue. As the ultimate "proof text," however, she has no voice; she serves as the legitimizing patron, or spectator, of the display of male rhetoric and knowledge. Organized as a didactic monologue in which the author instructs an imaginary male friend, the treatise reproduces at the structural level the belief that reason and learning should be modeled as masculine, in tacit acceptance of the loquacity and instability of women, which had just been so mercilessly caricatured by Valera's overtly misogynist opponents, Martínez de Toledo and Torrellas.

This formal structure is an act of what Bourdieu calls symbolic power and violence, "that invisible power which can be exercised only with the complicity of those who do not want to know that they are subject to it or even that they themselves exercise it" (*Language and Symbolic Power*, p. 164). Though it is identical in its ideological intent to what Judith Fetterley has termed "imasculation" (women's experience distorted by the masculinist assumptions and structures of the texts they are reading), as feminist critics have long pointed out, there is no guarantee that such complicity is either inevitable or absolute.[41] There is plenty of evidence in the debate that women's intellectual inferiority was not merely taken for granted, as an unspoken component of the doxa, but subject to debate. There are also examples of women acting as resisting readers of misogynist texts, as Weissberger has shown in her study of the sentimental romances by Juan de Flores.[42] The example with which I wish to close is more ambiguous, and for that very reason it is worth considering as an instance of the dilemma in which the debate caught noblewomen.

Following Torrellas, the only two extensive poems written by male courtiers against women were those by Juan de Tapia, who wrote a poetic gloss on Torrellas's misogynist "Yerra con poco saber," and Hernán Mexía, who actually retracted an earlier defense of women in order to write his own diatribe (see bibliography). The point is that both men wrote on the instigation of noble ladies. Are these instances of abjection, of the subaltern legitimizing her own oppression through willing complicity with symbolic power? This may be a simple answer, but it may simply be correct. On the other hand, given women's material exclusion as direct agents in the creation of literature, their exclusion as writers, rather than as spectators and patrons, we need to read the nature of this act of patronage with particular care. Their insistence on reproducing misogyny is by no means a subversive gesture, though it could be read as a transgressive one. They might not "misrecognize" their role within the game; but, deprived of the resources to speak—the symbolic and cultural capital, the appropriate habitus, a legitimate position in the field—they urge men to transgress their own codes of gentility and to become associates of Torrellas.[43] They cannot write directly about the contradiction between the "ennoblement" of the reified woman of courtly love and her abased material conditions of existence, but their patronage has perhaps made it more visible. This may be too hopeful a reading; but at least the women may have derived some satisfaction from the fact that Hernán Mexía did in fact become remembered as an ignoble accomplice to Torrellas.

Love Your Destiny?

The questions this act of patronage raises about the consensual model of social reproduction that underpins much of Bourdieu's thinking about the relation between habitus and field can be extended to include other aspects of the debate that I have so far ignored. The habitus is a set of durable and generative principles that predispose agents to love their destiny, in an act of *amor fati,* like a compass point turning ineluctably northward, or "a train bringing along its own rails."[44] In this brief section, I wish to raise the possibility—albeit in very schematic form—that some male participants in the debate were in fact highly ambivalent about their relationship to their "destined" role in life, and that in addition to being an exercise in symbolic violence enacted on women, the debate also symbolizes their ambivalence toward the sources and objects of their power, as well as toward the reproduction of their culture.

Several participants in the debate attempt to articulate reasons why women act in the way they do. Besides the usual naturalizing moves of moral and physiological arguments, some also gesture toward social, and hence man-made and mutable, explanations. Torrellas, for example, argues that women are so secretive because they feel that "son subjectas/ e sin ningún poderío,/ a fin d'aver senyorío/ tienen engañosas sectas" [they are subjected/ and powerless,/ in order to gain dominion/ they form deceitful sects; ed. Bach y Rita, p. 207). If this sounds like a classic case of projection onto the "other" of one's own anxieties, it is because that is precisely what it is. Before I return to the point, some more examples from the opposing side: Diego de Valera, though he believes women to be subject to man's authority, also believes that their fates are fundamentally intertwined, and cites a philosophical maxim to that effect: "El mayor mal que las mugeres han, es ser engendradas por onbres, y el mayor mal que los onbres han, es ser fijos de mugeres" [Women's greatest ill is to have been engendered by men, and men's greatest ill is to be sons of women; ed. Suz Ruiz, p. 58]. In his riposte to Torrellas, Suero de Ribera pens an unintentionally eloquent stanza that deserves to be quoted in full:

En boca de gentil hombre
mala está la villanía,
usando por otra vía
conviene que mude nombre,
que donas naturalmente,
si complazen nuestro modo,
nosotros somos en todo
la causa de accidente. (ll. 25–32) (emphasis mine)

[In the mouth of a nobleman/ baseness is wrong,/ unless he behaves differently [?]/ he should change his name,/ *for women by nature,/ if they follow our behavior,/ we are completely/ the cause of the accident.*][45]

While it is possible to paraphrase the italicized lines, it is also significant that this is the only syntactical obscurity in the whole poem, and it occurs precisely at the point at which Suero pauses his rather facile rambling on the theme of gentility to articulate the "natural" relationship between men and women. As he does so, the syntax cracks. Symptomatic, perhaps, of doubts? *Are* men the "essence" and women the "accident"? What *is* "nuestro modo" and how *do* women fit ("complazer")? Women start the clause as the grammatical subject but end as an abstracted object—which is the fundamental ideological move of the entire debate.

These passages tie in with the way in which some defenses of women manipulate the conventional argument that men should respect women because they are of woman born. Though often unstructured, such defenses sometimes use mothers as conclusions to their case. Valera is one such example (ed. Suz Ruiz, p. 60), and Diego de San Pedro offers another very instructive instance. Leriano, the hero of his romance *Cárcel de amor,* lies dying from love for his *belle dame sans merci,* Laureola. Women are excluded from his deathbed rebuttal of misogyny (he embraces his fate willingly), but when he dies his mother is wheeled in to provide the legitimizing pathos for his noble defense of womanhood. His mother gives voice to an unspoken aspect of his "tragedy," namely not only did he die *for* a woman, but he was produced *by* a woman. It is "noble" but also "tragic" because woman does not have to love her destiny, which is, in theory, to submit to male authority (the theoretical relationship is visually underscored in the woodcut to the 1493 Catalan translation, in which the grieving mother is placed on the same plane as a dead dog, the ultimate symbol of fidelity).[46]

Examples of this contradictory attitude could be multiplied—it lies, after all, at the heart of much aristocratic literature. As Mercedes Roffé has remarked concerning the name of the archmisogynist Torrellas (lexically divisible into "torre" [tower] and "ellas" [feminine plural pronoun]), "la ironía del misógino es llevar en su nombre inscripto el nombre de lo que teme" [the irony of the misogynist is to carry inscribed in his name the name of what he fears].[47] Even when transformed into the habitus of gentility, with its self-serving claptrap of tragic pathos and *noblesse oblige,* this contradiction illustrates to perfection the paradoxical mix of fear and desire that, according to Peter Stallybrass and Allon White, characterizes the dynamic relation between the dominant and the dominated:

A recurrent pattern emerges: the "top" attempts to reject and eliminate the "bottom" for reasons of prestige and status, only to discover, not only that it is frequently dependent upon that low-Other [. . .], but also that the top *includes* that low symbolically, as a primary eroticized constituent of its own fantasy life. The result is a mobile, conflictual fusion of power, fear and desire in the construction of subjectivity: a psychological dependence upon precisely those Others which are being rigorously opposed and excluded at the social level. It is for this reason that what is *socially* peripheral is so frequently *symbolically* central. [. . .] The low-Other is despised and denied at the level of political organization and social being whilst it is instrumentally constitutive of the shared imaginary repertoires of the dominant culture.[48]

When male courtiers argue both for and against women, gesture toward
the fundamental interdependence of the sexes, or project onto women
their fears about themselves, it is in part due to the political and cultural
structures of court life. Women were an essential part of the production of
courtly culture, but their access to cultural and symbolic capital needed to
be controlled. Male courtiers, as Joan Kelly persuasively argues in her discussion of Castiglione, were symbolically feminized, in that they were represented as being subject to seemingly irrational and unpredictable political
forces that governed their lives and identities.[49] But the debate is also related to the deeper economic structures of late feudal society. As recent
studies have shown, the fifteenth century in Spain saw the final consolida-
tion of agnatic lines of descent and their patterns of inheritance (the dominance of *mayorazgo,* or property rights of male primogeniture) and
changing forms of dowries, all of which excluded noblewomen economically at the same time as they emphasized their centrality in the transmission of wealth and lineage.[50] Adeline Rucquoi, for example, amply
documents how the urban oligarchy consolidated its economic and political power within the city by conducting a politics of "apertura de linaje"
[opening of lineage], which forged marriage alliances with selected individuals from classes both above (the landed aristocracy) and below
(wealthy merchants, tradesmen, converted Jews, clerics from the administrative caste).[51] All this accounts for the obsessive emphasis on chastity as
the defining characteristic of "woman" [i.e., noblewoman], and for the
equally obsessive anxiety over her "inconstancy." It is not that women are
mutable (at least not more mutable than men), but that material conditions
and political and economic structures that created men's privilege could
never guarantee absolute control. This is the paradoxical destiny that the
debate encourages men to embrace, in their symbolic as well as in their
physical conduct toward women; voiced, rather mutedly it is true, as a
querelle—both question and lament—is the dilemma, are we men really
making a virtue out of necessity? If they could have answered the question
directly, it would have been in the affirmative.

Entering the Debate:
Marcia Belisarda and the Subject of Change

The paradox of the court ladies who "patronized" Hernán Mexía and
Juan de Tapia was a common obstacle for women as they struggled for
the cultural legitimacy necessary to write. As numerous studies have
shown, the struggle was not simply a question of improving material
conditions but of working with and through the internalized sense of inferiority in the literary field, and of breaking away from the masculinist

assumptions that were built into the literary discourses that they had in-herited. Negotiating Petrarchism, for example, was both empowering and restricting for Renaissance women poets like Gaspara Stampa and Louise Labé. In Spain, the few surviving verses of Florencia Pinar (late fifteenth century) speak of the pain of sexual love, but even more poignantly of the pain of writing sexually as a woman; in the religious sphere, there is the case of the nun Teresa de Cartagena (born 1420/35) whose defense of her writing entails a "rhetoric of femininity" (the phrase coined by Alison Weber in her brilliant study of Teresa de Ávila), which adapts conventional patriarchal notions of female humility and modesty as strategies to legitimize her own writing. In this respect, both Teresas were anticipated by two anonymous noblewomen who, in the mid-fifteenth century, employed similar rhetorical ploys, paradoxes, and arguments during a fascinating debate over female literacy with the minor nobleman Fernando de la Torre. Later testimony has also survived of three dozen or so *puellae doctae* from the reigns of Isabel I and Carlos V: The obstacles they faced in establishing a firm foothold in humanist circles are eloquently symbolized by the Latin correspondence of the humanist Lucio Marineo Sículo and his pupil Juana de Contreras, who, in 1504, resolutely defended the Latinity of the term *heroina* and her right to use it.[52] Thanks to the work of numerous feminist scholars, the strategies and struggles of Hispanic women writers, both secular and lay, have been increasingly recognized.[53]

A particularly interesting example of an explicit engagement with the formal debate I have been studying here is to be found in the work of Marcia Belisarda, the pseudonym of sor María de Santa Isabel. A nun from Toledo who lived in the first half of the seventeenth century, she was the author of approximately 146 sacred and profane poems, which, though apparently intended for publication in print, survive only in a single contemporary manuscript.[54] I have chosen one poem of hers as an epilogue to this essay for two related reasons. Firstly, in responding to slanders of female inconstancy, Belisarda—on one level at least—continues to situate her defense within the habitus of courtliness, just as many defenders of women had attacked Torrellas over two hundred years before. Secondly, however, her poem allows glimpses of a more unsettled, and unsettling, kind of opposition: For in this work, Belisarda puts into question the very language in which men think and speak about women, and in doing so, she takes us back to the associations between the world, mutability, and women that opened this essay. Although I lack the space to develop the point here, it is significant that her questioning of gender assumptions takes place at a time of profound change in the political, economic, and social status of the nobility in Baroque Spain.[55]

The poem in question is headed by a rubric that announces theme, circumstance, and poetic mode: "Décimas, escritas muy de prisa, en respuesta de otras en que ponderaban la mudanza de las mujeres" [*Décimas* written in great haste, in reply to others which weighed up the fickleness of women]. This rubric, I think, shares the irony that characterizes the poem itself and that was a common strategy in women's polemical writing of the period.[56] For in contemporary usage, *ponderar* could mean 'to reflect thoughtfully' but also 'to exaggerate or extol'.[57] There is also the tongue-in-cheek contrast between the original poem (now either lost or discarded; or was it just a fictional pretext?), which "thoughtfully" weighed up the fickleness of women, and her own lines, modestly dashed off in swift response, which I quote in full below:

> Hombres, no deshonoréis
> con título de inconstantes
> las mujeres, que diamantes
> son si obligarlas sabéis.
> Si alguna mudable veis,
> la mudanza es argumento
> de que antes quiso de asiento;
> mas en vuestra voluntad,
> antes ni después, verdad
> no se halló con fundamento.
>   Si mujer dice mudanza,
> el hombre mentira dice;
> y si en algo contradice,
> es que el juicio no lo alcanza.
> Si se ajusta por igual balanza,
> por la cuenta se hallaría:
> en él, mentir cada día,
> y en mudarse cada mes.
> Que el mentir vileza es,
> mudar de hombres mejoría.

[Men, do not dishonor women/ by calling them inconstant/ because they are diamonds/ if you know how to oblige them./ If you see a mutable woman/ her mutability is a sign/ that once she did love firmly and truly;/ but your desire/ whether before or after (a love affair),/ lacks all foundation in truth.// If woman means mutability/ man means lie;/ and if he denies something,/ it is because it surpasses his understanding (or: if this is contradictory, it is because it surpasses our understanding)./ If one weighs this in an equal balance/ the scales will reveal:/ in him, lying every day, / and in (her?) changing every month./ For lying is villainy,/ changing men is an improvement]

It is hard for an English rendering to capture the puns and paradoxes that organize this densely eloquent poem. As the rubric's wordplay suggests, and as the poem itself confirms, Marcia Belisarda anticipates what Electa Arenal and Amanda Powell have termed the "prismatic method," which was later deployed by the great Mexican feminist Sor Juana Inés de la Cruz (1648/51–1695) in her struggle to unpick patriarchal thought and authority. According to Arenal and Powell, this method of writing "explores and exploits the interplay among words, their etymological roots and cognate forms, their denotations and connotations."[58] I shall start, however, by considering the overall structure of the work. It is structured by a dynamic process: The opening apostrophe and direct addresses of the first stanza modulate into the playful detachment of the second half, where the author speaks not to but about men, specifically about the discourse of misogyny. This move does not entail women's disillusioned withdrawal from the patriarchal world depicted by her famous contemporary, the novelist María de Zayas, who, in the conclusion to her *Desengaños amorosos* ([*The Disenchantments of Love*] 1647), has her female protagonists retire to the silence of a convent in order to end their debate with men and to escape the depredations wrought by social and sexual intercourse with them. Perhaps because she has already found the convent to be "a catalyst for female autonomy" (to borrow the title of a pioneering article by Electa Arenal), Sor María de Santa Isabel can speak back to men from across the convent walls.[59] Despite differences in tone, both authors project a sense of an achieved critical distance and an awareness of the fundamentally social— hence changeable—bases of patriarchy, both of which, as Gerda Lerner has argued, are the necessary preconditions for the creation of a feminist consciousness.[60] Marcia Belisarda creates critical leverage through the distancing effects of irony, which turns misogynist language back upon itself. Women are not inconstant, she argues, but diamonds, "si obligarlas sabéis" [if you know how to oblige them]. This metaphorical diamond is almost as multifaceted as the literal object itself: signifying everlasting constancy (after all, "diamonds are forever," according to De Beers marketing agents), but also hardness and resistance.[61] We women, suggests the poet, will be constant if you treat us with deference and respect ("oblige" us, in one of its senses), but we will also resist if you force us (that other kind of "obligation"). This duality indicates how women are caught up in a web of pressures that are apparently in contradiction (deference and coercion) but are in fact mutually supportive. Women are subject to a coercive deference that "treasures" them only insofar as they submit to their social "obligation" to be a reliable exchange object of constant value. For, like a diamond, which is worth little in its natural state and whose market value derives from its cut and polish, women are prized as a resource that can be manufactured into a worldly commodity. Their alleged inconstancy is a symptom of the fact that they are active, not passive, participants in this process, endowed with the diamantine power to resist and an independent, and hence changeable, will. And the meaning and implications of this power to change are explored in the dense and paradoxical lines that follow: "Si alguna mudable veis,/ la mudanza es argumento/ de que antes quiso de asiento" [If you see a mutable woman/ her mutability is a sign/ that once she did love firmly and truly].

As the editors point out in their notes to these lines, "querer de asiento" is a pun on *asiento*, meaning stability and permanence, and *hombre de asiento*, a wise and prudent person. The pun seems to suggest that in contrast to men, whose desire at any stage of love is a mere lie (lines 8–10), women's desire is at least grounded in the truth of the moment and thus possesses an experiential reality. The paradox Belisarda sets up here (change is a sign of permanence and prudence) is not new in the discourse of the European love lyric. Garcilaso de la Vega, who introduced into Spain the language and themes of the Petrarchan love sonnet in the early decades of the sixteenth century, ended his famous sonnet 23 ("En tanto que de rosa y azucena") in a similar fashion. In his sensual elaboration of the Horatian motif of *carpe diem,* he urges a virginal young girl to "pluck the fruit" of her beauty before it is withered by time: "Todo lo mudará la edad ligera/ por no hacer mudanza en su costumbre" [Fleeting time will change everything/ so as not to make a change in its own custom].[62] Since the only stable thing is change itself, it is prudent to capture the present moment. There is already in Garcilaso's well-worn classical paradox an unspoken but clear association between time and female beauty, which facilitates the ideological conflation of woman and mutability, with sex symbolizing man's vain attempt to pin down both woman and time.[63] Marcia Belisarda appropriates the logic of permanent impermanence, or of time changing so as not to change, and makes it part of her defense of woman. (As we shall see, at the end of the poem, Belisarda's references to menstruation add another layer to her conceptual play on notions of female changeability.) Her move anticipates later instances of marginalized and oppressed groups who reclaim the language of the dominant ideology and give positive valence to a previous term of abuse—black, queer. . . . This was also an important strategy for María de Zayas, who in the prologue to her first collection of tales, *Novelas amorosas y ejemplares* (1637), reversed physiological arguments for women's alleged intellectual inferiority and transformed them into evidence to support her own authority to write.[64]

But what is most intriguing about Marcia Belisarda's poem is the way in which she sets one paradox inside another larger, more corrosive one. For the ironic playfulness of the first stanza is itself enclosed by the paradox that opens the second half of the poem: "Si mujer dice mudanza,/ el hombre mentira dice" [If woman means mutability/ man means lie]. Structurally and conceptually, then, the poem hinges upon the most basic of all paradoxes, namely that the truth of Marcia's arguments about mutability depends upon them being a lie. The following gloss on this paradox can be read in two ways: "y si en algo contradice/ es que el juicio no lo alcanza." These two lines mean either, if man denies this ("y si en algo contradice") it is just that his understanding ("juicio") cannot grasp it; alternatively, they could mean, "if *this* is contradictory [supplying the neuter pronoun "esto," and with the paradox itself as antecedent], it is just that *our* understanding cannot grasp it." I see little value in trying to resolve the ambiguity: From a patriarchal standpoint the limitations specific to a man or to man in general can often be a moot point. As we have already seen, Suero de Ribera was one male defender of women to suggest that women were socially and historically conditioned by men, "que donas naturalmente,/ si complazen nuestro modo,/ nosotros somos en todo/ la causa de accidente" [for women by nature,/ if they follow our behavior,/ we are completely/ the cause of the accident]. I return to Suero's poem because his phrasing—the Aristotelian terminology of cause and accident—might help to explain the most puzzling, indeed bizarre, aspect of Belisarda's poem.

If everything is weighed equally, continues Belisarda, the scales will reveal: "en él, mentir cada día,/ y en mudarse cada mes" [in him, lying every day/ and in (her?) changing every month]. As Olivares and Boyce point out, the reader needs to supply the pronoun "ella" after the preposition in the second line. Both the syntactic parallelism and the sense of the whole poem urge us to fill in the gap created by the demands of a regular octosyllabic meter. Metaphorically, one might say that "she" is easily suppressed as excessive and unnecessary within the grammar and syntax, so to speak, of the patriarchal order. But just as the syntax and sense of the poem force us to keep this absent "she" in mind, to bring her back into the center of the textual construction of meaning, so the social world's ideological construction of itself needs the disorderly and abnormal, that is, the very elements that it reviles and marginalizes, to define the boundaries of its own normality and regular functioning.

The poem's absent "ella" as well as the need to supply her are telling instances of woman's symbolic status under patriarchy: As an accident of Nature, an imperfect man, she represents all that has been pushed to the edges of man's scientific explanation of the world. "And that there is no knowledge of the accidental is clear," wrote Aristotle, "for all knowledge deals either with what holds always or with what holds for the most part (for how else could one either learn it or teach it to someone else?)."[65] In the case of woman, her mutability is physiologically conditioned, since, as Belisarda points out, she changes "cada mes" [every month]. Although she exists in a state of bodily flux, and although menstruation was widely regarded as a sign of women's inferiority and imperfection, female mutability was not entirely indeterminate, random, and hence a sign of the unknowable. For one thing, menstruation occurs every month and as such it is part of that paradox of permanent impermanence that I mentioned above: Change is necessary for stability, since stability requires not stasis but regeneration. Moreover, though the presence of a menstruating woman was despised physically as a contaminating threat, as well as symbolically as a paradigmatically female sign of the human Fall, menstruation was also viewed as a necessary and healthy process of purgation, of bodily renewal.[66]

Belisarda's strategy of attributing positive connotations to change and female mutability takes yet another turn in the poem's final couplet: "Que el mentir vileza es,/ mudar de hombres mejoría." The phrasing and vocabulary indicate that this is more than a simple reaffirmation of the superiority of women's mutability over men's mendacity. Though it may be determined by the rhyme, the preference for the noun *mejoría* over the adverb *mejor* is suggestive. It is not just that change is *better* than lying, but that change brings an *improvement—mejoría* connotes material enrichment, or recovery from a particular physical or emotional condition: In short, change is progress. But in what does that progress consist? Yet again, Belisarda's elliptical expression is wittily open-ended, and the ambiguity is created by the semantic possibilities of the phrase "mudar de" compounded by the suppression of the required main verb "to be ("es" being understood through the parallelism with the previous line). "Mudar de hombres mejoría" could mean "changing men is an improvement" (i.e., "Mudar de hombres *es* mejoría"), and so be a plea for women's sexual freedom, whether by exchanging different male lovers (as in Juan de Flores's earlier romance *Triunfo de amor*), or even by discarding men as lovers. The radical implications of the latter reading are strengthened if we shift the placement of the silent main verb *es*: "Mudar *es* de hombres mejoría" suggests that "change is recuperation from men," an idea that immediately calls to mind notions of the convent as place of escape from men, a female space that allows for spiritual, emotional, and physical recovery from the sickness of patriarchy.

As we review how Belisarda shapes her response to misogyny, we see how the battle is waged in large measure upon the terrain of form. Ideas and values do not exist independently of their formal mode of expression, and challenging dominant ideologies means entering into the politics of language. Most obviously, Belisarda counters the accusation of female fickleness, and all the cultural freight that this slander carries, by rejecting the normative and unitary usage of the word "mudar." If woman is to be reduced to this linguistic sign, then the ideological effect of the sign can be challenged by opening the sign to a variety of perspectives. And the key word here is "if": Note how the poem is structured around a series of four hypothetical clauses. It is highly symbolic (though perhaps not a calculated gesture) that when, in the final four lines, Belisarda weighs men and women on the scales of equality, the two words that are missing are "ella" and "es." As Howard Bloch has argued (though his case is surely overstated), the statement "she is" plus a predicate constitutes the primary discursive strategy of misogyny.[67] The silencing of these two words illustrates to perfection how the poem enacts the very plurality it advocates.

Belisarda's conceptual wit, the *conceptismo* so beloved by Baroque culture, demonstrates how subaltern groups can draw their oppositional strength from the modes of thought and forms of expression of the dominant culture. But her wit is itself part of a larger display of *sprezzatura,* that nonchalance and scorn for affectation that characterizes the late medieval and early modern courtier (as the poem's rubric reminds us, the work was tossed off as a rapid response). *Sprezzatura,* of course, is highly charged ideologically. By naturalizing the external makeup of the ideal courtier, it presents as part of his very flesh and sinew what in fact were the learned cosmetics of his social caste, such as music, dancing, literacy, and the proper manners in the conduct of love and the enjoyment of female beauty.[68] In Belisarda's poem, it is as if one of the integral components of that cosmetic—woman as contradictory object of desire and revulsion—speaks back. *Sprezzatura,* recovering some of its etymological force of 'contempt,' modulates from masculine nonchalance into scorn for men.

This form of argumentation, which exploits the double-edged and paradoxical elements of misogyny, takes us back to Zeno of Elea (ca. 500 B.C.E.), called by Aristotle the inventor of dialectic because of his method of drawing contradictory conclusions from the premises of his opponents. Zeno, of course, was famous for his paradoxes (Achilles and the hare, the bow and arrow), which were designed to undermine the existence of plurality and motion in favor of his defense of monism, or indivisible reality. One might say that Marcia Belisarda, on the practical terrain of politics in its broadest sense (she is not philosophizing about the world, after all, but trying to change it), upends the originary paradox and argues for the existence and need for plurality and change: Her poem, which illustrates Joan Scott's contention that the history of feminism is marked by women with "only paradoxes to offer," constitutes one more twist and turn in a long and as yet unfinished revolution.[69]

Notes

1. Both Mena's text and Hernán Núñez's commentary are quoted from the second, revised version of the humanist scholar's edition: *Las trezientas del*

famosíssimo poeta Juan de Mena con glosa (Granada: Juan Varela, 1505), fols. 3r–
v. Varro's actual definition is: "Mundus ornatus muliebris dictus a munditia"
[*Mundus* is a woman's toilet set, named from *munditia,* 'neatness'], *De lingua
latina,* 5.129; text and translation quoted from *Varro: On the Latin Language,*
ed. and trans. Roland G. Kent, Loeb Classical Library, 2 vols. (Cambridge,
Mass.: Harvard University Press, 1938). For the etymological problems of
the term and the relations between its three main semantic fields ('earth',
the 'universe' in general, and the adjective 'clean'), see A. Ernout and A.
Meillet, *Dictionnaire étymologique de la langue latine: Histoire des mots,* 4th ed.
(Paris: Klincksieck, 1985), which reviews various hypotheses and concludes
that there is no clear etymology ["pas d'étymologie claire"]. Equally spec-
ulative is the *Oxford Latin Dictionary,* ed. P. G. W. Clare (Oxford: Clarendon,
1982), where a parallel is drawn between *mundus* and the (much wider) semantic range of the Greek κόσμος, the etymon of the English 'cosmetic':
order, behavior, form, government, ornament—especially of women, but
also of men, horses, speech—honor, ruler, universe, earth.

2. My translation of the passage quoted in Ernout and Meillet, *Dictionnaire
   étymologique,* p. 420.

3. R. Howard Bloch, *Medieval Misogyny and the Invention of Western Romantic
   Love* (Chicago: University of Chicago Press, 1991), pp. 39–47, quotation
   from 39–40. In note 11, he cites examples of the Greek pun on κόσμος as
   'ornament' and 'world.'

4. As Michael Solomon has remarked, "collapsing all antifeminist writing into
   the transhistorical [. . .] undermines attempts to analyze institutions and
   ideologies that foster misogynist discourse." See *The Literature of Misogyny
   in Medieval Spain: The "Arcipreste de Talavera" and the "Spill"* (Cambridge:
   Cambridge University Press, 1997), p. 3. For the common view of the debate as a courtly game, see Ronald E. Surtz, *Writing Women in Late Medieval
   and Early Modern Spain: The Mothers of Saint Teresa de Ávila* (Philadelphia:
   University of Pennsylvania Press, 1995), p. 17.

5. The most substantial recent contribution is *Queer Iberia: Sexualities, Cul-
   tures, and Crossings from the Middle Ages to the Renaissance,* ed. Josiah Blackmore and Gregory S. Hutcheson (Durham, N.C.: Duke University Press,
   1999), especially the broad sociopolitical treatment by Linde M. Brocato,
   "'Tened por espejo su fin': Mapping Gender and Sex in Fifteenth- and
   Sixteenth-Century Spain," pp. 325–65. Shorter, but also valuable, is Louise
   M. Haywood, ed., *Cultural Contexts / Female Voices,* Papers of the Medieval
   Hispanic Research Seminar 27 (London: Queen Mary & Westfield Col-
   lege, 2000). Essays from both collections are cited below.

6. In addition to Barbara F. Weissberger's contribution to the present volume,
   see her "Male Sexual Anxieties in the *Carajicomedia:* A Response to Female
   Sovereignty," in *Poetry at Court in Trastamaran Spain: From the "Cancionero de
   Baena" to the "Cancionero General,"* ed. E. Michael Gerli and Julian Weiss
   (Tempe, Ariz.: Medieval and Renaissance Texts and Studies, 1998), pp.
   222–34. She has just completed a book on the subject, *Repairing Spain's
   Broken Body: Gender Ideology in the Age of Isabel the Catholic.*

7. On Catherine's physique, see Fernán Pérez de Guzmán, *Generaciones y semblanzas*, ed. R. B. Tate (London: Tamesis, 1965), p. 9. For the close bonds between the queen and such gifted and powerful women as Leonor López de Córdoba, Inés de Torres, and Constanza de Castilla, and the alarm that their political power could provoke, see Surtz, *Writing Women in Late Medieval and Early Modern Spain*, pp. 41–3. About one hundred years later, there is the figure of Germaine de Foix, widow and alleged poisoner of Ferdinand the Catholic (d. 1516), who as vice-reine of Valencia presided over an important literary court; see Nancy Marino, "The *Cancionero de Valencia, Questión de Amor* and the Last Medieval Courts of Love," in *Cultural Contexts*, ed. Haywood, pp. 41–9.

8. The best-known source for the rumor is the contemporary historian and moralist Fernán Pérez de Guzmán, *Generaciones y semblanzas*, ed. Tate, pp. 40–41; see Gregory S. Hutcheson, "Desperately Seeking Sodom: Queerness in the Chronicles of Álvaro de Luna," in *Queer Iberia*, pp. 222–49.

9. See Barbara F. Weissberger, "'¡A tierra, puto!': Alfonso de Palencia's Discourse of Effeminacy," in *Queer Iberia*, pp. 291–324; William D. Phillips, Jr., *Enrique IV and the Crisis of Fifteenth-Century Castile, 1425–1480* (Cambridge, Mass.: The Medieval Academy of America, 1978), pp. 81–95.

10. Jacob Ornstein, "La misoginia y el profeminismo en la literatura castellana," *Revista de Filología Hispánica* 3 (1941): 219–32. This highly dated article is still being cited as a basic point of departure by modern scholars, e.g., Surtz, *Writing Women*, p. 17.

11. Raymond Williams, *Marxism and Literature* (Oxford: Oxford University Press, 1975), pp. 108–14 (quotation on p. 112). See also Terry Eagleton, *Ideology: An Introduction* (London: Verso, 1991), pp. 112–21.

12. Alcuin Blamires, *The Case for Women in Medieval Culture* (Oxford: Clarendon Press, 1997), p. 9. Blamires's approach is essentially thematically based, although important observations on formal aspects are scattered throughout the book, particularly in chapter 2. Suggestive generalizations about the four "presiding structural principles" of misogynist diatribes are also made in *Woman Defamed and Woman Defended: An Anthology of Medieval Texts*, ed. Alcuin Blamires, with Karen Pratt and C. W. Marx (Oxford: Clarendon, 1992), pp. 9–11.

13. Bloch has commented on the "repetitive monotony" of misogyny, and "the uniformity of its terms" over the past two thousand years (*Medieval Misogyny*, pp. 2–7). Contrast Blamires's remark that "misogyny was not unvariegated" (*Woman Defamed*, p. 9), and his call for the need to historicize more precisely the medieval discourse on women (*The Case for Women*, pp. 17–18).

14. This approach is best illustrated by María Cruz Muriel Tapia, *Antifeminismo y subestimación de la mujer en la literatura medieval castellana* (Cáceres: Guadiloba, 1991), pp. 304–45. This is, nonetheless, the best overview of the ideas brandished by both sides in the debate, as well as of previous misogynist literature. Her insistence on the ideological identity between pro- and antifeminine positions marks a fundamental advance on most earlier

treatments, e.g., by Ornstein, "La misoginia y el profeminismo"; Barbara Matulka, *The Novels of Juan de Flores and Their European Diffusion: A Study in Comparative Literature* (Geneva: Slatkine, 1974 [1931]); María Jesús Lacarra, "Algunos datos para la historia de la misoginia en la edad media," in *Studia in honorem profesor Martín de Riquer,* ed. Carlos Alvar et al. (Barcelona: Quaderns Crema, 1986–87), 1:339–61; for an anthology of debate texts, see Miguel Ángel Pérez Priego, ed., *Poesía femenina en los cancioneros* (Madrid: Castalia, 1989). Though narrower in scope than the book by Muriel Tapia, a similar emphasis on the ideological identity between pro- and antifeminine camps may be found in Antony van Beysterveldt, "Los debates feministas del siglo XV y las novelas de Juan de Flores," *Hispania* (USA, 64 (1981): 1–13. Two case studies that include valuable discussion of the broader context of the debate are Mercedes Roffé, *La cuestión del género en "Grisel y Mirabella" de Juan de Flores* (Newark, Del.: Juan de la Cuesta, 1996), and Rosanna Cantavella, *Els cards i el llir: una lectura de l'Espill de Jaume Roig* (Barcelona: Quaderns Crema, 1992).

15. See Raymond Williams, *Marxism and Literature,* pp. 151–57, 173–79, 186–91; Tony Bennett, *Formalism and Marxism* (London: Routledge, 1979). I explore the ideological relation between thirteenth-century lyric conventions and the construction of masculinity in "On the Conventionality of the *Cantigas de amor,*" *La Corónica* 26.1 (fall 1997): 63–83.

16. Deborah Cameron, *Feminism and Linguistic Theory* (London: Macmillan, 1985), p. 14.

17. For the medical postulates of the antifeminine arguments, see Solomon, *The Literature of Misogyny;* for the connections with race, see Barbara F. Weissberger's contribution to this volume, and more broadly, Louise Mirrer, *Women, Jews, and Muslims in the Texts of Reconquest Castile* (Ann Arbor: University of Michigan Press, 1996). Although scholars often acknowledge the moral grounds of the debate (e.g., Muriel Tapia, *Antifeminismo y subestimación,* p. 334), the debate's construction of the moral order has yet to be subjected to thorough ideological critique.

18. In French, the earliest documented attestation of "misogyne" is 1564, though it is then rare until the mid-eighteenth century; along with "misogynie," the term was consolidated by the successive early-nineteenth-century dictionaries of C. P. V. Boiste; see *Le Grand Robert de la langue française,* 12th ed. (Paris: Le Robert, 1985). In English, both "misogyny" and "misogynist" emerge in the seventeenth century (according to the OED), as does "misògino" in Italian, with "misoginia" acquiring currency in the early nineteenth century; see *Grande Dizionario della lingua italiana* (Turin: Unione Tipografico, Editrice Torinense, 1978). In these cases, one notes the tendency for the agent to be recognized before the general practice itself. In Castilian, whether because of the notoriously slow-turning wheels of the Real Academia or the equally notorious patriarchal attitudes of its denizens, "misoginia" and related terms are not included in that institution's dictionaries until 1925. This is not to say that the terms

were not more current before that. See J. Corominas and J. A. Pascual, *Diccionario crítico etimológico castellana e hispánica*, 6 vols. (Madrid: Gredos, 1991), s.v. "Miso-."

19. "[W]hen there is a quasi-perfect correspondence between the objective order and the subjective principles of organization [. . .] the natural and social world appears as self-evident. This experience we shall call *doxa*, so as to distinguish it from an orthodox or heterodox belief implying awareness and recognition of the possibility of different or antagonistic beliefs." See *Outline of a Theory of Practice*, trans. Richard Nice (Cambridge: Cambridge University Press, 1977), pp. 164–71 (at p. 164).

20. The account in this essay by necessity simplifies the complexity of Bourdieu's thought. It is based on *Outline of a Theory of Practice*, trans. Nice, and on various essays anthologized in *Language and Symbolic Power*, ed. John B. Thompson, trans. Gina Raymond and Matthew Adamson (Cambridge, Mass.: Harvard University Press, 1991). I have also learned from the critical engagement with Bourdieu's work in Toril Moi, "Appropriating Bourdieu: Feminist Theory and Pierre Bourdieu's Sociology of Culture," in *What Is a Woman? And Other Essays* (Oxford: Oxford University Press, 1999), pp. 264–99 [originally published in *New Literary History* 22 (1991): 1017–49]; John B. Thompson, *Studies in the Theory of Ideology* (Berkeley and Los Angeles: University of California Press, 1984), pp. 42–72. My interest in Bourdieu was first sparked by Mark D. Johnston's path-breaking essay "Cultural Studies on the *Gaya Ciencia*," in *Poetry at Court in Trastamaran Spain,* ed. Gerli and Weiss, pp. 235–53.

21. E. Michael Gerli, "La Religión de Amor y el antifeminismo en las letras castellanas del siglo XV," *Hispanic Review* 49 (1981): 65–96. The most recent overview, with ample bibliography, on Martínez de Toledo is by Sara Mañero, *"El arcipreste de Talavera" de Alfonso Martínez de Toledo* (Toledo: Instituto Provincial de Investigaciones y Estudios Toledanos, 1997). For an acute queer reading, see Catherine Brown, "Queer Representation in the *Arçipreste de Talavera*, or, The *Maldezir de mugeres* Is a Drag," in *Queer Iberia*, pp. 73–103.

22. *Cancionero de Juan Alfonso de Baena*, ed. José María Azáceta, Clásicos Hispánicos, 3 vols. (Madrid: CSIC, 1966), 1:5.

23. See, for example, the response of the Friar Diego de Valencia, who, when reluctantly drawn into a debate over the Holy Trinity by the nobleman Sánchez Calavera, retorted that theology was "muy más fonda que la poetría" [far deeper than poetry]; *Cancionero de Baena*, ed. Azáceta, 3:1066. I discuss this more fully in *The Poet's Art: Literary Theory in Castile, c. 1400–60*, Medium Aevum Monographs, n.s., 14. (Oxford: The Society for the Study of Medieval Languages and Literature, 1990), pp. 14–17, 32–40.

24. Significantly, the debt to Andreas Capellanus is from book 3 of *De amore*, the "Reprobatio amoris" (for the earlier Catalan translation of which, see appended bibliography). Martínez de Toledo thus carries out a structural inversion of his prime source: pursuit of women/love followed by retraction.

In spite of their multiple ironies, these texts combine to form a chiasmus that maps a shift in the relationship between clerical and lay courtly culture. In earlier centuries, the struggle over courtliness was played out in the literary genre of the knight/clerk debate, and fought through the voices and over the bodies of noblewomen, a prime resource in the cultural and symbolic capital of courtliness.

25. See Johnston, "Cultural Studies," pp. 243–52 (quotations from pp. 248, 250).

26. The poem is usually dated later, variously 1440–60; but the work needs to be assigned an earlier date since Torrellas penned a retraction to one Juana de Aragón, identified by Dutton as Giovanna II d'Angiò Durazzo, queen of Naples, who died in 1435. Matulka, however, believes the retraction was dedicated to a later Juana de Aragón, wife of Ferrante I of Naples in 1476 (*Novels of Juan de Flores,* p. 103). For the MSS and dating of the poem, see Brian Dutton, *El cancionero del siglo XV, c. 1360–1520,* Biblioteca Española del Siglo XV, Maior, 7 vols. (Salamanca: Universidad de Salamanca, 1990–91); the information is located through the ID number assigned to the poem, 0043. On Torrellas and his work, see Martí de Riquer, *Història de la literatura catalana* (Esplugues de Llobregat: Ariel, 1964), 3:161–86. Torrellas finds an ardent modern acolyte in Nicasio Salvador Miguel, who displays his noxious admiration for the medieval poet's "excelente conocimiento de la naturaleza feminina" [excellent knowledge of female nature] in *La poesía cancioneril: El "Cancionero de Estúñiga"* (Madrid: Alhambra, 1977), pp. 228–29.

27. Quoted, with minor orthographic modernization, from the edition of Pedro Bach y Rita, *The Works of Pere Torroella, a Catalan Writer of the Fifteenth Century* (New York: Instituto de las Españas, 1930), pp. 192–215. This final stanza and its variants are listed on p. 214.

28. As far as I am aware, no one has discussed the implications of this fact. Although there is a substantial body of "women's lyric" in the form of the *Cantigas de amigo* (twelfth and thirteenth centuries), in which men represent fictional, usually idealized, women singing, when it comes to representing *real* women, the professional *soldadeiras* are portrayed as pornographic bodies, never once as singers practicing their art. This silencing cannot be explained purely in terms of class contempt, since male minstrels were often satirized precisely as poets. It is part of the gendering of the literary field (see further in this essay). The quantity of female-voiced lyric declined dramatically in fifteenth-century Castile; see Vicenta Blay Manzanera, "El varón que finge voz de mujer en las composiciones de cancionero," in *Cultural Contexts / Female Voices,* pp. 9–26.

29. *Els cards i el llir,* p. 36, where Cantavella rightly underscores the importance of Catalonia in introducing the debate into Castile.

30. *Cancionero de Baena,* ed. Azáceta, 1:209.

31. *Knights at Court: Courtliness, Chivalry, and Courtesy from Ottonian Germany to the Italian Renaissance* (Berkeley and Los Angeles: University of California

Press, 1991), p. 310. I derive this quotation from Johnston, "Cultural Studies," p. 237. On the rhetoric of display and dissimulation, see my "Álvaro de Luna, Juan de Mena, and the Power of Courtly Love," *Modern Language Notes* 106 (1991): 241–56.

32. Ed. Bach y Rita, p. 217 (poem, pp. 217–20).

33. Alfredo d'Ambrosio, *Storia di Napoli dalle origini ad oggi* (Naples: Edizioni Nuova, 1995), p. 86. I am indebted to Marcella Salvi for this information.

34. Walter J. Ong, *Orality and Literacy: The Technologizing of the Word* (London: Methuen, 1982), pp. 31–77. This is the place to point out that we cannot speak of "the" text of Torrellas's poem, because it survives in various formats, with additional stanzas, in a state of textual "mouvance."

35. All references are from the edition by María Ángeles Suz Ruiz (Madrid: El Archipiélago, 1983).

36. On Valera and the contemporary debate over knighthood, see Jesús D. Rodríguez Velasco, *El debate sobre la caballería en el siglo XV: la tratadística caballeresca castellana en su marco europeo* (Salamanca: Junta de Castilla y León, 1996), esp. pp. 350–59 for Valera's aspirations to redefine the culture of the knight. For the contemporary practice of applying the methods of gloss and *accessus* to vernacular lay literature, see Weiss, *The Poet's Art*, pp. 107–42.

37. See Weiss, *The Poet's Art*, esp. pp. 11–24; Jeremy N. H. Lawrance, "The Spread of Lay Literacy in late Medieval Castile," *Bulletin of Hispanic Studies* 62 (1985): 79–94.

38. See Manuel Castillo, ed., *Libro de las claras e virtuosas mujeres,* 2nd ed. (Valencia: Prometeo, 1917); for the frequency of *refranes,* see Brian Dutton's *El cancionero del siglo XV,* where they are clearly identified and catalogued; for the misogynist tendencies of this popular wisdom, see Muriel Tapia, *Antifeminismo,* pp. 285–301. Santillana's quotation refers to the popular ballads; I discuss its implications in *The Poet's Art,* pp. 195–96.

39. For the reading process as an integral ingredient in "the noble mind," and for the ways in which "reposado estudio" [meditative study] was thematized as prudence, defined as the ability to make rational decisions in the active life, see Weiss, *The Poet's Art,* pp. 143–64.

40. Antonio Cortijo Ocaña has also remarked that the debate was related to the new position women occupied within courtly vernacular culture: "The Complication of the Narrative Technique in 15th Century Prose Literature on Love: The *Somni de Francesc Alegre recitant lo procés d'una qüestió enamorada,"* *Catalan Review* 11 (1997), 49–64, at p. 60.

41. Judith Fetterley, *The Resisting Reader: A Feminist Approach to American Fiction* (Bloomington: Indiana University Press, 1978).

42. Barbara F. Weissberger, "Resisting Readers and Writers in the Sentimental Romances and the Problem of Female Literacy," in *Studies on the Sentimental Romance,* ed. E. Michael Gerli and Joseph Gwara (London: Tamesis, 1997), pp. 173–90. Praise of women's role in cultural production is most pronounced in Rodríguez del Padrón's *Triunfo de las donas;* see Muriel Tapia, *Antifeminismo,* p. 339, and Francisco López Estrada, "Las

mujeres escritoras en la Edad Media castellana," in *La condición de la mujer en la Edad Media: actas del coloquio celebrado en la Casa de Velázquez, del 5 al 7 de noviembre de 1984,* ed. Yves-René Fonquerne and Alfonso Esteban (Madrid: Casa de Velázquez, 1986), pp. 9–38 (at pp. 18–19). For an important, though little-known, defense of female literacy, see the epistles by the two anonymous noblewomen included in *La obra literaria de Fernando de la Torre,* ed. María Jesús Díez Garretas (Valladolid: Universidad, 1983), pp. 128–49.

43. John Thompson argues that symbolic violence need not imply complicity between the dominated and the dominant, and that Bourdieu lays too great an emphasis on a consensual model of social reproduction; see *Studies in the Theory of Ideology,* pp. 58–72.

44. *Outline of a Theory of Practice,* trans. Nice, p. 79.

45. Quoted from E. Michael Gerli, ed., *Poesía cancioneril castellana* (Madrid: Akal, 1994), p. 282.

46. See Diego de San Pedro, *Obras completas, 2: Cárcel de amor,* ed. Keith Whinnom (Madrid: Castalia, 1971), p. 175.

47. Roffé, *La cuestión del género,* p. 207. For other famous examples of locating the source of one's masculine identity in the unstable feminine, see Diego de San Pedro's extraordinary poem that begins, "El mayor bien de quereros/ es querer un no quererme" [the greatest good in loving you/ is loving a dislike of myself; literally "loving a not loving of myself"], in Gerli, *Poesía cancioneril,* p. 296; or Juan de Mena's celebrated representation of the grieving mother in his *Laberinto de Fortuna* (stanzas 201–7). Her lament over the body of her doomed son, Lorenzo Dávalos, who died "tragically" young, is likened to the cries of a lioness—in bestiary terms, the lion cub is born unformed, and takes shape only through the roaring of the lioness. Birth, identity formation, and death are conflated in a single image of feminized pathos.

48. Peter Stallybrass and Allon White, *The Politics and Poetics of Transgression* (Ithaca, N.Y.: Cornell University Press, 1986), p. 5. Stallybrass and White have also influenced the gender analyses by Weissberger, "Male Sexual Anxieties in the *Carajicomedia,*" and E. Michael Gerli, "Dismembering the Body Politic: Vile Bodies and Sexual Underworlds in *Celestina,*" in *Queer Iberia,* pp. 369–93.

49. Joan Kelly-Gadol, "Did Women Have a Renaissance?" in *Becoming Visible: Women in European History,* ed. Renate Bridenthal et al., 2nd ed. (Boston: Houghton Mifflin, 1987), pp. 175–201.

50. With regard to urban women, historians have remarked on the freer economic conditions of the earlier Iberian frontier society. See Heath Dillard, *Daughters of the Reconquest: Women in Castilian Town Society, 1100–1300* (Cambridge: Cambridge University Press, 1984). On the fifteenth century, see Isabel Beceiro Pita and Ricardo Córdoba de la Llave, *Parentesco, poder y mentalidad: la nobleza castellana, siglos XII-XV* (Madrid: CSIC, 1990). Especially significant is their discussion of the importance of noblewomen in

transmitting the status of lineage, particularly for second-born sons, with the maternal coats of arms sometimes displayed alongside the paternal, albeit in secondary position (pp. 83–84). More details in Isabel Beceiro Pita, "La mujer noble en la baja edad media castellana," in *La condición de la mujer en la edad media: actas del coloquio celebrado en la Casa de Velázquez, del 5 al 7 de noviembre de 1984,* pp. 297–301.

51. *Valladolid en la edad media,* vol. 2: *El mundo abreviado (1367–1474)* (Valladolid: Junta de Castilla y León, 1987), pp. 190–213.

52. On Florencia Pinar, see Barbara Fulks, "The Poet Named Florencia Pinar," *La Corónica* 18 (1989–90): 33–44; the context of Pinar's work is traced in a valuable panorama by Pilar Lorenzo Gradín, "Voces de mujer y mujeres con voz en las tradiciones hispánicas medievales," in *Breve historia feminista de las literatura española (en lengua castellana),* ed. Iris M. Zavala (Barcelona: Anthropos, 1997), 4:13–81. On Teresa de Cartagena, see Dayle Seidenspinner-Núñez, "'El solo me leyó': Gendered Hermeneutics and Subversive Poetics in *Admiración operum Dey* of Teresa de Cartagena," *Medievalia* 15 (1993): 14–23; Surtz, *Writing Women,* pp. 21–40; see also Alison Weber, *Teresa de Ávila and the Rhetoric of Femininity* (Princeton, N.J.: Princeton University Press, 1990). For the anonymous female interlocutors of Fernando de la Torre, see note 42, and Jane Whetnall, "Isabel González of the *Cancionero de Baena* and Other Lost Voices," *La Corónica* 21 (1992–93): 59–82. For Juana de Contreras and other women prose writers, see María-Milagros Rivera Garretas, "Las prosistas del humanismo y del Renacimiento," in *Breve historia feminista,* 4:83–129.

53. For representative examples of this scholarship, see Electa Arenal and Stacy Schlau, *Untold Sisters: Hispanic Nuns in Their Own Works* (Albuquerque: University of New Mexico Press, 1989); Stephanie Merrim, *Early Modern Women's Writing and Sor Juana Inés de la Cruz* (Nashville, Tenn.: Vanderbilt University Press, 1999); Anita K. Stoll and Dawn L. Smith, *Gender, Identity, and Representation in Spain's Golden Age* (Lewisburg, Pa.: Bucknell University Press; London: Associated University Presses, 2000); the last two works provide ample bibliographical coverage of recent developments in the field. For a broader European treatment, see Constance Jordan, *Renaissance Feminism: Literary Texts and Political Models* (Ithaca, N.Y.: Cornell University Press, 1990.

54. For an extensive selection of her verse, see Julián Olivares and Elizabeth S. Boyce, *Tras el espejo la musa escribe: lírica femenina de los Siglos de Oro* (Madrid: Siglo XXI, 1993), pp. 327–90, from which the poem in this essay is quoted.

55. For a review of recent thinking on this vast topic, see Bartolomé Yun Casalilla, "The Castilian Aristocracy in the Seventeenth Century: Crisis, Refeudalisation, or Political Offensive?" in I. A. A. Thompson and Bartolomé Yun Casalilla, *The Castilian Crisis of the Seventeenth Century: New Perspectives on the Economic and Social History of Seventeenth-Century Spain* (Cambridge: Cambridge University Press, 1994), pp. 277–300. For the

impact of the new urban nobility upon the short story, with particular emphasis upon gender relations, see Nieves Romero-Díaz, *Nueva nobleza, nueva novela: re-escribiendo la cultura del Barroco,* unpublished Ph.D dissertation, University of Oregon, 1999, currently being revised for publication.

56. See, for example, Amy Williamsen, "Challenging the Code: Irony as Comic Challenge in María de Zayas," *Romance Languages Annual* 3 (1991): 642–47.

57. According to the *Diccionario de Autoridades* (1726) of the Spanish Royal Academy, the verb means "examinar, considerar y pensar con particular cuidado, atención y diligencia alguna cosa" [to examine, consider, and reflect with particular care, attention, and diligence upon something], and also "exagerar y encarecer alguna cosa" [to exaggerate and extol something]; quoted from *Diccionario de Autoridades,* facsimile ed., 3 vols. (Madrid: Real Academia Española, 1984), s.v. "ponderar."

58. See Sor Juana Inés de la Cruz, *The Answer/ La Repuesta, Including a Selection of Poems,* ed. and trans. Electa Arenal and Amanda Powell (New York: The Feminist Press at the City University of New York, 1994), p. 19.

59. Electa Arenal, "The Convent as Catalyst for Autonomy: Two Hispanic Nuns of the Seventeenth Century," in *Women in Hispanic Literature: Icons and Fallen Idols,* ed. Beth Miller (Berkeley and Los Angeles: University of California Press, 1983), pp. 147–83. In the two decades since this article, there has been much progress in our understanding of the conventual writing of early modern Spain and the New World, thanks both to new readings and to the publication of new texts. For a recent example, with ample bibliography on gender issues, see Fernando Itúrburu, *(Auto)biografía y misticismo femeninos en la Colonia: la "Relación" escrita por Madre Josefa de la Providencia sobre Madre Antonia Lucía Maldonado* (New Orleans, La.: University Press of the South, 2000); for a valuable survey, see Alison Weber, "Recent Studies on Women and Early Modern Religion in Spanish," *Renaissance Quarterly* 52 (1999): 197–206.

60. See Gerda Lerner, *The Creation of Feminist Consciousness: From the Middle Ages to 1870* (New York: Oxford University Press, 1993), p. 14.

61. See the entry in the *Diccionario de Autoridades,* s.v. "diamante": "Metafóricamente vale dureza, constancia y resistencia" [Metaphorically it means hardness, constancy, and resistance].

62. Quoted from *Poesías castellanas completas,* ed. Elias Rivers (Madrid: Castalia, 1984), p. 59.

63. Though the healthful properties of sex were the subject of debate, authorities like Albertus Magnus feared that men were aged more than women by frequent sexual intercourse; see Joan Cadden, *Meanings of Sex Difference in the Middle Ages: Medicine, Science, and Culture* (Cambridge: Cambridge University Press, 1993), p. 176. The anxiety was (if I may be forgiven the pun) disseminated in the Renaissance by Castiglione's *Book of the Courtier,* trans. George Bull (Harmondsworth: Penguin, 1976), p. 223.

64. Zayas argued that women's lack of literary achievement was the result of social exclusion, and was not biologically determined; but challenging contemporary humoral theory, she adds that women may in fact be more

suited to intellectual pursuits since they are "quizá más agudas por ser de natural más frío, por consistir en humedad el entendimiento, como se ve en las respuestas de repente y en los engaños de pensado, que todo lo que se hace con maña, aunque no sea virtud, es ingenio" [perhaps more acute since they are colder by nature, and since the understanding consists of the moist humor, as one can see in the sudden replies and calculated deceits; for everything that is done with cunning, although it may not be virtue, is wit]. Quoted from *Tres novelas amorosas y ejemplares y tres desengaños amorosos,* ed. Alicia Redondo Goicoechea (Madrid: Castalia, 1989), p. 48. Zayas thus unequivocally aligns herself with those who rejected the view, expressed in the major treatises on wit, that women lacked the physiological requisites for learning. For the variable range of opinions on the relation between gender and wit in the Spanish Golden Age, see Sharon D. Voros, "Fashioning Feminine Wit in María de Zayas, Ana Caro, and Leonor de la Cueva," in Stoll and Smith, ed., *Gender, Identity, and Representation,* pp. 156–77. For the medical view that the coldness of women precluded mental acuity, see Ian Maclean, *The Renaissance Notion of Woman: A Study in the Fortunes of Scholasticism and Medical Science in European Intellectual Life* (Cambridge: Cambridge University Press, 1980), pp. 32, 35.

65. Quoted from Jonathan Barnes, *Aristotle* (Oxford: Oxford University Press, 1982), p. 57.

66. For the range of ambivalent, "complex and unsettled" views on menstruation during the Middle Ages, see Cadden, *Meanings of Sex Difference,* pp. 173–77. For male fear of being contaminated by menses, see Solomon, *The Literature of Misogyny,* pp. 80–81. Maclean points out, however, that by the end of the sixteenth century there was less emphasis on the malignant nature of menstruation, and the majority of authors discuss its purgative value; see *The Renaissance Notion of Woman,* pp. 39–40.

67. Bloch maintains that the effect of such generalizing speech acts "is to make of woman an essence, which, as essence, is eliminated from the world historical stage. [. . .] [A]ny essentialist definition of woman, whether negative or positive, whether made by a man or a woman, is the fundamental definition of misogyny" (*Medieval Misogyny,* pp. 5–6). Bloch takes no account of the discursive situation of such statements and leaves no room for declarations of political solidarity.

68. These qualities were given their most eloquent expression throughout Castiglione's *Book of the Courtier.* For a concise summary, see Peter Burke, *The Fortunes of the Courtier: The European Reception of Castiglione's "Cortegiano"* (University Park: Pennsylvania State University Press, 1996), pp. 19–38. They are hardly a Renaissance invention: similar lists of abilities have been described for the medieval courtier by C. Stephen Jaeger, *The Origins of Courtliness: Civilizing Trends and the Formation of Courtly Ideals 939–1210* (Philadelphia: University of Pennsylvania Press, 1985), pp. 127–75.

69. See Joan Wallach Scott, *Only Paradoxes to Offer: French Feminists and the Rights of Man* (Cambridge, Mass.: Harvard University Press, 1996), especially pp. 1–18. I am grateful to the following for their bibliographical suggestions and advice on the content and structure of this essay: E. Michael Gerli, Amanda Powell, Marcella Salvi, Nieves Romero-Díaz, Alison Weber, and Julián Olivares. Though they have done much to improve it, none of them can be held responsible for the inadequacies that remain.

BIBLIOGRAPHY OF PRIMARY TEXTS
IN SPANISH, CA. 1430–1520

The goal of this bibliography is to provide a basic overview of the major primary texts in which women are defamed, defended, or otherwise debated. For reasons of space, I exclude secondary material except when I consider that the text may be hard to locate through the usual bibliographical sources. To facilitate identification and locate the texts and MS sources of the shorter poems, I provide the identification number given by Brian Dutton in *El cancionero del siglo XV.* Although it constitutes a substantial revision to Ornstein's list, it is not intended to be definitive: The boundaries of formal debate are blurred on the one hand by the implicitly epideictic nature of much courtly love literature, and on the other by the scurrilous personal invectives aimed at individual women (for this reason, I exclude texts like Guevara's *Coplas que hizo de maldezir contra una muger* [Dutton ID 6754]).

Non-Hispanists should know that like "Italy," the term "Spain" is a handy, though anachronistic, shorthand: My specialization is Castilian, and Catalan specialists may be able to add to the list of Catalan texts I provide here, which is derived largely from Rosanna Cantavella. Although they fall outside the chronology of my study, I provide under "Miscellaneous" some Catalan texts by Eiximenis and Metge, for example, that provide what I believe to be the "cultural capital" of one of the originators of the debate, Pere Torrellas. As someone who held posts in the Aragonese court in Naples and who conversed with such Italian humanists as Giovanni Pontano, Torrellas should remind us that the relevance of the corpus is not limited to the Iberian Peninsula. The Italian connection is illustrated by courtiers such as Suero de Ribera, Carvajal, and Juan de Tapia; by the influence (initially through Catalan) of Boccaccio; by the translation into Italian of *Celestina* (Venice, 1508: a book about whores for the city of *cortegiane*). Other international connections are worth pursuing, e.g., the first English translation of *Celestina* by John Rastell, which accompanied Catherine of Aragon to the Tudor court—or the French connection: the translation of Alain Chartier, or, in the other direction, of the translation of Rodríguez del Padrón's *Triunfo de las donas* for the Burgundian court. Clearly the international traffic in noblewomen was accompanied by the cultural traffic of discourse about women, which in some cases possessed explicitly nationalist overtones.

What is more, many of the texts listed here were widely read until the late sixteenth century, so they also ought to be considered in any discussion of the

Renaissance theories of gender. They provide a broader context, for example, for Castiglione's *Cortegiano* (translated into Renaissance Castilian by Boscán), or for Cristóbal Castillejo's debate about women, the *Diálogo de mujeres* (Venice, 1544—note the place of publication—plus about a dozen independent editions before 1615, and half a dozen more included in his complete works, 1577–1600), by an author whom conventional wisdom describes as an archaic remnant of an earlier esthetic and ethos. These late medieval texts may have been transposed in time but not, of course, without new meanings and investments, which future scholars need to explore.

Clerical Treatises

Alfonso Martínez de Toledo. *Arcipreste de Talavera o "Corbacho"* (1438). Direct address to male reader, a compendium of sermons and medical and astrological theory, compiled in condemnation of courtly love and evil women. Boccaccio's *Corbaccio* and Capellanus's *De amore* III among models and sources. Printed 1498, 1499, 1500, 1518, 1529, 1547 (with author's ironic retraction).

Alonso de Cartagena (bishop of Burgos). *Tratado de mugeres* (pre-1454). Gloss on misogynist passage from Seneca's play *Hyppolitus*. Included in compilation of Senecan translations *Cinco libros de Séneca* (printed 1491 with numerous sixteenth-century reprints). No modern ed.

Fray Martín de Córdoba. *Jardín de nobles donzellas* (ca. 1468). Addresses Princess Isabel, future queen. Defends her ability to rule, drawing on biblical, medical, moral, and historical arguments. Isabel fit to rule if she denies and controls her female condition. Printed 1500, 1542.

Joan Roís de Corella. *Triunfo de les dones* (2nd half of 15th c.). Catalan prose defense of women, whose title evokes the popular *Triunfo de las donas* by Rodríguez del Padrón (see below). Author (a master of theology, though not ordained) places his eulogy in the mouth of personified Truth.

Fray Antonio de Medina. *Coplas contra los vicios y deshonestidades de las mugeres* (2nd half 15th c.). Litany of female corruption, structured around 100 anaphoric repetitions of demonstrative pronouns (e.g., "This foul body, this evil whoring, those dark pleasures . . ."). Dutton ID 2947. Ed. E. Michael Gerli, "A Late Fifteenth-Century Antifeminist Poem: Fray Antonio de Medina's *Coplas contra los vicios y deshonestidades de las mugeres,*" *La Corónica* 8 (1979–80): 210–14.

Fray Íñigo de Mendoza. *Coplas en vituperio de las malas hembras, e en loor de las buenas* (ca. 1480). Twelve stanzas on evil women, twelve on good. Some nationalist tendencies. Dutton ID 0271. In his *Cancionero*, ed. Julio Rodríguez-Puértolas. Madrid: Espasa-Calpe, 1968. Pp. 223–32.

Luis Ramírez de Lucena. *Repetición de amores* (pre-1497). Parodic academic lecture, based on Torrellas's thesis "Quien bien amando persigue donas, a sí mesmo destruye." Concludes: "Mulier est hominis confusio." Published with his treatise on chess, which states that love and chess are allegories of war, and outlines new rules in which Queen (*dama*) is given greater freedom of movement and power.

Aristocratic, Courtly, or Secular Authors

Pere Torrellas. *Coplas de las calidades de las donas* (pre-1435, but often dated *ad quem* 1458). The "classic" misogynist poem of fifteenth-century Spain. Aristotelian diatribe, his own beloved exception to the rule; provoked numerous refutations and endorsements. A courtier in Naples, Torrellas later fictionalized as archetypical woman hater. Nineteen MSS. First printed in the *Cancionero general 1511*, which was republished throughout the sixteenth century. Dutton ID 0043.

———. "Yerra con poco saber." Canción on women's inconstancy. Dutton ID 1095. Ed. Bach y Rita, p. 270. The attribution to Mena discounted by Carla de Nigris, ed., Juan de Mena, *Poesie minori*. Naples: Liguori, 1988, p. 478. Glossed by Juan de Tapia (see below).

———. Three palinodes in defense of women: prose *Razonamiento en defensión de las donas* (ed. Bach y Rita, pp. 296–306), Dutton ID 2146; a *glosa* (verse gloss) (1435) on final stanza of his famous *Coplas*, eulogizing the *infanta* Juana de Aragón, whose "divine virtue" disproves his critique of women, Dutton ID 2390 G 0043; poem beginning "A quien basta el conocer" (ed. Bach y Rita, pp. 217–20).

Francesc Ferrer. *Lo conhort* (1425–58?). Catalan poem citing stanzas from thirteen poets (ranging from Bernart de Ventadorn to Ausias March) in a 730-line "antologia del misoginisme." Riquer, *Història* 3:33. Cantavella, *Els cards i el llir*, p. 38.

Ramon Boter, "Pus en lo mon sou feta singular" (early 2nd half of 15th c.), female sex redeemed by poet's Virgin-like beloved (Cantavella, *Els cards i el llir*, p. 38).

Diego de Valera. *Tratado en defensa de las virtuosas mujeres* (pre-1445). Dedicated to María of Castile. Refutes "new sect" of misogynists. Imaginary instruction of male friend, in form of learned treatise with author's glosses and *accessus*. Women morally equal, yet subordinate to men, as disciple to master. Their sins caused by men. Catalogue of famous (chaste) women. Ovid and Boccaccio impotent old men.

Juan Rodríguez del Padrón (or de la Cámara). *Triunfo de las donas* (pre-1445). Dedicated to María of Castile. Paired with treatise on nobility addressed to young male courtiers, rebutting *Corbacho*. Adduces 50 reasons in support of superiority of women. French translation for Burgundian court (1460) tones down original's nationalist discourse.

Álvaro de Luna. *Libro de las claras e virtuosas mujeres* (pre-1453). Compendium of famous women (biblical, classical, saints). Demonstrates moral and spiritual equality of women. Man responsible for original sin. Defends the new intellectual values of aristocratic class and compatibility of arms and letters.

Fernando de la Torre and anonymous women. *Libro de las veinte cartas e qüistiones* (mid-15th c.). Includes: epistolary exchanges with two anonymous ladies debating relative intellectual qualities of men and women, and *Un tratado de despido a una dama de religión*, farewell letter to beloved on entering a convent. Praises virtuous and blames inconstant women. Ed. Díez Garretas, pp. 128–49 and 170–84.

Mossén Hugo d'Urríes. *Coplas en loor de las mugeres* (mid-15th c.). Forty stanzas using arguments from natural philosophy. In *Cancionero de Vindel* (NH2), part of thematic grouping: 1) Torrellas, 2) Montoro, 3) Urríes. Dutton ID 2365. Torrellas dedicated to this author his prose retraction, the *Razonamiento*.

———[?]. *De los galanes* (mid-15th c.). Three hundred–line poem attacking insincere and deceitful courtiers who slander women. Dutton lists as anon. ID 2188.

Jacme Roig. *El Espill, o Llibre de les dones* [*The Mirror, or Book of Women*] (1459–60). Cynically misogynist Catalan poem (16,000 lines) relating protagonist's encounters with women of all ages, classes, and occupations.

Juan de Tapia. Poetic gloss on Torrellas's "Yerra con poco saber" (2nd half of 15th c.). Castilian courtier in Aragonese court in Naples. Dutton ID 6619 G 1095.

Hernán Mexía. Censures misogynists, e.g., Torrellas (2nd half of 15th c.). Attributes some *coplas de maldezir de las mugeres* to friend, the poet Juan Álvarez Gato. Twenty of one hundred lines praise women, the rest condemn slanderous language, which blemishes the work of art that is the ideal courtier. Dutton ID 3125.

Juan Álvarez Gato. Reply to Mexía (2nd half of 15th c.). Denies authorship of poem, turns to women for "justice," declaring in 40 anaphoric lines his loyalty and eulogizing female virtue. Dutton ID 3126 R 3125.

Hernán Mexía. "Recantation." Four hundred lines. Allegedly commissioned by two ladies, to test his rhetorical skills. Emphasizes female excess, woman as symbol of disorder, who cannot be represented and restrained by male language. His diatribe is a purging fire, the "holy spirit" in a trinity of Boccaccio (the Father) and Torrellas (the Son). In *Cancionero general,* reprinted throughout the sixteenth century. Dutton ID 6097.

Suero de Ribera. *Respuesta en defensión de las donas* (2nd half of 15th c.). Male detractors impotent. Women source of male courtliness. Ribera a courtier in Naples, 1446–73. Dutton ID 0199.

Antón de Montoro. Two epigrammatic poems (2nd half of 15th c.). Obscure invective against Torrellas, comparing him with the *mandrágola* [mandrake]. Followed by retraction: Woman's unpredictability and power over man. Dutton ID 2364 R 0043.

Gómez Manrique. *Contrafactum* of Torrellas's poem (2nd half of 15th c.). Torrellas an unrequited lover. Men the "weaker" sex. Women naturally good (Lucretia, Virgin Mary paradigmatic), their sins caused by men. Woman capable of ruling the earth. In some MSS, Manrique's stanzas intertwined with Torrellas's, a layout that points up the lack of relationship between their arguments. Dutton ID 0043 Y 2770.

Carvajal. *Respuesta en defensión del amor* (2nd half of 15th c.). Torrellas a frustrated, ungrateful lover and heretic. A Castilian courtier in Naples. Dutton ID 0657 R 0043.

Pedro de Cartagena. Untitled [fragment?] (2nd half of 15th c.). Obscure two-stanza commentary on beloved in light of Torrellas's poem. Dutton ID 1821.

Francesc Moner. *Bendir de dones* (late fifteenth century). Catalan misogynist poem, influenced by Torrellas. Cantavella, *Els cards i el llir,* pp. 38–39.

Rodrigo de Reinosa. *Pater noster trobado* (1480 *a quo*). Parody of the Lord's Prayer, requesting salvation from evil, inconstant women. Dutton ID 5040. See also under "Miscellaneous."

Juan del Encina. *Contra los que dizen mal de mugeres* (ca. 1496). Misogynist slanderers like Torrellas condemned to Hell. Slander "unmanly" and ungrateful. Women superior, source of virtue, their sins caused by men. Encina sought patronage of Isabel la Católica. Dutton ID 3962 R 0043.

Pedro Manuel de Urrea. *Coplas en alabança de las mugeres* (pre-1516). Posthumous attack on Torrellas and Hernán Mexía. Illegitimate, slanderous speech like that of Jews, friars, and Muslims. Women source of gentility, etc. Represent a perfection always out of man's reach. Dutton ID 7545.

Íñigo Beltrán de Valdelomar (ca. 1520). Attacks slanderers. Women source of virtue, power, etc. One hundred lines of anaphora, "Ellas son . . ." [women are . . .]. Dutton ID 5020 R 0043.

The Debate Embedded or Performed in Narrative Fiction and Drama

Francesc de la Via. *Libre de Fra Bernat* (early fifteenth century). Catalan verse fabliau, in which friar deceived by nun, attacks women and rejects narrator's defense. Cantavella, *Els cards i el llir,* p. 37.

"FADC" (anon. author). *Triste deleytación* (1458–67). Includes lengthy discussion between young lady and her stepmother comparing the behavior of men and women in love. Explicit condemnation of the social bases of women's oppression, and unusual emphasis on class and economic aspects of sexual relationships. Cites Torrellas and Rodríguez del Padrón. In Castilian, but single MS in Catalan hand.

Joanot Martorell and Martí Joan de Galba. *Tirant lo Blanc* (2nd half of 15th c.). Chapters 172–73 entail brief debate on women between protagonist and Princess Carmesina. Chapter 309 includes a list of famous women, drawn from Bernat Metge's *Lo somni.* Cantavella, *Els cards i el llir,* pp. 37–38.

Diego de San Pedro. *Cárcel de amor* (ca. 1490). Relates Leriano's unrequited passion for Laureola, a princess. Thematizes female autonomy and relation between love and power. Before suicide, Leriano defends women, cataloguing thirty-five (conventional) arguments, and numerous historical examples of female "goodness" (i.e., chastity). In sixteenth century: 22 Spanish editions; 9 French; 9 Italian; 2 English. In seventeenth century: 5 German. For diffusion, see Keith Whinnom, *The Spanish Sentimental Romance 1440–1550: A Critical Bibliography.* London: Grant & Cutler, 1983, pp. 43–44.

Juan de Flores. *Grisel e Mirabella* (ca. 1480). Torrellas is torn limb from limb by women, thus enacting the violence implicit in the verse debate. Five sixteenth-century Spanish eds. Translated into Italian, French, German, English, Polish (including tri- and quadrilingual editions). See Whinnom, *The Spanish Sentimental Romance,* pp. 58–59.

———. *Grimalte e Gradissa* (ca. 1480). Tragic and violent continuation of Boccaccio's *Elegia di Madonna Fiammetta.* Dramatizes conflict between sexes. French trans. Maurice Scève (1535). See Whinnom, *The Spanish Sentimental Romance,* p. 59.

———. *Triunfo de amor* (1470–85). Concludes with debate between men and women over relative sexual freedom and equality. God of Love intervenes to invert sexual roles, which are viewed as product of custom and habit. Some nationalist tendencies.

Fernando de Rojas. *Celestina* (1499). Problematizes (*inter alia*) question of female autonomy and power (located primarily in the realm of whores and witches). Explores how social identity is constructed in language. Numerous sequels and adaptations. About 100 sixteenth-century Spanish editions. Translated into Italian (18 eds. before 1551), French (3 trans. in 12 eds.), German, Flemish, Hebrew, Portuguese, Latin. Two English versions, including Rastell's moral adaptation, *The Beauty and Good Properties of Women* (ca. 1525), a female conduct book for the Tudor court.

Juan del Encina. *Égloga de Fileno e Cardonio* (ca. 1496). Women slandered because of unrequited love. Panegyric of virtuous woman. Ed. Ana María Rambaldo, *Obras completas*. Madrid: Espasa-Calpe, 1983, 4:156–83.

Miscellaneous

Andreas Capellanus. *De amore.* Fourteenth-century Catalan translation. Ed. Amadeu Pagès, *De Amore, text llatí amb la traducció catalana del segle XIV.* Castellón de la Plana: Sociedad Castellonense de Cultura, 1930.

Friar Francesc Eiximenis. *Lo libre de les dones* (1396). Catalan treatise on duties and classes of women. Castilian translation owned by Isabel la Católica. *Lo libre de les dones,* ed. Frank Naccarato et al. Barcelona: Curial Edicions Catalanes, 1981. *Texto y concordancias del "Libro de las donas,"* ed. Gracia Lozano López [on microfiche]. Madison, Wis.: Hispanic Seminary of Medieval Studies, 1992.

Giovanni Boccaccio. *Corbaccio.* Catalan translation by Narcís Franch (1397). *El "Corbatxo" de Giovanni Boccaccio; traduït en català per Narcís Franch (segle XIV),* ed. Francesc de B. Moll. Mallorca: Edicions de l'Obra del Diccionari, 1935.

Bernard Metge. *Lo somni* (1399). Catalan dialogue in four books. Book 3 based heavily on *Corbaccio.* Book 4 praise of women (influenced in part by Petrarch and Boccaccio's *De mulieribus claris*). Invective against men (substantially original).

Enrique de Villena. *Los doze trabajos de Hércules* (1417). Allegorical treatise, written first in Catalan, then trans. by author into Castilian. Hercules's twelfth labor a moral allegory eulogizing chastity and obedience of women. Though the weaker sex, their fortitude an example to men.

Clemente Sánchez de Vercial (d. 1438). Two exemplum collections containing examples of the wiles of women: *Espéculo de los legos* and *Libro de los exemplos por a.b.c.* See Lacarra, "Algunos datos," p. 353.

Fernán Pérez de Guzmán. *La doctrina que dieron a Sarra.* Mid-fifteenth verse conduct book for obedient women. Dutton ID 1938. Ed. Caroline B. Bourland, "*La doctrina que dieron a Sarra:* Poema de Fernán Pérez de Guzmán," *Revue Hispanique* 22 (1910): 648–86.

Teresa de Cartagena. *Arboleda de los enfermos y Admiración operum Dei* (1440–60). Deaf nun vindicates her right to literacy in spiritual treatises. English trans. by Dayle Seidenspinner-Núñez. *The Writings of Teresa de Cartagena.* Cambridge: D. S. Brewer, 1998.

Florencia Pinar. Six love lyrics (late fifteenth century). Only extant female-au-
thored fifteenth-century verse (apart from few fragments). Addresses destructive
effects of courtly love. Reprinted throughout sixteenth century in *Cancionero
general*. Dutton ID 0754, 0766, 0768, 6240, 6241, 6407.

Sor Isabel de Villena (d. 1490). *Vita Christi* (published 1497). Lengthy vernacular
life of Christ written for convent of Holy Trinity in Valencia, where author was
abbess. Considered by some to be (in part) an answer to the misogyny of *Spill*
by Jacme Roig (see above), who had contacts with her convent.

Giovanni Boccaccio. *De mulieribus claris*. Anon. Castilian trans. Zaragoza: Pablo
Hurus,1494. Facsimile ed. *De las ilustres mujeres en romance (Zaragoza, 1494). Sale
nuevamente a luz reproducida en facsimile por acuerdo de la Real Academia Española*.
Madrid: Real Academia Española, 1951.

Alain Chartier. "La Belle dame sans Merci." Catalan trans. by Francesc Oliver. Ed.
Martí de Riquer, *Alain Chartier, "La belle dame sans merci." Amb la traducció catalana del segle XV de fra Francesc Oliver*. Barcelona: Edicions del Quaderns Crema,
1983.

Anon. "Pleito del manto" (ca. 1500). Obscene debate between the relative power
of the *coño* [cunt] and *carajo* [prick]. Dutton ID 6921. With additions by García
d'Astorga. ID 6922 A21, ID 6923 R 6921.

Rodrigo de Reinosa. *Coplas de las comadres* and *Coplas de la chinagala* (ca. 1500).
Popular satires of low-class women and courtesans, repeating many of the
stereotypes of the misogynist debate. Dutton ID 5028 and 5041.

Anon. *Carajicomedia* (ca. 1515). Obscene and misogynist parody of Juan de Mena's
Laberinto de Fortuna and learned commentary, detailing the limp exploits of the
phallus in a brothel populated by sexually voracious whores. Thinly veiled allusions to Isabel la Católica.

Juvenal. *Sexta sátira* (Sixth Satire, but also includes no. 10). Trans Jerónimo de Ville-
gas. Valladolid: Arnaldo Guillén de Brocar, 1519. Brocar also printed the 1518 ed.
of Martínez de Toledo's *Arcipreste de Talavera*. Juvenal a popular university author.

BIOGRAPHIES

PAMELA J. BENSON is Professor of English at Rhode Island College. She has published *The Invention of the Renaissance Woman: The Challenge of Female Independence in the Literature and Thought of Italy and England* (1992) and the anthology *Italian Tales from the Age of Shakespeare* (1996).

ALCUIN BLAMIRES is Reader in English at Goldsmiths College, University of London. He has published *The Case for Women in Medieval Culture* (1997) and edited the anthology *Woman Defamed and Woman Defended* (1992).

THELMA FENSTER, Professor of French at Fordham University, has edited and translated several works by Christine de Pizan. She has also edited *Arthurian Women: A Casebook* (1995).

MARGARET FRANKLIN is Assistant Professor of Art History at Wayne State University in Detroit. She has published on *uomini famosi/donne illustri* images, including Raphael's *Parnassus,* the papal portraits in the Sistine Chapel, and Mantegna's *Dido.*

ROBERTA KRUEGER, Professor of French at Hamilton College, is the author of *Women Readers and the Ideology of Gender in Old French Romance* (1993) and the editor of *The Cambridge Companion to Medieval Romance* (2000). Her current research is on conduct literature written for women in late medieval France.

CLARE A. LEES is Professor of Medieval Literature and the History of the English Language at King's College London. She is the author of *Tradition and Belief: Religious Writing in Late Anglo-Saxon England* (1999), editor of *Medieval Masculinities: Regarding Men in the Middle Ages* (1994), and co-author (with Gillian Overing) of *Double Agents: Women and Clerical Culture in Anglo-Saxon England* (2001).

E. ANN MATTER is Professor of Religious Studies at the University of Pennsylvania. She has published four books, among which: *The Voice of My*

Beloved: The Song of Songs in Western Medieval Christianity (1990) and (co-edited with John Coakley) *Creative Women in Medieval and Early Modern Italy: A Religious and Artistic Renaissance,* 1994.

GILLIAN R. OVERING, Professor of English at Wake Forest University, is the author of *Language, Sign, and Gender in "Beowulf"* (1990), co-author (with Marijane Osborn) of *Landscape of Desire: Partial Stories of the Medieval Scandinavian World* (1990), and co-editor (with Britton J. Harwood) of *Class and Gender in Early English: Intersections* (1994). She is co-author (with Clare Lees) of *Double Agents: Women and Clerical Culture in Anglo-Saxon England* (2001).

KAREN PRATT is Senior Lecturer in French at King's College London. She is the author of *Meister Otte's Eraclius as an Adaptation of Eracle by Gautier d'Arras* and editor or co-editor of numerous essay collections. Along with C. W. Marx, she assisted Alcuin Blamires in editing *Woman Defamed and Woman Defended: An Anthology of Medieval Texts.*

ANN MARIE RASMUSSEN is Associate Professor of German and Women's Studies at Duke University. She is the author *of Mothers and Daughters in Medieval German Literature* (1997), and a past President of the Society for Medieval Feminist Scholarship. Her current research focuses on expanding her essay in this volume into a book-length study.

HELEN SOLTERER teaches French literature and culture at Duke University. She is the author of *The Master and Minerva: Disputing Women in French Medieval Culture* (1995), and of essays on hate speech and gender in pre-modern Paris, and on Christine de Pizan.

JULIAN WEISS is lecturer in the Department of Spanish and Spanish American Studies at Kings College London. He is the co-editor (with E. Michael Gerli) of *Poetry at Court in Trastamaran Spain* (1998), and the author of *The Poet's Art: Literary Theory in Castile, c. 1400–60* (1990), as well as of other publications on medieval and early modern Spanish literary, cultural and gender studies.

BARBARA F. WEISSBERGER is Associate Professor of Spanish at the University of Minnesota-Twin Cities. She has published feminist analyses of various late-fifteenth century Spanish literary genres, especially romance. Her recently-completed book manuscript is entitled *Repairing Spain's Broken Body: Gender Ideology in the Age of Isabel the Catholic.*

INDEX

All works with known authors are cited under author names